Conference of the North American Chapter of the Association for Computational Linguistics: Human Language Technologies (NAACL HLT 2018)

Industry Papers

New Orleans, Louisiana, USA
1 – 6 June 2018

ISBN: 978-1-5108-6348-4

NAACL HLT 2018

**The 2018 Conference of the
North American Chapter of the
Association for Computational Linguistics:
Human Language Technologies**

**Proceedings of the Conference
Volume 3 (Industry Papers)**

June 1-June 6, 2018
New Orleans, Louisiana

Introduction

It is our pleasure to welcome you to the inaugural Industry Track in the *ACL family of conferences at NAACL 2018.

The idea of organizing an industry track stemmed from the challenging issues encountered while attempting to apply state-of-the-art techniques to real-world language problems. As those who have attempted these problems know, practical applications are rarely as well defined as in laboratory settings and the data never as clean. In addition, there may be practical constraints such as computational requirements, processing speed, memory footprint, latency requirements, ease of updating a deployed solution that need to be balanced judiciously, and capability to be embedded as part of a larger system. The NAACL 2018 Industry Track was born out of the desire to provide a forum for researchers, engineers and application developers who are experienced in these issues to exchange ideas, share results and discuss use-cases of successful development and deployments of language technologies in real-world settings.

Although we thought that the time is ripe in the NLP field for such a forum, and hoped that the community will embrace the opportunity to share their experience with others, it was nonetheless a guessing game as to the amount of interest the track would actually generate. As submissions drew to a close in late February, we were happy to report that we received 91 submissions, far exceeding our expectations (which led to last-minute scrambling to recruit more reviewers, but we're not complaining!). Six of the papers were desk rejects due to non-conformance with submission requirements, and the remaining 85 papers were reviewed by 65 reviewers. We accepted 28 papers – an acceptance rate of 32.9% (one paper was subsequently withdrawn after acceptance) of which 19 papers will be presented in oral sessions that run as a parallel track during the main conference, and 8 papers will be presented during poster sessions. Of course, none of this would have been possible without the participation of authors and reviewers, and we would like to convey our heartfelt "thank you" to all the authors for submitting papers and the reviewers for their efforts in the paper selection process.

We analyzed our submissions along a couple of dimensions and would like to share some interesting statistics. First we looked at the submissions with respect to the distribution of author affiliations. As one would expect, the industry track focuses on problems that manifest themselves more readily in industry than in academia. Indeed, of the 85 papers reviewed, 55 papers are authored by researchers/engineers in industry laboratories. The particularly encouraging statistic, however, is that 25 papers are the results of collaboration between those in industry and academia. it would be interesting to track these statistics in future years to see if the collaboration increases as the field continues to mature. The second dimension we analyzed is the geographic distribution of authors by contact author. This being a NAACL conference, it is no surprise that 62% of the papers came from North America. We are pleased with the participation of authors from other regions, including 22% from Europe, 14% from Asia, and 1% from Africa.

In addition to paper presentations, we will have two plenary keynote speeches. For the keynote speeches, we aimed to feature researchers who also have first hand experience applying research results to practical applications. To that end, we are honored to have two illustrious members of NLP community – Daniel Marcu, who co-founded Language Weaver more than 15 years ago and is now the director of MT/NLP at Amazon, and Mari Ostendorf, professor at the University of Washington, who led a team of students to build a social bot that won the 2017 Alexa Prize competition. We are confident that their experiences would be of immense interest to the larger NLP community.

Another highlight of the industry track includes two panel discussions on topics of increasing importance in the community. The first panel, "Careers in Industry", moderated by Philip Resnik, professor at University of Maryland, is primarily geared toward students and recent graduates who are exploring careers in industry versus academia. The panel will feature experienced professionals who have worked in both environments to share their experience and offer advice, based on questions gathered from the *ACL community earlier this year . The second panel, "Ethics in NLP", will be moderated by Dirk Hovy, professor at Università Bocconi, and will focus on raising awareness of the emerging issues of biases present in NLP/AI solutions, the social implications of such biases, and what we, as NLP practitioners, can do to reduce them.

With the overwhelming response to the call for papers, the language community has unambiguously endorsed the relevance of the Industry track in the milieu of annual conferences. As organizers, we have attempted to amplify this endorsement by bringing to the participants a invigorating technical program. We hope through your engaging discussions and active participation during the sessions, you will unanimously support and nurture the concept of an Industry track in NLP conferences over the years to come.

Srinivas Bangalore (Interactions Labs)
Jennifer Chu-Carroll (Elemental Cognition)
Yunyao Li (IBM Research - Almaden)

NAACL 2018 Industry Track Co-Chairs

Organizers:

Srinivas Bangalore, Interactions Labs
Jennifer Chu-Carroll, Elemental Cognition
Yunyao Li, IBM Research - Almaden

Program Committee:

Apoorv Agarwal,Columbia University (United States)
Alan Akbik,Zalando Research (Germany)
Miguel Ballesteros,IBM Research (United States)
Loïc Barrault,LIUM, Le Mans University (France)
Akash Bharadwaj,Carnegie Mellon University (United States)
Ciprian Chelba,Google (United States)
John Chen,Interactions LLC (United States)
Minhua Chen,Interactions LLC (United States)
Laura Chiticariu,IBM Research - Almaden (United States)
Deborah Dahl,Conversational Technologies (United States)
Lingjia Deng,Bloomberg (United States)
Giuseppe Di Fabbrizio,Rakuten Institute of Technology (United States)
Christine Doran,Self (United States)
Kavita Ganesan,uiuc (United States)
Anna Lisa Gentile,IBM Research Almaden (United States)
Yufan Guo,University of Cambridge (United Kingdom)
Bo Han,RedMarker/Kaplan Inc. (Australia)
Peter Heeman,OHSU / CSLU (United States)
John Henderson,MITRE (United States)
Lynette Hirschman,MITRE (United States)
Dirk Hovy,Bocconi University (Italy)
Badrinath Jayakumar,Interactions LLC (United States)
Michael Johnston,Interactions Corporation (United States)
Adi Kalyanpur,Elemental Cognition (United States)
Doo Soon Kim,Adobe Research (United States)
Kevin Knight,USC/ISI (United States)
Gourab Kundu,IBM T.J. Watson Research Center (United States)
Gakuto Kurata,IBM Research (Japan)
Yocheved Levitan,Interactions LLC (United States)
Bing Liu,University of Illinois at Chicago (United States)
Alexander Loeser,Beuth-University of Applied Sciences Berlin (Germany)
Stephanie Lukin,US Army Research Laboratory (United States)
Xiaoqiang Luo,Google (United States)
Yuji Matsumoto,Nara Institute of Science and Technology (Japan)
Irina Matveeva,NexLP, Inc (United States)
David McClosky,Google (United States)
Mahnoosh Mehrabani,Interactions LLC (United States)
Marie Meteer,Brandeis University (United States)
Margaret Mitchell,Google Research and Machine Intelligence (United States)
Helena Moniz,INESC-ID, FLUL/Unbabel (Portugal)
Stefano Pacifico,Elemental Cognition (United States)

Shimei Pan,UMBC (United States)
Youngja Park,IBM T. J. Watson Research Center (United States)
Siddharth Patwardhan,Apple (United States)
Alexandros Potamianos,National Technical University of Athens (Greece)
John Prager,IBM Research (United States)
Rashmi Prasad,Interactions Corporation (United States)
Jerry Quinn,IBM Research (United States)
Preethi Raghavan,IBM Research TJ Watson (United States)
Owen Rambow,Columbia University (United States)
Ehud Reiter,University of Aberdeen (United Kingdom)
Giuseppe Riccardi,University of Trento (Italy)
Stefan Riezler,Heidelberg University (Germany)
Brian Roark,Google Inc. (United States)
Nicholas Ruiz,Interactions, LLC (United States)
Frank Seide,Microsoft Research (United States)
Ethan Selfridge,Interactions Corp (United States)
Chaitanya Shivade,IBM Research (United States)
Svetlana Stoyanchev,Interactions Corporation (United States)
Fabian Suchanek,Telecom ParisTech University (France)
Aniruddha Tammewar,Interactions Corporation (India)
Isabel Trancoso,INESC-ID / IST (Portugal)
Ling Tsou,SDL (United States)
Gokhan Tur,Uber (United States)
Jason D Williams,Microsoft Research (United States)
Fei Xia,University of Washington (United States)
Luke Zettlemoyer,University of Washington (United States)

Keynote Speaker:

Daniel Marcu, Amazon
Mari Ostendorf, University of Washington

Panel Moderator:

Philip Resnik, University of Maryland - College Park
Dirk Hovy, Università Bocconi

Table of Contents

Conference Program

Saturday, June 2, 2018

10:30–11:30   Machine Learning – Classification

10:30–10:47   *Scalable Wide and Deep Learning for Computer Assisted Coding*
Marilisa Amoia, Frank Diehl, Jesus Gimenez, Joel Pinto, Raphael Schumann, Fabian Stemmer, Paul Vozila and Yi Zhang

10:48–11:05   *Neural Network based Extreme Classification and Similarity Models for Product Matching*
Kashif Shah, Selcuk Kopru and Jean David Ruvini

11:06–11:23   *A Scalable Neural Shortlisting-Reranking Approach for Large-Scale Domain Classification in Natural Language Understanding*
Young-Bum Kim, Dongchan Kim, Joo-Kyung Kim and Ruhi Sarikaya

11:30–12:30   Dialog

11:30–11:47   *What we need to learn if we want to do and not just talk*
Rashmi Gangadharaiah, Balakrishnan Narayanaswamy and Charles Elkan

11:48–12:05   *Data Collection for Dialogue System: A Startup Perspective*
Yiping Kang, Yunqi Zhang, Jonathan K. Kummerfeld, Lingjia Tang and Jason Mars

12:05–12:23   *Bootstrapping a Neural Conversational Agent with Dialogue Self-Play, Crowdsourcing and On-Line Reinforcement Learning*
Pararth Shah, Dilek Hakkani-Tur, Bing Liu and Gokhan Tur

10:30am–12:00pm Session Posters and Demos: Generation

Quality Estimation for Automatically Generated Titles of eCommerce Browse Pages
Nicola Ueffing, José G. C. de Souza and Gregor Leusch

10:30–12:00 Session Posters and Demos: NLP Applications -

Atypical Inputs in Educational Applications
Su-Youn Yoon, Aoife Cahill, Anastassia Loukina, Klaus Zechner, Brian Riordan
and Nitin Madnani

Using Aspect Extraction Approaches to Generate Review Summaries and User Profiles
Christopher Mitcheltree, Veronica Wharton and Avneesh Saluja

SystemT: Declarative Text Understanding for Enterprise
laura chiticariu, Marina Danilevsky, Yunyao Li, Frederick Reiss and Huaiyu Zhu

Construction of the Literature Graph in Semantic Scholar
Waleed Ammar, Dirk Groeneveld, Chandra Bhagavatula, Iz Beltagy, Miles Crawford, Doug Downey, Jason Dunkelberger, Ahmed Elgohary, Sergey Feldman, Vu Ha, Rodney Kinney, Sebastian Kohlmeier, Kyle Lo, Tyler Murray, Hsu-Han Ooi, Matthew Peters, Joanna Power, Sam Skjonsberg, Lucy Wang, Chris Willhelm, Zheng Yuan, Madeleine van Zuylen and oren etzioni

14:00–15:00 Industry Track Keynote 1

14:00–15:00 *Building a Socialbot: Lessons Learned from 10M Conversations*
Mari Ostendorf

10:30–11:30   Machine Learning – Domain Adaptation

10:30–10:47   *Selecting Machine-Translated Data for Quick Bootstrapping of a Natural Language Understanding System*
Judith Gaspers, Penny Karanasou and Rajen Chatterjee

10:48–11:05   *Fast and Scalable Expansion of Natural Language Understanding Functionality for Intelligent Agents*
Anuj Kumar Goyal, Angeliki Metallinou and Spyros Matsoukas

11:05–11:22   *Bag of Experts Architectures for Model Reuse in Conversational Language Understanding*
Rahul Jha, Alex Marin, Suvamsh Shivaprasad and Imed Zitouni

11:30–12:30   Named Entity and Language Generation

11:30–11:47   *Multi-lingual neural title generation for e-Commerce browse pages*
Prashant Mathur, Nicola Ueffing and Gregor Leusch

11:48–12:05   *A Novel Approach to Part Name Discovery in Noisy Text*
Nobal Bikram Niraula, Daniel Whyatt and Anne Kao

12:06–12:23   *The Alexa Meaning Representation Language*
Thomas Kollar, Danielle Berry, Lauren Stuart, Karolina Owczarzak, Tagyoung Chung, Lambert Mathias, Michael Kayser, Bradford Snow and Spyros Matsoukas

10:30–12:00   **Session Posters and Demos: Social Media and Computational Social Science**

Document-based Recommender System for Job Postings using Dense Representations
Ahmed Elsafty, Martin Riedl and Chris Biemann

Scalable Wide and Deep Learning for Computer Assisted Coding

Marilisa Amoia[†], Frank Diehl[†], Jesus Gimenez[†], Joel Pinto[†], Raphael Schumann[‡],
Fabian Stemmer[†], Paul Vozila[†], Yi Zhang[†1]
[†]Nuance Communications
[‡]Institute for Computational Linguistics, Heidelberg University, Germany
{marilisa.amoia, frank.diehl, jesus.gimenez, joel.pinto, fabian.stemmer, paul.vozila,
yi.zhang}@nuance.com
rschuman@uni-heidelberg.de

Abstract

In recent years the use of electronic medical records has accelerated resulting in large volumes of medical data when a patient visits a healthcare facility. As a first step towards reimbursement healthcare institutions need to associate ICD-10 billing codes to these documents. This is done by trained clinical coders who may use a computer assisted solution for shortlisting of codes. In this work, we present our work to build a machine learning based scalable system for predicting ICD-10 codes from electronic medical records. We address data imbalance issues by implementing two system architectures using convolutional neural networks and logistic regression models. We illustrate the pros and cons of those system designs and show that the best performance can be achieved by leveraging the advantages of both using a system combination approach.

1 Introduction

Medical classification, also called medical coding, plays a vital role for healthcare providers. Medical coding is the process of assigning ICD-10 codes (2018) to a patient's visit in a healthcare facility. In the inpatient case these ICD-10 codes are further combined into Diagnosis-Related Groups (DRG) which classify inpatient stays into billing groups for the purposes of reimbursement.

Traditionally, medical coding is a manual process which involves a medical coder. The medical coder examines the complete encounter of a patient – the set of all associated Electronic Medical Records (EMRs) – and assigns the relevant ICD-10 codes. Medical classification is a complex task in many dimensions though. In the inpatient case the ICD-10 codes split into the Clinical Modification Coding System ICD-10-CM for diagnosis coding and the Procedure Coding System ICD-10-PCS for procedure coding. As of January 2018, there are 71704 ICD-10-CM codes and 78705 ICD-10-PCS codes (ICD-10, 2018).

Besides the sheer amount of possible codes, the coding process is further hampered by the unstructured nature of EMRs. Dependent on the individual encounter the set of associated EMRs can be very diverse (Scheurwegs et al., 2015). The EMRs may be composed out of discharge summaries, emergency room notes, imaging diagnoses, anesthesia process notes, laboratory reports, etcetera. In addition, EMRs typically stem from different physicians and laboratories. This results in large amounts of redundant information yet presented in different writing styles but without guarantee to be complete (Weiskopf et al., 2013; Cohen et al., 2013). Some of the EMRs may be composed out of free form written text whereas others contain dictated text, tables or a mixture of tables and text. Overall, when working with EMRs one is faced with severe data quality issues (Miotto et al., 2016).

To reduce the complexity of the medical coding task Computer Assisted Coding (CAC) was introduced. CAC is meant to automatically predict the relevant ICD-10 codes from the EMRs (Perotte et al., 2014; Scheurwegs et al., 2017; Shi et al., 2018; Pakhomov et al., 2006). Ideally CAC comes up with the exact set of codes which describe an encounter. However, due to the complexity of the task this is hardly possible. Instead CAC is typically designed to assist the medical coder by providing a list of most probable codes.

---

[1] Authors are listed in alphabetic order with respect to their family names.

Proceedings of NAACL-HLT 2018, pages 1–7
New Orleans, Louisiana, June 1 - 6, 2018. ©2017 Association for Computational Linguistics

In the paper on hand we present our work to design such a CAC system. The emphasis lies on industrial aspects as the scale and the scaling of the system. We describe the design of a system which models 3000 ICD-10-CM codes and applies up to 234k encounters to build the model. To address data imbalance issues a system combination approach was followed combining a wide and a deep modeling strategy (Heng et al., 2016). Finally, scaling aspects were examined by increasing the number of encounters used for training and development from 81k to 234k.

This paper is organized as follows. In Section 2 we state the problem under investigation. Section 3 gives a detailed description of the data, and Section 4 describes the methods we apply to approach the problem. Section 5 provides experiments and results, and Section 6 closes with the conclusions.

2 Problem description

The presented work studies the case of diagnosis code prediction for the inpatient case which corresponds to the prediction of ICD-10-CM codes. Typically, there are several ICD-10-CM codes which apply to an encounter making ICD-10-CM code prediction a multi-label classification task (Zhang and Zhou, 2014). Ultimately, the task consists in mapping a patient's encounter to all or a subset of the 71704 possible ICD-10-CM codes.

Traditionally, rule-based approaches which leverage linguistic expertise were used to address this problem (Farkas and Szarvas, 2008; Goldstein et al., 2007). Rule based methods don't rely on training data. Yet, this advantage is dearly bought by a lack of scalability and the need for linguistic expert knowledge which results in an expensive development phase and high maintenance costs.

The work on hand investigates the use of statistical methods for the CAC task. Statistical approaches have the advantage that they offer ways of continued learning. This can be leveraged to scale and improve the system over time which are important features in the dynamic environment healthcare providers are faced with.

3 Data and data preparation

The data used for this work stems from ten healthcare providers and covers 17 months of data. For the analysis of scalability aspects, the data was split into two partitions. Partition A covers 6 months of data and partition B covers additional 10 months of data. The remaining one month of data served as test set. For both partitions, 5% of the data was segregated and used as development (dev) set. The dev set is meant for threshold tuning, the generation of early stopping metrics and the estimation of interpolation weights. Table 1 provides some key statistics of the data.

One peculiarity of the data are encounters which are quite long, see Figure 1. The average and the median encounter length was found to be 11676 and 7238 tokens, respectively. In addition, the encounter length distribution exhibits a long tail. At the upper end there are 1422 encounters (0.63%) with more than 100k tokens and the maximum encounter length reaches 857k tokens.

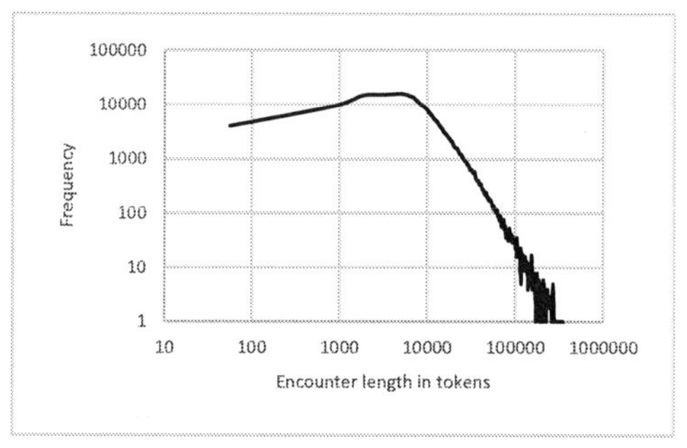

Figure 1: Encounter length distribution.

Figure 2 shows the ranked frequency distribution over the target codes. From Figure 2 it is apparent that out of the 18846 codes seen in the data about two-thirds appear less than ten times. This code sparsity issue had a direct impact on the system design as many of the codes can hardly be modeled.

Data preprocessing was kept at a minimum. After concatenating all EHRs of one encounter into one document lowercasing was applied. Date and time expressions as well as URLs, phone numbers and other numerical expressions were

	Partition-A Train/Dev	Partition-B Train/Dev	Test
#months of data	6	16	1
#encounters	81k	234k	14.1k
#tokens	0.9G	2.6G	160M
#running codes	870k	2.5M	143k
#codes types	13094	18846	6863

Table 1: Data statistics.

canonicalized. Finally, after applying some shallow normalization (hyphens, underscores) tokenization was done using whitespace as token separators.

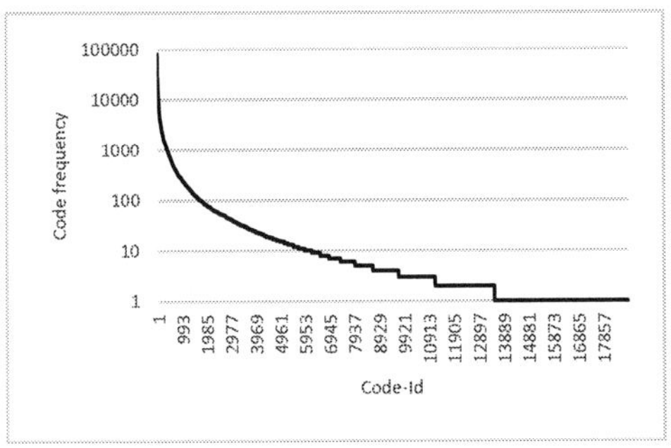

Figure 2: Code frequency over code-IDs.

4 Models and methods

As mentioned in Section 3 we had to operate over a set of codes with a wide range of occurrence probabilities. For some of the target codes training material was abundant whereas for others we were faced by severe data sparsity. To address this issue, we followed a system combination strategy combining a set of Logistic Regression (LR) classifiers, with a Convolutional Neural Network (CNN).

To cope with the multi-label nature of the classification problem we applied a first-order modeling strategy tackling the task in a code-by-code manner thus ignoring the coexistence of other codes (Zhang and Zhou, 2014). In case of LR this modeling strategy was strict, meaning that one LR model was built per target code. In the CNN case a relaxed version of this strategy was applied. One common CNN was built, with the target codes modeled conditionally independent by the loss function.

Regularized binary cross-entropy was applied for both the LR and the CNN objective function. In all cases model training was followed by a threshold tuning step to determine optimal decision thresholds. Finally, all test results are presented in terms of micro-F1 (Wu and Zhou, 2017).

4.1 Logistic regression

LR is a well understood and robust classification method. It is expected to perform well even for low frequency classes. The problem is convex and typically applied in conjunction with a L1 or a L2 regularization, the $\|w\|$ term in the LR objective function (1).

$$\min_{w} \; C\|w\| + \sum_{i=1}^{l} \log\left(1 + e^{-y_i w^T x_i}\right) \quad (1)$$

For solving the LR problem we used LibLinear (Fan et al., 2008) which is a large-scale linear classification library. The LibLinear solver exhibits the advantage that there is only one free hyperparameter to tune, namely the regularization weight C.

4.2 Convolutional neural networks

Compared to LR a CNN features an increased complexity. This higher modeling capability comes though with the need for more training data which makes it more suited for high frequency classes.

The CNN design we applied for this work follows the work described in Kalchbrenner et al. (2014) and Conneau et al. (2016). The basic architecture consists of one convolutional layer which is followed by max-pooling resulting in one feature per convolutional filter and document. As input to the convolutional layer word embeddings apply which were pre-trained using word2vec (Mikolov et al., 2013). The feature extraction layer is succeeded by the classification part of the network consisting of a feed-forward network of one fully-connected hidden layer and the final output layer. The output layer is formed by one node with sigmoid activation for each ICD-10 code, effectively modeling the code's probability.

Additional convolutional layers are added in conjunction with highway layers connecting each convolutional layer directly with the classification part of the network. The highway connections and the output of the last convolutional layer are followed by the same max-pooling operation described above. The convolutional layers are connected by a sliding-window max-pooling operation. For each filter of the lower convolutional layer a max-pooling operator of kernel-width 3 is applied to the stream of filter output values. With a stride of one the layer's output consists of a vector-feature stream which is of the same length as the input token sequence and a vector-dimension equal to the number of filters of the lower convolutional layer.

For our CNN implementation Theano (2017) was used. All CNNs were built using a NVIDIA P6000 GPU with 22GByte GPU-memory.

4.3 System combination

System combination was implemented by linearly interpolating the hypothesized predictions from the LR system and the CNN system. The interpolation weights were optimized maximizing dev set micro-F1. In case of codes which were not modeled by the CNN the LR predictions were directly used.

5 Experiments and results

For practical reasons it was not possible to model all ICD-10-CM codes. Most of the 71704 ICD-10-CM codes are never seen in the available data and even many of the seen codes are too rare to be modeled, see Figure 2. We therefore restricted our models to the most frequent codes seen within the first seven month of data. For the LR systems we used the most frequent 3000 codes. The CNN was restricted to model only the most frequent 1000 codes which reflects the data sparsity issues discussed in Section 3. With these settings a code coverage of >95% for the LR systems and >87 % for the CNN systems was obtained. Table 2 gives detailed code coverage statistics of the training data.

Model testing was directly affected by the target

Parti- tion	Data statistics	Top 200/1k/3k and All seen codes			
		200	1000	3000	All
A	#running codes	560k	768k	836k	870k
A	#code coverage	64.4%	88.3%	96.2%	100%
B	#running codes	1.6M	2.1M	2.3M	2.5M
B	#code coverage	63.3%	87.3%	95.2%	100%

Table 2: Code coverage statistics.

code restrictions. Out of the 143k running codes of the test set 6189 instances are not covered by the 3000 modeled codes and 71 of the 3000 modeled codes do even not appear in the test set.

The following experiments give results for the most frequent (top) 200, 1000, and 3000 codes and all codes seen in the test set. Note that for the case of 1000 codes and the case of 3000 codes there are 17653 and 6189 code instances, respectively, which are not modeled. These instances always entered the F1 calculation as false negatives when scored on all seen codes.

5.1 Basic system development

This phase of the project focused on basic system design question. All experiments were carried out using data-partition A.

In case of the LR system we model a document as a 'bag-of-ngrams' up to an ngram-length of three. With a frequency cutoff of 20 this gave 4.1M features. Using higher order ngram-features or a smaller cutoff value didn't provide any improvements. For all LR experiments described in this work indicator features apply.

Table 3 lists the results of two LR systems. Both systems apply the same feature file which is used for all 3000 code specific classifiers. The basic LRa system applies a common regularization weight C for all codes. In case of system LRa2 the regularization weight C was tuned individually for each code using 4-fold cross-validation over the training set. Tuning the regularization weights resulted in micro-F1 gains of ~0.8% absolute. Using an increased fold number didn't provide any improvements.

For the CNN experiments we first used the CNN design with one convolutional layer described in Section 4. After some initial experiments the convolutional layer of the network was fixed to 900 filters with a filter width of five tokens. The hidden layer was fixed to 1024 nodes and the output layer models the most frequent 1000 ICD-10-CM codes. Max-pooling was followed by Relu-activations.

All models were trained with RMSPROB. The convolutional layer used L2-regularization and L1-regularization was used for the hidden layer and the output layer. Dropout was applied to the output of the max-pool operation. Best results were achieved with a batch size (encounter level) of 32.

The result named CNa1 in Table 3 follows the

System	Micro-F1 for the top 200/1k/3k codes and All seen codes			
	200	1000	3000	All
LRa1	70.37	64.03	61.59	60.19
LRa2	71.48	64.81	62.38	60.96
CNa1	73.96	66.31	63.31	61.79
CNa2	74.82	67.25	64.24	62.71
LRa2 & CNa2	75.38	68.61	65.65	64.14

Table 3: Partition-A test results. LRa1: LR no c-tuning; LRa2: LR with c-tuning, CNa1: CNN 1 convolutional layer; CNa2: CNN 2 convolutional layers; LRa2 & CNa2: interpolated system.

design with one convolutional layer. The CNa1 system was initialized with 50-dimensional word embeddings which were pre-trained on the training data with word2vec (Mikolov et al., 2013). These embeddings were further refined during network training. This gave a final micro-F1 of 66.31% absolute when scored over the 1000 modeled codes. Best results were obtained with 50-dimensional embeddings and without batch normalization within the convolutional layer.

In a second step some initial experiments with the two convolutional layers CNN design were carried out. This network featured 300 filters and 900 filters in the first and second convolutional layer, respectively. The filter width was set to five and Relu-activations were used for the first layer.

Table 3 shows that the two convolutional layers system CNa2 achieves the best performance of a single system with an absolute increase in micro-F1 of ~0.9% over the CNa1 system with its one convolutional layer. In contrast to the setup with one convolutional layer the use of batch normalization turned out to be essential in the two-convolutional layer setup. Dropping it gave worse results compared to the one-convolutional layer design.

Finally, we explored the combination of the LR approach with the CNN approach. Linearly interpolating the LRa2 system with the CNa2 system gave the best results with 64.44% micro-F1 (65.37% precision, 63.53% recall) clearly outperforming the underlying individual systems. We also examined other system combination strategies following the work from Heng et al. (2016). However, the linear interpolation approach described in this work turned out to work best.

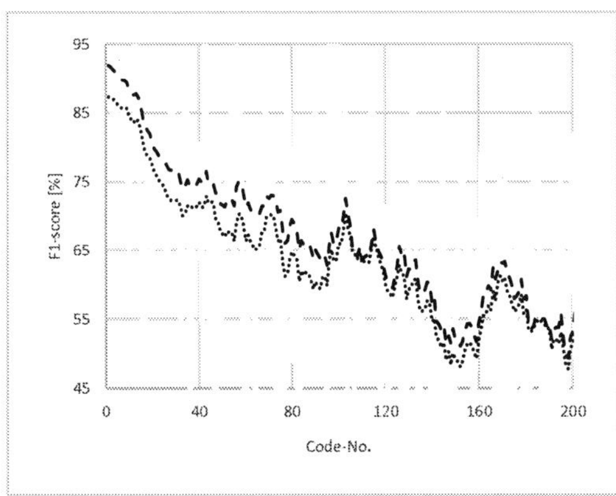

Figure 3: F1-scores, top 200 codes, CNN (dashed line) versus LR (dotted line).

Investigating the performance of the LRa2 system and the CNa2 system on code level, we found our assumption confirmed that the CNN is more suited to model high frequency codes whereas the LR system does better for low frequency codes. Figure 3 shows that the CNN does better for the most frequent 200 codes. However, after a transition region covering roughly the next 300 codes, the LR system starts to outperform the CNN sys-

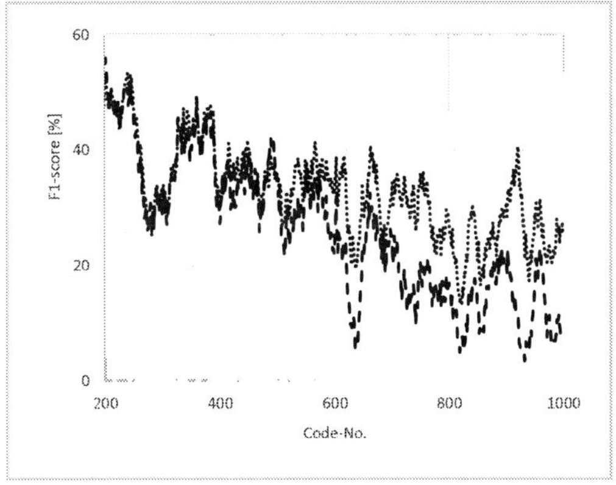

Figure 4: F1-scores, top 201-1000 codes, CNN (dashed line) versus LR (dotted line)

tem consistently, starting approximately from code position 500 on, see Figure 4.

These finding were reconfirmed when checking for the relative improvements of the combined LRa2 & CNa2 system over the CNa2 system. Comparing the scores for the most frequent 200 codes and the most frequent 1000 codes one finds 0.75% and 2.02% relative improvements, respectively. The LR system also fills up the 2000 codes not modeled by the CNN giving in a relative micro-F1 win of 2.19% when scoring over 3000 codes.

An integral part of the model building process was the tuning of the decision thresholds. Though individual thresholds per code are possible best micro-F1 results were always achieved with a common decision threshold over all codes. This behavior reflects again the data sparsity issues as not all modeled codes appear in the dev set and many other codes are so sparse that no robust threshold estimation was possible.

5.2 System refinements

In this phase of the project we focused on improved training recipes and the use of more training data given by data-partition B. We kept on modeling the same set of codes as used in Section 5.2. This lead

		Micro-F1 for the top 200/1k/3k codes and All seen codes			
System	#features	200	1000	3000	All
LRa2	4.1M	71.48	64.81	62.38	60.96
LRb1	9.2M	72.62	66.18	63.83	62.39
LRb2	149k	72.78	66.41	64.05	62.59
LRb3	7 - 5113	73.45	66.70	64.18	62.72

Table 4: Partition-B LR test results. LRa2: Partition-A reference system; LRb1: Same as LRa2 but with Phase-B data; LRb2: Same as LRb1 but with feature reduction; LRb3: system with per-code quadratic-kernel features.

to a slight reduction in code coverage, see Table 2, but guaranteed the comparability of the results.

For LR a bootstrapping approach was followed aiming to refine the system step-by-step from one model to the next model. We built up on the training recipe used to build system LRa2, see Section 5.1, i.e. L1 regularized LR with per-code tuned regularization constants C. First, we switched to the larger data-partition B which added additional 10 months of data to the original 6 months of data. Comparing the resulting LRb1 system with the LRa2 system, see Table 4, we found that the additional data improved micro-F1 by ~1.2% absolute.

The use of more data increased the features space from 4.1M features to 9.2M features. To ease subsequent development work, we applied a feature reduction approach taking advantage of the feature selection property of the L1 regularization (Andrew Ng, 2004). Reducing the feature space of the LRb1 system to all features with none-zero model weights reduced the features space by a factor of 62 giving 149k features. This feature selection step also improved system performance by ~0.2% absolute micro-F1, see LRb2 in Table 4.

LR is a linear classification method fitting a hyperplane as decision boundary into feature space. To leverage the increased modeling capabilities of a none-linear modeling regime, we applied a quadratic kernel to the feature space. With a features dimension of 149k this is yet a prohibitive endeavor. Instead we used code specific reduced features spaces. Based on the most prominent 400 features per code the quadratic kernel was applied which gave up to 80.2k squared features per code. After model building these features spaces were reduced again to all features with none-zero model weights.

	Micro-F1 for the top 200/1k/3k codes and All seen codes			
System	200	1000	3000	All
CNa1	73.96	66.31	63.31	61.79
CNb1	74.19	67.34	64.36	62.85
CNa2	74.82	67.25	64.24	62.71
LRb3 & CNa2	75.71	69.07	66.11	64.60

Table 5: Partition-B CNN and combined test results. CNa1: Partition-A 1-convolutional layer reference system; CNb1: Same as CNa1 but with Partition-B data; CNa2: Partition-A 2-convolutional layer reference system; LRb3 & CNa2: interpolated system.

Table 4 lists the corresponding results as LRb3. For the most frequent 200 codes absolute micro-F1 improvements of ~0.7% are observed with respect to the LRb2 system. For the less frequent codes this effect is nearly washed out though.

The partition B data was also applied to the CNN. Table 5 compares the corresponding 1-convolutional layer system built on the partition B data with the CNNs built on the partition A data[2]. We found that the additional 10 month of training data provide a ~0.2% - ~1% improvement in absolute micro-F1. Note that system CNb1 outperforms system CNa2 when soring over all 1000 modeled codes but that system CNa2 is better when scoring only over the top 200 codes, see Table 5. We attribute this behavior to the change in the code distribution when switching from partition A to partition B.

Finally, the best LR system, LRb3, was combined with the CNa2 system giving the best overall results with a micro-F1 of 64.60% (68.10% precision, 61.60% recall). Compared to the best single systems, CNa2 and CNb1, absolute micro-F1 improvements of ~1.8% - ~1.9% are observed.

6 Conclusions

In this work we have presented our work on building a machine learnable CAC system. The focus lies on aspects developers are faced with in practice. Data peculiarities like data amount, imbalances in code frequencies or sample length were discussed. We provide evidence that the imbalance issues are best addressed by a dedicated modeling approach for each datatype. Finally, with our combined LR-CNN system which models 3000 ICD-10-CM codes we achieved a micro-

---

[2] At the time of writing this paper the results for the 2-convolutional layer CNN which was built on the partition B data was still not available.

F1 score of 64.60% when scored over all codes seen in the test set.

References

Alexis Conneau, Holger Schwenk, Loïc Barrault, Yann Lecun, Very Deep Convolutional Networks for Text Classification. In *Proceedings of the 15th Conference of the European Chapter of the Association for Computational Linguistics*, 2016, pages 1107-1116. https://arxiv.org/pdf/1606.01781.pdf

Andrew Ng, Feature selection, L1 vs. L2 regularization, and rotational invariance. In *Proceedings of the 21st International Conference on Machine Learning*, Association for Computational Linguistics, 2004, page 78. http://ai.stanford.edu/~ang/papers/icml04-l1l2.pdf

A. Perotte, R. Pivovarov, K. Natarajan, N. Weiskopf, F. Wood, N. Elhadad, 2014, Diagnosis code assignment: models and evaluation metrics. In the *Journal of the American Medical Informatics Association*. https://www.ncbi.nlm.nih.gov/pmc/articles/PMC3932472/pdf/amiajnl-2013-002159.pdf

Diagnosis-related group. Design and development of the Diagnosis Related Group (DRG). https://www.cms.gov/

Elyne Scheurwegs, Boris Cule, Kim Luyckx, Léon Luyten, Walter Daelemans, Selecting Relevant Features from the Electronic Health Record for Clinical Code Prediction. *Preprint submitted to Journal of Biomedical Informatics*, 2017. http://win.ua.ac.be/~adrem/bibrem/pubs/confcov.pdf

Elyne Scheurwegs, Kim Luyckx, Léon Luyten, Walter Daelemans, Tim Van den Bulcke, Data integration of structured and unstructured sources for assigning clinical codes to patient stays. In the *Journal of the American Medical Informatics Association*, 2015 https://www.clips.uantwerpen.be/~walter/papers/2015/slldv15.pdf

Haoran Shi, Pengtao Xie, Zhiting Hu, Ming Zhang, Eric Xing, Towards Automated ICD Coding Using Deep Learning. In *https://arxiv.org/*, 2018. https://arxiv.org/pdf/1711.04075.pdf

Heng-Tze Cheng, Levent Koc, Jeremiah Harmsen, Tal Shaked, Tushar Chandra, Hrishi Aradhye, Glen Anderson, Greg Corrado, Wei Chai, Mustafa Ispir, Rohan Anil, Zakaria Haque, Lichan Hong, Vihan Jain, Xiaobing Liu, Hemal Shah. Wide & Deep Learning for Recommender Systems. In *https://arxiv.org/*, 2016, https://arxiv.org/pdf/1606.07792.pdf

I. Goldstein, A. Arzumtsyan, O. Uzuner, Three Approaches to Automatic Assignment of ICD-9-CM Codes to Radiology Reports, In *AMIA Annual Symposium Proceedings*, 2007, pages 279–283, https://www.ncbi.nlm.nih.gov/pmc/articles/PMC2655861/pdf/amia-0279-s2007.pdf

M. L. Zhang, Z. H. Zhou, A review on multi-label learning algorithms, In *IEEE Transactions on Knowledge and Data Engineering*, 2014, pages 1819-1837. http://ieeexplore.ieee.org/stamp/stamp.jsp?arnumber=6471714

Nal Kalchbrenner, Edward Grefenstette, Phil Blunsom, Phil, A Convolutional Neural Network for Modeling Sentences. In *Proceedings of the 52nd Annual Meeting of the Association for Computational Linguistics (Volume 1: Long Papers)*, Association for Computational Linguistics, 2014, pages 655-665. https://arxiv.org/pdf/1404.2188.pdf

N. G. Weiskopf, G. Hripcsak, S. Swaminathan,C. Weng, Defining and measuring completeness of electronic health records for secondary use. In Journal of Biomedical Informatics, 2013. https://www.ncbi.nlm.nih.gov/pmc/articles/PMC3810243/

R. Cohen, M. Elhadad, N. Elhadad, Redundancy in electronic health record corpora: analysis, impact on text mining performance and mitigation strategies, In *BMC Bioinformatics*, 2013. https://bmcbioinformatics.biomedcentral.com/articles/10.1186/1471-2105-14-10

Richárd Farkas, György Szarvas, Automatic construction of rule-based ICD-9-CM coding systems, In *BMC Bioinformatics*, 2008, https://bmcbioinformatics.biomedcentral.com/articles/10.1186/1471-2105-9-S3-S10

R.-E. Fan, K.-W. Chang, C.-J. Hsieh, X.-R. Wang, and C.-J. Lin, LIBLINEAR: A library for large linear classification. In *Journal of Machine Learning Research*, 2008, pages 1871-1874. https://www.csie.ntu.edu.tw/~cjlin/papers/liblinear.pdf

R. Miotto, L. Li, B. A. Kidd, J. T. Dudley, Deep Patient: An Unsupervised Representation to Predict the Future of Patients from the Electronic Health Records. In *Nature Scientific Reports*, 2016 https://www.nature.com/articles/srep26094/

S. Pakhomov, J. D. Buntrock, C. G. Chute, Automating the Assignment of Diagnosis Codes to Patient Encounters Using Example-based and Machine Learning Techniques. In the *Journal of the American Medical Informatics Association*, 2006. https://www.ncbi.nlm.nih.gov/pmc/articles/PMC1561792/pdf/516.06001186.pdf

Theano, http://deeplearning.net/software/theano/

Tomas Mikolov, Kai Chen, Greg Corrado, Jeffrey Dean, Efficient Estimation of Word Representations in Vector Space. In, *ICLR Workshop, 2013*. https://arxiv.org/pdf/1301.3781.pdf

World Health Organization ICD. World Health Organization, International classification of diseases, http://www.who.int/classifications/icd/en/

Xi-Zhu Wu 1 Zhi-Hua Zhou, A Unified View of Multi-Label Performance Measures, In *https://arxiv.org/*, 2017. https://arxiv.org/pdf/1609.00288.pdf

Neural Network based Extreme Classification and Similarity Models for Product Matching

Kashif Shah, Selcuk Kopru, Jean-David Ruvini

eBay Research, Hamilton Avenue San Jose, CA 95125, USA

{skshah,skopru,jean-david.ruvini}@ebay.com

Abstract

Matching a seller listed item to an appropriate product has become a fundamental and one of the most significant step for e-commerce platforms for product based experience. It has a huge impact on making the search effective, search engine optimization, providing product reviews and product price estimation etc. along with many other advantages for a better user experience. As significant and vital it has become, the challenge to tackle the complexity has become huge with the exponential growth of individual and business sellers trading millions of products everyday. We explored two approaches; classification based on shallow neural network and similarity based on deep siamese network. These models outperform the baseline by more than 5% in term of accuracy and are capable of extremely efficient training and inference.

1 Introduction

E-commerce marketplaces such as Amazon and eBay provide platforms where millions of people trade online every day. The growth of such marketplaces has been exponential in recent years with millions of active sellers and billions of live items listed at any point in time, bringing new interesting challenges.

On the buying side, while it provides buyers with more options and flexibility, it renders searching for a specific item and comparing items difficult. On the selling side, it dilutes the visibility of the sellers' items both on the marketplace and on external search engines such as Google and Bing. Also, it requires the sellers to provide a lot of details about the goods they are listing.

The product based experience is an enticing search experience that helps fulfill both buyers and sellers needs. The buyers can easily search, compare and make a decision on the product they wish to purchase while the sellers can speed up their listing process by using product details and stock photos from existing product catalog resulting in a professional-looking listing, more appealing in search results.

The process of automatically mapping items[1] to products become critical. Different sellers may describe the same item in very different ways, using very different terminologies. While some business sellers provide rich, structured description of their listings, the vast majority only provide short and sometimes insufficient information. The problem become even harder when information provided is not specific enough to identify the corresponding products. Lots of studies have been focused on structuring the products inventory by extracting and enriching attribute-value pairs (Mauge et al., 2012; Ghani et al., 2006) from various sources, and feed them into a matching function. The direction towards learning automatic semantic relationships on unstructured sequence of e-commerce text has been of less focus.

Neural based methods have recently shown to work well to capture the meanings and semantic relationships among words in textual data. In this paper, we aim at studying such approaches for e-commerce domain. We explored two neural network architectures for our product matching task; a simple shallow neural network model based on the *fastText* (Joulin et al., 2016b; Bojanowski et al., 2016; Joulin et al., 2016a) library and a deep siamese network model based on bidirectional long short term memory (Neculoiu et al., 2016; Mueller and Thyagarajan, 2016). We approach the problem in two ways, as a classification task where we have access to item listings and

---

[1] An *item* is an offer from a seller for a specific good containing seller specific information (description, condition, return, etc.). A *product* is the catalog (manufacturer) description of a good.

Proceedings of NAACL-HLT 2018, pages 8–15

New Orleans, Louisiana, June 1 - 6, 2018. ©2017 Association for Computational Linguistics

corresponding product ids, and as a similarity task where we also have access to product information. These approaches constitute different objective functions; classification aims at classifying an input instance into the identity classes, while similarity objective is to minimize the intra-class distance while maximizing the inter-class distance.

In the next section, we will discuss the challenges, section 3 contains the approaches and models we explored, and section 4 discusses the experiments and results. We will conclude after briefly reviewing the related work in section 5.

2 Challenges

Product matching is a difficult task due to the wider spectrum of products, many alike but different products, often missing or wrong values, and frequent variation in textual nature of products. In the following sections, we will briefly cover the challenges that make the task of product matching hard.

2.1 Data Sparsity

While some business and professional sellers provide rich information of their item listings, a vast majority of medium and small sellers provide short, unstructured and sometimes incomplete descriptions. This results in a lot of data sparsity due to missing values that are important to identify the products.

2.2 Product Duplicates

Data sparsity and erroneous information automatically extracted from unstructured or semi-structured sources may result into creation of the same product twice or multiple times called duplicates. The product duplicates are not only one of the biggest source of bad product experience, but also makes the product matching harder as multiple entities of the same product exists with overlapping information. The duplicates can have many fatal effects, including preventing machine learning algorithms from discovering important consistencies in product representations.

2.3 Single Source Products

There are many rare products such as antiques, collectibles, books, sculptures, etc. that are offered by only a particular single or business seller. Such products are often referred as single source products. In such cases, the description of the product can not be cross-validated in the absence of alternative sources. This causes a *one-shot* learning problem, which consists of learning a class from a single labeled example.

2.4 Product Bundles and Lots

Bundles are defined as multiple different products being grouped together and sold as a single offer. If the offer contains multiples of the same product these offers are referred as a *lot*. They make data ambiguous such as a number in product description could be a lot quantity or variation of product edition. Such product offers exhibit another level of complexity requiring special treatment or a separate model to identify lots and bundles.

2.5 Extreme Classification

Traditionally, multi-class classification solutions have been scalable up-to few hundred classes. As the number of classes grow, the time and space complexity increase exponentially to the extent that standard models do not scale up. For the task of product matching, the number of products are in millions and hence the methods that can scale up to million classes are required.

2.6 Open Set Classification

The number of classes are usually pre-defined for classification tasks and models are designed to predict one of those pre-defined classes for a given instance. For the task for product matching, new products are created everyday and they become part of inventory incrementing the amount of products daily. It either requires to re-train the models frequently with newly created products with additional classes or to employ models capable of handling unseen products.

3 Text Classification vs Similarity

The aim of text classification is to assign some piece of text (source) to one or more predefined classes or labels (targets). The piece of text could be a document, news article, listing offers, email, product review etc. Depending upon the task, the target labels are usually topic, category, product, sentiment id or name. Traditional classification approaches are employed to learn feature representation on the source and attempt to predict the target label. There are cases where inputs are text pairs along with their relevance score such as question-answer, query-document, source-translation pairs etc. Both input texts can be encoded with rich representations. For such cases similarity based methods are natural architecture to learn differentiation among them.

We research both classification and similarity algorithms for product matching. Classification based approach using shallow neural network based on *fastText* library turns out to be very efficient with good performance but it requires to re-train the models for newly created products as mentioned in previous section. The similarity based method does not have this bottle neck as it is tailored towards open class set problem given a sufficient amount of paired dataset. The similarity based method also allows to use product side data in more natural way to model our paired item-product data.

3.1 Shallow Neural Network - *fastText*

Learning word representations has a long history in natural language processing. These representations are typically learned from large corpora either using count statistics or distributed semantic representations. Recently, (Mikolov et al., 2013) proposed simple log-bilinear models to learn continuous representations of words on very large corpora efficiently using Continuous Bag Of Words (CBOW) and Skip-gram models. Both of these are shallow neural networks which map word(s) to the target variable which is also a word(s). Both of these methods learn weights which act as word vector representations. The assumption of these models is that semantically or grammatically related words are mapped to similar geometric locations in a high-dimensional continuous space. The probability distribution is thus much smoother and therefore the model has a better generalization power on unseen events.

Recently proposed *fastText* (Joulin et al., 2016b)[2] library extended these models for supervised classification tasks. This architecture is similar to the CBOW model of (Mikolov et al., 2013), where the center word is replaced by a label. They also incorporated bag-of-ngram as additional features to capture some partial information about the local word order. The n-grams features are efficiently implemented by using the hashing trick (Goodman, 2001).

The output layer consists of a softmax function that assigns a probability distribution to each of the

target label. The loss function aims at minimizing the negative log-likelihood over the classes. Because full-softmax is not scalable for large number of classes, *fastText* offers hierarchical-softmax as an alternate approach. This implementation uses huffman tree to reduce the complexity to logarithmic while incurring minor performance degradation. The hierarchical softmax function is the key factor that makes the task scalable to our million class dataset. For full details, we refer the reader to the original paper (Joulin et al., 2016b).

For our product matching task, these models not only offer the benefit of the rich distributed representation of item listings but also allow to deal with millions of classes while reducing the training time from days to minutes, and keeping good performance in terms of accuracy.

3.2 Siamese Networks

Siamese networks are a special type of neural network architecture having two identical structure trained simultaneously with shared weights. Instead of a model learning to classify its inputs, the neural network learns to differentiate between two inputs. In our case, we are interested in finding similarity between the item listings and corresponding products given pairs whose semantic similarity has been labeled. Our siamese network consists of two parallel neural networks, each taking one of the two inputs, listings or products in our case, along with a binary score (1 for match and 0 for mismatch).

Different kind of parallel structures has been explored for various tasks including Convolutional Neural Networks (CNN), Skip-thought vectors, Tree-LSTM etc. Recurrent Neural Networks (RNN) have shown promising performance on textual sequence of data for various NLP tasks. The Long Short Term Memory (LSTM) networks proved to be superior to basic RNNs for learning long range dependencies through its use of memory cell units that can store/access information across lengthy input sequences. The Bidirectional LSTM networks can leverage the knowledge present on both sides of the current word to encode the text and have shown good performance on various NLP tasks like named entity recognition (Huang et al., 2015; Wang et al., 2015) and text similarity (Neculoiu et al., 2016).

In this work, we studied BiLSTMs for our siamese network architecture that is very similar

---

[2]https://github.com/facebookresearch/fastText

to (Mueller and Thyagarajan, 2016) in architecture but we employed BiLSTM along with the contrastive loss function (instead of Manhattan LSTM) [3]. The network consists of three hidden layers and each layer consists of 50 hidden units. The LSTM units of our bidirectional network contain a memory state having an input, forget and output gate with the logistic function on the gates and the hyperbolic tangent (tanh) on the activations:

$$i_t = \sigma(W_{xi}x_t + W_{hi}h_{t-1} + b_i)$$
$$f_t = \sigma(W_{xf}x_t + W_{hf}h_{t-1} + b_f)$$
$$o_t = \sigma(W_{xo}x_t + W_{ho}h_{t-1} + b_o)$$
$$j_t = \tanh(W_{xj}x_t + W_{hj}h_{t-1} + b_j)$$
$$c_t = f_t \otimes c_{t-1} + i_t \otimes j_t$$
$$h_t = \tanh(c_t) \otimes o_t$$

where σ is the logistic sigmoid function, $\mathbf{W}_{hi}, \mathbf{W}_{hf}, \mathbf{W}_{ho}, \mathbf{W}_{hj}$ are recurrent weight matrices and $\mathbf{W}_{xi}, \mathbf{W}_{xf}, \mathbf{W}_{xo}, \mathbf{W}_{xj}$ are projection matrices. b are the bias terms in equations.

The inputs are represented as a sequence of words with a maximum length of 100 and (shorter sequences are padded). The output of the combined model at each time step is simply the concatenation of the outputs from the forward and backward networks. The outputs of the last layer are averaged over time and the output vectors are fed to the contrastive loss function:

$$E = \frac{1}{2N} \sum_{n=1}^{N} (y)\, D + (1 - y) \max(m - d, 0)$$

where $D = ||a_n - b_n||_2^2$ is euclidean distance between the outputs a_n and b_n of the two parallel networks. In our case, y is either 1 or 0. If the inputs are from the same class, then the value of y is 1, otherwise y is 0. $m > 0$ denotes a margin which acts as a boundary (with the radius m). The motivation behind this loss function is that similar pairs tend to be as close as possible and dissimilar pairs must be separated by a distance defined by the margin. The network is optimized using Adam optimizer along with dropout to prevent over-fitting.

4 Experiments and Results

We performed a set of experiments on an *eBay* dataset. The data has been collected over the years and contain millions of products and billions of listings. We divided the data into meta-categories and models are trained on these categories separately. This partition into categories not only keep the data size to a affordable level given the resources but also allow us to train the models in parallel for each category being independent.

In this paper, we only report the experiments for three categories namely Electronics, Clothes, Shoes and Accessories (CSA), and Collectibles as the proof-of-concept. In the next sections, we will briefly explain how this historical data has been created.

4.1 Dataset

Many branded items have unique identifiers that help buyers recognize and find them, including the items *brand*, Manufacturer Part Number (*mpn*), and Global Trade Item Number (*gtin*). The *gtin* can include an items Universal Product Code (*upc*), European Article Number (*ean*), or International Standard Book Number (*isbn*). Around 80% of our training data is created with these identifiers. The remaining 20% data is either adopted[4] by sellers or made available from third party sources. The statistics about the data used for experiments reported in the paper are given in table 1.

Our dataset consists of four fields, the *title* that are available for all instances, *gtin*, *brand* and *mpn* that are partially available as shown in Table 1. The classification experiments are based on combination of these inputs for item listings along with *product-id* as label. The inputs are just concatenated to make a single sequence of text. For similarity experiments, we made use of corresponding product *title*, *gtin*, *brand* and *mpn*. For the test set, we sampled the data randomly from our training set and performed manual validation. The validation is done against multiple sources available online such as other marketplaces etc. The validation score is simply a 1/0 label, 1 if the product against the item listing is correct, otherwise 0.

Basic data normalization is performed such as tokenization, lower casing, removing noise words (e.g. doesn't apply, not applicable etc). We removed the instances that contain a single word as they do not convey any meaningful information. Exact same listings are merged into a single in-

---

[3]we adapted an open source implementation for our task: https://github.com/dhwajraj/deep-siamese-text-similarity

[4]The sellers chose among the existing products in the catalog for their item listings.

Category	#listings	gtin	brand	mpn	#products	test
Electronics	9.38	5.60	7.19	6.45	3.17	6468
CSA	21.09	6.73	11.96	3.75	9.78	3549
Collectibles	0.80	0.28	0.58	0.38	0.58	1999

Table 1: Data Statistics (all numbers are in millions except the test set). *gtin*, *brand* and *mpn* column show the total number of these fields available for item listings.

| Category | baseline | *fastText* | | | | Siamese |
		title	title+gtin	title+brand+mpn	title+gtin+brand+mpn	all
Electronics	84.4	81.1	86.2	85.9	87.9	**89.9**
CSA	75.7	73.9	76.7	76.2	78.8	**82.4**
Collectibles	92.8	89.3	94.5	93.7	96.4	**97.1**

Table 2: Accuracy for 3 Meta-Categories: Electronics, CSA, and Collectibles

Category	pre-emb	product-data	accuracy
	yes	-	88.4
Electronics	-	yes	88.2
	yes	yes	**88.8**

Table 3: Accuracy with *fastText* models for Electronics using pre-embeddings and additional product data.

stance.

4.2 Results

Our baseline models are based on a waterfall approach. The first two modules are based on lookup tables for unique identifiers. In a first module, if the item listing has a *gtin* and it matches with the product in the inventory, then the item is adopted to matching product. The second module is based on *brand-mpn* lookup tables. Finally, if none of the unique identifiers are available, then the item listing is adopted to a product with highest string match[5].

We trained many *fastText* models with various combination of inputs. For all of our models, the embedding dimension is set 300, learning rate to 0.5, and number of epochs to 10. The n-gram parameter is set to 3 and it brings nice improvements than the models without these additional features. The hierarchical-softmax has been used as a loss function.

The results are shown in table 2. The combination of features produce better results than the models trained with *title* only even though *gtin*, *brand* and *mpn* are partially available. The combination of all features give the best perfor-

mance followed by models with combination of *title+gtin*. This is because of the fact that the *brand* or *mpn* are sometimes already available in *title* while *gtin* rarely appear in listing *title*. Therefore, inclusion of additional *brand* and *mpn* do not bring as much additional information as *gtin*.

We also trained the *fastText* models using pre-trained embedding and product data as additional resource for Electronics. The pre-embeddings are learned with *fastText* using unsupervised CBOW model on all of the listings available for the respective category. In a second setting, we simply merge the product data in our training set. The results are shown in table 3. Even though our initial dataset is quite large but it is evident from the results that these additional resources bring further improvements as they offer more coverage and completeness.

For Siamese Network, the models are trained using the item-product pairs as described in section 3.2. We set the embedding dimensions to 300, number of epochs to 100 and mini-batch size to 128. During inference for a given item listing, we first need to generate the item-product pairs to measure the similarity. It is prohibitively impractical to compare each item with all the products in the given category particularly for inference during production. Therefore, we first reduced the target space by generating top 500-best products with *fastText* models. Then, these pairs are fed to the Siamese network to calculate the similarity. The pair having highest similarity score is picked as matching. We also explored the n-gram matching approach to reduce the target space but n-best with *fastText* method turns out to be bet-

---

[5]any unigram overlap.

Category	*fastText*		Siamese	
	train	infer	train	infer
Electronics	56s	5ms	20mins	15ms
CSA	90s	8ms	30mins	21ms
Collectibles	20s	3ms	10mins	11ms

Table 4: *fastText* versus Siamese training (per epoch) and inference time (per instance), mins=minutes, s=seconds, ms=milliseconds

ter. Siamese models show the same trend as with *fastText* models on different combination of inputs showing best performance when using all of them (the last column in table 2).

In table 4, we present the training (per epoch) and inference time (per instance) for both kind of models[6]. The *fastText* models are extremely efficient to train as compared to the Siamese network. These classification models can be trained everyday to cope with open class set problem as mentioned in section 2.6. Siamese network though take longer training time, but they do not need everyday re-training and shown to be better in term of performance.

4.3 Product Deduplication

Our product matching method resulted into an another interesting findings for product deduplication. The *fastText* models produce the probability score along with predicted product for a given item listing. The probability score encodes the confidence score for the predicted label. We have collected the instances in our test set where the confidence score is very high (i.e closer to 1) and predictions do not agree with the labels in our sampled test set. Manual inspection of this data revealed that many predictions are actually correctly adopted to another duplicate product in the catalog.

For these experiments, we manually evaluated the test set for the Electronics category and sampled the data based on disagreement where the confidence score is equal or higher than 0.99. This yields 2% of the instances of our test set. The result showed 89% accuracy demonstrating the potential of using confidence score for product deduplication. As we drop the threshold, the coverage increases but accuracy starts to degrade as ex-

---

[6]All *fastText* models are trained on Intel(R) Core(TM) i7-5930K CPU @ 3.50GHz and all Siamese models are trained on 4 Nvidia GPUs GM200 [GeForce GTX TITAN X] with 64GB total memory.

pected. We plan to further investigate this in our future work along with Siamese Network based product deduplication on inter-product similarity score.

5 Related Work

The problem of product matching has been largely focused on attribute-value pair extraction to retrieve a unique set of attributes or in other words structuring the e-commerce inventory (Mauge et al., 2012; Ghani et al., 2006). The attribute and feature extraction studies go from regular expression (Köpcke et al., 2012) to named entity recognition methods based on CRF models (Melli, 2014; Ristoski and Mika, 2016). There are wide range of matching algorithms studied from various string matching (Vandic et al., 2012; Thor, 2010) to more advance methods. We refer the reader to Ristoskia et al. (2017) and Kannan et al. (2011) for a good brief overview of these studies.

Many of these methods aim to convert the free text into a structured representation and employ matching models by weighting the attributes based on their significance. In this paper, we do not model explicitly to first structure the offers and products. In our case, both offers and products are sequence of free text, and we let the models learn representations based on large historical data. Vector based models such as word2vec (Mikolov et al., 2013), glove (Pennington et al., 2014) and skip-thought (Kiros et al., 2015) have shown promising results on textual data to learn semantic representations. Sequence models based on neural networks is a hot topic in the NLP community and variety of models have been researched for different kind of tasks including more recently convolutional and recurrent networks (RNN). Convolutional networks based siamese network have been successful to find image similarity (Chopra et al., 2005; Koch, 2015). Many variants of siamese recurrent neural networks have been studies on textual sequences including manhattan-LSTM (Mueller and Thyagarajan, 2016) and bidirectional LSTM (Neculoiu et al., 2016). Our work takes the motivation from these siamese LSTM models and studied them on e-commerce domain for product matching task along with *fastText* models for extreme classification using hierarchical softmax.

6   Conclusion

We have proposed classification and similarity based approaches for product matching task. The inputs to our models are sequence of texts unlike many of the previous studies where more focus has been on structured text for such tasks. The classification approach based on the *fastText* models can scale up to millions of classes, outperforms the baseline and is extremely efficient to train. The similarity approach based on siamese network makes use of both item listings and product text. They not only improves the accuracy further but also have the advantage of avoiding frequent retraining. As a by-product, we also have shown the potential to use our models for product deduplication, which we plan to explore further in our future work. Finally, our models can accommodate any information (beyond *title*, *gtin*, *brand* and *mpn*) easily amenable into a textual form. We are now planning to extend them with image data.

References

Piotr Bojanowski, Edouard Grave, Armand Joulin, and Tomas Mikolov. 2016. Enriching word vectors with subword information. *arXiv preprint arXiv:1607.04606*.

Sumit Chopra, Raia Hadsell, and Yann LeCun. 2005. Learning a similarity metric discriminatively, with application to face verification. In *Computer Vision and Pattern Recognition, 2005. CVPR 2005. IEEE Computer Society Conference on*, volume 1, pages 539–546. IEEE.

Rayid Ghani, Katharina Probst, Yan Liu, Marko Krema, and Andrew Fano. 2006. Text mining for product attribute extraction. *ACM SIGKDD Explorations Newsletter*, 8(1):41–48.

Joshua Goodman. 2001. Classes for fast maximum entropy training. In *Acoustics, Speech, and Signal Processing, 2001. Proceedings.(ICASSP'01). 2001 IEEE International Conference on*, volume 1, pages 561–564. IEEE.

Zhiheng Huang, Wei Xu, and Kai Yu. 2015. Bidirectional lstm-crf models for sequence tagging. *arXiv preprint arXiv:1508.01991*.

Armand Joulin, Edouard Grave, Piotr Bojanowski, Matthijs Douze, Hérve Jégou, and Tomas Mikolov. 2016a. Fasttext.zip: Compressing text classification models. *arXiv preprint arXiv:1612.03651*.

Armand Joulin, Edouard Grave, Piotr Bojanowski, and Tomas Mikolov. 2016b. Bag of tricks for efficient text classification. *arXiv preprint arXiv:1607.01759*.

Anitha Kannan, Inmar E Givoni, Rakesh Agrawal, and Ariel Fuxman. 2011. Matching unstructured product offers to structured product specifications. In *Proceedings of the 17th ACM SIGKDD international conference on Knowledge discovery and data mining*, pages 404–412. ACM.

Ryan Kiros, Yukun Zhu, Ruslan Salakhutdinov, Richard S Zemel, Antonio Torralba, Raquel Urtasun, and Sanja Fidler. 2015. Skip-thought vectors. *arXiv preprint arXiv:1506.06726*.

Gregory Koch. 2015. *Siamese Neural Networks for One-Shot Image Recognition*. Ph.D. thesis, University of Toronto.

Hanna Köpcke, Andreas Thor, Stefan Thomas, and Erhard Rahm. 2012. Tailoring entity resolution for matching product offers. In *Proceedings of the 15th International Conference on Extending Database Technology*, pages 545–550. ACM.

Karin Mauge, Khash Rohanimanesh, and Jean-David Ruvini. 2012. Structuring e-commerce inventory. In *Proceedings of the 50th Annual Meeting of the Association for Computational Linguistics: Long Papers-Volume 1*, pages 805–814. Association for Computational Linguistics.

Gabor Melli. 2014. Shallow semantic parsing of product offering titles (for better automatic hyperlink insertion). In *Proceedings of the 20th ACM SIGKDD international conference on Knowledge discovery and data mining*, pages 1670–1678. ACM.

Tomas Mikolov, Ilya Sutskever, Kai Chen, Greg S Corrado, and Jeff Dean. 2013. Distributed representations of words and phrases and their compositionality. In *Advances in neural information processing systems*, pages 3111–3119.

Jonas Mueller and Aditya Thyagarajan. 2016. Siamese recurrent architectures for learning sentence similarity. In *Thirtieth AAAI Conference on Artificial Intelligence*.

Paul Neculoiu, Maarten Versteegh, and Mihai Rotaru. 2016. Learning text similarity with siamese recurrent networks. In *Proceedings of the 1st Workshop on Representation Learning for NLP*, pages 148–157.

Jeffrey Pennington, Richard Socher, and Christopher Manning. 2014. Glove: Global vectors for word representation. In *Proceedings of the 2014 conference on empirical methods in natural language processing (EMNLP)*, pages 1532–1543.

Petar Ristoski and Peter Mika. 2016. Enriching product ads with metadata from html annotations. In *International Semantic Web Conference*, pages 151–167. Springer.

Petar Ristoskia, Petar Petrovskia, Peter Mikab, and Heiko Paulheima. 2017. A machine learning approach for product matching and categorization. *Semantic web*.

Andreas Thor. 2010. Toward an adaptive string similarity measure for matching product offers. In *GI Jahrestagung (1)*, pages 702–710.

Damir Vandic, Jan-Willem Van Dam, and Flavius Frasincar. 2012. Faceted product search powered by the semantic web. *Decision Support Systems*, 53(3):425–437.

Peilu Wang, Yao Qian, Frank K Soong, Lei He, and Hai Zhao. 2015. A unified tagging solution: Bidirectional lstm recurrent neural network with word embedding. *arXiv preprint arXiv:1511.00215.*

A Scalable Neural Shortlisting-Reranking Approach for Large-Scale Domain Classification in Natural Language Understanding

Young-Bum Kim **Dongchan Kim** **Joo-Kyung Kim** **Ruhi Sarikaya**

Amazon Alexa

{youngbum, dongchan, jookyk, rsarikay}@amazon.com

Abstract

Intelligent personal digital assistants (IPDAs), a popular real-life application with spoken language understanding capabilities, can cover potentially thousands of overlapping domains for natural language understanding, and the task of finding the best domain to handle an utterance becomes a challenging problem on a large scale. In this paper, we propose a set of efficient and scalable neural shortlisting-reranking models for large-scale domain classification in IPDAs. The shortlisting stage focuses on efficiently trimming all domains down to a list of k-best candidate domains, and the reranking stage performs a list-wise reranking of the initial k-best domains with additional contextual information. We show the effectiveness of our approach with extensive experiments on 1,500 IPDA domains.

1 Introduction

Natural language understanding (NLU) is a core component of intelligent personal digital assistants (IPDAs) such as Amazon Alexa, Google Assistant, Apple Siri, and Microsoft Cortana (Sarikaya, 2017). A well-established approach in current real-time systems is to classify an utterance into a domain, followed by domain-specific intent classification and slot sequence tagging (Tur and de Mori, 2011). A domain is typically defined in terms of a specific application or a functionality such as weather, calendar and music, which narrows down the scope of NLU for a given utterance. A domain can also be defined as a collection of relevant intents; assuming an utterance belongs to the calendar domain, possible intents could be to create a meeting or cancel one, and possible extracted slots could be people names, meeting title and date from the utterance. Traditional IPDAs cover only tens of domains that share a common schema. The schema is designed to separate out the domains in an effort to minimize language ambiguity. A shared schema, while addressing domain ambiguity, becomes a bottleneck as new domains and intents are added to cover new scenarios. Redefining the domain, intent and slot boundaries requires relabeling of the underlying data, which is very costly and time-consuming. On the other hand, when thousands of domains evolve independently without a shared schema, finding the most relevant domain to handle an utterance among thousands of overlapping domains emerges as a key challenge.

The difficulty of solving this problem at scale has led to stopgap solutions, such as requiring an utterance to explicitly mention a domain name and restricting the expression to be in a predefined form as in "Ask ALLRECIPES, how can I bake an apple pie?" However, such solutions lead to an unintuitive and unnatural way of conversing and create interaction friction for the end users. For the example utterance, a more natural way of saying it is simply, "How can I bake an apple pie?" but the most relevant domain to handle it now becomes ambiguous. There could be a number of candidate domains and even multiple overlapping recipe-related domains that could handle it.

In this paper, we propose efficient and scalable shortlisting-reranking neural models in two steps for effective large-scale domain classification in IPDAs. The first step uses light-weight BiLSTM models that leverage only the character and word-level information to efficiently find the k-best list of most likely domains. The second step uses rich contextual information later in the pipeline and applies another BiLSTM model to a list-wise ranking task to further rerank the k-best domains to find the most relevant one. We show the effectiveness of our approach for large-scale domain classification with an extensive set of experiments on 1,500 IPDA domains.

Proceedings of NAACL-HLT 2018, pages 16–24

New Orleans, Louisiana, June 1 - 6, 2018. ©2017 Association for Computational Linguistics

2 Related Work

Reranking approaches attempt to improve upon an initial ranking by considering additional contextual information. Initial model outputs are trimmed down to a subset of most likely candidates, and each candidate is combined with additional features to form a hypothesis to be re-scored. Reranking has been applied to various natural language processing tasks, including machine translation (Shen et al., 2004), parsing (Collins and Koo, 2005), sentence boundary detection (Roark et al., 2006), named entity recognition (Nguyen et al., 2010), and supertagging (Chen et al., 2002).

In the context of NLU or SLU systems, Morbini et al. (2012) showed a reranking approach using k-best lists from multiple automatic speech recognition (ASR) engines to improve response category classification for virtual museum guides. Basili et al. (2013) showed that reranking multiple ASR candidates by analyzing their syntactic properties can improve spoken command understanding in human-robot interaction, but with more focus on ASR improvement. Xu and Sarikaya (2014) showed that multi-turn contextual information and recurrent neural networks can improve domain classification in a multi-domain and multi-turn NLU system. There have been many other pieces of prior work on improving NLU systems with pre-training (Kim et al., 2015b; Celikyilmaz et al., 2016; Kim et al., 2017e), multi-task learning (Zhang and Wang, 2016; Liu and Lane, 2016; Kim et al., 2017b), transfer learning (El-Kahky et al., 2014; Kim et al., 2015a,c; Chen et al., 2016a; Yang et al., 2017), domain adaptation (Kim et al., 2016; Jaech et al., 2016; Liu and Lane, 2017; Kim et al., 2017d,c) and contextual signals (Bhargava et al., 2013; Chen et al., 2016b; Hori et al., 2016; Kim et al., 2017a).

To our knowledge, the work by Robichaud et al. (2014); Crook et al. (2015); Khan et al. (2015) is most closely related to this paper. Their approach is to first run a complete pass of all 3 NLU models of binary domain classification, multi-class intent classification, and sequence tagging of slots across all domains. Then, a hypothesis is formed per domain using the semantic information provided by the domain-intent-slot outputs as well as many other contextual and cross-hypothesis features such as the presence of a slot tagging type in any other hypotheses. Reranking the hypotheses with Gradient Boosted Decision Trees (Friedman, 2001; Burges et al., 2011) has been shown to improve domain classification performance compared to using only domain classifiers without reranking.

Their approach however suffers from the following two limitations. First, it requires running all domain-intent-slot models in parallel across all domains. Their work considers only 8 or 9 distinct domains, and the approach has serious practical scaling issues when the number of domains scales to thousands. Second, contextual information, especially cross-hypothesis features, that is crucial for reranking is manually designed at the feature level with a sparse representation.

Our work in this paper addresses both of these limitations with a scalable and efficient two-step shortlisting-reranking approach, which has a neural ranking model capturing cross-hypothesis features automatically. To our knowledge, this work is the first in the literature on large-scale domain classification for a real IPDA production system with a scale of thousands of domains. Our LSTM-based list-wise ranking approach also makes a novel contribution to the existing literature in the context of IPDA and NLU systems. In this work, we limit our scope to first-turn utterances and leave multi-turn conversations for future work.

3 Shortlisting-Reranking Architecture

Our shortlisting-reranking models process an incoming utterance as follows. (1) *Shortlister* performs a naive, fast ranking of all domains to find the k-best list using only the character and word-level information. The goal here is to achieve high domain recall with maximal efficiency and minimal information and latency. (2) For each domain in the k-best list, we prepare a hypothesis per domain with additional contextual information, including domain-intent-slot semantic analysis, user preferences, and domain index of popularity and quality. (3) A second ranker called *Hypotheses Reranker (HypRank)* performs a list-wise ranking of the k hypotheses to improve on the initial naive ranking and find the best hypothesis, thus domain, to handle the utterance.

Figure 1 illustrates the steps with an example utterance, "*play michael jackson.*" Based on character and word features, *shortlister* returns the k-best list in the order of CLASSIC MUSIC, POP MUSIC, and VIDEO domains. CLASSIC MUSIC outputs PlayTune intent, but without any slots, low domain popularity, and no usage history for the user, its ranking is adjusted to be last. `POP MUSIC` outputs `PlayMusic` intent and `Singer` slot for "*michael jackson*", and with frequent user usage history, it is determined to be the best domain to handle the utterance.

In our architecture, key focus is on efficiency and scalability. Running full domain-intent-slot semantic analysis for thousands of domains imposes a significant computational burden in terms of memory footprint, latency and number of machines, and it is impractical in real-time systems. For the same reason, this work only uses contextual information in the reranking stage, and the utility of including it in the shortlisting stage is left for future work.

4 Shortlister

Shortlister consists of three layers: an orthography-sensitive character and word embedding layer, a BiLSTM layer that makes a vector representation for the words in a given utterance, and an output layer for domain classification. Figure 2 shows the overall shortlister architecture.

Embedding layer In order to capture character-level patterns, we construct an orthography-sensitive word embedding layer (Ling et al., 2015; Ballesteros et al., 2015). Let $\mathcal{C}$, $\mathcal{W}$, and $\oplus$ denote the set of characters, the set of words, and the vector concatenation operator, respectively. We represent an LSTM as a mapping $\phi : \mathbb{R}^d \times \mathbb{R}^{d'} \to \mathbb{R}^{d'}$ that takes an input vector x and a state vector h to output a new state vector $h' = \phi(x, h)$[1]. The model parameters associated with this layer are:

Char embedding: $e_c \in \mathbb{R}^{25}$ for each $c \in \mathcal{C}$

Char LSTMs: $\phi_f^{\mathcal{C}}, \phi_b^{\mathcal{C}} : \mathbb{R}^{25} \times \mathbb{R}^{25} \to \mathbb{R}^{25}$

Word embedding: $e_w \in \mathbb{R}^{100}$ for each $w \in \mathcal{W}$

Let $(w_1, \ldots, w_m)$ denote a word sequence where word $w_i \in \mathcal{W}$ has character $w_i(j) \in \mathcal{C}$ at position j. This layer computes an orthography-sensitive word representation $v_i \in \mathbb{R}^{150}$ as:[2]

$$f_j^{\mathcal{C}} = \phi_f^{\mathcal{C}}\left(e_{w_i(j)}, f_{j-1}^{\mathcal{C}}\right) \qquad \forall j = 1 \ldots |w_i|$$
$$b_j^{\mathcal{C}} = \phi_b^{\mathcal{C}}\left(e_{w_i(j)}, b_{j+1}^{\mathcal{C}}\right) \qquad \forall j = |w_i| \ldots 1$$
$$v_i = f_{|w_i|}^{\mathcal{C}} \oplus b_1^{\mathcal{C}} \oplus e_{w_i}$$

---

[1] We omit cell variable notations for simple LSTM formulations.

[2] We randomly initialize state vectors such as $f_0^{\mathcal{C}}$ and $b_{|w_i|+1}^{\mathcal{C}}$.

BiLSTM layer We utilize a BiLSTM to encode the word vector sequence $(v_1, \ldots, v_m)$. The BiLSTM outputs are generated as:

$$f_i^{\mathcal{W}} = \phi_f^{\mathcal{W}}\left(v_i, f_{i-1}^{\mathcal{W}}\right) \qquad \forall i = 1 \ldots m$$
$$b_i^{\mathcal{W}} = \phi_b^{\mathcal{W}}\left(v_i, b_{i+1}^{\mathcal{W}}\right) \qquad \forall i = m \ldots 1$$

where $\phi_f^{\mathcal{W}}, \phi_f^{\mathcal{W}} : \mathbb{R}^{150} \times \mathbb{R}^{100} \to \mathbb{R}^{100}$ are the forward LSTM and the backward LSTM, respectively. An utterance representation $h \in \mathbb{R}^{200}$ is induced by concatenating the outputs of the both LSTMs as:

$$h = f_m^{\mathcal{W}} \oplus b_1^{\mathcal{W}}$$

Output layer We map the word LSTM output h to a n-dimensional output vector with a linear transformation. Then, we take a softmax function either over the entire domains ($softmax_a$) or over two classes (in-domain or out-of-domain) for each domain ($softmax_b$).

$softmax_a$ is used to set the sum of the confidence scores over the entire domains to be 1. We can obtain the outputs as:

$$o = softmax\left(W \cdot h + b\right)$$

where W and b are parameters for a linear transformation.

For training, we use cross-entropy loss, which is formulated as follows:

$$\mathcal{L}_a = -\sum_{i=1}^{n} l_i \log o_i \qquad (1)$$

where l is a n-dimensional one-hot vector whose element corresponding to the position of the ground-truth hypothesis is set to 1.

$softmax_b$ is used to set the confidence score for each domain to be between 0 and 1. While $softmax_a$ tends to highlight only the ground-truth domain while suppressing all the rest, $softmax_b$ is designed to produce a more balanced confidence score per domain independent of other domains. When using $softmax_b$, we obtain a 2-dimensional output vector for each domain as follows:

$$o^i = softmax\left(W^i \cdot h + b^i\right)$$

where W^i is a 2 by 200 matrix and b^i is a 2-dimensional vector; o_1^i and o_2^i denote the in-domain probability and the out-of-domain probability, respectively. The loss function is formulated as follows:

$$\mathcal{L}_b = -\sum_{i=1}^{n} \left\{ l_i \log o_1^i + \frac{1 - l_i}{n - 1} \log o_2^i \right\} \qquad (2)$$

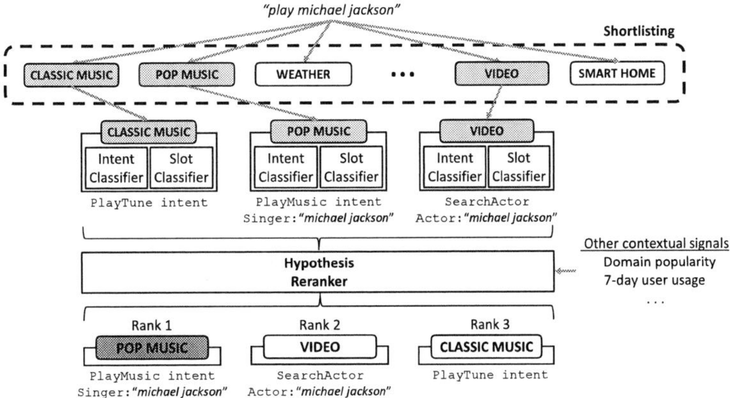

Figure 1: A high-level flow of our two-step shortlisting-reranking approach given an utterance to an IPDA.

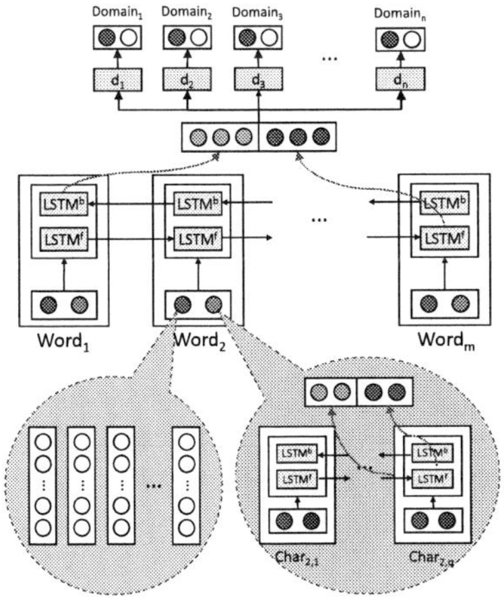

Figure 2: The architecture of our neural shortlisting model that uses character and word-level information of a given utterance.

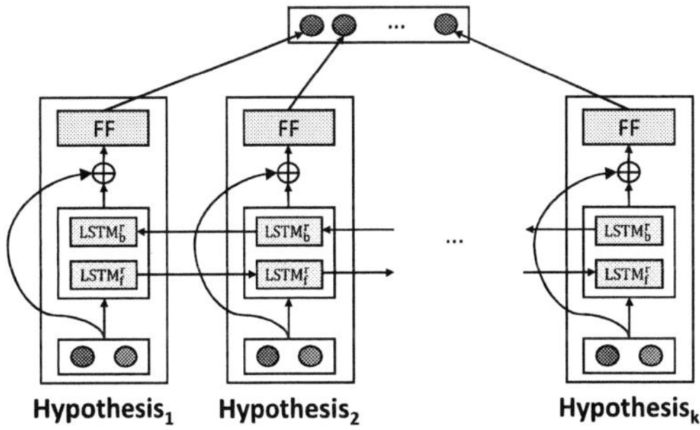

Figure 3: The architecture of our neural Hypotheses Reranker model that takes in k hypotheses with rich contextual information for more refined ranking.

where we divide the second term by $n - 1$ so that o_1^i and o_2^i are balanced in terms of the ratio of the training examples for a domain to those for other domains.

5 Hypotheses Reranker (HypRank)

Hypotheses Reranker (HypRank) comprises of two components: hypothesis representation and a BiLSTM model for reranking a list of hypotheses. We use the term reranking since we improve upon the initial ranking from Shortlister's k-best list. In our problem context, a hypothesis is formed per domain with additional semantic and contextual information, and selecting the highest-scored hypothesis means selecting the domain represented in that hypothesis for final domain classification.

HypRank, illustrated in Figure 3, is a list-wise ranking approach in that it considers the entire list of hypotheses before giving a reranking score for each hypothesis. While previous work manually

encoded cross-hypothesis information at the feature level (Robichaud et al., 2014; Crook et al., 2015; Khan et al., 2015), our approach is to let a BiLSTM layer automatically capture that information and learn appropriate representations at the model level. In addition to giving detail of useful contextual signals for IPDAs, we also introduce the use of pre-trained domain, intent and slot embeddings in this section.

5.1 Hypothesis Representation

A hypothesis is formed for each domain with the following three categories of contextual information: NLU interpretation, user preferences, and domain index.

NLU interpretation Each domain has three corresponding NLU models for binary domain classification, multi-class intent classification, and sequence tagging for slots. From the domain-intent-slot semantic analysis, we use the confidence score from the shortlister, the intent classification confidence, Viterbi path score of the slot sequence from a slot tagger, and the average confidence score of the tagged slots[3].

To pre-train domain embeddings, we use a word-level BiLSTM with each utterance as a sequence of word embedding vector $\in \mathbb{R}^{100}$ in the input layer. The BiLSTM outputs, each a vector $\in \mathbb{R}^{25}$, are concatenated and projected to an output vector for all domains in the output layer. The learned projection weight matrix is extracted as domain embeddings. The output vector dimension used was $\in \mathbb{R}^{1500}$ for the large-scale setting and $\in \mathbb{R}^{20}$ for the traditional small-scale setting in our experiments (Section 6.1). For intent and slot embeddings, we take the same process with the only difference in the output vector with the dimension $\in \mathbb{R}^{6991}$ for all unique intents across all domains and with the dimension $\in \mathbb{R}^{2845}$ for all unique slots.

Once pre-trained, the domain or intent embeddings are used simply as a lookup table per domain or per intent. For slot embeddings, there can be more than one slot per utterance, and in case of multiple tagged slots, we sum up each slot embedding vector to combine the information. In summary, these are the three domain-intent-slots embeddings we used: $e^d \in \mathbb{R}^{50}$ for a domain vector, $e^i \in \mathbb{R}^{50}$ for an intent vector, and $e^s \in \mathbb{R}^{50}$ for a vector of slots.

User Preferences User-specific signals are designed to capture each user's behavioral history or preferences. In particular, we encode whether a user has specific domains enabled in his/her IPDA setting and whether he/she triggered certain domains within 7, 14 or 30 days in the past.

Domain Index From this category, we encode domain popularity and quality as rated by the user population. For example, if the utterance "*I need a ride to work*" can be equally handled by TAXI_A domain or TAXI_B domain but the user has never used any, the signals in this category could give a boost to TAXI_A domain due to its higher popularity.

5.2 HypRank Model

The proposed model is trained to rerank the domain hypotheses formed from Shortlister results. Let $(p_1, \ldots, p_k)$ be the sequence of k input hypothesis vectors that are sorted in decreasing order of Shortlister scores.

We utilize a BiLSTM layer for transforming the input sequence to the BiLSTM output sequence

Category	$|\mathcal{D}|$	Example
Device	177	smart home, smart car
Food	99	recipe, nutrition
Ent.	465	movie, music, game
Info.	399	travel, lifestyle
News	159	local, sports, finance
Shopping	39	retail, food, media
Util.	162	productivity, weather
Total	1,500	

Table 1: The categories of the 1,500 domains for our large-scale IPDA. $|\mathcal{D}|$ denotes the number of domains.

$(h_1, \ldots, h_k)$ as follows:

$$f_i^r = \phi_f^r\left(p_i, f_{i-1}^r\right)$$
$$b_i^r = \phi_b^r\left(p_i, b_{i+1}^r\right)$$
$$h_i = f_i^r \oplus b_i^r \qquad \forall i \in \{1, \ldots, k\},$$

where ϕ_f^r and ϕ_b^r are the forward LSTM and the backward LSTM, respectively.

Since the BiLSTM utilizes both the previous and the next sub-sequences as the context, each of the BiLSTM outputs is computed considering cross-hypothesis information.

For the i-th hypothesis, we either sum or concatenate the input vector and the BiLSTM output to utilize both of them as an intermediate representation as $g_i = d_i \oplus h_i$. Then, we use a feed-forward neural network with a single hidden layer to transform g to a k-dimensional vector p as follows:

$$p_i = W_2 \cdot \sigma\left(W_1 \cdot g_i + b_1\right) + b_2 \quad \forall i \in \{1, \ldots, k\},$$

where σ indicates scaled exponential linear unit (SeLU) for normalized activation outputs (Klambauer et al., 2017); the outputs of all the hypotheses are generated by using the same parameter set $\{W_1, b_1, W_2, b_2\}$ for consistency regardless of the hypothesis order.

Finally, we obtain a k-dimensional output vector o by taking a softmax function:

$$o = softmax\left(p\right).$$

$argmax_i\{o_1, .., o_k\}$ is the index of the predicted hypothesis after the reranking. Cross entropy is used for training as follows:

$$\mathcal{L}_r = -\sum_{i=1}^{k} l_i \log o_i, \tag{3}$$

where l is a k-dimensional ground-truth one-hot vector.

6 Experiments

This section gives detail of our experimental setup, followed by results and discussion.

---

[3]We use off-the-shelf intent classifiers and slot taggers achieving 98% and 96% accuracies on average, respectively.

	SL train	SL dev	HR train	HR dev	test
Traditional	3M	415K	715K	20K	420K
Large-Scale	5M	530K	830K	20K	530K

Table 2: The number of train, development and test utterances. SL denotes Shortlister and HR denotes HypRank.

	Traditional IPDA		Large-Scale IPDA	
	smx_a	smx_b	smx_a	smx_b
1-best	95.58	95.56	81.38	81.49
3-best	98.45	98.43	92.53	92.81
5-best	**98.81**	**98.77**	**95.77**	**95.93**

Table 3: The k-best classification accuracies (%) of Shortlister using different softmax functions in the traditional and large-scale IPDA settings.

6.1 Experimental Setup

We evaluated our shortlisting-reranking approach in two different settings of traditional small-scale IPDA and large-scale IPDA for comparison:

Traditional IPDA For this setting, we simulated the traditional small-scale IPDA with only 20 domains that are commonly present in any IPDAs. Since these domains are built-in, which are carefully designed to be non-overlapping and of high quality, the signals from user preferences and domain index become irrelevant compared to the large-scale setting. The dataset comprises of more than 4M labeled utterances in text evenly distributed across 20+ domains.

Large-Scale IPDA This setting is a large-scale IPDA with 1,500 domains as shown in Table 1 that could be overlapping with a varying level of quality. For instance, there could be multiple domains to get a recipe, and a high quality domain could have more recipes with more capabilities such as making recommendations compared to a low quality one. The dataset comprises of more than 6M utterances having strict invocation patterns. For instance, we extract *"get me a ride"* as a preprocessed sample belonging to *TAXI* skill for the original utterance, *"Ask {TAXI} to {get me a ride}."*

Shortlister For Shortlister, we show the results of using 2 different softmax functions of $softmax_a$ (smx_a) and $softmax_b$ (smx_b) as described in Section 4. The results are shown in k-best classification accuracies, where the 5-best accuracy means the percentage of test samples that have the ground-truth domain included in the top 5 domains returned by Shortlister.

Hypotheses Reranker We also evaluate different variations of the reranking model for comparison.

- SL: Shortlister 1-best result, which is our baseline without using a reranking model.
- LR: LR point-wise: A binary logistic regression model with the hypothesis vector as features (see Section 5.1). We run it for each hypothesis made from Shortlister's k-best list and select the highest-scoring one, hence the domain in that hypothesis.
- N^{PO}: Neural point-wise: A feed-forward (FF) layer between the hypothesis vector and the nonlinear output layer. We run it for each hypothesis made from Shortlister's k-best list and select the highest-scoring hypothesis.
- N^{PA}: Neural pair-wise: A FF layer between the concatenation of two hypothesis vectors and the nonlinear output layer. We run it k - 1 times for a pair of hypotheses in a series of tournament-like competitions in the order of the k-best list. For instance, the 1st and 2nd hypothesis compete first and the winner of the two competes with the 3rd hypothesis next and so on until the kth hypothesis.
- N^{CH}: Neural quasi list-wise with manual cross-hypothesis features added to N^{PO}, following past approaches (Robichaud et al., 2014; Crook et al., 2015; Khan et al., 2015) such as the ratio of Shortlister scores to the maximum score, relative number of slots across all hypotheses, etc.
- $LSTM^{O}$: Using only the BiLSTM output vectors as the input to the FF-layer.
- $LSTM^{S}$: Summing up the hypothesis vector and the BiLSTM output vectors as the input to the FF-layer, similar to residual networks (He et al., 2016).
- $LSTM^{C}$: Concatenating the hypothesis vector and the BiLSTM output vectors as the input to the FF-layer.
- $LSTM^{CH}$: Same as $LSTM^{C}$ except that manual cross-hypothesis features used for N^{CH} were also added to see if combining manual and automatic cross-hypothesis features help.
- $UPPER$: Upper bound of HypRank accuracy set by the performance of Shortlister.

6.2 Methodology

Table 2 shows the distribution of the training, development and test sets for each setting of traditional and large-scale IPDAs. Note that we ensure

Model	Traditional IPDA		Large-Scale IPDA	
	smx_a	smx_b	smx_a	smx_b
SL	95.58	95.56	81.38	81.49
LR	95.50	95.59	86.74	87.50
N^{PO}	95.26	95.46	88.65	90.38
N^{PA}	96.08	96.37	88.29	90.82
N^{CH}	96.20	96.65	88.43	91.13
$LSTM^O$	94.36	94.45	81.37	82.98
$LSTM^S$	97.44	97.54	92.43	93.79
$LSTM^C$	**97.47**	**97.55**	**92.49**	**93.83**
$LSTM^{CH}$	97.22	97.34	92.18	93.46
$UPPER$	98.81	98.77	95.77	95.93

Table 4: The final classification accuracies (%) for different Shortlisting-HypRank models under the traditional and large-scale IPDA settings. The input hypothesis size is 5.

no overlap between the Shortlister and HypRank training sets so that HypRank is not overly tuned on Shortlister results. For the NLU models, the intent and slot models are trained on roughly 70% of the available training data.

In our experiments, all the models were implemented using Dynet (Neubig et al., 2017) and were trained with Adam (Kingma and Ba, 2015). We used the initial learning rate of 4×10^{-4} and left all the other hyper-parameters as suggested in Kingma and Ba (2015). We also used variational dropout (Gal and Ghahramani, 2016) for regularization.

6.3 Results and Discussion

Table 3 summarizes the k-best classification accuracy results for our Shortlister. With only 20 domains in the traditional IPDA setting, the accuracy is over 95% even when we take 1-best or top domain returned from Shortlister. The accuracy approaches 99% when we consider Shortlister correct if the ground-truth domain is present in the top 5 domains. The results suggest that the character and word-level information by itself, coupled with BiLSTMs, can already show significant discriminative power for our task.

With a scale of 1,500 domains, the results indicate that just using the top domain returned from Shortlister is not enough to have comparable performance shown in the traditional IPDA setting. However, the performance catches up to close to 96% as we include more domains in the k-best list, and although not shown here, it starts to level off at 5-best list. The k-best results from Shortlister set an upper bound for HypRank performance. We note that it could be possible to include more contextual information at the shortlisting stage to bring Shortlister's performance up with some trade-offs in terms of real-time systems,

which we leave for future work. In addition, using smx_b shows a tendency of slightly better performance compared to using smx_a, which takes a softmax over all domains and tends to emphasize only the top domain while suppressing all others even when there are many overlapping and very similar domains.

The classification performance after the reranking stage with HypRank using Shortlister's 5-best results is summarized in Table 4. SL shows the results of taking the top domain from Shortlister without any reranking step, and UPPER shows the performance upper bound of HypRank set by the shortlisting stage. In general, the pair-wise approach is shown to be better than the point-wise approaches, with the best performance coming from the list-wise ones. Looking at the lowest accuracy from $LSTM^O$, it suggests that the raw hypothesis vectors themselves are important features that should be combined with the cross-hypothesis contextual features from the LSTM outputs for best results. Adding manual cross-hypothesis features to the automatic ones from the LSTM outputs do not improve the performance.

The performance trend is very similar for smx_a and smx_b, but there is a gap between them in the large-scale setting. An explanation for this is similar to that for Shortlister results that smx_a emphasizes only the top domain while suppressing all the rest, which might not be suitable in a large-scale setting with many overlapping domains. For both traditional and large-scale settings, the best accuracy is shown with the list-wise model of $LSTM^C$.

7 Conclusion

We have described an efficient and scalable shortlisting-reranking neural models for large-scale domain classification. The models first efficiently prune all domains to only a small number of k candidates using minimal information and subsequently rerank them using additional contextual information that could be more expensive in terms of computing resources. We have shown the effectiveness of our approach with 1,500 domains in a real IPDA system and evaluated using different variations of the shortlisting model and our novel reranking models, in terms of point-wise, pair-wise, and list-wise ranking approaches.

Acknowledgments

We thank Sunghyun Park and Sungjin Lee for helpful discussion and feedback.

References

Miguel Ballesteros, Chris Dyer, and Noah A. Smith. 2015. Improved transition-based parsing by modeling characters instead of words with LSTMs. In *Proceedings of the 2015 Conference on Empirical Methods in Natural Language Processing (EMNLP)*. pages 349–359.

Roberto Basili, Emanuele Bastianelli, Giuseppe Castellucci, Daniele Nardi, and Vittorio Perera. 2013. *Kernel-based discriminative re-ranking for spoken command understanding in HRI*, Springer International Publishing, Cham, pages 169–180.

A. Bhargava, Asli elikyilmaz, Dilek Z. Hakkani-Tur, and Ruhi Sarikaya. 2013. Easy contextual intent prediction and slot detection. *IEEE International Conference on Acoustics, Speech and Signal Processing* pages 8337–8341.

Christopher J C Burges, Krysta M Svore, Paul N. Bennett, Andrzej Pastusiak, and Qiang Wu. 2011. Learning to Rank Using an Ensemble of Lambda-Gradient Models. *Journal of Machine Learning Research (JMLR)* 14:25–35.

Asli Celikyilmaz, Ruhi Sarikaya, Dilek Hakkani-Tür, Xiaohu Liu, Nikhil Ramesh, and Gökhan Tür. 2016. A new pre-training method for training deep learning models with application to spoken language understanding. In *Interspeech*. pages 3255–3259.

John Chen, Srinivas Bangalore, Michael Collins, and Owen Rambow. 2002. Reranking an n-gram supertagger. In *Proceedings of the Sixth International Workshop on Tree Adjoining Grammar and Related Frameworks (TAG+ 6)*. pages 259–268.

Yun-Nung Chen, Dilek Hakkani-Tür, and Xiaodong He. 2016a. Zero-shot learning of intent embeddings for expansion by convolutional deep structured semantic models. In *Acoustics, Speech and Signal Processing (ICASSP), 2016 IEEE International Conference on*. pages 6045–6049.

Yun-Nung Chen, Dilek Hakkani-Tür, Gokhan Tur, Jianfeng Gao, and Li Deng. 2016b. End-to-end memory networks with knowledge carryover for multi-turn spoken language understanding. In *Interspeech*.

Michael Collins and Terry Koo. 2005. Discriminative reranking for natural language parsing. *Computational Linguistics* 31(1):25–70.

Paul A Crook, Jean-Philippe Martin, and Ruhi Sarikaya. 2015. Multi-language hypotheses ranking and domain tracking for open domain. In *Interspeech*.

Ali El-Kahky, Xiaohu Liu, Ruhi Sarikaya, Gokhan Tur, Dilek Hakkani-Tur, and Larry Heck. 2014. Extending domain coverage of language understanding systems via intent transfer between domains using knowledge graphs and search query click logs. In *IEEE International Conference on Acoustics, Speech and Signal Processing (ICASSP)*. IEEE, pages 4067–4071.

Jerome H. Friedman. 2001. Greedy function approximation: A gradient boosting machine 29(5):1189–1232.

Yarin Gal and Zoubin Ghahramani. 2016. A theoretically grounded application of dropout in recurrent neural networks. In *Advances in Neural Information Processing Systems 29 (NIPS)*. pages 1019–1027.

Kaiming He, Xiang Zhang, Shaoqing Ren, and Jian Sun. 2016. Deep residual learning for image recognition. In *IEEE Conference on Computer Vision and Pattern Recognition (CVPR)*. pages 770–778.

Chiori Hori, Takaaki Hori, Shinji Watanabe, and John R Hershey. 2016. Context-sensitive and role-dependent spoken language understanding using bidirectional and attention lstms. *Interspeech* pages 3236–3240.

Aaron Jaech, Larry Heck, and Mari Ostendorf. 2016. Domain adaptation of recurrent neural networks for natural language understanding. In *Interspeech*.

Omar Zia Khan, Jean-Philippe Robichaud, Paul A. Crook, and Ruhi Sarikaya. 2015. Hypotheses ranking and state tracking for a multi-domain dialog system using multiple ASR alternates. In *Interspeech*.

Young-Bum Kim, Minwoo Jeong, Karl Stratos, and Ruhi Sarikaya. 2015a. Weakly supervised slot tagging with partially labeled sequences from web search click logs. In *Proceedings of the 2015 Conference of the North American Chapter of the Association for Computational Linguistics: Human Language Technologies*. pages 84–92.

Young-Bum Kim, Sungjin Lee, and Ruhi Sarikaya. 2017a. Speaker-sensitive dual memory networks for multi-turn slot tagging. In *Automatic Speech Recognition and Understanding Workshop (ASRU), 2017 IEEE*. IEEE, pages 547–553.

Young-Bum Kim, Sungjin Lee, and Karl Stratos. 2017b. Onenet: Joint domain, intent, slot prediction for spoken language understanding. In *Automatic Speech Recognition and Understanding Workshop (ASRU), 2017 IEEE*. IEEE, pages 547–553.

Young-Bum Kim, Karl Stratos, and Dongchan Kim. 2017c. Adversarial adaptation of synthetic or stale data. In *Proceedings of the 55th Annual Meeting of the Association for Computational Linguistics*. Association for Computational Linguistics, pages 1297–1307.

Young-Bum Kim, Karl Stratos, and Dongchan Kim. 2017d. Domain attention with an ensemble of experts. In *Proceedings of the 55th Annual Meeting of the Association for Computational Linguistics*. volume 1, pages 643–653.

Young-Bum Kim, Karl Stratos, and Ruhi Sarikaya. 2015b. Pre-training of hidden-unit crfs. In *Proceedings of the 53rd Annual Meeting of the Association for Computational Linguistics and the 7th International Joint Conference on Natural Language Processing*. volume 2, pages 192–198.

Young-Bum Kim, Karl Stratos, and Ruhi Sarikaya. 2016. Frustratingly easy neural domain adaptation. In *Proceedings of COLING 2016, the 26th International Conference on Computational Linguistics: Technical Papers*. pages 387–396.

Young-Bum Kim, Karl Stratos, and Ruhi Sarikaya. 2017e. A framework for pre-training hidden-unit conditional random fields and its extension to long short term memory networks. *Computer Speech & Language* 46:311–326.

Young-Bum Kim, Karl Stratos, Ruhi Sarikaya, and Minwoo Jeong. 2015c. New transfer learning techniques for disparate label sets. In *Proceedings of the 53rd Annual Meeting of the Association for Computational Linguistics and the 7th International Joint Conference on Natural Language Processing*. volume 1, pages 473–482.

Diederik Kingma and Jimmy Ba. 2015. ADAM: A method for stochastic optimization. In *International Conference on Learning Representations (ICLR)*.

Günter Klambauer, Thomas Unterthiner, Andreas Mayr, and Sepp Hochreiter. 2017. Self-normalizing neural networks. In *Advances in Neural Information Processing Systems 30 (NIPS)*. pages 972–981.

Wang Ling, Chris Dyer, Alan W Black, Isabel Trancoso, Ramon Fermandez, Silvio Amir, Luis Marujo, and Tiago Luis. 2015. Finding function in form: Compositional character models for open vocabulary word representation. In *Proceedings of the 2015 Conference on Empirical Methods in Natural Language Processing (EMNLP)*. pages 1520–1530.

Bing Liu and Ian Lane. 2016. Attention-based recurrent neural network models for joint intent detection and slot filling. In *Interspeech*. pages 685–689.

Bing Liu and Ian Lane. 2017. Multi-domain adversarial learning for slot filling in spoken language understanding. In *NIPS Workshop on Conversational AI*.

F. Morbini, K. Audhkhasi, R. Artstein, M. Van Segbroeck, K. Sagae, P. Georgiou, D. R. Traum, and S. Narayanan. 2012. A reranking approach for recognition and classification of speech input in conversational dialogue systems. In *IEEE Spoken Language Technology Workshop (SLT)*. pages 49–54.

Graham Neubig, Chris Dyer, Yoav Goldberg, Austin Matthews, Waleed Ammar, Antonios Anastasopoulos, Miguel Ballesteros, David Chiang, Daniel Clothiaux, Trevor Cohn, et al. 2017. Dynet: The dynamic neural network toolkit. *arXiv preprint arXiv:1701.03980* .

Truc-Vien T Nguyen, Alessandro Moschitti, and Giuseppe Riccardi. 2010. Kernel-based reranking for named-entity extraction. In *Proceedings of the 23rd International Conference on Computational Linguistics: Posters*. Association for Computational Linguistics, pages 901–909.

Brian Roark, Yang Liu, Mary Harper, Robin Stewart, Matthew Lease, Matthew Snover, Izhak Shafran, Bonnie Dorr, John Hale, Anna Krasnyanskaya, et al. 2006. Reranking for sentence boundary detection in conversational speech. In *IEEE International Conference on Acoustics, Speech and Signal Processing (ICASSP)*.

Jean-Philippe Robichaud, Paul A. Crook, Puyang Xu, Omar Zia Khan, and Ruhi Sarikaya. 2014. Hypotheses ranking for robust domain classification and tracking in dialogue systems. In *Interspeech*. pages 145–149.

Ruhi Sarikaya. 2017. The technology behind personal digital assistants: An overview of the system architecture and key components. *IEEE Signal Processing Magazine* 34(1):67–81.

Libin Shen, Anoop Sarkar, and Franz Josef Och. 2004. Discriminative reranking for machine translation. In *Proceedings of the Human Language Technology Conference of the North American Chapter of the Association for Computational Linguistics: HLT-NAACL 2004*.

Gokhan Tur and Renato de Mori. 2011. *Spoken Language Understanding: Systems for Extracting Semantic Information from Speech*. New York, NY: John Wiley and Sons.

Puyang Xu and Ruhi Sarikaya. 2014. Contextual domain classification in spoken language understanding systems using recurrent neural network. In *IEEE International Conference on Acoustics, Speech and Signal Processing (ICASSP)*. pages 136–140.

Zhilin Yang, Ruslan Salakhutdinov, and William W Cohen. 2017. Transfer learning for sequence tagging with hierarchical recurrent networks. *International Conference on Learning Representation (ICLR)* .

Xiaodong Zhang and Houfeng Wang. 2016. A joint model of intent determination and slot filling for spoken language understanding. In *International Joint Conference on Artificial Intelligence (IJCAI)*. pages 2993–2999.

What we need to learn if we want to *do* and not just *talk*

Rashmi Gangadharaiah, Balakrishnan (Murali) Narayanaswamy, Charles Elkan
Amazon AI Lab
{rgangad@,muralibn@,elkanc@}amazon.com

Abstract

In task-oriented dialog, agents need to generate both fluent natural language responses and correct external actions like database queries and updates. We show that methods that achieve state of the art performance on synthetic datasets, perform poorly in real world dialog tasks. We propose a hybrid model, where nearest neighbor is used to generate fluent responses and Sequence-to-Sequence (Seq2Seq) type models ensure dialogue coherency and generate accurate external actions. The hybrid model on an internal customer support dataset achieves a 78% relative improvement in fluency, and a 200% improvement in external call accuracy.

1 Introduction

Many commercial applications of artificial agents require task-oriented conversational agents that help customers achieve a specific goal, such as making or cancelling a payment or reservation (Zue et al., 2000; Bennacef et al., 1996). These chatbots must extract relevant information from the user, provide relevant knowledge to her, and issue appropriate system calls to achieve the goal.

Supervised approaches such as seq2seq models (Vinyals and Le, 2015; Shang et al., 2015; Serban et al., 2015; Sordoni et al., 2015b), have recently gained attention in non-task oriented dialog, due to their ability to perform end-to-end learning from expert dialogues[1], removing the need for many of the independent modules in traditional systems such as, natural language understanding, dialog state tracker and natural language generator.

Seq2Seq models have also shown promising results on small domain or synthetic task-oriented dialog datasets. However, performance was much worse when we applied these models to real world datasets. This is in part because end-to-end methods, in general, require large amounts of data before they are able to generate fluent textual responses. In real world settings, words chosen by human users and agents are not constrained to a fixed vocabulary, and hence we see many lexical variations even among semantically similar dialogs.

To ensure that information is both conveyed and understood, we want responses to be *fluent* as well as *coherent*. We say a response is *coherent* if it is a sensible response in the dialogue context. Table 1 shows responses generated by a variant of the seq2seq model, when trained on real customer-agent chat transcripts. The response of the chatbot during the fourth turn[2] in Table 1, accepting the customer's expression of gratitude, is coherent and fluent. Coherence of a response does not necessarily guarantee fluency. The generated response during the second turn is coherent but not fluent.

On our customer support dataset, seq2seq models performed well with salutations, but performed poorly both in terms of fluency and coherency on intermediate responses. The reason being, salutations contain minimal lexical variations across dialogs and occur more frequently when compared to other utterances. (Koehn and Knowles, 2017) use beam search decoding in Neural Machine Translation to mitigate fluency issues on larger translation datasets. Typically increasing the beam size improves translation quality, however, increasing beam sizes in Neural MT has shown to produce poor translations (Koehn and Knowles, 2017).

We propose nearest neighbor based approaches that can directly use and replay available expert utterances. This removes the need for the models to learn the grammar of the language, and allows the models to focus on learning what to say, rather than how to say it. The nearest neighbor-based

---

[1] We refer to an entire session of text exchanges between an agent and a customer as a *dialogue*.

[2] We define a *turn* as a pair of text exchanges between the customer and the agent.

Proceedings of NAACL-HLT 2018, pages 25–32
New Orleans, Louisiana, June 1 - 6, 2018. ©2017 Association for Computational Linguistics

Table 1: Generated dialogue on customer support data. *masked* used for anonymization.

Turn	User's Utterance	Agent's Response	Generated Chatbot Response
1	got charged for <masked> membership after trial i did not want to continue.	hello , my name is <PERSON> . i 'm here to help you today .	hello <PERSON> , my name is <PERSON> . i 'm here to help you .
2	<SILENCE>	thank you for being a <masked> member .	thank , for you <masked> member
3	<SILENCE>	i 'm sorry to hear that you were charged with our membership . no worries . i 'll do my best	<SILENCE>
4	thank you , i did not know that it would auto renew after the trial	you 're welcome	you 're most welcome
5	<SILENCE>	*api_call* cancel_refund	*api_call* cancel_refund
6	<SILENCE>	i hope my actions helped you out today	you 're most welcome
7	very appreciated	thank you for contacting <masked>	thank you for contacting <masked>

methods we propose naturally generate more fluent responses, since they use actual agent responses. However, our results in Table 3 show that they perform poorly in predicting external actions and at ensuring dialogue level coherency. In contrast, the skip-connection seq2seq models we propose here, learn when to produce external actions and produce more coherent dialogues. We propose a hybrid model that brings together the strengths of both the approaches.

The contributions of this paper are as follows:

- We propose skip-connections to handle multi-turn dialogue that outperforms previous models.

- We propose a hybrid model where nearest neighbor-based models generate fluent responses and skip-connection models generate accurate responses and external actions. We show the effectiveness of the belief state representations obtained from the skip-connection model by comparing against previous approaches.

- To the best of our knowledge, our paper makes the first attempt at evaluating state of the art models on a large real world task with human users. We show that methods that achieve state of the art performance on synthetic datasets, perform poorly in real world dialog tasks. Comparing Tables 2 and 3, we see the impact of moving from synthetic to real world datasets, and as a result, find issues with previously proposed models that may have been obscured by the simplicity and regularity of synthetic datasets.

2 Related Work

Although seq2seq models have been applied in task-oriented settings (Wen et al., 2017; Williams and Zweig, 2016; Bordes and Weston, 2016; Zhao and Eskénazi, 2016), they have only been evaluated on small domain or synthetic datasets.

More recent work has focused on representation learning for multi-turn dialogue. Sordoni et al. (2015b) use a single bag-of-words representation of the entire dialog history. Such a representation ignores the order of responses, which is crucial to ensure that utterances are coherent across turns. An alternative approach is to use a hierarchical encoder-decoder network (HRED) (Sordoni et al., 2015a) which uses a complex three layered RNN network, a query level encoder, a session level encoder and a decoder. Attentional networks (Bordes and Weston, 2016; Dodge et al., 2015) use a weighted combination of all the context vectors upto the current turn. Attentional networks proved to be a stronger baseline over HRED during our evaluation. We propose models that learn fixed size representations of the history using simpler skip-connection models showing comparable performance with attentional networks (Bordes and Weston, 2016; Dodge et al., 2015).

Our work is closely related to retrieval-based chatbots. Williams and Zweig (2016), select a response from a small set of templates. Zhou et al. (2016); Yan et al. (2016) perform multi-turn dialogue by treating the dialogue history as the query, and perform classification with the number of classes equal to the number of possible responses. They evaluate precision@K, from a restricted list, but do not indicate how this list is obtained in practice. In our real world dataset, the number of possible responses grows with the dataset size. In addition, responses are unevenly distributed with salutations occurring frequently. As a

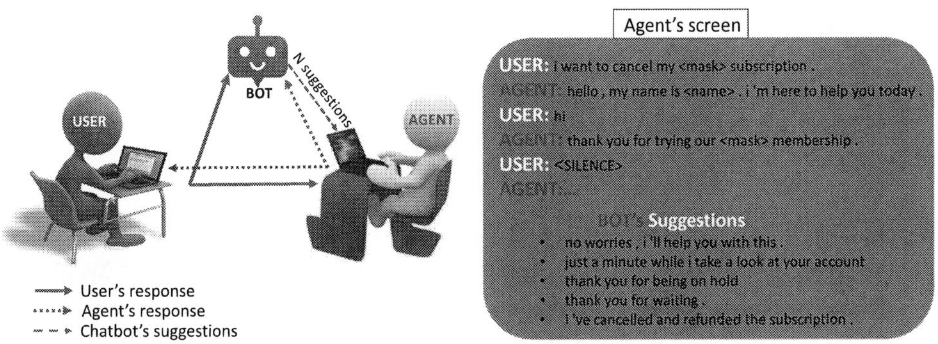

Figure 1: System Description. A human agent plays an intermediary role between the chatbot and the user.

result, the classification based approach performed poorly, with most of the outputs being salutations.

3 Proposed Approach

Complete automation of customer service is still not possible as chatbots are not perfect yet. However, automation where possible in the workflow could still result in considerable savings. In order to ensure that the end user experience is not substandard, in live user testing, we ask a human agent to play intermediary role between the chatbot and the user. A user initiates a chat by entering an initial query or an issue that requires resolution (Figure 1). The chatbot responds with 5 diverse responses. The agent selects the most relevant response, and may choose to modify it. If the response is not relevant, she may type a different response. During offline testing, the chatbot returns only one response and no human agent is used. The following section describes our skip connection seq2seq model for representation learning and our nearest neighbor approach for response selection. First we describe the datasets and metrics we use.

3.1 Dataset and Metrics

We use data from bAbI (Task1 and Task2) (Bordes and Weston, 2016) to evaluate our models. Other dialog tasks in bAbI require the model to mimic a knowledge base i.e., memorize it. This is not a suitable strategy for our application, since in practice knowledge bases undergo frequent changes, making this infeasible. In the bAbI task, the user interacts with an agent in a simulated restaurant reservation application, by providing her constraints, such as place, cuisine, number of people or price range. The agent or chatbot performs external actions or SQL-like queries (api_call) to retrieve information from the knowledge base of restaurants. We used 80% of the data for training (of which 10% was used for validation) and the remaining 20% for testing.

We also evaluate our models on an internal customer support dataset of 160k chat transcripts containing 3 million interactions. We limit the number of turns to 20. We will refer to this dataset as CS_large. We perform spell correction, de-identification to remove customer sensitive information, lexical normalization particularly of lingo words such as, *lol* and *ty*. Generalizing such entities reduces the amount of training data required. The values must be reinserted, currently by a human in the loop. We have also masked product and the organization name in the examples.

The use of MT evaluation metrics to evaluate dialogue fluency with just one reference has been debated (Liu et al., 2016). There is still no good alternative to evaluate dialog systems, and so we continue to report fluency using BLEU (BiLingual Evaluation Understudy (Papineni et al., 2002)), in addition to other metrics and human evaluations. Coherency also requires measuring correctness of the external actions which we measure using a metric we call, Exact Query Match (EQM), which represents the fraction of times the api_call matched the ground truth query issued by the human agent. We do not assign any credit to partial matches. In addition, we report the precision (P), recall (R) and accuracy (Acc) achieved by the models in predicting whether to make an api_call (positive) or not (negative). Obtaining and aligning api_calls with the chat transcripts is often complex as such information is typically stored in multiple confidential logs. In order to measure coherency with respect to api_calls, we randomly sampled 1000 chat tran-

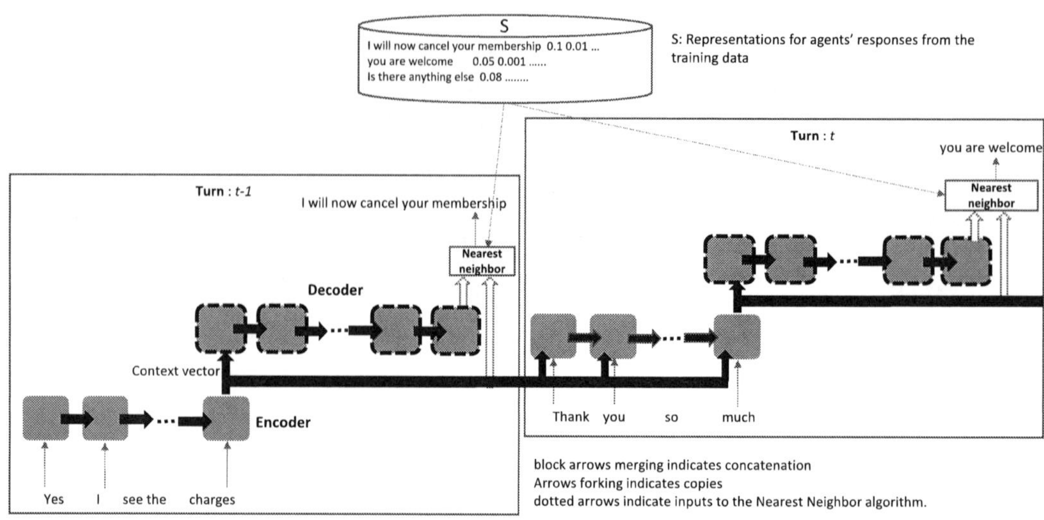

Figure 2: Proposed embeddings for finding the nearest neighbor.

scripts and asked human agents to hand annotate the api_calls wherever appropriate. We will refer to this labeled dataset as CS_small.

3.1.1 Skip Connection Seq2Seq Model

Seq2seq models are an application of Long Short-Term Memory (Hochreiter and Schmidhuber, 1997) architecture where inputs and outputs are variable length sequences. We unroll the basic seq2seq model and make one copy for each turn. This is illustrated in Figure 2. Input words are one hot encoded, and projected using a linear layer to obtain x_k^t for the input word at position k in turn t, resulting in a sequence $X_t = \{x_1^t, x_2^t, ...x_L^t\}$. The output sequence to be generated is represented by $Y_t = \{y_1^t, y_2^t, ...y_{L'}^t\}$. The encoder at turn t receives the user's projected input, as well as the context vectors from the final hidden units of the encoder and the decoder at turn $t - 1$, forming a skip connection. This ensures that a fixed size vector is used to represent the dialogue history at every turn. Orange-solid-square boxes in Figure 2 represent LSTM cells of the encoder. $h_{L,enc}^t$ is the context vector which is sent to every LSTM cell in the decoder (dec) at any turn t (Cho et al., 2014).

Green-dashed-square cells in the decoder represent the LSTM and dense layers with a softmax non-linearity. These are trained to predict each word in the agent's utterance. Each of the seq2seq copies share the same parameters. Once the training is complete, we use only one copy of the seq2seq model to make predictions.

3.1.2 Results with Skip-Connections

The results obtained with the vanilla seq2seq model on the bAbI dataset is shown in the first row (**Model 1**) of Table 2. The EQM is 0%, even though the BLEU scores look reasonable. **Model 2** is the skip-connection seq2seq model, where only the output of the hidden states from the decoder at turn $t - 1$ is appended to the input at time t, i.e., $h_{L,enc}^{t-1}$ from the *encoder* history is not explicitly presented to turn t.

Model 3 extends Model 1 by adding an attentional layer. Model 3 is a variant of Bordes and Weston (2016); Dodge et al. (2015) where the output of the attentional layer is sent to the decoder for generating the responses rather than classifying as one of the known responses. This variant performed better on the customer support data compared to a direct implementation of Bordes and Weston (2016). The reason being, salutations occurred more frequently in the customer support data and hence, the classification based approach originally proposed by Bordes and Weston (2016) classified most of the outputs as salutations. Finally, **Model 4** extends Model 2 by providing $h_{L,enc}^{t-1}$ to turn t.

We see that explicitly adding skip-connections substantially improves performance in EQM, from 0 or 6% to 55%, and has a positive effect on BLEU. The models show similar behavior on CS_small. In this case, when an api_call is executed, the result is treated as a response and sent as input to the next turn. Although Model 4 performed the best

Table 2: Results with variants of the seq2seq model on the bAbI dataset.

Model	Type	Description	BLEU	P	Acc	EQM
Model 1	Basic Seq2Seq	dependencies between turns absent	88.3	0.60	0.87	0.00
Model 2	Skip connection	append $h_{L',dec}^{t-1}$	90.2	1.00	1.00	0.06
Model 3	Seq2Seq	Model 1 with an attention layer	93.4	1.00	1.00	0.26
Model 4	Skip connection	Model 2 + $h_{L,enc}^{t-1}$	95.8	1.00	1.00	0.55

Table 3: Results with the Nearest Neighbor approach on customer support data (CS_small).

Model	Description	BLEU	P	R	Acc	EQM
Model 4	Skip connection	9.91	0.34	0.79	0.81	0.30
Model 6	Nearest Neighbor using Word2Vec	11.06	0.31	0.24	0.86	0.10
Model 7	Nearest Neighbor using Sent2Vec	14.39	0.29	0.26	0.85	0.09
Model 8	Nearest Neighbor using discounted Sent2Vec	16.43	0.56	0.60	0.91	0.21
Model 9	Nearest neighbor using output of encoder	15.14	0.38	0.35	0.86	0.13
Model 10	Nearest neighbor using output of decoder	16.34	0.36	0.31	0.86	0.16
Model 11	Best Of both (Models 4+10)	17.67	0.33	0.73	0.80	0.30

on CS_small and CS_large, our analysis showed that the generated responses were most often incoherent and not fluent, a phenomenon that did not arise in the synthetic dataset. We now proceed to explain the nearest neighbor based approach, which we show is able to produce reasonable responses that are more fluent.

3.2 Nearest Neighbor-based approach

In our nearest neighbor approach, an agent's response is chosen from human generated transcripts or the training data - ensuring fluency. However, this does not necessarily ensure that the responses are coherent in the context of the dialogue. The nearest neighbor approach starts with a representation of the entire dialogue history $bs_{t,i}$ for turn t and dialogue i. Together with $a_{t,i}$, the action the agent took while in this state i.e., the natural language response or api_call query issued by the agent, this results in a tuple $< bs_{t,i}, a_{t,i} >$. The entire training data is converted into a set of tuples S, that contains pairwise relationships between dialog state representations and agent actions.

In the online or test phase, given an embedding of the dialogue so far, $testVec$, we find the nearest neighbor $bs_{testVec}$ in S. We return the nearest neighbor's corresponding response, $a_{testVec}$, as the predicted agent's response. We use ball trees (Kibriya and Frank, 2007) to perform efficient nearest neighbor search. Since we want to provide more flexibility to the human agent in choosing the most

appropriate response, we extended this approach to find $k = 100$ responses and then used a diversity-based ranking approach (Zhu et al., 2007) to return 5 diverse responses. To construct the adjacency matrix for diversity ranking, we use word overlap between responses after stop word removal.

Numerous techniques have been proposed for representating text including word2vec and sent2vec (Mikolov et al., 2013b,a; Pagliardini et al., 2017; Pennington et al., 2014). In the following sections, we compare these approaches against our proposed representations using skip connections.

3.2.1 Dialogue Embeddings from Word/Sentence Embeddings

In our first baseline, **Model 6**, for a dialogue, i, the user's response at turn t, $user_t$, is concatenated with his/her responses in previous turns ($user_{i,1:t-1}$) and the agent's responses upto turn $t - 1$ ($agent_{i,1:t-1}$), to obtain, $p_{i,t} = (user_{i,1:t}, agent_{i,1:t-1})$. We obtain a belief state vector representation as the average of the word2vec (Mikolov et al., 2013b) representations of words in $p_{i,t}$. We then apply the nearest neighbor approach described in Section 3.2. Results obtained with this approach on CS_small are in Table 3.

We emphasize a subtle but important oracle advantage that we give this baseline algorithm. When we obtain the embeddings of a test dialogue, we use the true utterances of the expert agent so far,

Table 4: Results with the Nearest Neighbor approach on customer support data (CS_large).

Model	Description	BLEU	Online-BLEU
Model 4	Skip connection	8.9	46.2
Model 5	Lucene	8.4	39.2
Model 10	Nearest neighbor using output of decoder	13.5	90.8

which would not be available in practice. However, we will show that our proposed representation, described in Section 3.3, performs better, even without access to this information.

Pagliardini et al. (2017) recently described a method that leads to better sentence-level representations. We use their approach as another baseline. bs_t is represented by the average of the sentence embeddings of all agent's responses upto turn $t - 1$ and user's responses upto turn t. We also explore geometric discounting to give higher importance to recent responses. We use a similar process to obtain representations for the user's responses during the test phase. As done with word-embeddings, we provide true agent responses upto turn $t - 1$ for predicting the agent's response at turn t. Results obtained on CS_small by averaging (**Model 7**) and discounted averaging (**Model 8**) are given in Table 3. Model 8 performs better than Model 7 across all measures. A comparison between Model 6, 7 and 8 with Model 4 in Table 3, would not be a fair one as Model 4 does not use previous *true* agent responses to predict the agent's next response.

3.3 Hybrid model: Nearest Neighbor with Seq2Seq Embeddings

We suggest using the outputs of the hidden units in the decoder of our skip connection seq2seq model, as suitable representations for the belief states. The seq2seq model for handling multi-turn dialogue is trained as before (Section 3.1.1). Once the parameters have been learned, we proceed to generate representations for all turns in the training data. The output of the last hidden unit of the encoder or the decoder before turn t is used to represent the belief state vector at turn t. As before, we obtain a set S consisting of pairs of belief state vectors and next actions taken by the agent.

We test the models as done in Section 3.1.1, except now we select responses using the nearest neighbor approach (Figure 2). Results obtained are in Table 3 (Models 9 and 10). **Model 9** uses the output of the last hidden unit of the encoder. **Model 10** uses previous turn's decoder's last hidden unit.

Both the models show a significant improvement in BLEU when compared to generating the agent's response (Model 4). Although Model 10 was not exposed to the past true agent responses, it still achieved comparable performance to that of Model 8. Appending both the encoder and the decoder outputs did not have significant impact.

The results also show that the seq2seq model achieved a better EQM when compared to the nearest neighbor approach. The final hybrid model, we propose (**Model 11**) combines both strategies. We run both the Models 4 and 10 in parallel. When Model 4 predicts an API response, we use the output generated by Model 4 as the agent's response, otherwise we use the output of Model 10 as the predicted agent's response. This model achieved the best results among all models we study, both in terms of fluency (BLEU) as well as correctness of external actions (EQM). The hybrid model achieves a 78% relative improvement (from 9.91 to 17.67) in fluency scores, and 200% improvement in EQM over previous approaches (from 0.10 to 0.30).

Table 4 shows results obtained on CS_large (column 3) using models that performed the best on the other datasets. Another obvious baseline is to use traditional retrieval approaches. (query, agent response) pairs are created for each agent response, with a query constructed by concatenating all the agent's responses upto turn $t - 1$ and user's responses upto turn t, for an agent response at time t. For a given dialogue history query, the corresponding agent response is retrieved using Lucene[3]. Since CS_large did not contain labeled api_calls, we report results using Model 10. As seen, Model 10 provides a substantial boost in performance.

3.4 Manual Online Evaluation

One caveat to the above evaluations is that they are based on customer responses to the actual human agent interactions, and are not fully indicative of how customers would react to the real automated system in practice. Another disadvantage of using

---

[3]https://lucene.apache.org/

Table 5: Sample responses show interesting human behaviors learned by the approach.

Example	User's Utterance	Agent's Response
1	YES YES YES , get it done .	done :)
	perfect	sir , thanks for waiting
2	it was clearly your fault	i understand sir
	when should i return it and how	you can keep it or you can donate or else you can dispose it off .

automated evaluation with just one reference, is that the score (BLEU) penalizes valid responses that may be lexically different from the available agent response. To overcome this issue, we conducted online experiments with human agents.

We used 5 human users and 2 agents. On average each user interacted with an agent on 10 different issues that needed resolution. To compare against our baseline, each user interacted with the Model 4, 5 and 10 using the same issues. This resulted in $\approx$ 50 dialogues from each of the models. After every response from the user, the human agent was allowed to select one of the top five responses the system selected. We refer to the selected response as A. The human agent was asked to make minimal modifications to the selected response, resulting in a response A'. If the responses suggested were completely irrelevant, the human agent was allowed to type in the most suitable response.

We then computed the BLEU between the system generated responses (As) and human generated responses ($A's$), referred to as Online-BLEU in Table 4. Since the human agent only made minimal changes where appropriate, we believe the BLEU score would now be more correlated to human judgments. Since CS_large did not contain any api_calls, we only report BLEU scores. The results obtained with models 4, 5 and 10 on CS_large are shown in Table 4 (column 4). Model 10 performs better than Models 4 and 5. We do not measure inter-annotator agreement as each human user can take a different dialog trajectory.

We noticed that the approach mimics certain interesting human behavior. For example, in Table 5, the chatbot detects that the user is frustrated and responds with smileys and even makes exceptions on the return policy.

4   Conclusion and Future Work

We demonstrated limitations of previous end-end dialog approaches and proposed variants to make them suitable for real world settings. In ongoing work, we explore reinforcement learning techniques to reach the goal state quicker thereby reducing the number of interactions.

References

S. Bennacef, L. Devillers, S. Rosset, and L. Lamel. 1996. Dialog in the railtel telephone-based system. In *Spoken Language, 1996. ICSLP 96. Proceedings., Fourth International Conference on.* volume 1, pages 550–553 vol.1.

Antoine Bordes and Jason Weston. 2016. Learning end-to-end goal-oriented dialog. *CoRR* abs/1605.07683.

Kyunghyun Cho, Bart van Merrienboer, Çaglar Gülçehre, Fethi Bougares, Holger Schwenk, and Yoshua Bengio. 2014. Learning phrase representations using RNN encoder-decoder for statistical machine translation. *CoRR* .

Jesse Dodge, Andreea Gane, Xiang Zhang, Antoine Bordes, Sumit Chopra, Alexander H. Miller, Arthur Szlam, and Jason Weston. 2015. Evaluating prerequisite qualities for learning end-to-end dialog systems. *CoRR* abs/1511.06931.

Sepp Hochreiter and Jürgen Schmidhuber. 1997. Long short-term memory. *Neural Comput.* 9(8):1735–1780.

Ashraf M. Kibriya and Eibe Frank. 2007. An empirical comparison of exact nearest neighbour algorithms. In *Proceedings of the 11th European Conference on Principles and Practice of Knowledge Discovery in Databases.* Springer-Verlag, Berlin, Heidelberg, PKDD 2007, pages 140–151.

Philipp Koehn and Rebecca Knowles. 2017. Six challenges for neural machine translation. *CoRR* abs/1706.03872.

Chia-Wei Liu, Ryan Lowe, Iulian Vlad Serban, Michael Noseworthy, Laurent Charlin, and Joelle Pineau. 2016. How NOT to evaluate your dialogue system: An empirical study of unsupervised evaluation metrics for dialogue response generation. *CoRR* abs/1603.08023.

Tomas Mikolov, Kai Chen, Greg Corrado, and Jeffrey Dean. 2013a. Efficient estimation of word representations in vector space. *CoRR* abs/1301.3781.

Tomas Mikolov, Ilya Sutskever, Kai Chen, Greg Corrado, and Jeffrey Dean. 2013b. Distributed representations of words and phrases and their compositionality. In *Proceedings of the 26th International Conference on Neural Information Processing Systems - Volume 2*. Curran Associates Inc., USA, NIPS'13, pages 3111–3119.

Matteo Pagliardini, Prakhar Gupta, and Martin Jaggi. 2017. Unsupervised learning of sentence embeddings using compositional n-gram features. *CoRR* abs/1703.02507.

Kishore Papineni, Salim Roukos, Todd Ward, and Wei-Jing Zhu. 2002. Bleu: A method for automatic evaluation of machine translation. In *Proceedings of the 40th Annual Meeting on Association for Computational Linguistics*. Association for Computational Linguistics, Stroudsburg, PA, USA, ACL '02, pages 311–318.

Jeffrey Pennington, Richard Socher, and Christopher Manning. 2014. Glove: Global Vectors for Word Representation. In *Proceedings of the 2014 Conference on Empirical Methods in Natural Language Processing (EMNLP)*. Association for Computational Linguistics, Doha, Qatar, pages 1532–1543.

Iulian Vlad Serban, Ryan Lowe, Peter Henderson, Laurent Charlin, and Joelle Pineau. 2015. A survey of available corpora for building data-driven dialogue systems. *CoRR* abs/1512.05742.

Lifeng Shang, Zhengdong Lu, and Hang Li. 2015. Neural responding machine for short text conversation. *ACL* .

Alessandro Sordoni, Yoshua Bengio, Hossein Vahabi, Christina Lioma, Jakob Grue Simonsen, and Jian-Yun Nie. 2015a. A hierarchical recurrent encoder-decoder for generative context-aware query suggestion. In *Proceedings of the 24th ACM International on Conference on Information and Knowledge Management*. ACM, New York, NY, USA, CIKM '15, pages 553–562.

Alessandro Sordoni, Michel Galley, Michael Auli, Chris Brockett, Yangfeng Ji, Margaret Mitchell, Jian-Yun Nie, Jianfeng Gao, and Bill Dolan. 2015b. A neural network approach to context-sensitive generation of conversational responses. *CoRR* abs/1506.06714.

Oriol Vinyals and Quoc V. Le. 2015. A neural conversational model. *CoRR* abs/1506.05869.

Tsung-Hsien Wen, Milica Gasic, Nikola Mrksic, Lina M Rojas-Barahona, Pei-Hao Su, Stefan Ultes, David Vandyke, and Steve Young. 2017. A network-based end-to-end trainable task-oriented dialogue system. *EACL* .

Jason D. Williams and Geoffrey Zweig. 2016. End-to-end lstm-based dialog control optimized with supervised and reinforcement learning. *CoRR* abs/1606.01269.

Rui Yan, Yiping Song, and Hua Wu. 2016. Learning to respond with deep neural networks for retrieval-based human-computer conversation system. In *Proceedings of the 39th International ACM SIGIR Conference on Research and Development in Information Retrieval*. ACM, New York, NY, USA, SIGIR '16, pages 55–64.

Tiancheng Zhao and Maxine Eskénazi. 2016. Towards end-to-end learning for dialog state tracking and management using deep reinforcement learning. *CoRR* abs/1606.02560.

Xiangyang Zhou, Daxiang Dong, Hua Wu, Shiqi Zhao, Dianhai Yu, Hao Tian, Xuan Liu, and Rui Yan. 2016. Multi-view response selection for human-computer conversation. In *EMNLP*. pages 372–381.

Xiaojin Zhu, Andrew Goldberg, Jurgen Van Gael, and David Andrzejewski. 2007. Improving diversity in ranking using absorbing random walks. *HLT-NAACL* pages 97–104.

Victor Zue, Stephanie Seneff, James Glass, Joseph Polifroni, Christine Pao, Timothy J. Hazen, and Lee Hetherington. 2000. Jupiter: A telephone-based conversational interface for weather information. *IEEE Trans. on Speech and Audio Processing* 8:85–96.

Data Collection for a Production Dialogue System: A Clinc Perspective

Yiping Kang   **Yunqi Zhang**   **Jonathan K. Kummerfeld**   **Parker Hill**
Johann Hauswald   **Michael A. Laurenzano**   **Lingjia Tang**   **Jason Mars**

Clinc, Inc.

Ann Arbor, MI, USA

{yiping,yunqi,jkk,parkerhh,johann,mike,lingjia,jason}@clinc.com

Abstract

Industrial dialogue systems such as Apple Siri and Google Assistant require large scale diverse training data to enable their sophisticated conversation capabilities. Crowdsourcing is a scalable and inexpensive data collection method, but collecting high quality data efficiently requires thoughtful orchestration of crowdsourcing jobs. Prior study of data collection process has focused on tasks with limited scope and performed intrinsic data analysis, which may not be indicative of impact on trained model performance. In this paper, we present a study of crowdsourcing methods for a user intent classification task in one of our deployed dialogue systems. Our task requires classification over 47 possible user intents and contains many intent pairs with subtle differences. We consider different crowdsourcing job types and job prompts, quantitatively analyzing the quality of collected data and downstream model performance on a test set of real user queries from production logs. Our observations provide insight into how design decisions impact crowdsourced data quality, with clear recommendations for future data collection for dialogue systems.

1   Introduction

Large, high quality corpora are crucial in the development of effective machine learning models in many areas, including Natural Language Processing (NLP). The performance of the machine learning models, especially deep learning models, depend heavily on the quantity and quality of the training data. Developing dialogue systems such as Apple Siri, Google Assistant and Amazon Alexa poses a significant challenge for data collection as we need to do rapid prototyping and bootstrapping to train new virtual assistant capabilities. The use of crowdsourcing has enabled the creation of large corpora at relatively low cost (Snow et al., 2008) and is critical in collecting the quantities of data required to train models with high accuracy. However, designing effective methodologies for data collection with the crowd is largely an open research question (Sabou et al., 2014).

From the perspective of Clinc, a young AI company creating innovative conversational AI experiences, there exists a major challenge when collecting data to build a dialogue system. We have observed that the complexity of building production-grade dialogue system is often substantially greater than those studied in the research community. For example, one of our production deployed dialogue systems requires intent classification among 47 different intents to meet product specifications, whereas most academic datasets for text classification only have a small number (i.e., 2–14) of classes (Zhang et al., 2015). The few datasets that have a large number of classes, such as RCV-1 (Lewis et al., 2004), distribute intents across many distinct topics. We address the significantly more challenging problem of handling many intents within a single domain, specifically personal finance and wealth management, requiring the classifier to carefully distinguish between nuanced intent topics. Therefore, a large amount of high-quality training data tailored to our targeted problem is critical for creating the best user experience in our production dialogue system.

Crowdsourcing offers a promising solution by massively parallelizing data collection efforts across a large pool of workers at relatively low cost. Because of the involvement of crowd workers, collecting high-quality data efficiently requires careful orchestration of crowdsourcing jobs, including their instructions and prompts. In order to collect the large-scale tailored dataset we need via crowdsourcing, there are several research questions we need to answer:

- How can we evaluate the effectiveness of crowdsourcing methods and the quality of the datasets collected via these methods?

Proceedings of NAACL-HLT 2018, pages 33–40
New Orleans, Louisiana, June 1 - 6, 2018. ©2017 Association for Computational Linguistics

- During the data collection process, how can we identify the point when additional data would have diminishing returns on the performance of the downstream trained models?

- Which crowdsourcing method yields the highest-quality training data for intent classification in a production dialogue system?

There is limited work on effective techniques to evaluate a crowdsourcing method and the data collected using that method. Prior work has focused on intrinsic analysis of the data, lacking quantitative investigation of the data's impact on downstream model performance (Jiang et al., 2017). In this paper, we propose two novel model-indepedent metrics to evaluate dataset quality. Specifically, we introduce (1) `coverage`, quantifying how well a training set covers the expression space of a certain task, and (2) `diversity`, quantifying the heterogeneity of sentences in the training set. We verify the effectiveness of both metrics by correlating them with the model accuracy of two well-known algorithms, SVM (Cortes and Vapnik, 1995) and FastText (Joulin et al., 2017; Bojanowski et al., 2017). We show that while `diversity` gives a sense of the variation in the data, `coverage` closely correlates with the model accuracy and serves as an effective metric for evaluating training data quality.

We then describe in detail two crowdsourcing methods we use to collect intent classification data for our deployed dialogue system. The key ideas of these two methods are (1) describing the intent as a scenario or (2) providing an example sentence to be paraphrased. We experiment multiple variants of these methods by varying the number and type of prompts and collect training data using each variant. We perform metric and accuracy evaluation of these datasets and show that using a mixture of different prompts and sampling paraphrasing exmples from real user queries yield training data with higher `coverage` and `diversity` and lead to better performing models. These observations have impacted the way that we collect data and are improving the quality of our production system.

2 Many-intent Classification

We focus on a specific aspect of dialogue systems: intent classification. This task takes a user utterance as input and classifies it into one of the predefined categories. Unlike general dialogue annotation schemes such as DAMSL (Core and Allen, 1997), intent classification is generally domain-specific. Our system requires classification over 47 customer service related intents in the domain of personal finance and wealth management. These intents cover a large set of topics while some of the intents are very closely related and it requires the classifier to identify the nuanced differences between utterances. For example, user's queries to see a list of their banking transactions can often be very similar to their queries to see a summary of historical spending, e.g., *"When did I spend money at Starbucks recently?"* vs. *"How much money did I spend at Starbucks recently?"*.

Test Methodology   Our test data contains a combination of real user queries from a deployed system and additional cases manually constructed by developers. This combination allows us to effectively measure performance for current users, while also testing a broad range of ways to phrase queries. Our test set contains 3,988 sentences labelled with intents.

3 Training Data Quality Metrics

When we look to improve a model's performance, there are generally two approaches that we can take: improve the model and inference algorithm and/or improve the training data. There is currently no reliable way to help us identify whether the training data or the model structure is the current bottleneck. One solution is to train actual models using the training set and measure their accuracy with a pre-defined test set. However, if only a single algorithm is used, over time this evaluation may lead to a bias, as the training data is tuned to suit that specific algorithm. Using a suite of different algorithms avoids this issue, but can be very time consuming. We need an algorithm-independent way to evaluate the quality of training data and its effectiveness at solving the target task. In this section, we introduce two metrics to achieve this, `diversity` and `coverage`.

Diversity   We use `diversity` to evaluate the heterogeneity of the training data. The idea behind `diversity` is that the more diverse the training data is, the less likely a downstream model will overfit to certain words or phrases and the better it will generalize to the testing set.

We first define a pairwise sentence distance measure. For a given pair of sentences, a and b, we calculate the reverse of the mean Jaccard Index between the sentences' n-grams sets to represent the semantic distances between the two sentences:

$$D(a,b) = 1 - \sum_{n=1}^{N} \frac{|n\text{-grams}_a \cap n\text{-grams}_b|}{|n\text{-grams}_a \cup n\text{-grams}_b|} \quad (1)$$

where N is the maximum n-gram length. We use $N = 3$ in our experiments.

Our pairwise score is similar to the PINC score (Chen and Dolan, 2011), except that we use the n-grams from the union of both sentences instead of just one sentence in the denominator of Equation 1. This is because the PINC score is used in paraphrasing tasks to measures how much a paraphrased sentence differ from the original sentence and specifically rewards n-grams that are unique to the paraphrsed sentence. Our metric measures the semantic distance between two sentences and treat the unique n-grams in both sentences as equal contribution to the distance.

We define the `diversity` of a training set as the average distance between all sentence pairs that share the same intent. For a training set X, its `diversity` ($DIV(X)$) is:

$$DIV(X) = \frac{1}{|I|} \sum_{i=1}^{I} \frac{1}{|X_i|^2} \left[\sum_{a}^{X_i} \sum_{b}^{X_i} D(a,b) \right] \quad (2)$$

where I is the set of intents and X_i is the set of sentences with intent i in the training set X.

Coverage We now introduce `coverage`, a new metric designed to model how well a training dataset covers the complete space of ways an intent can be expressed. We use our test set as an approximate representation of the expression space for our classification task. As described in § 2, our test set is constructed primarily with real user queries collected from the log of a deployed system and annotated by engineers.

To measure `coverage` of a training set given a test set, we first identify, for each test sentence, the most similar training sentence with the same intent, according to the pairwise sentence distance measure $D(a,b)$ defined in Equation 1. We then derive `coverage` by averaging the shortest distances for all sentences in the test set. For a given test set, we would want the training set to have as high `coverage` as possible. Specifically, for a

training set X and a test set Y:

$$CVG(X,Y) = \frac{1}{|I|} \sum_{i=1}^{I} \frac{1}{|Y_i|} \sum_{b}^{Y_i} \max_{a}^{X_i} (1 - D(a,b)) \quad (3)$$

where I is the set of intents and X_i and Y_i are the sets of utterances labeled with intent i in the training (X) and test (Y) sets, respectively.

Correlating Metrics with Model Accuracy In order to evaluate the effectiveness of `diversity` and `coverage` at representing the training data quality, we collect training data via different methods and of varying sizes, train actual models, measure their accuracy and investigate the correlation between the metrics and the accuracy. We consider two well-known algorithms that have publicly available implementations: a linear SVM and FastText, a neural network-based algorithm.

SVM Support Vector Machines (Cortes and Vapnik, 1995) are a widely used and effective approach for classification tasks. We use a linear model trained with the SVM objective as a simple baseline approach.

FastText We also consider a recently developed neural network approach (Joulin et al., 2017; Bojanowski et al., 2017). This model has three steps: (1) look up vectors for each n-gram in the sentence, (2) average the vectors, and (3) apply a linear classifier. The core advantage of this approach is parameter sharing, as the vector look-up step places the tokens in a dense vector space. This model consistently outperforms linear models on a range of tasks.

For all experiments we apply a consistent set of pre-processing steps designed to reduce sparseness in the data: we lowercase the text, remove punctuation, replace each digit with a common symbol, expand contractions, and lemmatize (using NLTK for the last two).

4   Crowdsourcing Data Collection Methods

We consider two aspects of a crowdsourcing setup: the *template* style, and the *prompt*. The template defines the structure of the task, including its instructions and interface. Prompts are intent-specific descriptions or examples that define the scope of each task and guide workers to supply answers related to the target intent. We define a set of prompts for each intent and populate a

React to a Scenario
Suppose you have a device that has a Siri-like app for your bank account that acts as a customer service agent and can handle questions about **your bank account's balance.**
Given the original scenario described below that is related to your bank account, **supply 5 creative ways of asking the intelligent device to assist your situation.**
"You want to ask about the balance of your bank account."

Figure 1: An example of scenario-driven task instructions. The template sets up a real-world situation and asks workers to provide a response as if they are in that situation. The prompt shown here is for collecting data for the intent 'balance'.

template with each prompt to create a complete crowdsourcing job. We study two types of templates: scenario-driven (§ 4.1) and paraphrasing (§ 4.2), and two methods of generating prompts: manual generation (§ 4.1 and 4.2) and test set sampling (§ 5.3). A data collection method is the combination of a template and a prompt generation method. In this section, we describe each method and its variants.

4.1 Scenario-driven

The instructions for a scenario-driven job describe a real-world situation and ask the worker to provide a response as if they are in the situation. Figure 1 shows an example job for the intent of "asking about your bank account balance". Table 1 shows additional example prompts for generic and specific scenarios. Scenario-driven jobs simulate real world situations and encourage workers to create natural questions and requests resembling real user queries.

We consider two variations on the scenario-driven setup. Generic scenarios describe the situation in which the target intent applies, without specific constraints. For example, a generic scenario for the intent 'balance' is *"You want to know about your account balance"*. Specific scenarios refine the description by adding details. These are intended to encourage workers to write responses with more entities and constraints. These jobs also add specific information that the worker needs to include in their response. For example, a specific scenario for the intent 'balance' is *"You'd like to know the balance of one of your accounts. (Please specify the account you want to inquire about in your responses)"*.

For each intent, we use one generic scenario and three specific scenarios. To evaluate the differ-

Paraphrase Sentence
Given the following sentence, **supply 5 creative ways of rephrasing the same sentence.**
Assume the original question is in regards to **your bank account's balance.**
"What is the balance of my bank account?"

Figure 2: An example of a paraphrasing task instructions.

ent scenario types, we collected data with either generic scenarios only, specific scenarios only, or a combination of both. The mixed setting contains equal contributions from all four scenarios (one generic and three specific). In our experiments, we keep the number of training samples per intent balanced across intents regardless of the number of total training examples.

4.2 Paraphrasing

Paraphrasing jobs provide an example sentence and ask workers to write several creative paraphrases of it. Figure 2 shows an example of job instructions for paraphrasing the sentence *"What is the balance of my bank account?"* To make sure we can directly compare the results of paraphrasing and scenario-driven jobs, we convert each scenario used in § 4.1 into a user question or command, which is provided as the sentence to paraphrase. As a result, there are two types of paraphrasing prompts: generic prompts and specific prompts. Table 1 shows example pairs of scenarios and paraphrasing prompts. Like in the scenario-driven case, we construct training sets with three different mixes of prompts, generic only, specific only and a combination of both.

5 Evaluation

In this section, we first verify that `diversity` and `coverage` provide insight regarding training data quality. We compare trends in these metrics with trends in model accuracy as the amount of training data is increased. We then evaluate the performance of the scenario-driven and paraphrase methods and their variants by comparing the quality of training data collected via these methods. Finally, we explore sampling paraphrasing examples from the test set and compare against manually generation by engineers.

Type	Scenario	Paraphrasing
Generic	You want to learn about your spending history.	"Show me my spending history."
Specific	You want to learn about your spending history during a specific period of time.	"Show me my spending history in the last month. (Use different time periods in your answers)."
Generic	You want to ask about your income.	"What's my income?"
Specific	You want to ask about your income from a specific employer.	"How much money did I make from Company A? (Use different employers in your answers.)"

Table 1: Examples of generic and specific scenario description and paraphrasing prompts.

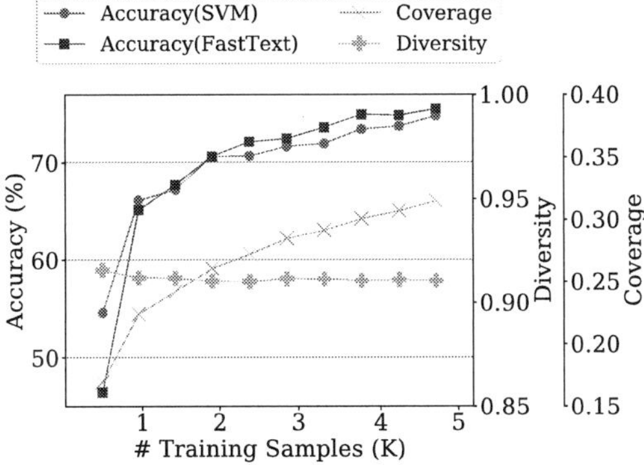

Figure 3: Accuracy, coverage and diversity for scenario-driven jobs as the training data size increases. This data is collected using a mixture of generic and specific scenarios.

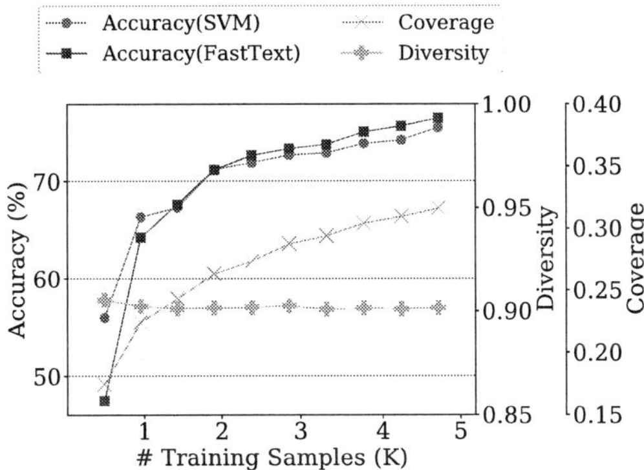

Figure 4: Accuracy, coverage and diversity for paraphrasing jobs as the training data size increases. This data is collected using a combination of generic and specific paraphrase examples.

5.1 Correlating Diversity and Coverage with Model Accuracy

Figure 3 and 4 show diversity, coverage, and accuracy of the SVM and FastText models as we vary the number of training examples for scenario-driven and paraphrase-based jobs, respectively. In this experiment, we use a combination of both generic and specific scenarios and paraphrasing examples.

We observe that for both scenario and paraphrase jobs, the diversity starts high (> 0.90) with a few hundred training samples and stay stable as training data size increases. This means that the new training examples generally have a low percentage of n-grams overlap and a long distance ($D(a, b)$) with the existing examples, therefore maintaining the overall high diversity. This indicates that the newly introduced examples are generally creative contributions from the crowd and not repeats or straightforward rephrase of the existing samples with the same words.

coverage starts low with a few hundred training examples and steadily increases as the training set grows. This indicates that the new training examples contain sentences that are semantically closer to the test set sentences than exisiting training examples, increasing the training set's scope to better cover the expression space represented by the test set. The accuracy of both SVM and FastText models follow a very similar trend to that of coverage, gradually increasing as more training samples are collected. The correlation between model accuracy and coverage shows that coverage is a more effective metric than diversity in evaluating the quality of a training set without training models.

We also observe diminishing returns in coverage as more data is collected. This trend roughly correlates with the diminishing return in accuracy of the SVM and FastText models. The trend in coverage provides insight into improvements in training data quality, which can inform the choice of when to stop collecting more data and start focusing on improving algorithms. This is further demonstrated by the way FastText consistently outperforms the SVM model when their accuracies and coverage of the training data saturate, indicating that the algorithm is the bottleneck for improving accuracy instead of the amount of training data.

Key Insights (1) diversity stays relatively constant with a high value as more training samples are collected, indicating that new distinct training examples are being introduced. (2) coverage continuously improves as data scales, showing that the training data is becoming more

| | | Accuracy | | | |
Template	Type	SVM	FastText	CVG	DIV
Scenario	Generic	68.49	69.70	0.30	0.90
	Specific	65.86	68.10	0.29	0.89
	Both	**74.77**	**75.48**	**0.32**	**0.91**
Paraphrase	Generic	68.60	70.50	0.30	0.88
	Specific	67.80	67.77	0.29	0.87
	Both	**75.46**	**76.44**	**0.32**	**0.90**

Table 2: Accuracy, `coverage` and `diversity` for the six template + prompt conditions considered, all with ~4.7K training samples.

effective at covering the expression space defined by the test set. The trend of `coverage` closely correlates with the trend in model accuracy, indicating that `coverage` is an effective metric at evaluating training data quality without requiring model training.

5.2 Comparing Scenario and Paraphrase Based Collection and Their Variants

Table 2 summarizes the model accuracy, `coverage` and `diversity` of both scenario-driven and paraphrase-based jobs. We studied three variants for each job type, where we use different mixtures of prompt type (generic prompts only, specific prompts only and combined prompts). All configurations are evaluated using training data of the same size (~4.7K) and on the same test set.

For both scenario and paraphrase jobs, using a mixture of both generic and specific prompts yields training data with higher `coverage` and models with higher accuracy than using only generic or specific prompts.

Table 2 compares scenario and paraphrasing jobs. As described in § 4.2, the paraphrasing examples were based on the scenario descriptions so we are only measuring the impact of different job types. The two approaches lead to similar results across all metrics. This shows that despite the instructions being distinctly different, scenario-driven and paraphrasing jobs generally yield training data of similar quality.

Key Insights (1) A mixture of generic and specific scenarios and paraphrasing examples yields the best training data given a fixed number of training examples, in terms of both `coverage` of the training set and the accuracy of the downstream models. (2) Scenario-driven and paraphrasing based crowdsourcing jobs yield similar quality training data despite having different job instructions and templates.

| | Accuracy | | | |
	SVM	FastText	CVG	DIV
Manual generation	75.46	76.44	0.32	0.90
Test set sampling	**83.05**	**84.69**	**0.40**	**0.92**

Table 3: Comparison of manually generating prompts and sampling from test set, evaluated on half of the test data (kept blind in sampling).

| # of paraphrasing | Accuracy | | | |
prompts	SVM	FastText	CVG	DIV
1	71.46	71.69	0.31	0.88
2	78.34	79.33	0.36	0.91
3	81.47	82.67	0.39	0.91
4	83.05	84.69	0.40	0.92
5	**84.61**	**85.96**	**0.41**	**0.92**

Table 4: Accuracy, `coverage` and `diversity` of paraphrasing jobs using 1-5 prompts sampled from the test set, with constant training set size (~4.7K).

5.3 Sampling Prompts from the Test Set

We now investigate a different way to generate the prompts used for the crowdsourcing jobs. In the context of scenario-driven and paraphrasing jobs, prompts are the scenario descriptions and the example sentences provided to workers to rephrase, respectively. In § 4.1 and 4.2, engineers manually generated the prompts based on the definition of each intent. While manual generation guarantees high quality prompts, it requires engineering effort and could potentially be biased by the engineer's perspective. One way to reduce such effort and bias is to automatically source prompts based on real user queries.

We divide the test set into two equal halves. For each intent, we randomly sample 5 utterances from the first half of the test set and use them as prompts to construct paraphrasing jobs. The second half of the test set is kept entirely blind and used for evaluation.

Manual Generation vs. Test Set Sampling Table 3 shows the accuracy, `coverage` and `diversity` of a training set collected with 4 manually generated paraphrasing examples vs. with 4 paraphrasing examples sampled from the first half of the test set. The accuracy for both methods is evaluated on the second half of the test set (kept blind from prompt sampling). The results show that sampling from the test set leads to a training set that has 8% higher `coverage`, 2% higher `diversity` and yields models with 8% higher accuracy, compared to manual generation.

Varying the Number of Prompts Table 4 shows the accuracy, `coverage` and `diversity` of training data collected using a varying number (1-5) of unique paraphrasing examples sampled from the test set. We observe that test set accuracy improves as we use more unique prompts but eventually there are diminishing returns. Increasing the number of prompts from 1 to 2 increases the accuracy by 6.9% and 7.6% for SVM and FastText, respectively, while increasing the number of prompts from 4 to 5 improves their accuracy by only 1.6% and 1.3%.

6 Related work

This study complements a line of work on understanding how to effectively collect data with non-expert workers. The closest work is Jiang et al. (2017)'s study of a range of interface design choices that impact the quality and diversity of crowdsourced paraphrases. However, their work focused on intrinsic evaluation of the paraphrases only, whereas we explore the impact on performance in a downstream task. The variations we consider are also complementary to the aspects covered by their study, providing additional guidance for future data collection efforts.

In terms of the variations we consider, the closest work is Rogstadius et al. (2011), who also considered how task framing can impact behavior. Their study made a more drastic change than ours though, attempting to shift workers' intrinsic motivation by changing the perspective to be about assisting a non-profit organization. While this shift did have a significant impact on worker behavior, it is often not applicable.

More generally, starting with the work of Snow et al. (2008) there have been several investigations of crowdsourcing design for natural language processing tasks. Factors that have been considered include quality control mechanisms (Rashtchian et al., 2010), payment rates and task descriptions (Grady and Lease, 2010), task naming (Vliegendhart et al., 2011), and worker qualification requirements (Kazai et al., 2013). Other studies have focused on exploring variations for specific tasks, such as named entity recognition (Feyisetan et al., 2017). Recent work has started to combine and summarize these observations together into consistent guidelines (Sabou et al., 2014), though the range of tasks and design factors makes the scope of such guidelines large. Our work adds to this literature, introducing new metrics and evaluation methods to guide crowdsourcing practice.

7 Conclusion

Training data is the key to building a successful production dialogue system, and efficiently collecting large scale robust training data via crowdsourcing is particularly challenging. In this work, we introduce and characterize two training data quality evaluation metrics. We verify their effectiveness by training models of well-known algorithms and correlating the metrics with model accuracy. We show that an algorithm-independent `coverage` metric is effective at providing insights into the training data and can guide the data collection process. We also studied and compared a range of crowdsourcing approaches for collecting training data for a many-intent classification task in one of our deployed dialogue systems. Our observations provide several key insights that serve as recommendations for future dialogue system data collection efforts, specifically that using a mixture of generic and specific prompts and sampling prompts from the real user queries yields better quality training data.

References

Piotr Bojanowski, Edouard Grave, Armand Joulin, and Tomas Mikolov. 2017. Enriching word vectors with subword information. *Transactions of the Association for Computational Linguistics*, 5:135–146.

David Chen and William Dolan. 2011. Collecting highly parallel data for paraphrase evaluation. In *Proceedings of the 49th Annual Meeting of the Association for Computational Linguistics: Human Language Technologies*, pages 190–200, Portland, Oregon, USA.

Mark G. Core and James F. Allen. 1997. Coding dialogs with the damsl annotation scheme. In *Working Notes of the AAAI Fall Symposium on Communicative Action in Humans and Machines*, pages 28–35, Cambridge, MA.

Corinna Cortes and Vladimir Vapnik. 1995. Support-vector networks. *Machine Learning*, 20(3):273–297.

Oluwaseyi Feyisetan, Elena Simperl, Markus Luczak-Roesch, Ramine Tinati, and Nigel Shadbolt. 2017. An extended study of content and crowdsourcing-related performance factors in named entity annotation. *Semantic Web*.

Catherine Grady and Matthew Lease. 2010. Crowdsourcing document relevance assessment with mechanical turk. In *Proceedings of the NAACL HLT 2010 Workshop on Creating Speech and Language Data with Amazon's Mechanical Turk*, pages 172–179, Los Angeles.

Youxuan Jiang, Jonathan K. Kummerfeld, and Walter S. Lasecki. 2017. Understanding task design trade-offs in crowdsourced paraphrase collection. In *Proceedings of the 55th Annual Meeting of the Association for Computational Linguistics (Volume 2: Short Papers)*, pages 103–109, Vancouver, Canada.

Armand Joulin, Edouard Grave, Piotr Bojanowski, and Tomas Mikolov. 2017. Bag of tricks for efficient text classification. In *Proceedings of the 15th Conference of the European Chapter of the Association for Computational Linguistics: Volume 2, Short Papers*, pages 427–431, Valencia, Spain.

Gabriella Kazai, Jaap Kamps, and Natasa Milic-Frayling. 2013. An analysis of human factors and label accuracy in crowdsourcing relevance judgments. *Information Retrieval*, 16(2):138–178.

David D. Lewis, Yiming Yang, Tony G. Rose, and Fan Li. 2004. Rcv1: A new benchmark collection for text categorization research. *J. Mach. Learn. Res.*, 5:361–397.

Cyrus Rashtchian, Peter Young, Micah Hodosh, and Julia Hockenmaier. 2010. Collecting image annotations using amazon's mechanical turk. In *Proceedings of the NAACL HLT 2010 Workshop on Creating Speech and Language Data with Amazon's Mechanical Turk*, pages 139–147, Los Angeles.

Jakob Rogstadius, Vassilis Kostakos, Aniket Kittur, Boris Smus, Jim Laredo, and Maja Vukovic. 2011. An assessment of intrinsic and extrinsic motivation on task performance in crowdsourcing markets. In *International AAAI Conference on Web and Social Media*.

Marta Sabou, Kalina Bontcheva, Leon Derczynski, and Arno Scharl. 2014. Corpus annotation through crowdsourcing: Towards best practice guidelines. In *Proceedings of the Ninth International Conference on Language Resources and Evaluation (LREC-2014)*.

Rion Snow, Brendan O'Connor, Daniel Jurafsky, and Andrew Ng. 2008. Cheap and fast – but is it good? evaluating non-expert annotations for natural language tasks. In *Proceedings of the 2008 Conference on Empirical Methods in Natural Language Processing*, pages 254–263, Honolulu, Hawaii.

Raynor Vliegendhart, Martha Larson, Christoph Kofler, Carsten Eickhoff, and Johan Pouwelse. 2011. Investigating factors influencing crowdsourcing tasks with high imaginative load. In *Proceedings of the Workshop on Crowdsourcing for Search and Data Mining (CSDM) at the Fourth ACM International Conference on Web Search and Data Mining*, pages 27–30.

Xiang Zhang, Junbo Zhao, and Yann LeCun. 2015. Character-level convolutional networks for text classification. In *Proceedings of the 28th International Conference on Neural Information Processing Systems - Volume 1*, NIPS'15, pages 649–657, Cambridge, MA, USA. MIT Press.

Bootstrapping a Neural Conversational Agent with Dialogue Self-Play, Crowdsourcing and On-Line Reinforcement Learning

Pararth Shah[1], Dilek Hakkani-Tür[1], Bing Liu[2]*, Gokhan Tür[1]
[1]Google AI, Mountain View, CA, USA
`pararth@google.com, {dilek,gokhan.tur}@ieee.org`
[2]Carnegie Mellon University, Pittsburgh, PA, USA
`liubing@cmu.edu`

Abstract

End-to-end neural models show great promise towards building conversational agents that are trained from data and on-line experience using supervised and reinforcement learning. However, these models require a large corpus of dialogues to learn effectively. For goal-oriented dialogues, such datasets are expensive to collect and annotate, since each task involves a separate schema and database of entities. Further, the Wizard-of-Oz approach commonly used for dialogue collection does not provide sufficient coverage of salient dialogue flows, which is critical for guaranteeing an acceptable task completion rate in consumer-facing conversational agents. In this paper, we study a recently proposed approach for building an agent for arbitrary tasks by combining dialogue self-play and crowd-sourcing to generate fully-annotated dialogues with diverse and natural utterances. We discuss the advantages of this approach for industry applications of conversational agents, wherein an agent can be rapidly bootstrapped to deploy in front of users and further optimized via interactive learning from actual users of the system.

1 Introduction

Goal-oriented conversational agents enable users to complete specific tasks like restaurant reservations, buying movie tickets or booking a doctor's appointment, through natural language dialogue via a spoken or a text-based chat interface, instead of operating a graphical user interface on a device. Each task is based on a database *schema* which defines the domain of interest. Developing an agent to effectively handle all user interactions in a given domain requires properly dealing with variations in the dialogue flows (what information the users choose to convey in each utterance), surface forms (choice of words to convey the same information),

database states (what entities are available for satisfying the user's request), and noise conditions (whether the user's utterances are correctly recognized by the agent). Moreover, the number of potential tasks is proportional to the number of transactional websites on the Web, which is in the order of millions.

Popular consumer-facing conversational assistants approach this by enabling third-party developers to build dialogue "experiences" or "skills" focusing on individual tasks (e.g. DialogFlow[1], Alexa Skills (Kumar et al. (2017)), wit.ai[2]). The platform provides a parse of the user utterance into a developer defined *intent*, and the developer provides a *policy* which maps user intents to system *actions*, usually modeled as flow charts[3]. This gives the developer full control over how a particular task is handled, allowing her to incrementally add new features to that task. However, some limitations are that (i) the developer must anticipate all ways in which users might interact with the agent, and (ii) since the programmed dialogue flows are not "differentiable", the agent's dialogue policy cannot be improved automatically with experience and each improvement requires human intervention to add logic to support a new dialogue flow or revise an existing flow.

Recently proposed neural conversational models (Vinyals and Le (2015)) are trained with supervision over a large corpus of dialogues (Serban et al. (2016, 2017); Lowe et al. (2017)) or with reinforcement to optimize a long term reward (Li et al. (2016a,b)). End-to-end neural conversational models for task-oriented dialogues (Wen et al. (2016); Liu and Lane (2017a)) leverage annotated dialogues collected with an expert to embed the expert's dialogue policy for a given task in

---

* Work done while the author was an intern at Google.

[1]https://dialogflow.com
[2]https://wit.ai
[3]https://dialogflow.com/docs/dialogs

41

Proceedings of NAACL-HLT 2018, pages 41–51
New Orleans, Louisiana, June 1 - 6, 2018. ©2017 Association for Computational Linguistics

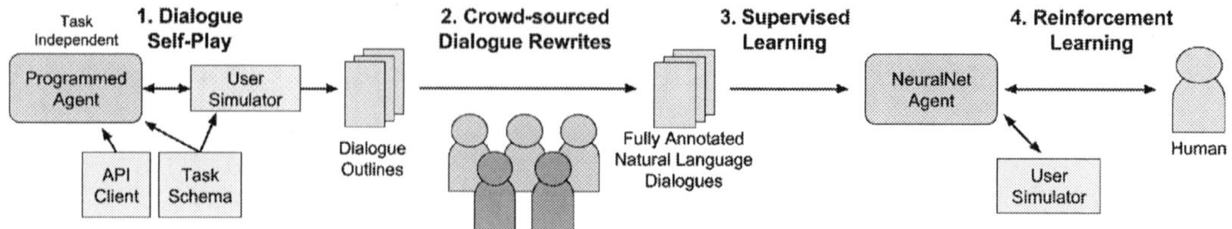

Figure 1: Bootstrapping a neural conversational agent.

the weights of a neural network. However, training such models requires a large corpus of annotated dialogues in a specific domain, which is expensive to collect. Approaches that use reinforcement learning to find the optimal policy also rely on a pre-training step of supervised learning over expert dialogues in order to reduce the exploration space to make the policy learning tractable (Fatemi et al. (2016); Su et al. (2016b, 2017); Liu and Lane (2017b)). A further issue with application of reinforcement learning techniques is that the user simulator used for the policy training step may not entirely mimic the behavior of actual users of the system. This can be mitigated by continuously improving the deployed agent from interactions with actual users via on-line learning (Gašić et al. (2011); Su et al. (2015, 2016a)).

The Wizard-of-Oz setup (Kelley (1984); Dahlbäck et al. (1993)) is a popular approach to collect and annotate task-oriented dialogues via crowd-sourcing for training neural conversational models (Wen et al. (2016); Asri et al. (2017)). However, this is an expensive and lossy process as the free-form dialogues collected from crowd-workers might contain dialogues unfit for use as training data, for instance if the crowd workers use language that is either too simplistic or too convoluted, or may have errors in dialogue act annotations requiring an expensive manual filtering and cleaning step. Further, the corpus might not cover all the interactions that the dialogue developer expects the agent to handle. In contrast, the recently proposed Machines Talking To Machines (M2M) approach (Shah et al. (2018)) is a functionality-driven process for training dialogue agents, which combines a dialogue self-play step and a crowd-sourcing step to obtain a higher quality of dialogues in terms of (i) diversity of surface forms as well as dialogue flows, (ii) coverage of all expected user behaviors,

and (iii) correctness of annotations.

To apply these recent neural approaches to consumer-facing agents that must rapidly scale to new tasks, we propose the following recipe (Fig. 1): (1) exhaustively generate dialogue templates for a given task using *dialogue self-play* between a simulated user and a task-independent programmed system agent, (2) obtain natural language rewrites of these templates using crowd sourcing, (3) train an end-to-end conversational agent on this fully annotated dataset, achieving a reasonable task completion rate, and (4) deploy this agent to interact with users and collect user feedback, which serves as a reward value to continuously improve the agent's policy with on-line reinforcement learning updates. Consequently, a programmed dialogue agent's policy is distilled into a differentiable neural model which sustains a minimum task completion rate through guaranteed coverage of the interactions anticipated by the developer. Such an agent is safely deployable in front of actual users while also continuously improving from user feedback via lifelong learning.

The main contribution of this paper is two-fold:

1. an approach combining dialogue self-play, crowd-sourcing, and on-line reinforcement learning to rapidly scale consumer-facing conversational agents to new tasks.

2. discussion of practical solutions for improving user simulation and crowd-sourcing setups to guarantee coverage of salient dialogue flows and diversity of surface forms.

2 Approach

We present a brief overview of the Machines Talking To Machines (M2M) approach for bootstrapping a conversational agent. We direct the reader to the technical report Shah et al. (2018) for a detailed description of this approach.

Table 1: Sample dialogue outline and rewrite for movie ticket booking.

Outline		Rewrite
Annotations	**Template utterances**	**NL utterances**
S: greeting()	Greeting.	Hi, how can I help you?
U: inform(intent=book_movie, name=Inside Out, date=tomorrow, num_tickets=2)	Book movie with name is Inside Out and date is tomorrow and num tickets is 2.	I want to buy 2 tickets for Inside Out for tomorrow.
S: ack() request(time)	OK. Provide time.	Alright. What time would you like to see the movie?
U: inform(time=evening)	Time is evening.	Anytime during the evening works for me.
S: offer(theatre=Cinemark 16, time=6pm)	Offer theatre is Cinemark 16 and time is 6pm.	How about the 6pm show at Cinemark 16?
U: affirm()	Agree.	That sounds good.
S: notify_success()	Reservation confirmed.	Your tickets have been booked!

2.1 M2M

At a high level, M2M connects a *developer*, who provides the task-specific information, and a *framework*, which provides the task-independent information, for generating dialogues centered around completing the task. In this work we focus on database querying applications, which involve a relational database which contains entities that the user would like to browse and select through a natural language dialogue. The input to the framework is a task specification obtained from the developer, consisting of a *schema* of "slots" induced by the columns of the database and an *API client* which can be queried with a SQL-like syntax to return a list of matching candidate entities for any valid combination of slot values. For example, the schema for a movie ticket booking domain would include slots such as "movie name", "number of tickets", "date" and "time" of the show, etc. The API client would provide access to a database (hosted locally or remotely via the Web) of movie showtimes.

Outlines. With the task specification, the framework must generate a set of dialogues centered around that task. Each dialogue is a sequence of natural language utterances, i.e. dialogue *turns*, and their corresponding *annotations*, which include the semantic parse of that turn as well as additional information tied to that turn. For example, for the user turn "Anytime during the evening works for me", the annotation would be *"User: inform(time=evening)"*. The key idea in M2M is to separate the linguistic variations in the surface forms of the utterances from the semantic variations in the dialogue flows. This is achieved by defining the notion of a dialogue *outline* as a sequence of *template utterances* and their corresponding annotations. Template utterances are simplistic statements with language that is easy to generate procedurally. An outline encapsulates the semantic flow of the dialogue while abstracting out the linguistic variation in the utterances. The first two columns of Table 1 provide a sample dialogue outline for a movie ticket booking interaction, consisting of the annotations and template utterances, respectively.

Dialogue self-play. M2M proceeds by first generating a set of dialogue outlines for the specified task. A task-oriented dialogue involves the back and forth flow of information between a user and a system agent aimed towards satisfying a user need. Dialogue self-play simulates this process by employing a task-independent *user simulator* and *system agent* seeded with a task schema and API client. The user simulator maps a (possibly empty) dialogue history, a user profile and a task schema to a distribution over turn annotations for the next user turn. Similarly, the system agent maps a dialogue history, task schema and API client to a distribution over system turn annotations. Annotations are sampled from user and system iteratively to take the dialogue forward. The generated annotations consist of *dialogue frames* that encode the semantics of the turn through a *dialogue act* and a *slot-value map* (Table 1). For example "inform(date=tomorrow, time=evening)" is a dialogue frame that informs the system of the user's constraints for the date and time slots. We use the Cambridge dialogue act schema (Henderson et al. (2013)) as the list of possible dialogue acts. The process continues until either the user's goals are achieved and the user exits the dialogue with a "bye()" act, or a maximum number of turns are reached.

In our experiments we use an agenda-based user simulator (Schatzmann et al. (2007)) parameterized by a user goal and a user profile. The programmed system agent is modeled as a handcrafted finite state machine (Hopcroft et al. (2006)) which encodes a set of task-independent rules for constructing system turns, with each turn consisting of a *response* frame which responds to the user's previous turn, and an *initiate* frame which drives the dialogue forward through a predetermined sequence of sub-dialogues. For database querying applications, these sub-dialogues are: gather user preferences, query a database via an API, offer matching entities to the user, allow user to modify preferences or request more information about an entity, and finally complete the transaction (buying or reserving the entity) (Fig. 2). By exploring a range of parameter values and sampling a large number of outlines, dialogue self-play can generate a diverse set of dialogue outlines for the task.

Template utterances. Once a full dialogue has been sampled, a *template utterance generator* maps each annotation to a template utterance using a domain-general grammar (Wang et al. (2015)) parameterized with the task schema. For example, "inform(date=tomorrow, time=evening)" would map to a template *"($slot is $value) (and ($slot is $value))*"*, which is grounded as "Date is tomorrow and time is evening." The developer can also provide a list of templates to use for some or all of the dialogue frames if they want more control over the language used in the utterances. Template utterances are an important bridge between the annotation and the corresponding natural language utterance, as they present the semantic information of a turn annotation in a format understandable by crowd workers.

Crowd-sourced rewrites. To obtain a natural language dialogue from its outline, the framework employs crowd sourcing to paraphrase template utterances into more natural sounding utterances. The paraphrase task is designed as a "contextual rewrite" task where a crowd worker sees the full dialogue template, and provides the natural language utterances for each template utterances of the dialogue. This encourages the crowd

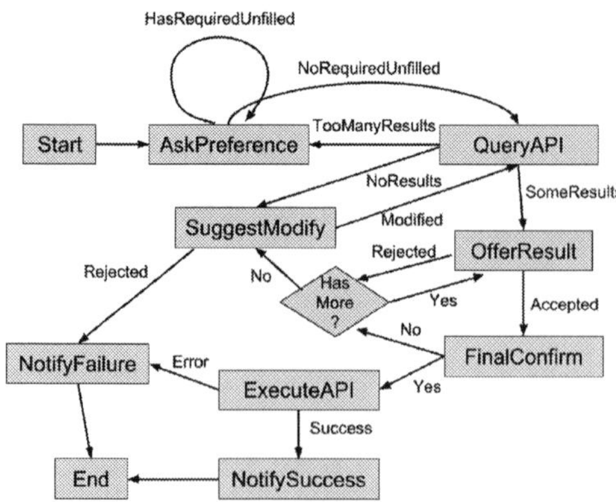

Figure 2: Finite state machine for a task-independent system agent for database querying applications.

worker to inject linguistic phenomena like coreference ("Reserve *that* restaurant") and lexical entrainment ("Yes, the *6pm show*") into the utterances. Fig. 5 in the Appendix provides the UI shown to crowd workers for this task. The same outline is shown to $K > 1$ crowd-workers to get diverse natural language utterances for the same dialogue. The third column of Table 1 presents contextual rewrites for each turn of an outline for a movie ticket booking task.

Model training. The crowd sourced dataset has natural language utterances along with full annotations of dialogue acts, slot spans, dialogue state and API state for each turn. These annotated dialogues are sufficient for training end-to-end models using supervision (Wen et al. (2016)). Dialogue self-play ensures sufficient coverage of flows encoded in the programmed system agent in the crowd sourced dataset. Consequently, the trained agent reads natural language user utterances and emits system turns by encoding the FSM policy of system agent in a differentiable neural model.

2.2 On-line reinforcement learning

A limitation of training a neural agent on the dataset collected with M2M is that it is restricted to the flows encoded in the user simulator or the programmed system agent, and utterances collected from crowd-workers. When deployed to interact with actual users, the agent may find itself in new dialogue states that weren't seen during training. This can be mitigated by continually improving the agent's language understanding as well as dialogue policy by using a feedback score on each dialogue interaction of the neural agent as a reward value to optimize the end-to-end model using policy gradient reinforcement learning (RL). The RL updates can be done in two phases (which could be interleaved):

RL with user simulator. Since RL requires training for thousands of episodes, we construct a simulated environment in which the user simulator emits a user turn annotation, and a natural language utterance is sampled from the set of utterances collected for that dialogue frame from crowd sourcing. This enables the neural agent to discover dialogue flows not present in the programmed agent. The reward is computed based on successful task completion minus a turn penalty (El Asri et al. (2014)), and the model is updated with the on-policy REINFORCE update after each episode (Liu et al. (2017)).

RL with human feedback. For the agent to handle user interactions that are not generated by the user simulator, the agent must learn from its interactions with actual users. This is accomplished by applying updates to the model based on feedback scores collected from users after each dialogue interaction (Shah et al. (2016)).

3 User simulation and dialogue self-play

M2M hinges on having a generative model of a user that is reasonably close to actual users of the system. While it is difficult to develop precise models of user behavior customized for every type of dialogue interaction, it is easier to create a task-independent user simulator that operates at a higher level of abstraction (dialogue acts) and encapsulates common patterns of user behavior for a broad class of dialogue tasks. Seeding the user simulator with a task-specific schema of intents, slot names and slot values allows the framework to generate a variety of dialogue flows tailored to that specific task. Developing a general user simulator targeting a broad class of tasks, for example database querying applications, has significant leverage as adding a new conversational pattern to the simulator benefits the outlines generated for dialogue interfaces to any database or third-party API.

Another concern with the use of a user simulator is that it restricts the generated dialogue flows to only those that are engineered into the

user model. In comparison, asking crowd workers to converse without any restrictions could generate interesting dialogues that are not anticipated by the dialogue developer. Covering complex interactions is important when developing datasets to benchmark research aimed towards building human-level dialogue systems. However, we argue that for consumer-facing chatbots, the primary aim is reliable coverage of critical user interactions. Existing methods for developing chatbots with engineered finite state machines implicitly define a model of expected user behavior in the states and transitions of the system agent. A user simulator makes this user model explicit and is a more systematic approach for a dialogue developer to reason about the user behaviors handled by the agent. Similarly, having more control over the dialogue flows present in the dataset ensures that all and only expected user and system agent behaviors are present in the dataset. A dialogue agent bootstrapped with such a dataset can be deployed in front of users with a guaranteed minimum task completion rate.

The self-play step also uses a programmed system agent that generates valid system turns for a given task. Since M2M takes a rule-based agent which works with user dialogue acts and emits a neural conversational agent that works with natural language user utterances, the framework effectively distills an expert dialogue policy combined with a language understanding module into a single learned neural network. The developer can customize the behavior of the neural agent by modifying the component rules of the programmed agent. Further, by developing a task-independent set of rules for handling a broad task like database querying applications (Fig. 2), the cost of building the programmed agent can be amortized over a large number of dialogue tasks.

4 Crowdsourcing

In the Wizard-of-Oz setting, a task is shown to a pair of crowd workers who are asked to converse in natural language to complete the task. The collected dialogues are manually annotated with dialogue act and slot span labels. This process is expensive as the two annotation tasks are difficult and therefore time consuming: identifying the dialogue acts of an utterance requires understanding the precise meaning of each dialogue act, and identifying all slot spans in an utterance requires checking the utterance against all slots in the schema. As a result, the crowd-sourced annotations may need to be cleaned by an expert. In contrast, M2M significantly reduces the crowd-sourcing expense by automatically annotating a majority of the dialogue turns and annotating the remaining turns with two simpler crowd-sourcing tasks: "Does this utterance contain this particular slot value?" and "Do these two utterances have the same meaning?", which are easier for the average crowd worker.

Further, the lack of control over crowd workers' behavior in the Wizard-of-Oz setting can lead to dialogues that may not reflect the behavior of real users, for example if the crowd worker provides all constraints in a single turn or always mentions a single constraint in each turn. Such low-quality dialogues either need to be manually removed from the dataset, or the crowd participants need to be given additional instructions or training to encourage better interactions (Asri et al. (2017)). M2M avoids this issue by using dialogue self-play to systematically generate all usable dialogue outlines, and simplifying the crowd-sourcing step to a dialogue paraphrase task.

5 Evaluations

We have released[4] two datasets totaling 3000 dialogues collected using M2M for the tasks of buying a movie ticket (Sim-M) and reserving a restaurant table (Sim-R). We present some experiments with these datasets.

5.1 Dialogue diversity

First we investigate the claim that M2M leads to higher coverage of dialogue features in the dataset. We compare the Sim-R training dialogues with the DSTC2 (Henderson et al. (2013)) training set which also deals with restaurants and is similarly sized (1611 vs. 1116 dialogues) (Table 2). M2M compares favorably to DSTC2 on the ratio of unique unigrams and bigrams to total number of tokens in the dataset, which signifies a greater variety of surface forms as opposed to repeating the same words and phrases. We also measure the *outline diversity*, defined as the ratio of unique outlines divided by total dialogues in the dataset. We calculate this for sub-dialogues of length $k = \{1, 3, 5\}$ as well as full dialogues. This

<hr>

[4]https://github.com/google-research-datasets/simulated-dialogue

Table 2: Comparing DSTC2 and M2M Restaurants datasets on diversity of language and dialogue flows.

Metric	DSTC2 (Train)	Sim-R (Train)
Dialogues	1611	1116
Total turns	11670	6188
Total tokens	199295	99932
Avg. turns per dialogue	14.49	11.09
Avg. tokens per turn	8.54	8.07
Unique tokens ratio	0.0049	0.0092
Unique bigrams ratio	0.0177	0.0670
Outline diversity (k=1)	0.0982	0.2646
Outline diversity (k=3)	0.1831	0.3145
Outline diversity (k=5)	0.5621	0.7061
Outline diversity (full)	0.9243	0.9292

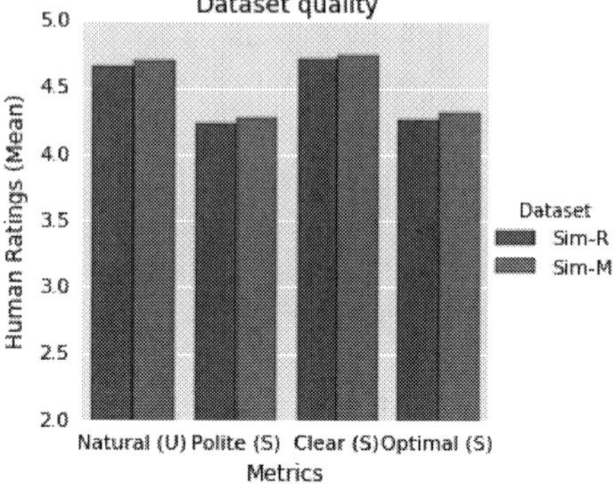

Figure 3: Crowd worker ratings for the quality of the user and system utterances of dialogues collected with M2M.

gives a sense of the diversity of dialogue flows in the dataset. M2M has fewer repetitions of sub-dialogues compared to DSTC2.

5.2 Human evaluation of dataset quality

To evaluate the subjective quality of the M2M datasets, we showed the final dialogues to human judges recruited via a crowd-sourcing service, and asked them to rate each user and system turn between 1 to 5 on multiple dimensions. Fig. 6 in the Appendix provides the UI shown to crowd workers for this task. Each dialogue was shown to 3 judges. Fig. 3 shows the average ratings aggregated over all turns for the two datasets.

5.3 Human evaluation of model quality

To evaluate the proposed method of bootstrapping neural conversational agents from a programmed system agent, we trained an end-to-end conversa-

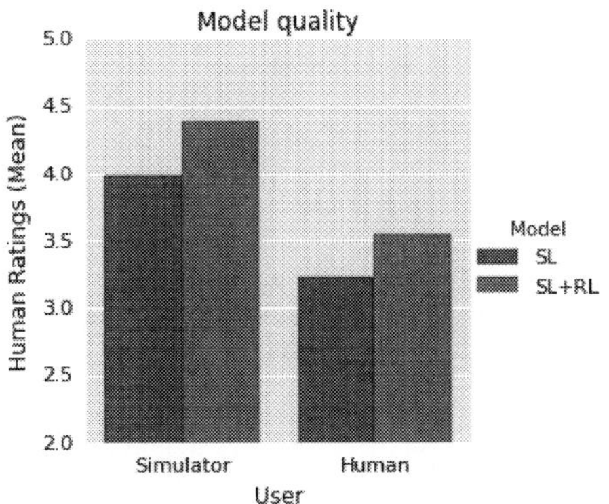

Figure 4: Average crowd worker ratings for the quality of the system utterances of neural conversational agents trained on Sim-M.

tional model (Liu et al. (2017)) using supervised learning (SL) on the Sim-M training set. This model is further trained with RL for 10K episodes with the user simulator as described in Section 2.2 (SL+RL). We performed two separate evaluations of these models:

Simulated user. We evaluate the neural agents in the user simulation environment for 100 episodes. We asked crowd-sourced judges to read dialogues between the agent and the user simulator and rate each system turn on a scale of 1 (frustrating) to 5 (optimal way to help the user). Each turn was rated by 3 different judges. Fig. 4 shows the average scores for both agents. End-to-end optimization with RL improves the quality of the agent according to human judges, compared to an agent trained with only supervised learning on the dataset.

Human user. We evaluate the neural agents in live interactions with human judges for 100 episodes each. The human judges are given scenarios for a movie booking task and asked to talk with the agent to complete the booking according to the constraints. After the dialogue finishes, the judge is asked to rate each system turn on the same scale of 1 to 5. Fig. 4 shows the average scores for both agents. End-to-end optimization with RL improves the agent's interactions with human users. The interactions with human users are of lower quality than those with the user simulator as human users may use utterances or dialogue flows unseen by the agent. Continual training of the agent with on-line reinforcement learning can close this gap with more experience.

6   Related work and discussion

We presented an approach for rapidly bootstrapping goal-oriented conversational agents for arbitrary database querying tasks, by combining dialogue self-play, crowd-sourcing and on-line reinforcement learning.

The dialogue self-play step uses a task-independent user simulator and programmed system agent seeded with a task-specific schema, which provides the developer with full control over the generated dialogue outlines. PyDial (Ultes et al. (2017)) is an extensible open-source toolkit which provides domain-independent implementations of dialogue system modules, which could be extended by adding dialogue self-play functionality. We described an FSM system agent for handling any transactional or form-filling task. For more complex tasks, the developer can extend the user simulator and system agents by adding their own rules. These components could also be replaced by machine learned generative models if available. Task Completion Platform (TCP) (Crook et al. (2016)) introduced a task configuration language for building goal-oriented dialogue interactions. The state update and policy modules of TCP could be used to implement agents that generate outlines for more complex tasks.

The crowd-sourcing step uses human intelligence to gather diverse natural language utterances. Comparisons with the DSTC2 dataset show that this approach can create high-quality fully annotated datasets for training conversational agents in arbitrary domains. ParlAI (Miller et al. (2017)), a dialogue research software platform, provides easy integration with crowd sourcing for data collection and evaluation. However, the crowd sourcing tasks are open-ended and may result in lower quality dialogues as described in Section 4. In M2M, crowd workers are asked to paraphrase given utterances instead of writing new ones, which is at a suitable difficulty level for crowd workers.

Finally, training a neural conversational model over the M2M generated dataset encodes the programmed policy in a differentiable neural model which can be deployed to interact with users. This model is amenable to on-line reinforcement learning updates with feedback from actual users of the system (Su et al. (2016a); Liu et al. (2017)), ensuring that the agent improves its performance in real situations with more experience.

References

Layla El Asri, Hannes Schulz, Shikhar Sharma, Jeremie Zumer, Justin Harris, Emery Fine, Rahul Mehrotra, and Kaheer Suleman. 2017. Frames: A corpus for adding memory to goal-oriented dialogue systems. *arXiv preprint arXiv:1704.00057* .

Paul Crook, Alex Marin, Vipul Agarwal, Khushboo Aggarwal, Tasos Anastasakos, Ravi Bikkula, Daniel Boies, Asli Celikyilmaz, Senthilkumar Chandramohan, Zhaleh Feizollahi, et al. 2016. Task completion platform: A self-serve multi-domain goal oriented dialogue platform. In *Proceedings of the 2016 Conference of the North American Chapter of the Association for Computational Linguistics: Demonstrations*. pages 47–51.

Nils Dahlbäck, Arne Jönsson, and Lars Ahrenberg. 1993. Wizard of oz studieswhy and how. *Knowledge-based systems* 6(4):258–266.

Layla El Asri, Romain Laroche, and Olivier Pietquin. 2014. Task completion transfer learning for reward inference. *Proc of MLIS* .

Mehdi Fatemi, Layla El Asri, Hannes Schulz, Jing He, and Kaheer Suleman. 2016. Policy networks with two-stage training for dialogue systems. In *Proceedings of the 17th Annual Meeting of the Special Interest Group on Discourse and Dialogue*. pages 101–110.

Milica Gašić, Filip Jurčíček, Blaise Thomson, Kai Yu, and Steve Young. 2011. On-line policy optimisation of spoken dialogue systems via live interaction with human subjects. In *Automatic Speech Recognition and Understanding (ASRU), 2011 IEEE Workshop on*. IEEE, pages 312–317.

Matthew Henderson, Blaise Thomson, and Jason Williams. 2013. Dialog state tracking challenge 2 & 3. http://camdial.org/~mh521/dstc/.

John E. Hopcroft, Rajeev Motwani, and Jeffrey D. Ullman. 2006. *Introduction to Automata Theory, Languages, and Computation (3rd Edition)*. Addison-Wesley Longman Publishing Co., Inc., Boston, MA, USA.

John F Kelley. 1984. An iterative design methodology for user-friendly natural language office information applications. *ACM Transactions on Information Systems (TOIS)* 2(1):26–41.

Anjishnu Kumar, Arpit Gupta, Julian Chan, Sam Tucker, Bjorn Hoffmeister, and Markus Dreyer. 2017. Just ask: Building an architecture for extensible self-service spoken language understanding. In *NIPS Conversational AI Workshop*.

Jiwei Li, Alexander H Miller, Sumit Chopra, Marc'Aurelio Ranzato, and Jason Weston. 2016a. Dialogue learning with human-in-the-loop. *arXiv preprint arXiv:1611.09823* .

Jiwei Li, Will Monroe, Alan Ritter, Dan Jurafsky, Michel Galley, and Jianfeng Gao. 2016b. Deep reinforcement learning for dialogue generation. In *Proceedings of the 2016 Conference on Empirical Methods in Natural Language Processing*. pages 1192–1202.

Bing Liu and Ian Lane. 2017a. An end-to-end trainable neural network model with belief tracking for task-oriented dialog. In *Interspeech*.

Bing Liu and Ian Lane. 2017b. Iterative policy learning in end-to-end trainable task-oriented neural dialog models. In *Proceedings of IEEE ASRU*.

Bing Liu, Gokhan Tur, Dilek Hakkani-Tur, Pararth Shah, and Larry Heck. 2017. End-to-end optimization of task-oriented dialogue model with deep reinforcement learning. In *NIPS Workshop on Conversational AI*.

Ryan Lowe, Nissan Pow, Iulian Vlad Serban, Laurent Charlin, Chia-Wei Liu, and Joelle Pineau. 2017. Training end-to-end dialogue systems with the ubuntu dialogue corpus. *Dialogue & Discourse* 8(1):31–65.

Alexander H Miller, Will Feng, Adam Fisch, Jiasen Lu, Dhruv Batra, Antoine Bordes, Devi Parikh, and Jason Weston. 2017. Parlai: A dialog research software platform. *arXiv preprint arXiv:1705.06476* .

Jost Schatzmann, Blaise Thomson, Karl Weilhammer, Hui Ye, and Steve Young. 2007. Agenda-based user simulation for bootstrapping a pomdp dialogue system. In *Human Language Technologies 2007: The Conference of the North American Chapter of the Association for Computational Linguistics; Companion Volume, Short Papers*. Association for Computational Linguistics, pages 149–152.

Iulian Vlad Serban, Alessandro Sordoni, Yoshua Bengio, Aaron C Courville, and Joelle Pineau. 2016. Building end-to-end dialogue systems using generative hierarchical neural network models. In *AAAI*. volume 16, pages 3776–3784.

Iulian Vlad Serban, Alessandro Sordoni, Ryan Lowe, Laurent Charlin, Joelle Pineau, Aaron Courville, and Yoshua Bengio. 2017. A hierarchical latent variable encoder-decoder model for generating dialogues. In *Thirty-First AAAI Conference on Artificial Intelligence*.

Pararth Shah, Dilek Hakkani-Tür, and Larry Heck. 2016. Interactive reinforcement learning for task-oriented dialogue management. In *NIPS Deep Learning for Action and Interaction Workshop*.

Pararth Shah, Dilek Hakkani-Tür, Gokhan Tür, Abhinav Rastogi, Ankur Bapna, Neha Nayak, and Larry Heck. 2018. Building a conversational agent overnight with dialogue self-play. *arXiv preprint arXiv:1801.04871* .

Pei-Hao Su, Paweł Budzianowski, Stefan Ultes, Milica Gasic, and Steve Young. 2017. Sample-efficient actor-critic reinforcement learning with supervised data for dialogue management. In *Proceedings of the 18th Annual SIGdial Meeting on Discourse and Dialogue*. pages 147–157.

Pei-Hao Su, Milica Gasic, Nikola Mrkšić, Lina M Rojas Barahona, Stefan Ultes, David Vandyke, Tsung-Hsien Wen, and Steve Young. 2016a. On-line active reward learning for policy optimisation in spoken dialogue systems. In *Proceedings of the 54th Annual Meeting of the Association for Computational Linguistics (Volume 1: Long Papers)*. volume 1, pages 2431–2441.

Pei-Hao Su, Milica Gasic, Nikola Mrksic, Lina Rojas-Barahona, Stefan Ultes, David Vandyke, Tsung-Hsien Wen, and Steve Young. 2016b. Continuously learning neural dialogue management. *arXiv preprint arXiv:1606.02689* .

Pei-Hao Su, David Vandyke, Milica Gašíc, Dongho Kim, Nikola Mrkšíc, Tsung-Hsien Wen, and Steve Young. 2015. Learning from real users: Rating dialogue success with neural networks for reinforcement learning in spoken dialogue systems. In *Proceedings of the Annual Conference of the International Speech Communication Association, INTERSPEECH*. volume 2015, pages 2007–2011.

Stefan Ultes, Lina M Rojas Barahona, Pei-Hao Su, David Vandyke, Dongho Kim, Inigo Casanueva, Paweł Budzianowski, Nikola Mrkšić, Tsung-Hsien Wen, Milica Gasic, et al. 2017. Pydial: A multi-domain statistical dialogue system toolkit. *Proceedings of ACL 2017, System Demonstrations* pages 73–78.

Oriol Vinyals and Quoc Le. 2015. A neural conversational model. *arXiv preprint arXiv:1506.05869* .

Yushi Wang, Jonathan Berant, Percy Liang, et al. 2015. Building a semantic parser overnight. *ACL* .

Tsung-Hsien Wen, David Vandyke, Nikola Mrksic, Milica Gasic, Lina M Rojas-Barahona, Pei-Hao Su, Stefan Ultes, and Steve Young. 2016. A network-based end-to-end trainable task-oriented dialogue system. *ACL* .

Figure 5: Contextual rewrite task interface for paraphrasing a dialogue outline with natural language.

Instructions

You'll be shown **a very unnatural computer generated conversation** between a user and an assistant.

Your task is to paraphrase the messages in the original conversation in order to create a new conversation that has the exact same meaning but sounds like a real conversation between a user and a professional assistant.
Feel free to be creative with your paraphrased messages, as long as they meet the following **important requirements**:

- User messages need to look like something you would type in a chat window.
- Assistant messages need to look formal -- just like chat replies from a human customer service agent.
- **All of your paraphrased messages must have the same meaning as the original message**.
- Your paraphrased conversation needs to make sense on it's own.

When done rewording/rephrasing the original phrases, you'll be asked to re-read the entire dialog as a whole and verify it makes sense as a stand alone dialog, as opposed to paraphrasing each sentence without looking at the result as a whole.

Task

Original conversation	Paraphrased conversation
Assistant: greetings	Hello
User: greetings AND buy movie tickets AND date is Wednesday	I would like to buy movie tickets for Wednesday.
Assistant: provide preference for: theatre name and time and number of tickets and movie	What theatre, movie, time, and number of tickets would you like?
User: unable to understand, must re-phrase your message	Sorry, I didn't understand. Could you repeat that?
Assistant: provide preference for: theatre name and time and number of tickets and movie	How many tickets would you like and what is the theatre, movie, and showtime?
User: movie is The Magnificent Seven and time is 4:00 pm and theatre name is Century 20 Great Mall and number of tickets is 6	I need 6 tickets for the 4:00 pm showing of The Magnificent Seven at the Century 20 Great Mall
Assistant: confirm the following: time is 4:00 pm	That was for 4:00 pm, right?
User: accept time is 4:00 pm	Yes, 4:00 pm.
Assistant: purchase confirmed with given details movie is The Magnificent Seven and number of tickets is 6 and time is 4:00 pm and date is March 08 and theatre name is Century 20 Great Mall	I have purchased 6 tickets for the Magnificent Seven at 4:00 o'clock on March 8 at the Century 20 Great Mall.
User: thank you AND goodbye	Thanks, bye.

After you are done paraphrasing, please read your paraphrased conversation from top to bottom.

Does it seem like a conversation between a user that sounds like you and an assistant that sounds formal?
⦿ Yes
◯ No, but I can't make it better

Does it have the same meaning as the original conversation, while still making sense on it's own?
⦿ Yes
◯ No, but I can't make it better

General comments/feedback (optional)
Please add any comments here

Figure 6: Dialogue quality evaluation task interface for rating the user and system turns of completed dialogues.

Instructions

You'll be shown **a machine-generated conversation** between a user and an assistant. The assistant is helping the user achieve a task such as booking a table at a restaurant, finding movie tickets, etc.

Your task is to evaluate the quality of the conversation by evaluating each message in it.

Examples

How to evaluate the assistant:
Focus on the conversation context and what the assistant is trying to accomplish with their last message (rather than the wording).
Then compare that with what an ideal human assistant would do in this same situation.
Here are some examples of what an ideal human assistant would do:

- Pay attention to the preferences expressed by the user and offer helpful suggestions
- Ask the user only for necessary information
- Offer alternatives when the user's request is not possible (e.g. reservation time is unavailable)

Here are some examples of what an ideal human assistant would **not** do:

- Make nonsensical offers such as dinner at 1 pm or alternative offers that are unrelated to the user's request
- Ask for information that the user already provided
- Easily get confused

Task

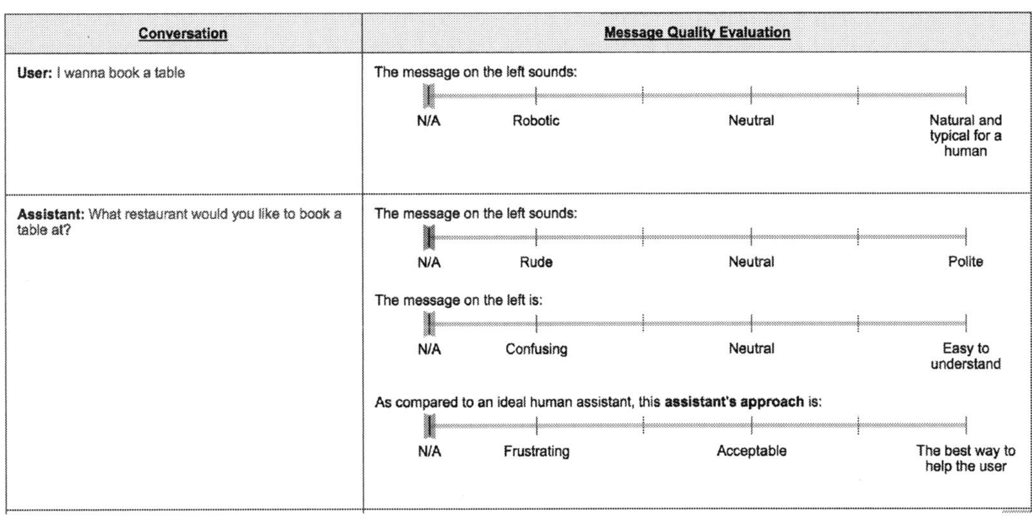

Quality Estimation for Automatically Generated Titles of eCommerce Browse Pages

Nicola Ueffing and **José G. C. de Souza** and **Gregor Leusch**

Machine Translation Science Lab

eBay Inc.

Kasernenstraße 25

Aachen, Germany

{nueffing, jgcdesouza, gleusch}@ebay.com

Abstract

At eBay, we are automatically generating a large amount of natural language titles for eCommerce browse pages using machine translation (MT) technology. While automatic approaches can generate millions of titles very fast, they are prone to errors. We therefore develop quality estimation (QE) methods which can automatically detect titles with low quality in order to prevent them from going live. In this paper, we present different approaches: The first one is a Random Forest (RF) model that explores hand-crafted, robust features, which are a mix of established features commonly used in Machine Translation Quality Estimation (MTQE) and new features developed specifically for our task. The second model is based on Siamese Networks (SNs) which embed the metadata input sequence and the generated title in the same space and do not require hand-crafted features at all. We thoroughly evaluate and compare those approaches on in-house data. While the RF models are competitive for scenarios with smaller amounts of training data and somewhat more robust, they are clearly outperformed by the SN models when the amount of training data is larger.

1 Introduction

On eCommerce sites, multiple items can be grouped on a common page called *browse page (BP)*. Each browse page contains an overview of various items which share some, but not necessarily all characteristics. The characteristics can be expressed as slot/value pairs. Figure 1 shows an example of a browse page with a title, with navigation elements leading to related browse pages as well as the individual items listed on this page.

The browse pages are linked among each other and can be organized in a hierarchy. This structure

Figure 1: Example of a browse page.

allows users to navigate laterally between different browse pages, or to dive deeper and refine their search. The example browse page in Figure 1 shows different white ACME smartphones with capacity 32GB. This page is linked from various browse pages, e.g. those for white ACME Smartphones, for ACME smartphones with 32GB, or for white smartphones with 32GB. It also links to browse pages with a higher number of slots, i.e. refining the set of listed items by additional features like network provider.

Different combinations of characteristics bijectively correspond to different browse pages, and consequently to different *browse page titles*. To show customers which items are grouped on a browse page, we need a human-readable description of the content of that particular page.

Large eCommerce sites can easily have tens of millions of such browse pages in many different languages. Each browse page has one to six slots to be realized. The number of unique slot-value pairs are in the order of hundreds of thousands. All these factors render the task of human creation of browse page titles infeasible. We have therefore developed several strategies to generate these human-readable titles automatically for

Proceedings of NAACL-HLT 2018, pages 52–59

New Orleans, Louisiana, June 1 - 6, 2018. ©2017 Association for Computational Linguistics

any possible browse page (Mathur, Ueffing, and Leusch, 2017). These strategies are based on MT technology and take the slot/value pairs mentioned in Section 1 as input. Examples of such slot/value pairs are the category to which the products belong, and characteristics like brand, color, size, storage capacity, which are dependant on the category. The slot/value pairs for the browse page from Figure 1 are shown in Table 1.

Slot Name	Value
Category	*Cell Phones & Smart Phones*
Brand	*ACME*
Color	*white*
Storage Capacity	*32GB*

Table 1: The underlying metadata for Figure 1.

These metadata are fed into an MT system and translated into natural language. We have developed three different MT-based systems, which are tailored towards different amounts of training data available across languages. These systems are shortly described in Section 4. In this paper, we compare our QE methods on output from different MT systems on English titles.

2 Approach

The automatically generated BP titles are regularly monitored, and quality is assessed by human experts, who label each title with one out of four error severity classes:

- Good: good quality, no issues,

- P3: minor issues, acceptable quality,

- P2: issues which impact the understandability of the title,

- P1: severe issues, like incorrect brand names.

We map these error classes to the two quality classes 'OK' and 'Bad': 'Good' and 'P3' represent acceptable title quality ('OK'), while 'P2' and 'P1' constitute 'Bad' titles. For English browse page titles, we have a large amount of these manually assigned labels available (see Section 3). For automatically predicting the quality of a BP title, we train different machine learning models on these annotated data. In MT(QE) terms, the metadata for a browse page is considered the source language, and the target language is the natural language, English, in our experiments.

2.1 Random Forests

Random Forests are ensemble classifiers that induce several decision trees using some source of randomness to form a diverse set of estimators (Breiman, 2001). There are two sources of randomness: (i) each individual decision tree is trained over a sub-sample of the training data and (ii) when building the tree, the node splitting step is modified to use the best split among splits using random subsets of features. In our experiments, we used the Random Forest (RF) implementation from the Scikit-learn toolkit (Pedregosa et al., 2011).

2.1.1 Features

We trained various RF classifiers, using several different feature types. Some of those features are commonly used in MTQE (Blatz et al., 2004; Specia et al., 2015). Additionally, we developed specific features which are well-suited for browse page title generation. Our features can be grouped into several different classes:

- MTQE: These are common features from quality estimation for MT, such as title length, language model score, or number of unique words in the title;

- Browse-page-specific: These are new features we developed specifically for BP titles, based on the browse page's metadata, such as the number of slots in the BP, binary indicators for the most frequent slot names, and indicators of incorrect brand names;

- Redundancy: These are features capturing redundancy, e.g. word repetitions, and within-title cosine distance based on word embeddings (Mikolov et al., 2013). We developed those because redundancy emerged as error pattern in the regular monitoring of the titles.

These features explore different sources of information. Some of them are based only on the title itself (e.g. title length and cosine distance between words) and capture the *fluency* of the title. Other features are based only on the browse page's metadata (e.g. number of slots in the browse page) and capture the *complexity* of the input for title generation. Some features explore both metadata and generated title (e.g. checking for brand names that are not reproduced exactly in the title) and capture the *adequacy* of the generated title given the input data.

Note that all features are black-box features independent of the underlying system which generated the BP titles. This is important for our application because we have different algorithms in production which generate the BP titles. All of them are described in (Mathur, Ueffing, and Leusch, 2017). As we will see in Section 4, the QE model works well for all of them. Another important aspect is that the features can be easily applied to different languages without requiring complex resources.

Hyper-parameter optimization We performed hyper-parameter search of the RF models with random search for 100 iterations and 5-fold cross-validation in each iteration.

2.2 Siamese Networks

As in other areas in machine learning, neural networks have recently gained much attention in MTQE and have contributed to pushing the state of the art of the task (Kim et al., 2017; Martins et al., 2017). One type of neural network that can be used to predict similarity between paired inputs is called Siamese networks. These networks were originally defined by Bromley et al. (1994) as a neural network composed by two symmetric sub-networks that compare two input patterns and outputs a similarity between these inputs. The authors proposed this architecture in the context of signature verification, i.e., estimating how similar two signatures are to each other. SN models have also been applied to face verification (Chopra et al., 2005), metric learning in speech recognition, to extract speaker-specific information (Chen and Salman, 2011) and text similarity (Yih et al., 2011). Grégoire and Langlais (2017) proposes a siamese network architecture to extract parallel sentences out of parallel corpora. This is a pre-print publication found upon completion of the work described here and we plan to have a detailed comparison in future work.

In this work, we build a QE model inspired by work on sentence similarity (Mueller and Thyagarajan, 2016), which uses SN models to learn a similarity metric between paired inputs. The motivation to apply such architecture to QE is that the problem can be seen as a sentence similarity problem but across two "languages": given a sentence in English and its corresponding translation

in French, we want to know if the translation is adequate and fluent with respect to the original sentence. In the problem described in this paper, we can reformulate the scenario as follows: given a segment of slot/value pairs representing the metadata and its corresponding title in English, we want to know if the title is adequate and fluent with respect to the metadata input.

2.2.1 Architecture

The SN architecture we are evaluating was built using a specific type of recurrent neural networks (RNNs) to model each segment input. RNNs are models well-suited to deal with variable-length input like natural language sentences. In RNNs, the standard feed-forward neural networks are adapted for sequence data $(x_1, \ldots, x_T)$, where at each time step $t \in 1, ..., T$, a hidden-state vector h_t is updated as $h_t = \sigma(Wx_t + Uh_{t-1})$, where x_t is the input at time t, W is the weight matrix from inputs to the hidden-state vector and U is the weight matrix on the hidden-state vector from the previous time step h_{t-1} and σ is the logistic function defined as $\sigma = (1 + e^{-x})^{-1}$.

Though RNNs can cope with variable-length sequences, the optimization of the weight matrices in RNNs is hard: when the gradients are back-propagated, they decrease to the point of becoming so small that the weights cannot be updated, specially over long input sequences. In order to alleviate this problem, Hochreiter and Schmidhuber (1997) proposed Long Short-Term Memory models (LSTMs), which are able to overcome the vanishing gradients problem by capturing long-range dependencies through its use of memory cell units that can store/access information across long input sequences. For more details on LSTMs we refer the interested reader to Greff et al. (2015).

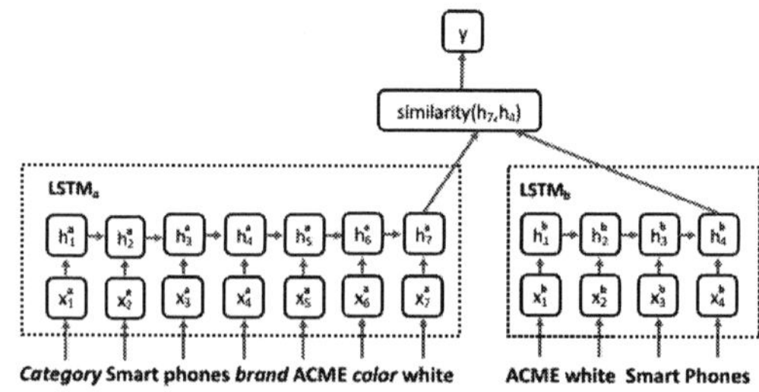

Figure 2: Example of an SN for title quality estimation. The left sequence represents the BP's metadata, the right sequence is the BP title.

The SN architecture we employ in this work is

depicted in Figure 2[1]. The architecture consists of two networks, LSTM_a and LSTM_b, one for each input sentence (the browse page's metadata on the left and the title on the right). Both LSTMs have tied weights, meaning that both networks have identical transformations in their paths in the experiments presented in this paper.

The architecture is defined in a supervised learning setting, in which each instance is a pair of sentences represented as a sequence of word vectors, $x_1^a, \ldots, x_{T_a}^a$ and $x_1^b, \ldots, x_{T_b}^b$, where $T_a \neq T_b$, and a binary label y that indicates whether the pair is similar or not. The two sequences of word embeddings are the input to their corresponding LSTM, which updates its hidden state at each sequence-index. The sentence is represented by the last hidden state h_T of the LSTM (h_7^a and h_4^b in Figure 2).

The similarity function is pre-defined and is used to compare the LSTM representations and infer their semantic similarity. In this paper, we use the cosine similarity between the final representations of each LSTM, $h_{T_a}^a$ and $h_{T_b}^b$:

$$s(h_T^a, h_T^b) = \frac{h_T^a \cdot h_T^b}{||h_T^a|| \cdot ||h_T^b||} \qquad (1)$$

The cumulative loss function for a training set $X = \{(x_i^a, x_i^b, y_i)\}_{i=1}^N$ is defined following (Neculoiu et al., 2016):

$$\mathcal{L}(X) = \sum_{i=1}^{N} L(x_i^a, x_i^b, y_i) \qquad (2)$$

In Equation 2, N is the number of instances in the training set X and L is the instance loss composed of two terms: one for similar pairs (L_+), and one for dissimilar pairs (L_-):

$$
L(x_i^a, x_i^b, y_i) = y_i \cdot L_+(x_i^a, x_i^b) \\
+ (1 - y_i) \cdot L_-(x_i^a, x_i^b), \qquad (3)
$$

where the loss functions for the similar and dissimilar cases are given by:

$$L_+(x_i^a, x_i^b) = (1 - s)^2$$

$$
L_-(x_i^a, x_i^b) = \begin{cases} s^2 & \text{if } s < 0 \\ 0 & \text{otherwise} \end{cases} \qquad (4)
$$

where s stands for the cosine similarity, as defined in Equation 1.

---

[1]Inspired by the figure in (Mueller and Thyagarajan, 2016), and adapted to our use case.

3 Data

3.1 Training Data

For English, we have a large amount of training data, consisting of the browse page's metadata (slot/value pairs and category name), a title generated by the rule-based system (see section 3.2), and manually assigned error severity (see section 2) for this title. Table 2 shows some examples of training data instances.

Category	MP3 Player Headphones & Earbuds
Brand	Sony
Connector	3.5mm (1/8in.)
Features	Volume Control
Title	Sony 3.5mm (1/8in.) MP3 Player Headphones & Earbuds with Volume Control
Quality	OK
Category	Nursery Bedding Sets
To Fit	Crib
Brand	My Baby Sam
Title	My Nursery Bedding Sets Sam Baby Crib Shoes
Quality	Bad

Table 2: Examples of metadata, automatically generated title, manually assigned quality class.

Table 3 shows statistics on the training data. When we started working on quality estimation for these titles, we only had the first set of data, labeled *train1*. The other set, *train2*, is much larger and became available later on. We use these two training sets for evaluating the impact of adding more data to model training.

Data set	# Browse Pages	Quality (%) OK	Bad
train1	81,251	65	35
train2	269,409	66	34
artificial P1	29,150	0	100

Table 3: Training data statistics.

The distribution of quality classes is similar across both training sets. The majority of titles is labeled as 'OK', and about one third are labeled as 'Bad'. Since the number of P1 samples in the training data is very low (approx. 1%), we generated 29k additional training samples with P1 issues semi-automatically, in order to increase their representation in the training data, and improve the models' prediction capabilities on this type of errors: We extracted BPs from the training data which contain "brand" slots, modified the curated reference title by misspelling the brand name, and added these modified titles to the training data with label 'Bad'.

Test Set	# BPs	Rule-based	Hybrid	APE
1	508	60 / 40	–	54 / 46
2	509	62 / 38	63 / 36	71 / 29
1+2	2,543	all combined : 63% OK 37% Bad		

Table 4: Evaluation data statistics. Numbers are % Good / % Bad in the three rightmost columns.

3.2 Evaluation Data

We constantly carry out human evaluation of title quality. From these evaluations, we have two test sets with approximately 500 browse pages each, called *test1* and *test2*. For those browse pages, we have automatically generated titles from three different systems along with manual assessment of title quality. The three different title generation systems are described in detail in (Mathur, Ueffing, and Leusch, 2017). In short, they are:

- a strictly rule-based approach with a manually created grammar. This is especially useful when the amount of human-curated training data is limited.

- a hybrid generation approach which combines rule-based language generation and statistical MT techniques for situations in which monolingual data for the language is available, but human-curated titles are not.

- an Automatic Post-Editing (APE) system which first generates titles with the rule-based approach, and then uses statistical MT techniques for automatically correcting the errors made by the rule-based approach.

See Table 4 for the amount of data and title quality across these different test sets and system outputs. Apart from the APE system, the class distribution is similar for all sets, and also similar to the distribution on the training data. The APE system was significantly improved between these two evaluation rounds, leading to a much higher percentage of 'OK' labels on *test2*. The hybrid system was manually evaluated only on *test2*.

4 Results

We evaluated our QE models in the following scenario: given a browse page's metadata and an automatically generated title, we want to decide whether the title meets the quality standards and should be presented on our website. Evaluation metrics are F1-score per class and total (weighted) F1-score, and Matthew's correlation.

4.1 Model comparison

We first compared QE models obtained using different learning algorithms and trained only on *train1* because model training is faster and we expect the observed trends to be independent of the amount of training data. Table 5 shows the results. The majority baseline (accepting all titles as 'OK') yields fairly low F1-score, because all bad titles are labeled incorrectly. For the RF

Model	F1(OK)	F1(Bad)	F1	MC
Majority ('OK')	0.77	0.00	0.48	0.00
Random Forest				
MTQE features	0.61	0.58	0.60	0.24
BP features	0.68	0.59	0.65	0.29
MTQE + BP	0.66	**0.64**	0.65	0.36
MTQE + BP + redun.	0.66	**0.64**	0.65	**0.37**
Siamese Network				
fastText, dim50	**0.80**	0.54	**0.70**	**0.37**
word2vec, dim50	0.79	0.55	**0.70**	**0.37**

Table 5: F1-scores and Matthew's correlation (MC) for different QE models. Training on *train1*, evaluation on *test1+2*. Best results in bold.

classifiers, we can see how adding information improves the model. The model based only on MTQE features achieves the worst performance (60 points F1 and correlation 0.24). Our newly developed browse-page-specific features in isolation perform 5 points better both in F1 and in correlation. Combining those two feature groups yields a significant improvement in correlation, though not in total F1. It significantly increases the F1-score for 'Bad' titles, but hurts a bit on the 'OK' titles, which are more frequent in the test data. The redundancy features additionally increase correlation by 1 point absolute.

Training data	F1(OK)	F1(Bad)	F1	MC
Random Forest				
train1	0.66	**0.64**	0.65	0.37
train1+2	0.76	**0.64**	0.72	0.41
train1+2 + artif.	0.78	**0.64**	0.73	0.43
Siamese Network				
train1	0.79	0.55	0.70	0.37
train1+2 + artif.	**0.82**	**0.64**	**0.75**	**0.48**

Table 6: QE performance for different amounts of training data. Evaluation on *test1+2*. RF with all features. SN with word2vec embeddings. Best results in bold.

We compared SN models with two different pre-trained word embeddings, using either word2vec (Mikolov et al., 2013) or fastText (Bojanowski et al., 2016). As we see in Table 5, their QE performance is almost identical, and we

Model	F1-score / Matthew's correlation				
	test1 RB	test2 RB	test1 APE	test2 APE	test2 hybrid
RF trained on *train1*	0.68 / 0.44	0.64 / 0.35	0.62 / 0.29	0.65 / 0.30	0.68 / 0.40
RF trained on all data	0.75 / 0.47	0.74 / 0.46	**0.70 / 0.39**	0.71 / 0.31	0.75 / 0.46
SN trained on *train1*	0.74 / 0.46	0.74 / 0.47	0.60 / 0.24	0.71 / 0.28	0.73 / 0.41
SN trained on all data	**0.79 / 0.57**	**0.81 / 0.59**	0.66 / 0.36	**0.72 / 0.32**	**0.79 / 0.54**

Table 7: QE performance per title generation system. RF with all features. SN with word2vec embeddings. Best results marked in bold. RB is rule-based.

will use the word2vec embeddings going forward. Both SN models significantly outperform the RF models in total F1-score, which increases by 5 points. This stems from much better classification of 'OK' titles, while 'Bad' titles are better recognized by the RF models. Matthew's correlation is at 0.37 both for the best RF and the SN models.

4.2 Impact of training data

After the original experiments described in section 4.1, we obtained a much larger amount of training data. We then trained RF models on the combined sets *train1* and *train2*, with 349k titles. As Table 6 shows, this yields a gain of 7 points in F1-score and 4 points in correlation, caused by improved classification on 'OK' titles. Manual analysis of QE performance showed that it was particularly low on titles with P1 issues. As described in section 3.1, we therefore generated artificial training data for better representing P1 errors in training. Adding these in training further improves the RF model, yielding total F1 of 73 points and correlation of 0.43. The effect of an increased amount of training data is even stronger for the SN models. QE performance increases by 5 points in F1 and 11 points in correlation. This SN trained on all 376k titles is the best QE model according to all metrics.

4.3 System-specific evaluation

We are constantly improving the system for BP title generation and have implemented different approaches. It is therefore important that the QE models work equally well for output from different title generation systems, i.e. they should not be heavily tailored to one specific system.

We evaluated the QE models per evaluation set (*test1* and *test2*) and per title generation system. The QE performance per system output is shown in Table 7, with notable difference in F1-score and Matthew's correlation across the five different sets. The SN models perform best on the titles from the rule-based generation system, i.e. when

training and test titles are similar – with F1-scores around 0.8 and Matthew's correlation in the high 50s. The worst classification performance is achieved for the APE titles on *test1*, which is the set with the lowest title quality (see Table 4). This is also the only set on which the RF models outperform the SN models. The RF models were trained with class weights adjusted inversely proportional to class frequencies in the training data, making them more robust w.r.t. the differences between training and test data. The neural network model does not have the same class imbalance treatment, which makes the model biased towards most frequent classes in training data sets in which the imbalance is high (e.g. the rule-based system). In future work, we plan to apply the same balancing to SN training. This setting could potentially improve the SN performance.

5 Conclusion

We developed different methods for automatically assessing the quality of browse page titles. One is a Random Forest classifier which combines well-studied QE features with new features which are specific to the task and explore information from the browse page's metadata. The second approach is a neural network model using a Siamese architecture. The classification performance of the methods was evaluated on in-house data, showing that: (i) Random Forest models are significantly improved by using new task-specific features; (ii) Siamese networks significantly outperform Random Forest models in most settings; (iii) Random Forest models show more robust quality estimation performance on titles where error distribution diverges from what was observed in training; (iv) unsurprisingly, a drastic increase in the amount of training data significantly improves QE performance for both model types; (v) adding artificial training data, which alleviates the imbalanced distribution of error types, improves both types of models. The Siamese architecture presented in this paper could also be employed in the context of machine translation or other language generation tasks in which one needs to estimate the output quality.

As future work, we plan to bring those research and pilot systems into production and gather experience on their use; as well as extending them to multi-class prediction for finer-grained QE, directly predicting the error severity classes (Good, P3, P2, P1). Furthermore, we plan to develop QE methods for languages other than English, where the amount of training data is much smaller.

6 Acknowledgements

We would like to thank our colleague Kashif Shah for the fruitful discussions.

Appendix: Examples

Table 8 shows examples of quality predictions from different QE models. The first block contains titles where both model types correctly predict quality, such as bad titles which have issues with fluency or repetition, or well-formed titles which contain all relevant aspects.

The second block shows examples where none of the models correctly predicts title quality. In the first two examples, the bad quality is caused by omissions of words ("Water" and "Row"), and none of the QE models detects this. This is probably due to the structure of the metadata input, with aspect slot/value pairs like {"Water Type": "Pond"}, which needs to be realized as "Pond Water" and not just "Pond" in the title – this type of omission is hard to capture for the QE models. Similar observations hold for the slot/value pair {"Row": "5"} in the next example. In the third and fourth example in the second block, there is a mismatch between the category name in the metadata input and the realization in the title, which might be the cause for the "Bad" QE predictions. Category names are "Sculptures & Carvings Direct from the Artist" and "Barware Glasses & Cups", respectively, and significant portions of the category names are dropped in both cases.

The third block of the table shows examples where the RF models perform better. The first example is an incorrect brand name ("aden anais"), for which we explicitly designed features in the RF models.

The last block of Table 8 contains titles which the SN models classified correctly, but the RF model did not. The first one is again a case of missing information and resulting disfluency in the title, which seems to be harder to capture for the RF models.

References

John Blatz, Erin Fitzgerald, George Foster, Simona Gandrabur, Cyril Goutte, Alex Kulesza, Alberto Sanchis, and Nicola Ueffing. 2004. Confidence estimation for machine translation. In *Proceedings of the 20th International Conference on Computational Linguistics*, COLING '04, Stroudsburg, PA, USA. Association for Computational Linguistics.

Piotr Bojanowski, Edouard Grave, Armand Joulin, and Tomas Mikolov. 2016. Enriching word vectors with subword information. *arXiv preprint arXiv:1607.04606.*

Leo Breiman. 2001. Random forests. *Machine Learning*, 45(1):5–32.

Jane Bromley, Isabelle Guyon, Yann LeCun, Eduard Säckinger, and Roopak Shah. 1994. Signature verification using a" siamese" time delay neural network. In *Advances in Neural Information Processing Systems*, pages 737–744.

Ke Chen and Ahmad Salman. 2011. Extracting speaker-specific information with a regularized siamese deep network. In J. Shawe-Taylor, R. S. Zemel, P. L. Bartlett, F. Pereira, and K. Q. Weinberger, editors, *Advances in Neural Information Processing Systems 24*, pages 298–306. Curran Associates, Inc.

Sumit Chopra, Raia Hadsell, and Yann LeCun. 2005. Learning a similarity metric discriminatively, with application to face verification. In *Computer Vision and Pattern Recognition, 2005. CVPR 2005. IEEE Computer Society Conference on*, volume 1, pages 539–546. IEEE.

Klaus Greff, Rupesh Kumar Srivastava, Jan Koutník, Bas R. Steunebrink, and Jürgen Schmidhuber. 2015. LSTM: A search space odyssey. *CoRR*, abs/1503.04069.

Francis Grégoire and Philippe Langlais. 2017. A deep neural network approach to parallel sentence extraction. *CoRR*, abs/1709.09783.

Sepp Hochreiter and Jürgen Schmidhuber. 1997. Lstm can solve hard long time lag problems. In *Advances in neural information processing systems*, pages 473–479.

Hyun Kim, Jong-Hyeok Lee, and Seung-Hoon Na. 2017. Predictor-estimator using multilevel task learning with stack propagation for neural quality estimation. In *Proceedings of the Second Conference on Machine Translation*, pages 562–568, Copenhagen, Denmark. Association for Computational Linguistics.

<table>
<thead>
<tr><th colspan="2" style="text-align:center">Title</th><th colspan="3" style="text-align:center">Quality</th></tr>
<tr><th>Automatic</th><th>Reference</th><th>RF</th><th>SN</th><th>Ref.</th></tr>
</thead>
<tbody>
<tr><td colspan="5">both correct</td></tr>
<tr><td>Telefunken Portable AM/FM Radios with Alarm</td><td>Telefunken Portable AM/FM Radios with Alarm</td><td>OK</td><td>OK</td><td>OK</td></tr>
<tr><td>Dog Standard Shampoos</td><td>Dog Standard Shampoos</td><td>OK</td><td>OK</td><td>OK</td></tr>
<tr><td>Samsung Cell Display: Lens Screens Parts for Verizon</td><td>Samsung Cellphone & Smartphone Lens Screens for Verizon</td><td>Bad</td><td>Bad</td><td>Bad</td></tr>
<tr><td>Science Fiction Fiction & Literature Books</td><td>Science Fiction Books in German</td><td>Bad</td><td>Bad</td><td>Bad</td></tr>
<tr><td colspan="5">both incorrect</td></tr>
<tr><td>Pond Aquarium Filter Media & Accessories</td><td>Pond Water Aquarium Filter Media and Accessories</td><td>OK</td><td>OK</td><td>Bad</td></tr>
<tr><td>3 5 Concert Tickets</td><td>Row 5 3 Concert Tickets</td><td>OK</td><td>OK</td><td>Bad</td></tr>
<tr><td>Less than 12in. Figurines Direct from the Artist</td><td>Less than 12" Direct from the Artist Figurines</td><td>Bad</td><td>Bad</td><td>OK</td></tr>
<tr><td>Whisky Glasses Barware</td><td>Barware Whisky Glasses</td><td>Bad</td><td>Bad</td><td>OK</td></tr>
<tr><td colspan="5">RF better</td></tr>
<tr><td>aden anais Cribskirts & Dust Ruffles</td><td>aden+anais Cribskirts & Dust Ruffles</td><td>Bad</td><td>OK</td><td>Bad</td></tr>
<tr><td>Full Sun Dry H2 (1 to 5°C) Cactus & Succulent Plants</td><td>Full Sun Dry H2 (1 to 5°C) Cactus & Succulent Plants</td><td>OK</td><td>Bad</td><td>OK</td></tr>
<tr><td colspan="5">SN better</td></tr>
<tr><td>Topshop Mid L32 Jeans for Women</td><td>Topshop Mid Rise L32 Jeans for Women</td><td>OK</td><td>Bad</td><td>Bad</td></tr>
<tr><td>Simulation Sony PlayStation 2 Manual Included PAL Video Games</td><td>Sony PlayStation 2 Simulation PAL Video Games with Manual</td><td>Bad</td><td>OK</td><td>OK</td></tr>
</tbody>
</table>

Table 8: Examples of quality predictions from the RF and SN models, and true label (Ref.)

André F. T. Martins, Fabio Kepler, and Jose Monteiro. 2017. Unbabel's participation in the WMT17 translation quality estimation shared task. In *Proceedings of the Second Conference on Machine Translation*, pages 569–574, Copenhagen, Denmark. Association for Computational Linguistics.

Prashant Mathur, Nicola Ueffing, and Gregor Leusch. 2017. Generating titles for millions of browse pages on an e-commerce site. In *Proceedings of the International Conference on Natural Language Generation*.

Tomas Mikolov, Kai Chen, Greg Corrado, and Jeffrey Dean. 2013. Efficient estimation of word representations in vector space. *arXiv preprint arXiv:1301.3781*.

Jonas Mueller and Aditya Thyagarajan. 2016. Siamese recurrent architectures for learning sentence similarity. In *AAAI*, pages 2786–2792.

Paul Neculoiu, Maarten Versteegh, and Mihai Rotaru. 2016. Learning text similarity with siamese recurrent networks. In *Proceedings of the 1st Workshop on Representation Learning for NLP*, pages 148–157.

F. Pedregosa, G. Varoquaux, A. Gramfort, V. Michel, B. Thirion, O. Grisel, M. Blondel, P. Prettenhofer, R. Weiss, V. Dubourg, J. Vanderplas, A. Passos, D. Cournapeau, M. Brucher, M. Perrot, and E. Duchesnay. 2011. Scikit-learn: Machine learning in Python. *Journal of Machine Learning Research*, 12:2825–2830.

Lucia Specia, Gustavo Henrique Paetzold, and Carolina Scarton. 2015. Multi-level translation quality prediction with QuEst++. In *Proceedings of ACL-IJCNLP 2015 System Demonstrations*, pages 115–120.

Wen-tau Yih, Kristina Toutanova, John C Platt, and Christopher Meek. 2011. Learning discriminative projections for text similarity measures. In *Proceedings of the Fifteenth Conference on Computational Natural Language Learning*, pages 247–256. Association for Computational Linguistics.

Atypical Inputs in Educational Applications

Su-Youn Yoon, Aoife Cahill, Anastassia Loukina,
Klaus Zechner, Brian Riordan, Nitin Madnani
Educational Testing Service
660 Rosedale Road, Princeton, NJ
`syoon, acahill, aloukina, kzechner, briodan, nmadnani@ets.org`

Abstract

In large-scale educational assessments, the use of automated scoring has recently become quite common. While the majority of student responses can be processed and scored without difficulty, there are a small number of responses that have atypical characteristics that make it difficult for an automated scoring system to assign a correct score. We describe a pipeline that detects and processes these kinds of responses at run-time. We present the most frequent kinds of what are called non-scorable responses along with effective filtering models based on various NLP and speech processing technologies. We give an overview of two operational automated scoring systems —one for essay scoring and one for speech scoring— and describe the filtering models they use. Finally, we present an evaluation and analysis of filtering models used for spoken responses in an assessment of language proficiency.

1 Introduction

An automated scoring system can assess constructed responses such as essays to open-ended questions faster than human raters, often at lower cost, with the resulting scores being consistent over time. These advantages have prompted strong demand for high-performing automated scoring systems for various educational applications. However, even state-of-the-art automated scoring systems face numerous challenges when used in a large-scale operational setting. For instance, some responses have atypical characteristics that make it difficult for an automated scoring system to provide a valid score. A spoken response, for example, with a lot of background noise may suffer from frequent errors in automated speech recognition (ASR), and the linguistic features generated from the erroneous ASR word hypotheses may be inaccurate. As a result, the automated score based on the inaccurate features may differ greatly from the score a human expert would assign. Furthermore, it may substantially weaken the *validity* of the automated scoring system.[1] More recently, some studies have systematically evaluated the impact of atypical inputs, particularly gaming responses, on the validity of automated scoring of essays (Lochbaum et al., 2013) and short-answers (Higgins and Heilman, 2014). They showed that automated scoring systems tend to be more vulnerable than human raters to students trying to game the system. Consistent with these findings, Zhang (2013) argued that the ability to detect abnormal performance is one of the most important requirements of a high-stakes automated scoring system. However, despite its importance, and compared to the large body of work describing the empirical performance of automated scoring systems, there has been little discussion of how NLP tools and techniques can contribute to improving the detection of atypical inputs.

In this paper we present a typical processing pipeline for automated scoring of essay and spoken responses and describe the points in the process where handling of atypical inputs and system failures can occur. In particular, we describe some of the NLP technologies used at each of these points and the role of NLP components as *filters* in an automated scoring pipeline. We present a case study on building automated filters to detect problematic responses in an assessment of spoken English.

2 Detecting Atypical Inputs

In this section, we give an overview of an automated scoring pipeline and describe how atypical

---

[1] Test validity is the extent to which a test accurately measures what it is supposed to measure.

Proceedings of NAACL-HLT 2018, pages 60–67
New Orleans, Louisiana, June 1 - 6, 2018. ©2017 Association for Computational Linguistics

inputs can be detected and processed in applications that automatically score the language quality of spoken responses and essays.

A typical automated scoring pipeline has three major components: (1) the student response is captured by the input capture module; (2) the system computes a wide range of linguistic features that measure various aspects of language proficiency using NLP and/or speech processing technologies; and (3) a pre-trained automated scoring model predicts a proficiency score using the linguistic features. The components above the dotted line in Figure 1 illustrate the typical processing sequence.

However, this scoring pipeline is a simplified version of what happens in a real-life operational system. In a large-scale assessment, there are usually a small number of atypical responses, where the automated scoring system would have difficulty in predicting *valid* scores.[2] We call these problematic responses *non-scorable*. In order to handle these problematic inputs in real-time, we can add *filtering models* (FMs) as sub-modules of the automated scoring systems. The filtering models detect and process different kinds of problematic inputs at different points in the typical pipeline. Figure 1 indicates three points at which filtering models could be employed in an operationally-deployed automated scoring system (below the dotted line). The points at which FMs could be introduced are after (1) input capture, (2) feature generation and (3) score generation. Responses that are flagged by the FMs are handled in different ways depending on the application context. The responses can receive an automated score (with a warning that it is unreliable), they can be rejected and receive no score, or they can be sent to a human rater for manual scoring.

Analogous to the FMs, non-scorable responses can also be classified into three main groups. Non-scorable responses in the feature generation and score generation groups are mostly system-initiated non-scorable responses, where system components had critical errors at the feature generation or score generation stages. Non-scoreable responses in the input capture group can be further classified into (a) system-initiated and (b) user-

initiated non-scorable responses. User-initiated non-scorable responses can occur for a number of reasons, both for good faith (where the students try their best to answer the question appropriately) and bad faith (where the students do not make a reasonable attempt to answer the question) attempts. Students making good-faith attempts to answer questions may still present an automated scoring system with atypical input. For example, in a speaking assessment, inappropriate distance to the microphone may result in a distorted recording; or in a written assessment a student may misread the question, and unintentionally write an off-topic response. Bad faith responses can come from unmotivated students, or students trying to game the system. These responses represent a wide range of (often very creative) inputs that can be troublesome for an automated scoring system that is ill-prepared to handle them. If system components fail or the system is not confident in its prediction, the automated processing pipeline also needs to be able to handle this correctly and fairly.

Next we describe some of the techniques that have been proposed for detecting non-scorable responses at each of the stages.

2.1 Input Capture Filtering Models

Some system-initiated errors that should be flagged at the input capture stage are: severe audio problems typically caused by equipment malfunction, background noise, or problems with test takers' recording level (speaking proficiency assessment) or text capture failures (writing proficiency assessment).

There is also a wide range of potential user-initiated non-scorable responses. Some of the most frequent categories include (a) response in non-target language; (b) off-topic; (c) generic responses;[3] (d) repetition of the question; (e) canned responses;[4] (f) banging on the keyboard; and (g) no-response.

Five of the categories mentioned relate to topicality. Off-topic responses and generic responses are unrelated to the prompt, while the prompt-repetition responses and canned responses can be considered repetition or plagiarism. For automated essay scoring, off-topic detection systems

---

[2]Many scoring systems could produce *some* score for these problematic responses, however it is unlikely to be correct. It is therefore important for the overall validity of the test and automated scoring system, to be able to identify such responses and treat them correctly.

[3]Responses that only include simple unrelated sentences such as "I don't know," "this is too difficult" "why do I have to answer," etc.

[4]Responses that only include memorized segments from external sources (often websites)

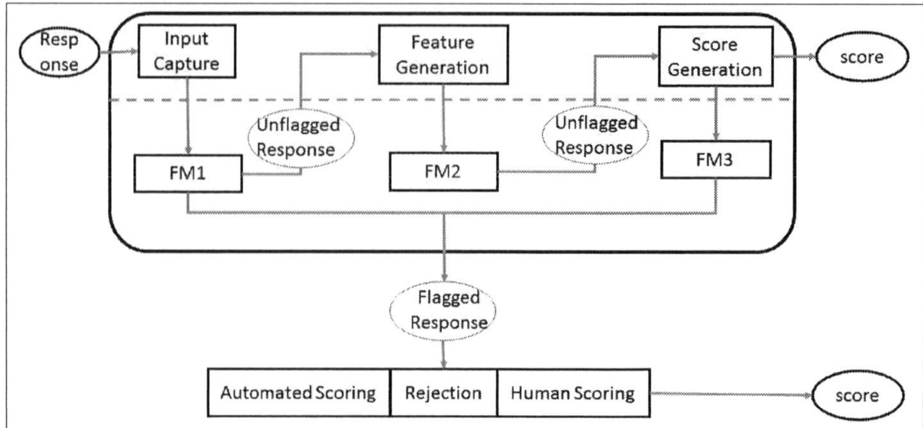

Figure 1: A diagram of the overall architecture of a generic automated scoring pipeline. Above the dotted line are the key stages in automated scoring. Below the dotted line are the possible additions to the pipeline to handle atypical inputs using filtering models (FMs).

have been developed based on question-specific content models, such as a standard vector space model (VSM) built for each question (Bernstein et al., 2000; Higgins et al., 2006; Louis and Higgins, 2010).

For speaking tests eliciting highly or moderately restricted speech, filtering models based on features derived from ASR systems such as normalized confidence scores and language model (LM) scores can achieve good performance in identifying topic-related non-scorable responses (van Doremalen et al., 2009; Lo et al., 2010; Cheng and Shen, 2011). However, this approach is not appropriate for a speaking test that elicits unconstrained spontaneous speech. More recently, similar to techniques that have been applied in essay scoring, systems based on document similarity measures and topic detection were developed to detect spoken non-scorable responses. In addition, neural networks and word embeddings, which have the advantage of capturing topically relevant words that are not identical, have been used in Malinin et al. (2017) and Yoon et al. (2017), and this has resulted in further improvements over systems using only traditional lexical similarity features.

Unlike off-topic responses, canned responses include pre-existing material. These can often be identified by matching responses to test preparation websites or other student responses. Potthast et al. (2014) give an overview of approaches to detecting plagiarism in written texts based on the systems that competed in the PAN-2014 shared

task on plagiarism detection. Wang et al. (2016) developed a spoken canned response detection system using similar techniques applied in essay plagiarism detection.

In addition, various speech processing and NLP techniques have also been used to detect other types of non-scorable responses: language identification technology for non-English detection (Yoon and Higgins, 2011) and speaker recognition technology for automated impostor detection (Qian et al., 2016). "Banging on the keyboard" can be identified by analyzing part-of-speech sequences and looking for ill-formed sequences (Higgins et al., 2006).

2.2 Feature Generation Filtering Models

The most typical way for a response to be flagged at the Feature Generation stage is for an internal component to fail. For example, in an automated speech scoring system the ASR system, or the speech-signal processing component may fail. In addition, parsers and taggers also sometimes fail to produce analyses, particularly on ill-formed language-learner responses. In order to detect sub-optimal ASR performance, filtering models have been developed using signal processing technology and features derived from ASR systems, e.g., confidence scores and normalized LM scores (Jeon and Yoon, 2012; Cheng and Shen, 2011).

It should be noted that while some of the user-initiated non-scorable responses undetected at the input capture stage would likely also cause feature generation failures (e.g., no-speech may cause empty ASR hypothesis which result in feature generation failure), other types (e.g., gaming responses) would simply cause subtle differences in feature values leading to potential inflation of the automated scores without causing clear sub-process failures.

2.3 Score Generation Filtering Models

It is also possible to identify responses that may not have received a correct score from the automated scoring system by looking at the output of the scoring model directly. van Dalen et al. (2015) developed an automated essay scoring system that uses a Gaussian process to not only generate proficiency scores, but also give a measure of the uncertainty of the generated score. They proposed a process that uses the uncertainty measure to filter responses with high uncertainty and send them to human raters for scoring.

2.4 Adjusting Scoring for non-scorable responses

We consider two main scoring scenarios:

- Human raters in the loop: there are several ways that human scoring can be combined with automated scoring. The two most common situations are co-grading (a majority of responses are scored by both human raters and the automated scoring system) and hybrid scoring (a majority of the responses are scored by the automated scoring system, while only subset of responses are scored by human raters for quality control purposes).

- Sole automated scoring: all responses are scored by only the automated scoring system; there are no humans involved in scoring. Such situations could include practice tests or classroom tools.

If a response is flagged as non-scorable in a scoring situation that has a human in the loop, the most typical behavior is for the response to be sent to a human rater for additional scoring. The score from the automated system may or may not be combined with human scores, depending on the use case and the kind of flag.

If a response is flagged as non-scorable in a sole scoring situation, there are two main ways to process the response. Either no score is given and a message is returned to the user that their response

could not be successfully processed. Or alternatively, a score is given with a warning that it is unreliable.

3 Practical Implementation of Filtering Models

In this section we describe two systems for automated scoring of CRs: (1) e-rater – an automated scoring system for essays and (2) $SpeechRater^{SM}$ – an automated scoring system for spoken responses. We describe the kinds of filters used by both systems.

3.1 Automated Essay Scoring

The e-rater system (Attali and Burstein, 2006) automatically evaluates the writing quality of essays by taking key aspects of writing into account. It aligns the writing construct, via scoring rubrics, to NLP methods that identify various linguistic features of writing. The feature classes include the following: (a) grammatical errors (e.g., subject-verb agreement errors), (b) word usage errors (e.g., their versus there), (c) errors in writing mechanics (e.g., spelling), (d) presence of essay-based discourse elements (e.g., thesis statement, main points, supporting details, and conclusions), (e) development of essay-based discourse elements, (f) a feature that considers correct usage of prepositions and collocations (e.g., powerful computer vs. strong computer), and (g) sentence variety. The features are combined in a simple linear model learned from an appropriate data sample for the target populations.

In a high-stakes testing scenario with e-rater, there is a human in the loop. The first step in the pipeline is that a human rater reviews the essay (*FM1*). If they deem the essay to be non-scorable (e.g., because it is off-topic, or gibberish), the essay is immediately sent to another human for adjudication and there is no automated score produced.

If the first human rater assigns a valid score to the essay, it is then passed to the e-rater engine. The e-rater engine applies a filter that does automated garbage detection as its first step and filters out responses that it detects as being non-English (*FM1*). This filter uses unusual POS tag sequences to identify non-English responses. The number of such responses should be very low with a human as the first filter. Non-garbage responses are then passed to the next stage of processing – feature extraction. At this point there are two different kinds of filters. The first kind of filter compares the response to other responses seen during the training of the model. If the current response is too dissimilar (in terms of length, vocabulary, etc.), it is flagged (*FM2*). These filters rely on typical textual-similarity techniques including content-vector analysis (Salton et al., 1975) and distributional similarity. The second kind of filter flags responses for which the engine cannot reliably determine a score because an internal component (e.g., a parser) has indicated that its output may be unreliable (*FM2*). In both cases flagged responses are sent to a human for adjudication.

Table 1 gives a summary of the frequency of each of the types of filters applied in a high-stakes standardized test of English proficiency. The values were computed using a large sample of over 2 million candidate essays. The final score for the responses can range from 0–5. It can be seen that the average final score assigned to most of the essays flagged is very low. The average final score assigned to essays automatically flagged as being too dissimilar to the training data is higher. Typically this category of flags are designed to be conservative and sometimes flag perfectly reasonable essays, simply to err on the side of caution.

	Freq. (%)	Avg. Score
FM1 (human)	0.47	0.04
FM1 (automated)	0.02	0.96
FM2 (dissimilar)	0.95	2.65
FM2 (engine uncertainty)	0.06	1.09

Table 1: Frequency of different kinds of filters in high-stakes e-rater deployment with the average final score assigned to the responses flagged by each filter.

3.2 Automated Speech Scoring

The $SpeechRater^{SM}$ system is an automated oral proficiency scoring system for non-native speakers' of English (Zechner et al., 2009). It has been operationally deployed to score low-stakes speaking practice tests. In order to score a spoken response, the input capture module in $SpeechRater^{SM}$ records the audio. Next, the ASR system generates word hypotheses and time stamps. The feature generation modules create a wide range of linguistic features measuring fluency, pronunciation and prosody, vocabulary and grammar usage based on the ASR outputs and NLP and speech processing technologies (e.g., a POS tagger, a dependency parser, pitch and energy analysis software). In addition, it generates a set of features to monitor the quality of ASR and the audio quality of input responses.

Because of the low-stakes nature of the tests, only limited types of non-scorable responses have so far been observed in the data. There were some system-initiated non-scorable responses. Of the user-initiated non-scorable responses, the majority are no-response and the proportion of gaming responses is close to none. As a result, the filtering models in $SpeechRater^{SM}$ system are much simpler than the e-rater system; it consists of just one FM at the location of FM2, comprised of a set of rules along with a statistical model based on a subset of $SpeechRater^{SM}$ features. A detailed description and evaluation of its performance is summarized in Section 4. Finally, non-flagged responses are scored by the automated scoring moduleand flagged responses are not scored.

4 Case Study: Developing filtering models for an Automated Speech Scoring System

In this section, we will introduce a filtering model for $SpeechRater^{SM}$ developed for a low-stakes English proficiency practice test comprised of multiple questions which elicit unconstrained and spontaneous speech with duration of 45 to 60 seconds. All responses were scored by the automated scoring system (sole automated scoring scenario).

We collected $6,000$ responses from $1,000$ test takers, and expert human raters assigned a score on a scale of 1 to 4, where 1 indicates a low speaking proficiency and 4 indicates a high speaking proficiency. In addition, the raters also annotated whether each response fell into the input capture non-scorable group.[5] A total of 605 responses (10.1%) were annotated as being non-scorable responses. The majority of them were due to recording failures (7.0%), followed by no-response (3.0%) and non-English (0.1%). The data was randomly partitioned into Model Training ($4,002$ responses) and Model Evaluation ($1,998$ responses).

The ASR system was based on a gender-independent acoustic model and a trigram lan-

---

[5]The human raters did not annotate any errors caused by system component failures (system errors at the feature generation and scoring model stage).

guage model trained on 800 hours of spoken responses extracted from the same English proficiency test (but not overlapping with the Model Building set) using the Kaldi toolkit (Povey et al., 2011). In a separate study, the ASR system achieved a Word Error Rate (WER) of 37% on the held-out dataset (Tao et al., 2016). Although the performance of our ASR on non-native speakers' spontaneous speech was a state-of-the art, it showed substantially high WER for a small number of responses. Our analysis showed that the feature values and the scores for such responses were unreliable.

Initially, we developed two FMs. The Baseline FM was comprised of a statistical model trained on the Model Training partition and a set of rules to detect no-responses and responses with poor audio quality (recording errors). The extended FM was comprised of the baseline FM and an additional rule, ASRErrorFilter to detect responses for which the ASR result is likely to be highly erroneous.

The performance of two FMs on the evaluation dataset is given in Table 2.

	% flagged	acc.	pre.	recall	fscore
Baseline	9%	0.96	0.83	0.80	0.81
Extended	13%	0.95	0.66	0.90	0.76

Table 2: Performance of FMs in detecting non-scorable.

The accuracy and fscore of the baseline FM was 0.96 and 0.81, respectively. The extended model achieved a higher recall with slightly lower accuracy and fscore than the baseline. This was an expected result, since the extended model was designed to detect responses with high ASR errors that are likely to cause high human-machine score difference (HMSD) and we choose to err on the side of caution and flag more responses at the risk of flagging some good ones.

In order to investigate to what extent the extended FM can identify responses with a large HMSD, we also calculated an absolute HMSD for each response. After excluding responses annotated as non-scorable by human raters, the remaining $1,775$ responses in the evaluation set were used in this analysis. Table 4 shows the distribution of absolute system-human score differences for flagged and unflagged responses by the extended FM.

	# response	HMSD		
		mean	SD	max
Flagged	77	0.83	0.58	2.38
Unflagged	1698	0.48	0.34	1.96

Table 3: Average human-machine score differences.

The average HMSD for the flagged responses was quite large (0.83), given that the proficiency score scale was 1 to 4. Furthermore, it was 1.73 times higher than that of unflagged responses (0.48). The extended FM indeed correctly identified responses for which the automated scores were substantially different from the human scores. In contrast, the number of responses flagged by the extended FM was substantially higher than the baseline FM. 4% of responses scorable by human raters were flagged and they could not receive scores.

5 Discussion and Conclusions

We discussed the issue of atypical inputs in the context of automated scoring. Non-scorable responses can cause critical issues in various sub-processes of automated scoring systems and the automated scores for these responses may differ greatly from the correct scores. In order to address this issue, we augmented a typical automated scoring pipeline and included a set of filtering models to detect non-scorable responses based on various NLP and speech processing technologies. Finally, we described two automated scoring systems deployed to score essay and spoken responses from large scale standardized assessments.

An alternative to the approach presented here (individual filtering models for different kinds of inputs), is to simply train one single classifier to detect non-scorable responses (perhaps as an additional score point). Depending on the context of the automated scoring system, this may be sufficient, however for our purposes, it was important to have more fine grained control over the different kinds of filters (setting thresholds, etc.). This gives us the freedom to treat and route each of the types of flags differently. This is particularly important if a system is being used in both high-stakes and low-stakes testing scenarios since the number and type of non-scorable responses varies by scenario.

Section 4, in its comparison between two FMs, highlights an important trade-off between the accuracy of automated scores and the percentage of filtered responses by the filtering model. By proactively filtering out non-scorable responses, the automated scoring system (the extended FM, in this study) can prevent the generation of erroneous scores and improve the quality and validity of the automated scores. However, this may result in a higher percentage of scoring failures which could cause higher costs (e.g., additional human scoring, or providing free retest or refund to the test takers). These two important factors should be carefully considered during system development.

References

Yigal Attali and Jill Burstein. 2006. Automated essay scoring with e–rater V.2. *Journal of Technology, Learning, and Assessment* 4(3).

J. Bernstein, J. DeJong, D. Pisoni, and B. Townshend. 2000. Two experiments in automated scoring of spoken language proficiency. In *Proceedings of the Workshop on Integrating Speech Technology in Learning*.

Jian Cheng and Jianqiang Shen. 2011. Off-topic detection in automated speech assessment applications. In *Proceedings of the 12th Annual Conference of the International Speech Communication Association*. pages 1597–1600.

Derrick Higgins, Jill Burstein, and Yigal Attali. 2006. Identifying off-topic student essays without topic-specific training data. *Natural Language Engineering* 12(2):145–159.

Derrick Higgins and Michael Heilman. 2014. Managing what we can measure: Quantifying the susceptibility of automated scoring systems to gaming behavior. *Educational Measurement: Issues and Practice* 33(3):36–46.

Je Hun Jeon and Su-Youn Yoon. 2012. Acoustic feature-based non-scorable response detection for an automated speaking proficiency assessment. In *Proceedings of the 13th Annual Conference of the International Speech Communication Association*. pages 1275–1278.

Wai-Kit Lo, Alissa M Harrison, and Helen Meng. 2010. Statistical phone duration modeling to filter for intact utterances in a computer-assisted pronunciation training system. In *Proceedings of the Conference on Acoustics, Speech and Signal Processing*. pages 5238–5241.

Karen E Lochbaum, Mark Rosenstein, Peter Foltz, and Marcia A Derr. 2013. Detection of gaming in automated scoring of essays with the IEA. *Presented at 75th Annual meeting of NCME* .

Annie Louis and Derrick Higgins. 2010. Off-topic essay detection using short prompt texts. In *Proceedings of the 5th Workshop on Innovative Use of NLP for Building Educational Applications*. pages 92–95.

Andrey Malinin, Kate Knill, Anton Ragni, Yu Wang, and Mark JF Gales. 2017. An attention based model for off-topic spontaneous spoken response detection: An initial study. In *Proceedings of the 7th Workshop on Speech and Language Technology in Education*. pages 144–149.

Martin Potthast, Matthias Hagen, Anna Beyer, Matthias Busse, Martin Tippmann, Paolo Rosso, and Benno Stein. 2014. Overview of the 6th international competition on plagiarism detection. In *Proceedings of the CLEF Conference on Multilingual and Multimodal Information Access Evaluation*.

Daniel Povey, Arnab Ghoshal, Gilles Boulianne, Lukas Burget, Ondrej Glembek, Nagendra Goel, Mirko Hannemann, Petr Motlicek, Yanmin Qian, Petr Schwarz, et al. 2011. The Kaldi speech recognition toolkit. In *Proceedings of the workshop on Automatic Speech Recognition and Understanding*.

Yao Qian, Jidong Tao, David Suendermann-Oeft, Keelan Evanini, Alexei V Ivanov, and Vikram Ramanarayanan. 2016. Noise and metadata sensitive bottleneck features for improving speaker recognition with non-native speech input. In *Proceedings of the 17th Annual Conference of the International Speech Communication Association*. pages 3648–3652.

G. Salton, A. Wong, and C. S. Yang. 1975. A vector space model for automatic indexing. *Communications of the ACM* pages 613–620.

Jidong Tao, Shabnam Ghaffarzadegan, Lei Chen, and Klaus Zechner. 2016. Exploring deep learning architectures for automatically grading non-native spontaneous speech. In *Proceedings of the Conference on Acoustics, Speech and Signal Processing*. pages 6140–6144.

Rogier C. van Dalen, Kate M. Knill, and Mark J. F. Gales. 2015. Automatically grading learners english using a gaussian process. In *Proceedings of the Workshop on Speech and Language Technology in Education*. pages 7–12.

Joost van Doremalen, Helmet Strik, and Cartia Cucchiarini. 2009. Utterance verification in language learning applications. In *Proceedings of the Workshop on Speech and Language Technology in Education*.

Xinhao Wang, Keelan Evanini, James Bruno, and Matthew Mulholland. 2016. Automatic plagiarism detection for spoken responses in an assessment of english language proficiency. In *Proceedings of the Workshop on Spoken Language Technology Workshop (SLT)*. pages 121–128.

Su-Youn Yoon and Derrick Higgins. 2011. Non-English response detection method for automated proficiency scoring system. In *Proceedings of the 6th Workshop on Innovative Use of NLP for Building Educational Applications*. pages 161–169.

Su-Youn Yoon, Chong Min Lee, Ikkyu Choi, Xinhao Wang, Matthew Mulholland, and Keelan Evanini. 2017. Off-topic spoken response detection with word embeddings. In *Proceedings of the 18th Annual Conference of the International Speech Communication Association*. pages 2754–2758.

Klaus Zechner, Derrick Higgins, Xiaoming Xi, and David M. Williamson. 2009. Automatic scoring of non-native spontaneous speech in tests of spoken English. *Speech Communication* 51:883–895.

Mo Zhang. 2013. Contrasting automated and human scoring of essays. *ETS R & D Connections* 21:1–11.

Using Aspect Extraction Approaches
to Generate Review Summaries and User Profiles

Christopher Mitcheltree[*]   **Veronica Wharton**[*]   **Avneesh Saluja**

Airbnb AI Lab

San Francisco, CA, USA

`firstname.lastname@airbnb.com`

Abstract

Reviews of products or services on Internet marketplace websites contain a rich amount of information. Users often wish to survey reviews or review snippets from the perspective of a certain aspect, which has resulted in a large body of work on aspect identification and extraction from such corpora. In this work, we evaluate a newly-proposed neural model for aspect extraction on two practical tasks. The first is to extract canonical sentences of various aspects from reviews, and is judged by human evaluators against alternatives. A k-means baseline does remarkably well in this setting. The second experiment focuses on the suitability of the recovered aspect distributions to represent users by the reviews they have written. Through a set of review reranking experiments, we find that aspect-based profiles can largely capture notions of user preferences, by showing that divergent users generate markedly different review rankings.

1 Introduction

Aspect extraction has traditionally been associated with the sentiment analysis community (Liu, 2012; Pontiki et al., 2016), with the goal being to decompose a small document of text (e.g., a review) into multiple facets, each of which may possess their own sentiment marker. For example, a restaurant review may comment on the ambiance, service, and food, preventing the assignment of a uniform sentiment over the entire review. A common approach to aspect extraction is to treat the aspects as latent variables and utilize latent Dirichlet allocation (LDA; Blei et al. (2003)) to extract relevant aspects from a collection of documents in an unsupervised (Titov and McDonald, 2008; Brody and Elhadad, 2010) or semi-supervised (Mukherjee and Liu, 2012) fash-

ion. Subsequent research has taken the latent variable approach further by encoding more complicated dependencies between aspects and sentiment (Zhao et al., 2010), or between aspects, ratings, and sentiment (Diao et al., 2014), using probabilistic graphical models (Koller and Friedman, 2009) to jointly learn the parameters.

However, it has been argued that the coherence of aspects extracted from the family of LDA-based approaches is low; words clustered together within a specific aspect are often unrelated, which can be attributed to the lack of word co-occurrence information in these models (Mimno et al., 2011), since conventional LDA assumes each word in a document is generated independently. Recently, He et al. (2017) proposed a neural attention-based aspect extraction (ABAE) approach, which like LDA, is an unsupervised model. The starting point is a set of word embeddings, where the vector representation of the word encapsulates co-occurrence[1]. The embeddings are used to represent a sentence as a bag-of-words, weighted with a self-attention mechanism (Lin et al., 2017), and learning amounts to encoding the resulting attention-based sentence embedding as a linear combination of aspect embeddings, optimized using an autoencoder formulation (§2). The attention mechanism thus learns to highlight words that will be pertinent for aspect identification.

In this work, we apply the ABAE model to a large corpus of reviews on Airbnb[2], an online marketplace for travel; users (guests) utilize the site to find accommodation (listings) all around the world, and a large number of these guests write reviews of the listing post-stay. We first provide additional details on the workings of the ABAE

---

[*]Equal contribution.

[1] words that co-occur with each other get mapped to points close to each other in the embedding space (Harris, 1968; Schütze, 1998).

[2] `www.airbnb.com`

Proceedings of NAACL-HLT 2018, pages 68–75

New Orleans, Louisiana, June 1 - 6, 2018. ©2017 Association for Computational Linguistics

model (§2). ABAE is then applied to two tasks: the first (§3.1) is to extract a representative sentence from a set of listing-specific reviews for a number of pre-defined aspects e.g., cleanliness and location, with the efficacy of extractive summarization evaluated by humans (§4.3). Surprisingly, we find that the k-means baseline performs very well on aspects that occur more frequently, but ABAE may be better for infrequent aspects.

In the second task (§3.2), we analyze the suitability of aspect embeddings to represent guest profiles. The hypothesis is that the content of guest reviews reveals the guest's preferences and priorities (Chen et al., 2015), and that these preferences correspond to extracted aspects. We investigate several ways to aggregate sentence-level aspect embeddings at the review and user levels and compute distances between user aspect and listing review embeddings, in order to personalize listing reviews by reranking them for each user. The correlation between guest profile distances (computed on pairs of guests) and review rank distances (computed on pairs of ordinal rankings over reviews) is then measured to evaluate our hypothesis (§4.4). We find a robust relationship between distances in the two spaces, with the correlation increasing at finer granularities like sentences compared to reviews or listings.

2 Background

To start, we provide a brief background of the ABAE model. For additional details, please refer to the original paper (He et al., 2017). At a high level, the ABAE model is an autoencoder that minimizes the reconstruction error between a weighted bag-of-words (BoW) representation of a sentence (where the weights are determined by a self-attention mechanism) and a linear combination of aspect embeddings. The linear combination represents the probabilities of the sentence belonging to each of the aspects.

The first step in ABAE is to compute the embedding $\mathbf{z}_s \in \mathbb{R}^d$ for a sentence s:

$$\mathbf{z}_s = \sum_{i=1}^{n} a_i \mathbf{e}_{w_i}$$

where $\mathbf{e}_{w_i}$ is the word embedding $\mathbf{e} \in \mathbb{R}^d$ for word w_i. As in the original paper, we use word vectors trained using the skip-gram model with negative sampling (Mikolov et al., 2013). The attention weights a_i are computed as a multiplicative self-attention model:

$$a_i = \text{softmax}(\mathbf{e}_{w_i}^{\mathrm{T}} \cdot \mathbf{M} \cdot \mathbf{y}_s)$$

$$\mathbf{y}_s = \sum_{i=1}^{n} \mathbf{e}_{w_i}$$

where $\mathbf{y}_s$ is simply the uniformly-weighted BoW embedding of the sentence, and $\mathbf{M} \in \mathbb{R}^{d \times d}$ is a learned attention model.

The next step is to compute the aspect-based sentence representation $\mathbf{r}_s \in \mathbb{R}^d$ in terms of an aspect embeddings matrix $\mathbf{T} \in \mathbb{R}^{K \times d}$, where K is the number of aspects:

$$\mathbf{p}_s = \text{softmax}(\mathbf{W} \cdot \mathbf{z}_s + \mathbf{b})$$

$$\mathbf{r}_s = \mathbf{T}^{\mathrm{T}} \cdot \mathbf{p}_s$$

where $\mathbf{p}_s \in \mathbb{R}^K$ is the weight (probability) vector over K aspect embeddings, and $\mathbf{W} \in \mathbb{R}^{K \times d}, \mathbf{b} \in \mathbb{R}^K$ are parameters of a multiclass logistic regression model.

The model is trained to minimize reconstruction error (using the cosine distance between $\mathbf{r}_s$ and $\mathbf{z}_s$) with a contrastive max-margin objective function (Weston et al., 2011). In addition, an orthogonality penalty term is added to the objective, which encourages the aspect embedding matrix $\mathbf{T}$ to produce diverse (orthogonal) aspect embeddings.

3 Tasks

To evaluate the utility of ABAE, we craft two methods of evaluation that mimic the practical ways in which aspect extraction can be used on a marketplace website with reviews.

3.1 Extractive Summarization

The first task is a direct evaluation of the quality of the recovered aspects: we use ABAE to select review sentences of a listing that are representative of a set of preselected aspects, namely cleanliness, communication, and location. "Cleanliness" refers to how clean the listing is, "communication" refers to communication between the listing host and the guest, and "location" refers to the qualities of or amenities in the listing's neighborhood. Refer to Table 3 for representative words for each aspect. Thus, aspect extraction is used to summarize listing reviews along several manually-defined topics.

We benchmark the ABAE model's extracted aspects against those from two baselines: LDA and k-means. For each experimental setup, the authors assigned one of four interpretable labels (corresponding to the identified aspects and the "other" category) to each unlabeled aspect by evaluating the 50 words most associated with that aspect[3]. LDA's topics are represented as distributions over words, so the most associated words correspond to those that occur with highest probability. For k-means and ABAE, each aspect is represented as a point in word embedding space[4], so we retrieve the 50 closest words to each point using cosine distance as a measure.

After aspect identification, we infer aspect distributions for the review sentences of an unseen test set of listings. For LDA, identification simply amounts to computing the (approximate) posterior over topic mixtures for a set of review sentences, and selecting the sentences with the highest probability in the specified aspect. For k-means, each sentence is represented as a uniformly-weighted BoW embedding, and we retrieve the sentences that are closest to the centroids that correspond to our preselected aspects. ABAE is similar, except the self-attention mechanism is applied to compute an attention-based BoW embedding, and we retrieve the sentences closest to the aspect embeddings corresponding to our aspects of interest. For some aspects (e.g., location and communication), there is a many-to-one mapping between the recovered word clusters and the aspect label. In these cases, we compute the average of the aspect embeddings, and the closest sentences to the resulting points are retrieved.

In our selection process, we retrieve the three most representative sentences (across all reviews of that listing) for each aspect. Three human annotators then evaluated the appropriateness of the selected aspect for each sentence via binary judgments. For example, an evaluator was presented with the sentence "Easy to get there from center of city by subway and bus.", along with the inferred aspect (*location*), for which a binary "yes/no" response suffices. Results aggregated by experimental setup and aspect are presented in §4.3.

3.2 Aspects as Profiles

An aspect extraction model provides a distribution over aspects for each sentence, and we can consider these distributions as interpretable sentence embeddings (since we can assign a meaning corresponding to an aspect for each of the extracted word clusters). These embeddings can be used to provide *guest profiles* by aggregating aspect distributions over review sentences that a user has written across different listings on the website. Such profiles arguably capture finer-grained information about guest preferences than an aggregate star rating across all aspects. Star ratings are also heavily positively-biased: more than 80% of reviews on Airbnb rate the maximum of 5 stars.

There are many conceivable ways to aggregate the sentence distributions, with some of the factors of variation being:

1. level of hierarchy: is the guest considered to be a bag-of-reviews (BoR), sentences (BoS), or words i.e., do we weight longer sentences or reviews with more sentences higher when computing the aggregated representation?
2. time decay: how do we treat more recently written reviews compared to earlier ones?
3. average or maximum: is the aggregate representation a (weighted) average, or should we consider the maximum value across each aspect and renormalize?

The same considerations also arise when computing the representations of the objects to be ranked e.g., a listing embedding as the aggregation of its component sentence embeddings.

For our evaluation (§4.4), guest profiles are computed by averaging distributions across a guest's review sentences uniformly (BoS), equivalent to a BoR representation weighted by the review length (number of sentences). We also experimented with a BoR representation using uniformly-weighted reviews, and the results are very similar to the BoS representation. We considered computing the guest profile by utilizing the maximum value (probability) of each aspect dimension across all review sentences written by the user and renormalizing the resulting embedding using the softmax function, but this approach resulted in high-entropic guest profiles with limited use downstream. More complex aggregation functions, like using an exponential moving average to upweight recent reviews, is an interesting future direction to explore.

4 Evaluation

We now look at the qualitative and quantitative performance of ABAE across the two tasks. After providing statistics on the review corpus that forms the basis of our evaluation, we qualitatively analyze the recovered aspects of the model,

---

[3]Inter-annotator agreements for each setup are provided in Table 3.

[4]The aspect embeddings in ABAE are initialized using the k-means centroids.

compared to k-means and LDA baselines. On a heldout evaluation set, human evaluators assessed whether the model-extracted aspects correspond to their understanding of the predefined ones by inspecting the top-ranked sentences for each aspect. Furthermore, the quality of the guest profile embeddings was evaluated by looking at the correlation between distances in the aspect space and the ordinal position of reviews on a given listing page, with the hypothesis that guests who write reviews with divergent content or aspects should receive rankings that are very different.

Our experiments were implemented using the pyTorch package[5]. Word vectors were trained using Gensim (Řehůřek and Sojka, 2010) with 5 negative samples, window size 5, and dimension 200, and Scikit-learn (Pedregosa et al., 2011) was used to run the k-means algorithm and LDA with the default settings. For ABAE, we used Adam with a learning rate of 0.001 (and the default β parameters) with a batch size of 50, 20 negative samples, and an orthogonality penalty weight of 0.1. All experiments were run on an Amazon AWS `p2.8xlarge` instance.

4.1 Datasets

The corpus was extracted from all reviews across all listings on Airbnb written between January 1, 2010 and January 1, 2017. We used spaCy[6] to segment reviews into sentences and remove non-English sentences. All sentences were subsequently preprocessed in the same manner as He et al. (2017), which entailed restricting the vocabulary to the 9,000 most frequent words in the corpus after stopword and punctuation removal. From the resulting set, we randomly sampled 10 million sentences across 5.8 million guests and 1.8 million listings to form a training set, and used the remaining unsampled sentences to select validation and test sets for the human evaluation (§4.3) and ranking (§4.4) experiments.

To select datasets for human evaluation, we identified all listings with at least 50 and at most 100 reviews in all languages and filtered out any *listing* in the training set, resulting in 900 listings which were split into validation and test sets. The validation set is used to select an appropriate number of aspects, by computing coherence scores (Mimno et al., 2011) as the number of aspects is varied in the ABAE model (§4.2). The test set was used to extract review sentences that

were presented to our human evaluators; we ensured that every listing in the test set has at least 3 non-empty English review sentences.

For the ranking correlation experiments, we first identified users who had written at least 10 review sentences in our corpus and removed those users that featured in the training set from this list. We then selected 20 users uniformly at random to form our validation set i.e., to compute guest profiles for[7]. A subset of the human evaluation test set was used to compute the correlation between aspect space and ranking order distances; we selected all listings that had at least 20 review sentences, resulting in 69 listings for evaluation. Table 1 presents a summary of corpus statistics for all of the datasets used in this work.

Set	Task	Tokens	Sentences	Guests	Listings
Train	-	68.0mil	10.0mil	5.8mil	1.8mil
Val	§3.1	91,124	14,173	3719	721
Test	§3.1	21,069	3389	920	168
Val	§3.2	3189	543	20	202
Test	§3.2	13,925	2269	587	69

Table 1: Corpus statistics for the datasets that we use. All numbers are computed after preprocessing.

4.2 Recovered Aspects

Table 2 presents coherence scores for the ABAE model as we varied the number of aspects. Similar to He et al. (2017), we considered a "document" to be a sentence, but treating reviews as documents or all reviews of a listing as a document revealed similar trends. The table shows that coherence score improvements taper off after 30 aspects, so we chose this aspect value for further experiments.

Num.	Num. Representative Words			Sum
Aspects	10	30	50	
5	-125	-1106	-2829	-4060
10	-148	-1244	-3017	-4409
15	-126	-1069	-2656	-3851
30	-101	-760	-1917	-2778
40	-84	-701	-1765	-2550

Table 2: Coherence scores as a function of the number of aspects and the number of representative words used to compute the scores (higher is better). The summed values indicate significant improvement from 15 to 30 aspects. For details on computing coherence score, see Mimno et al. (2011).

Next, for each 30-aspect experimental setup, we identified the word clusters corresponding to the set of preselected aspects by labeling

---

[5] http://pytorch.org/
[6] http://spacy.io/

[7] The most prolific guest in this set had written 66 review sentences.

	Aspects			
Setup	Location	Cleanliness	Communication	Fleiss' κ
k-means	union, music, minute, dozen, quarter, chain, zoo, buffet, nord, theater (3 clusters, 10.2%)	master, conditioners, boiler, fabric, roll, smelling, dusty, shutter, dirty, installed (1 cluster, 3.6%)	welcomed, sorted, proactive, fix, checkin, prior, replied, process, communicator, ahead (3 clusters, 9.9%)	0.58
LDA	restaurant, location, flat, walk, away, back, short, minute, bus, come (4 clusters, 16.2%)	house, comfortable, clean, bed, beach, street, part, modern, appartment, cool (1 cluster, 3.5%)	helpful, arrival, wonderful, coffee, loved, use, warm, communication, friendly, got (4 clusters, 14.5%)	0.46
ABAE	statue, tavern, woodsy, street, takeaway, woodland, cathedral, specialty, idyllic, attraction (6 clusters, 18.4%)	clean, neat, pictured, immaculate, spotless, stylish, described, uncluttered, tidy, classy (1 cluster, 3.5%)	dear, u, responsive, greeted, instruction, communicative, sent, contract, attentive, key (3 clusters, 10.1%)	0.46

Table 3: Representative words for each aspect of interest across experimental setups, along with the number of clusters mapped to that aspect in parentheses as well as the percentage of validation set sentences assigned to that cluster (the remaining sentences were assigned to "Other"). For the aspects with multiple clusters, we select a roughly equal number of words from each cluster. Misspellings are deliberate.

each revealed cluster with a value from the set $\{cleanliness, communication, location, other\}$. Note that the mapping from clusters to identified aspects is many-to-one (i.e., multiple clusters for the same aspect were identified for two of the three aspects, namely location and communication.) In fact, the number of clusters associated with each aspect is a proxy for the frequency with which these aspects occur in the corpus. To verify this claim, we computed aspect-based representations (§3.1) for each sentence in the validation set used for comparing coherence scores, and utilized these representations to compute sentence similarities to each cluster, followed by a softmax in order to assign fractional counts i.e., a soft clustering approach. For each setup, Table 3 provides the top 10 words associated with each aspect, the number of clusters mapped to that aspect, and the number of validation sentences assigned to the aspect. The location and communication aspects are 3 to 6 times more prevalent than the cleanliness aspect.

Qualitatively, the ABAE aspects are more coherent, especially in the cleanliness aspect, and do not include irrelevant words (often verbs) that are not indicative of any conceivable aspect, like "got", "use", or "come". k-means selects relevant words to indicate the aspect, but the aspects are relatively incoherent compared to ABAE. LDA has a difficult time identifying relevant words, indicating the importance of the attention mechanism in ABAE. Interestingly, we found that the inter-annotator agreement (Fleiss' κ) was slightly higher for the k-means baseline, but all scores are in the range of moderate agreement.

	Aspects		
Setup	Loc	Clean	Comm
k-means	**0.85/0.68**	0.30/0.26	**0.62/0.43**
LDA	0.16/0.17	0.09/0.10	0.11/0.13
ABAE	0.45/0.46	**0.45/0.32**	0.41/0.35

Table 4: Precision@1 and precision@3 for the extractive summarization task, as judged by our human evaluators.

4.3 Extracting Prototypical Sentences

Table 4 presents precision@1 and precision@3 results for each experimental setup-aspect pair, as evaluated by our human annotators. There are a total of 168 listings × 3 experimental setups × 3 aspects × 3 sentences per aspect = 4536 examples to evaluate; we set aside 795 examples to compute inter-annotator agreement, resulting in 2042 examples per annotator. Fleiss' $\kappa = 0.69$, which is quite high given the difficulty of the task[8].

The most surprising result is that the k-means baseline is actually the strongest performer in the location and communication aspects. Nonetheless, the result is encouraging since it suggests that, for some aspects of interest to us, a simple k-means approach and uniformly-weighted BoW embeddings suffices. It is interesting to note that the strong baseline performance occurs with the aspects that occur more frequently in the corpus, as discussed in §4.2, suggesting that ABAE is more useful with aspects that occur more rarely in our corpus (e.g., cleanliness). For future work, we propose to evaluate this hypothesis in more depth by applying the approaches in this paper to the long tail of rarer aspects. The disappointing performance of LDA shows that its lack of aware-

---

[8]The *communication* aspect (referring to host responsiveness and timeliness) is often easily confused with the friendliness of the host or staff.

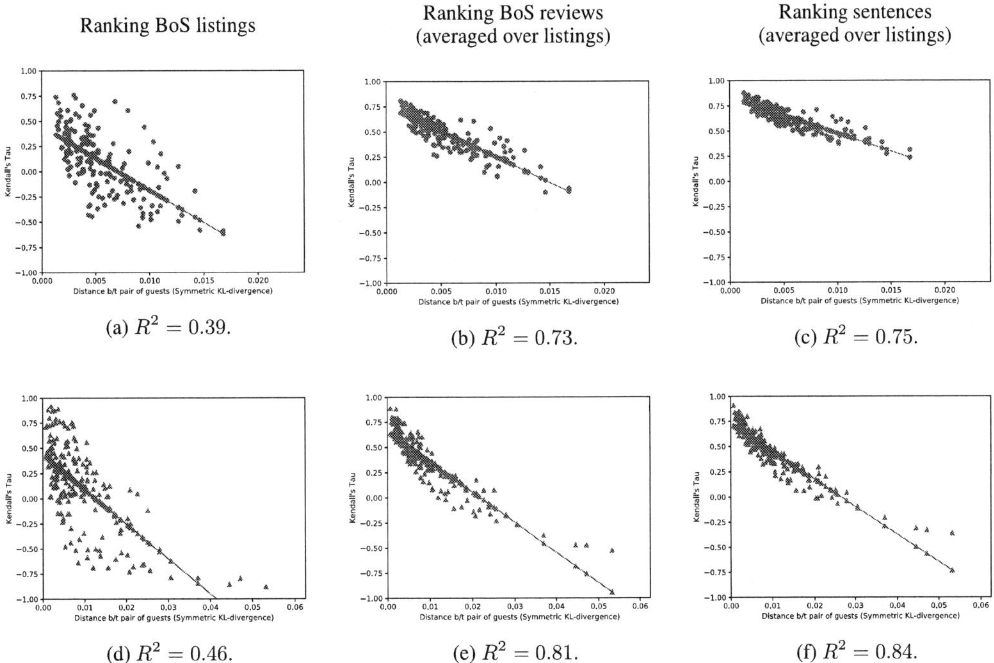

(a) $R^2 = 0.39$.   (b) $R^2 = 0.73$.   (c) $R^2 = 0.75$.

(d) $R^2 = 0.46$.   (e) $R^2 = 0.81$.   (f) $R^2 = 0.84$.

Figure 1: Plots showing the relationship between distance in aspect space and ranking space, for guest profiles computed as bag-of-sentences representations. Figures 1a, 1b, and 1c are produced with the ABAE model, and figures 1d, 1e, while 1f are produced with the k-means model.

ness for word co-occurrence is damaging for aspect identification.

4.4 Review Ranking

Figure 1 presents results for the ranking correlation experiments with the ABAE and k-means models. The validation set is used to compute pairwise distances between all $\binom{20}{2} = 190$ guest pairs using the symmetric KL divergence, since guest profiles are probability distributions over aspects. This divergence forms the x-axis for our plots. We then rerank several objects of interest, and compute the rank correlation coefficient (Kendall's τ) between pairs of rankings; this coefficient forms the y-axis for our plots. Lastly, the correlation between the distance in aspect space (between pairs of user profiles) and the distance in ranking space (between pairs of rankings over objects, as measured by Kendall's τ) with R^2 values stated in the captions.

With the guest profiles, we ranked the following objects using the symmetric KL divergence:

1. listings, where each listing is represented as a BoS (similar results were achieved when considering each listing as a BoR).
2. reviews within a listing: for each guest pair and listing, we ranked the reviews using each guest's profile and computed Kendall's τ between the ranked pair of reviews. That score was then averaged over the 69 listings to yield a single score for each guest pair.
3. sentences within a listing: similar to reviews within a listing, except Kendall's τ was computed over ranked sentences. The averaging step was the same as above.

Since ABAE extracts aspects at the sentence-level, we would expect to see sentence-based representations result in higher correlations than other representations. Indeed, if we rank smaller units (i.e., sentences vs. listings), the correlation with distances in aspect space is higher (0.75 vs. 0.39 in the case of ABAE, 0.84 vs. 0.46 in the case of k-means). Interestingly, the correlation results are slightly better for k-means: the range of values for the pairwise distances (x-axis) is much larger, so it seems like the k-means guest profiles are better at capturing extremely divergent users, and the resulting ranking pairs are more divergent too. Table 5 presents an example of divergent rankings over review sentences for a given listing from two different guest profiles using the ABAE model.

Rank	Guest 1	Guest 2
1	Room is cozy and clean only the washroom feel a little bit old.	Within walking distance to Feng Chia Night Market yet quiet enough when it comes time to rest.
2	Clean and comfortable room for the lone traveller or couples.	Nice and clean place to stay, very near to Fengjia night market.
3	The room is very good, as good as on the photos, and also clean.	Overall my TaiChung trip was good and really convenient place to stay at Nami's place.
4	Nice and clean place to stay, very near to Fengjia night market.	Ia a great place to stay, clean.
5	Within walking distance to Feng Chia Night Market yet quiet enough when it comes time to rest.	Near feng jia night market.

Table 5: From the experiment in §4.4, ranked review sentences for two different guest profiles for the same listing using the ABAE model. The first guest's profile focuses on the listing interior and cleanliness aspects, whereas the second guest is more interested in location.

5   Conclusion

In this work, we evaluated a recently proposed neural-based aspect extraction model in several settings. First, we used the inferred sentence-level aspects to select prototypical review sentences of a listing for a given aspect, and evaluated this aspect identification/extractive summarization task using human evaluators benchmarked against two baselines. Interestingly, the k-means baseline does quite well on frequently-occurring aspects. Second, the sentence-level aspects were also used to compute user profiles by grouping reviews that individual users have written. We showed that these embeddings are effective in reranking sentences, reviews, or listings in order to personalize this content to individual users.

For future work, we wish to investigate alternative ways to aggregate and compute user profiles and compute distances between objects to rank and user profiles. We would also like to utilize human evaluators to judge the rankings produced in the review reranking experiments.

Acknowledgments

We thank the authors of the ABAE paper (He et al., 2017) for providing us with their code[9], which we used to benchmark our internal implementation. We are also grateful to our human evaluators.

References

David Blei, Andrew Ng, and Michael Jordan. 2003. Latent dirichlet allocation. *Journal of Machine Learning Research*, 3:993–1022.

Samuel Brody and Noemie Elhadad. 2010. An unsupervised aspect-sentiment model for online reviews. In *Proceedings of NAACL-HLT*.

Li Chen, Guanliang Chen, and Feng Wang. 2015. Recommender systems based on user reviews: the state of the art. *User Modeling and User-Adapted Interaction*.

Qiming Diao, Minghui Qiu, Chao-Yuan Wu, Alexander J. Smola, Jing Jiang, and Chong Wang. 2014. Jointly modeling aspects, ratings and sentiments for movie recommendation (jmars). In *Proceedings of KDD*.

Zellig Harris. 1968. Mathematical structures of language. In *Interscience tracts in pure and applied mathematics*.

Ruidan He, Wee Sun Lee, Hwee Tou Ng, and Daniel Dahlmeier. 2017. An unsupervised neural attention model for aspect extraction. In *Proceedings of ACL*.

Daphne Koller and Nir Friedman. 2009. *Probabilistic Graphical Models: Principles and Techniques*. The MIT Press.

Zhouhan Lin, Minwei Feng, Cícero Nogueira dos Santos, Mo Yu, Bing Xiang, Bowen Zhou, and Yoshua Bengio. 2017. A structured self-attentive sentence embedding. In *Proceedings of ICLR*.

Bing Liu. 2012. *Sentiment Analysis and Opinion Mining*. Morgan & Claypool Publishers.

Tomas Mikolov, Ilya Sutskever, Kai Chen, Greg Corrado, and Jeffrey Dean. 2013. Distributed representations of words and phrases and their compositionality. *CoRR: abs/1310.4546*.

David Mimno, Hanna M. Wallach, Edmund Talley, Miriam Leenders, and Andrew McCallum. 2011. Optimizing semantic coherence in topic models. In *Proceedings of EMNLP*.

Arjun Mukherjee and Bing Liu. 2012. Aspect extraction through semi-supervised modeling. In *Proceedings of ACL*.

F. Pedregosa, G. Varoquaux, A. Gramfort, V. Michel, B. Thirion, O. Grisel, M. Blondel, P. Prettenhofer, R. Weiss, V. Dubourg, J. Vanderplas, A. Passos, D. Cournapeau, M. Brucher, M. Perrot, and E. Duchesnay. 2011. Scikit-learn: Machine learning

---

[9] `https://github.com/ruidan/Unsupervised-Aspect-Extraction`

in Python. *Journal of Machine Learning Research*, 12:2825–2830.

Maria Pontiki, Dimitris Galanis, Haris Papageorgiou, Ion Androutsopoulos, Suresh Manandhar, Mohammad AL-Smadi, Mahmoud Al-Ayyoub, Yanyan Zhao, Bing Qin, Orphee De Clercq, Veronique Hoste, Marianna Apidianaki, Xavier Tannier, Natalia Loukachevitch, Evgeniy Kotelnikov, Núria Bel, Salud María Jiménez-Zafra, and Gülşen Eryiğit. 2016. Semeval-2016 task 5: Aspect based sentiment analysis. In *Proceedings of SemEval*.

Radim Řehůřek and Petr Sojka. 2010. Software Framework for Topic Modelling with Large Corpora. In *Proceedings of the LREC 2010 Workshop on New Challenges for NLP Frameworks*.

Hinrich Schütze. 1998. Automatic word sense discrimination. *Computational Linguistics*, 24:97–123.

Ivan Titov and Ryan McDonald. 2008. Modeling online reviews with multi-grain topic models. In *Proceedings of WWW*.

Jason Weston, Samy Bengio, and Nicolas Usunier. 2011. Wsabie: Scaling up to large vocabulary image annotation. In *Proceedings of IJCAI*.

Wayne Xin Zhao, Jing Jiang, Hongfei Yan, and Xiaoming Li. 2010. Jointly modeling aspects and opinions with a maxent-lda hybrid. In *Proceedings of EMNLP*.

SystemT: Declarative Text Understanding for Enterprise

Laura Chiticariu[†] **Marina Danilevsky**[‡] **Yunyao Li**[‡] **Frederick R. Reiss**[‡] **Huaiyu Zhu**[‡]

[†]IBM Watson   [‡]IBM Research - Almaden

650 Harry Rd

San Jose, CA 95120

`{chiti,mdanile,yunyaoli,frreiss,huaiyu}@us.ibm.com`

Abstract

The rise of enterprise applications over unstructured and semi-structured documents poses new challenges to text understanding systems across multiple dimensions. We present SystemT, a declarative text understanding system that addresses these challenges and has been deployed in a wide range of enterprise applications. We highlight the design considerations and decisions behind SystemT in addressing the needs of the enterprise setting. We also summarize the impact of SystemT on business and education.

1 Introduction

With the proliferation of information in unstructured and semi-structured form, text understanding (TU) is becoming a fundamental building block in enterprise applications. Numerous tools, algorithms and APIs have been developed to address various text understanding sub-tasks, ranging from low-level text tasks (e.g., tokenization) and core natural language processing (e.g., syntactic and semantic parsing) to higher-level tasks such as document classification, entity and relation extraction, and sentiment analysis. Real world applications usually require several such components.

As an example, consider a *Financial Investment Research Analysis* application, which leverages financial market analyst reports such as the one in Fig. 1 to inform automatic trading and financial recommendations. Information is conveyed in both natural language (e.g., "*We thus downgrade US and global HY credits*") and tabular form, requiring both natural language understanding primitives (e.g., syntactic or semantic parsing) and document structure understanding primitives (e.g., table titles, row and column headers, and the association of table cells and headers). Furthermore, the business problem involves higher-level tasks such

High valuation risk to HY credits – look for opportunities elsewhere

Economic growth remains strong and synchronised across both DM and EM economies. This is a positive environment for risk assets. However, pricing is becoming increasingly stretched in a number of markets. For US and global HY credits, although default and downgrade risks are low, our measure of implied credit risk premia (compensation for bearing credit risk) has compressed even further. The margin of safety is very thin. We thus downgrade US and global HY credits from neutral to underweight.

Equities			Government bonds		
Asset class	View	View Move	Asset class	View	View Move
Global	OW	--	Developed Market (DM)	UW	--
US	N	--	US	UW	--
UK	N	--	UK	UW	--
Eurozone	OW	--	Eurozone	UW	--
Japan	OW	--	Japan	UW	--
Emerging Markets (EM)	OW	--	EM (local currency)	OW	--
CEE & Latam	N	--			

Figure 1: Fragment of investment report.

as financial entity extraction (e.g., equities, bonds, currencies) in natural language and tabular forms, and sentiment analysis for such entities.

While approaches for solving individual TU sub-tasks have proliferated, considerably less effort has been dedicated to developing systems that enable building end-to-end TU applications in a principled, systematic and replicable fashion. In the absence of such systems, building a TU application involves piecing together individual components in an *ad hoc* fashion, usually requiring custom code to address the impedance mismatch in data models between the different components, and to bridge gaps in functionality. Different implementations of the same application may yield vastly different runtime performance characteristics as well as, even more worryingly, different output semantics. For example, two developers may make disparate assumptions implementing even such a seemingly simple text operation as dictionary matching: Should dictionary terms match the input text only on token boundaries, or is matching allowed in the middle of a token? Which tokenization approach should be used? Is matching case sensitive or insensitive? In an enter-

Proceedings of NAACL-HLT 2018, pages 76–83

New Orleans, Louisiana, June 1 - 6, 2018. ©2017 Association for Computational Linguistics

prise environment, such *ad-hoc* approaches produce code repositories that are difficult to understand, maintain, reuse in new applications, or optimize for runtime performance.

This paper presents SystemT, an industrial-strength system for developing end-to-end TU applications in a declarative fashion. SystemT was developed at IBM Research and has been widely adopted inside and outside IBM (Sec. 4) Borrowing ideas from database systems, commonly used text operations are abstracted away as built-in operators with clean, well-specified semantics and highly optimized internal implementations, and exposed through a formal declarative language called AQL *(Annotation Query Language)*. Fig. 2 illustrates a fragment of AQL for extracting financial entities and associated sentiment from financial reports as in Fig. 1. The snippet illustrates several types of declarative TU structures (or rules) expressible in AQL, including sequential structures (*AssetClass*), semantic understanding structures (*RecommendationNU*), and table understanding structures (*RecommendationTable*). The rules leverage built-in text operators readily available in AQL, including dictionary matching (*AssetClassSuffixes*), core NLP operators such as Semantic Role Labeling (SRL) (*Verbs*, *Arguments*), and document structure operators such as table structure understanding (*AllCells*). Sec. 3 details the data model and semantics of AQL.

Architecture Overview. As illustrated in (Fig. 3), SystemT consists of two major components: the *Compiler* and the *Runtime*.

The *Compiler* takes as input a TU program specified in AQL and compiles it into an execution plan. AQL is a purely declarative language: the developer specifies *what* should be extracted, but not *how* to do it. The *Optimizer* computes the *how* automatically by enumerating multiple logical equivalent plans, and choosing a plan with the least estimated cost. Since each operator has well-specified semantics, the Optimizer can automatically determine when operators can be reordered, merged, or even discarded without affecting the output semantics, while significantly increasing the runtime performance of the TU program. The *Operator Graph* captures the execution plan generated by the *Optimizer* and is used by the *Runtime* to decide the actual sequence of operations.

The *Runtime* is a lightweight engine that loads the *Operator Graph* and then processes inputs

```
create dictionary AssetClassSuffixes
    with lemma_match
    as ('bond', 'credit', 'equity');

create view AssetClassSuffix as
    extract dictionary 'AssetClassSuffixes' on D.text as span
    from Document D;

create view AssetClass as
    extract pattern <G.span> <Token>{0,1} <S.span> as span
    from GeoRegion G, AssetClassSuffix S;

create dictionary RecommendVerbs as ('upgrade', 'downgrade');

create table PolarityAdj (polarity Text, adj Text)
    as values
    ('negative', 'underweight'),
    ('negative', 'UW'),
    ('neutral', 'neutral'),
    ('neutral', 'N'),
    ('positive', 'overweight'),
    ('positive', 'OW');

create view RecommendationNU as
    select E.span as entity, P.polarity
    from Verbs V, Arguments A, Contexts C, AssetClass E, PolarityAdj P
    where Equals (V.id, A.verbId)
        and Equals (V.id, C.verbId)
        and Contains (A.span, E.span)
        and MatchesDict(V.verbBase, 'RecommendVerbs')
        and Equals(C.type, 'to')
        and Equals(GetText(C.span), P.adj);

create view RecommendationTable as
    select C1.span as entity, P.polarity
    from AllCells C1, AllCells C2, PolarityAdj P
    where Equals(C1.colHeader,'Asset class')
        and Equals(C2.colHeader,'View')
        and Equals(C1.rowId, C2.rowId)
        and Equals(GetText(C2.span), P.adj);
```

Figure 2: Example AQL specifications expressing a sequential structure (*AssetClass*), a semantic structure (*RecommendationNU*) and a table structure (*RecommendationTable*). (Simplified for presentation.)

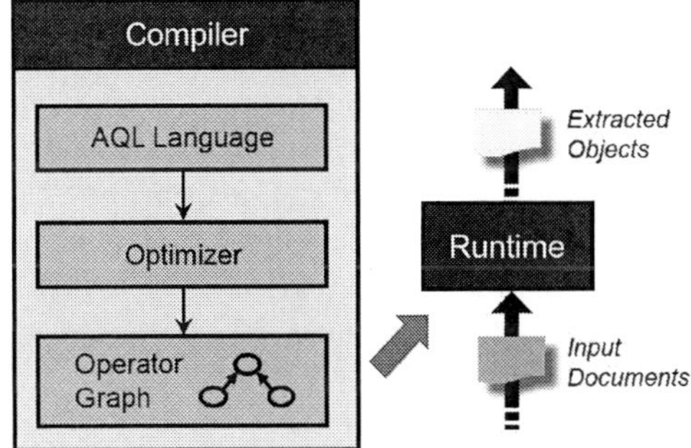

Figure 3: SystemT Overall Architecture

document-at-a-time (DAAT), with the text and metadata of each document acting like a separate "database" from the perspective of the AQL rules. This DAAT model speeds up join and aggregation operations within a document, as the entire document's data is in memory. It also simplifies scale-out processing and can be scaled up by utilizing multithreading and multiple processes, as well as various cluster and cloud environments.

Related Work. SystemT's declarative approach is a departure from other rule-based TU systems. Early systems (Cunningham et al., 2000; Boguraev, 2003; Drozdzynski et al., 2004) are based on the Common Pattern Specification Language (CPSL) (Appelt and Onyshkevych, 1998), a cascading grammar formalism where the input text is viewed as a sequence of annotations, and extraction rules are written as pattern/action rules over the lexical features of these annotations. Each grammar consists of a set of rules evaluated in a left-to-right fashion over the input annotations, with multiple grammars cascaded together and evaluated bottom-up.

As discussed in (Chiticariu et al., 2010), grammar-based systems suffer from two fundamental limitations: expressivity and performance. Formal studies of AQL semantics have shown that AQL is strictly more expressive than regular expression-based languages such as CPSL (Sec. 3.2.5). Furthermore, the rigid evaluation order imposed in grammar-based systems has significant runtime performance implications, as the system is effectively forced into a fixed pipeline execution strategy, leaving little opportunity for global optimization. While the expressivity of grammar-based systems has been extended in different ways, such as additional built-in constructs (Boguraev, 2003; Drozdzynski et al., 2004; Cunningham et al., 2000), or allowing a mix of sequential patterns and rules over dependency parse trees (Valenzuela-Escárcega et al., 2016), such extensions do not fundamentally address the inherent expressivity and performance limitations due to the intertwining of rule language semantics and execution strategy. In contrast, SystemT's declarative approach enables the optimizer to explore a variety of execution plans, resulting in orders of magnitude higher throughput and a lower memory footprint (Chiticariu et al., 2010).

2 Requirements for Enterprise TU

While the traditional accuracy requirement remains important, emerging enterprising applications introduce additional requirements for enterprise-scale TU systems.

Scalability. Compared to conventional TU task corpora, such as those available via the Linguistic Data Consortium, enterprise TU corpora comprise much larger volumes of data from a wider variety of sources, ranging from user-created content and public data, to proprietary data such as call-center logs. The TU system must scale for both documents (e.g., a single financial report runs in the tens of MBs) and document collections (e.g., 500 million new tweets posted daily on Twitter; terabytes of system logs produced hourly in a medium-size data center).

Expressivity. Enterprise TU must handle an ample variety of functionalities required by different enterprise applications, from known natural language processing tasks such as entity extraction to more practical challenges such as table structure understanding. Data may come from plain text, semi-structured text (e.g., HTML or XML), or the conversion of a binary format (PDF, Word) to text. Different degrees of noise may be present, from manually introduced noise such as typos and acronyms (e.g., in tweets) to systematic errors such as those resulting from format conversion.

Transparency. Enterprise TU must be transparent and enable ease of comprehension, debugging and enhancement, to avoid TU development becoming the bottleneck for building enterprise applications. Furthermore, as the underlying data or application requirements change, it must be easy to adapt existing TU programs in response.

Extensibility. Enterprise TU, no matter how well designed, might not provide all of the capabilities required by a real-world use case out-of-the-box. As such, it should be extensible to gracefully handle tasks that are not natively supported.

3 SystemT Highlights

We now describe the key design considerations and decisions behind SystemT and discuss how they help address the requirements in Sec. 2.

3.1 Preliminaries

Data model. AQL operates over a simple relational data model with three basic data structures: *field value*, *tuple*, and *view*. A tuple (aka an *annotation*) consists of a list of named and typed fields. The field values can be of the text-specific type *span*, representing a region of text within a document identified by its "begin" and "end" positions, or any of a collection of familiar data types such as *text*, *integer*, *scalar List*, and *null* (with 3-value logic, similar to SQL). A view is a set of tuples with the same schema (field name and field type).

Statements and modules. Each AQL statement defines a view as the result of some operations on one or more other views, which are defined by previous statements. A special view called *Document* is created automatically, which contains a single tuple with the document text. AQL code is organized in modules which provide a namespace for the views. The modules are compiled. At run time the modules are loaded on demand and executed.

3.2 Expressivity

AQL[1] is similar in syntax to the database language SQL, chosen for its expressivity and its familiarity to enterprise developers. It provides a number of TU constructs, including primitive extraction operators for finding parts of speech, matches of regular expressions and dictionaries, as well as set operators such as sequence, union, filter and consolidate. Each operator implements a single basic atomic operation, producing and consuming sets of tuples. AQL developers create TU programs by composing these operators together into sets of rules, or statements.

3.2.1 Basic Primitives

Three of the most basic operators of AQL include: *Extract* ($\mathcal{E}$) performs character level operations such as regular expression and dictionary matching over text, creating a tuple for each match.
Select (τ) applies a predicate to a set of tuples, and outputs all those tuples that satisfy the predicate.
Join ($\bowtie$) applies a predicate to pairs of tuples from two sets of input tuples, outputting all pairs that satisfy the predicate.

AQL also provides a sequence pattern notation, similar in its grammar-like syntax to that of CPSL (Appelt and Onyshkevych, 1998), which is translated internally into one or more select and extract statements. Other operators include *Detag* for removing HTML tags and retaining the locations of important HTML metadata such as section, lists and table markup, *PartOfSpeech* for part-of-speech detection, *Consolidate* for removing overlapping annotations, *Block* and *Group* for grouping together similar annotations occurring within close proximity to each other, as well as expressing more general types of aggregation, *Sort* and *Limit* for sorting and truncating output, and *Union* and *Minus* for expressing set union and set difference, respectively. Rules can also be easily customized to particular TU domains using external dictionary and table structures, which can be rapidly populated with relevant terms without the need to alter existing AQL code.

3.2.2 Advanced Primitives

SystemT has built-in multilingual support including tokenization, part of speech and lemmatization for over 20 languages. TU developers can utilize the multilingual support via AQL without having to configure or manage any additional resources. Language expansion is enabled as described in Sec. 3.4. SystemT also has advanced primitives for semantic role labeling (SRL), the task of labeling predicate-argument structure in sentences with shallow semantic information. Such advanced primitives enable the creation of cross-lingual TU programs (see, e.g., (Akbik et al., 2016).)

3.2.3 Extensions with Pre-Built Libraries

Corpora can introduce a variety of additional TU challenges, including having a high degree of noise (e.g., non-standard word forms or informal usage patterns), exposing data through non-free-text structures (e.g., tables), or existing in a difficult-to-digest format (e.g., PDF). We have extended the functionality of SystemT by creating pre-built libraries with advanced TU capabilities such as text normalization (Baldwin and Li, 2015), semantic table processing (Chen et al., 2017), and document format conversion.

3.2.4 An AQL Example

As discussed in Sec.1, Fig. 2 shows AQL snippets for extracting sentiment around financial assets from investment reports such as the one in Fig. 1. View *AssetClass* identifies financial entities using syntactic constructs: a geographical region followed within 0 to 1 tokens by a common suffix (e.g., 'credits', 'equities').

View *RecommendationNU* uses semantic parse primitives to identify recommendations expressed in natural language such as *'We downgrade ... from neutral to underweight'*. In order to assign the correct polarity to *'underweight'* and *'neutral'*, SRL information exposed in views *Verbs*, *Arguments* and *Contexts* is joined with the view *AssetClass* and the AQL table *PolarityAdj*, mapping domain terminology (e.g., *'UW'*, *'underweight'*) to sentiment polarities. The view uses several AQL built-in join and selection predicates (equality, span containment, dictionary matching.)

Finally, view *RecommendationTable* identifies recommendations present in tabular form. It leverages table semantic understanding primitives exposed through the view *AllCells*, which connects the span of each table cell with additional row and column metadata such as row and column ids and headers. *RecommendationTable* identifies all cells that appear in the same row under specific column headers, and assigns polarity using *PolarityAdj*.

---

[1]AQL manual: `https://ibm.biz/BdZpjX`.

3.2.5 Formal Analysis

Fagin *et al* (Fagin et al., 2013, 2016) formalized the semantics of relational-based extraction languages like AQL with the theoretical framework *document spanners*. The initial paper showed that a restricted version of document spanners are broadly equivalent in expressivity to regular-expression-based languages such as CPSL. The follow-on paper described how *consolidation*, a facility also supported by SystemT for addressing overlapping spans in intermediate results, extends the expressivity of the spanners framework.

3.3 Scalability

SystemT is architected to achieve scalability along three dimensions: (1) Cost-based Optimizer to select the most efficient execution plan for a given declarative specification and input documents; (2) Document-centric Runtime engine, scalable by trivial parallelization, leveraging the advances in parallel computing (e.g., via Hadoop/Spark); (3) Hardware acceleration for sped up computation.

3.3.1 Optimizer

Internally, the declarative AQL specification compiles into an algebra consisting of individual operators with well-specified semantics and properties that compose to form an execution plan. The SystemT Optimizer chooses an efficient execution plan among all possible equivalent execution plans for a given AQL specification. The Optimizer is inspired by relational query optimizers, which have been operational in commercial database systems for over 40 years (Astrahan et al., 1979), with one important difference: While SQL optimizers are designed to minimize I/O costs, the SystemT Optimizer focuses on minimizing CPU-intensive text operations. We briefly describe the two classes of optimization techniques used, and refer the reader to (Reiss et al., 2008) for a detailed description.

Cost-based optimizations are used to select an efficient join ordering for AQL statements that join two or more relations (as in Fig. 2). The search algorithm uses dynamic programming to build up larger sub-plan candidates from smaller sub-plans. The Optimizer uses a text-centric cost model to estimate the execution time of each operator based on the input size, selectivity of the join predicate, and choice of join algorithm.

Rewrite-based optimizations include plan rewrites known to always speed up the execution time, including (1) text-centric optimizations such as Shared Dictionary Matching and Shared Regex Matching, which group multiple dictionaries or regular expressions together to be executed in a single pass over the document; and (2) relational-style query rewrites, such as pushing down select and project operators.

3.3.2 Runtime

The SystemT Runtime engine is architected as a compact in-memory embeddable Java library (<2 MB). It is purely document-centric, leaving the storage of document collections and extracted artifacts to the embedding application. The engine exposes two low-level Java APIs: (1) *instantiate()* creates an *OperatorGraph instance*, an in-memory representation of the execution plan generated by the Optimizer, and (2) *execute()* takes as input an in-memory representation of the input document and returns an in-memory representation of the objects extracted from that document. The APIs are reentrant and thread safe. The *execute()* API is multithreaded (a single OperatorGraph instance can be used simultaneously by multiple threads, each annotating a different document.)

This document-centric in-memory design has provided the flexibility necessary to embed the SystemT Runtime in a variety of environments, including: (1) Big Data platforms (e.g., Hadoop, Spark) (2) Cloud platforms (e.g., Kubernetes), and (3) custom applications. We enable SystemT in Big Data and Cloud platforms by providing platform-specific APIs that mirror the low-level Java APIs, but are tailored to the platform's compute and data models. Custom applications not built on Big Data or Cloud platforms (e.g., a desktop email client, a travel app, or a compliance program) can embed the SystemT runtime in any way suitable for the application.

3.3.3 Hardware Acceleration

The separation of specification from implementation has the added advantage that new hardware can be relatively easy to take advantage of, with no changes in the declarative specification of the program. For example, recent work on hardware acceleration for low level text operators such as regular expressions (Atasu et al., 2013) can be leveraged by extending the Optimizer's search space and cost model to incorporate alternative hardware implementations of individual operators and associated cost model (Polig et al., 2018).

```
create function classifyPolarity (
 firstArg table(entity String,
             polarity String,
             numPolarity Integer) as locator)
return table( entity String, docLevelPolarity String)
external_name
'udfs/udf.jar:udf.ClassifyTableFn!eval'
language java
deterministic
called on null input;
```

(a) Declaring UDF Function

```
create view RecommendationAll as
    (select R.entity, R.polarity
        from RecommendationNU R)
    union all
    (select R.entity, R.polarity
        from RecommendationTable R);

create view RecommendationFeatures as
select GetText(E.entity) as entity, R.polarity,
        Count(E.polarity) as numPolarity
from RecommendationAll R
group by GetText(E.entity), R.polarity;

create view RecommendationDocLevel as
select T.entity, T.polarity
from classifyPolarity(RecommendationFeatures) T;
```

(b) Using UDF Function

Figure 4: Example UDF function: document-level sentiment classification

3.4 Extensibility

SystemT has been built with extensibility in mind. With a grey-box design, users are able to extend its capabilities via the following mechanisms.

User-Defined Functions (UDFs) can be defined to extend AQL by performing operations that are not supported natively by SystemT. Using a UDF requires three simple steps: (1) Implementing the function in Java or PMML; (2) Declaring it in AQL; and (3) Using it in AQL. Fig. 4 illustrates how to extend AQL to support a simple document-level sentiment classifier for asset classes using features extracted with sentiment extractors defined earlier in Sec. 3.2.4. The example illustrates several other AQL constructs, including unioning, grouping and counting annotations.

NLP Primitive API. Low-level language-dependent primitives such as tokenization, part-of-speech tagging, lemmatization or semantic role labeling are pluggable through an internal API, and automatically exposed to all AQL constructs. For example, the matching of *AssetClassSuffixes* dictionary on lemma form in Fig. 2 is enabled by the underlying tokenizer and lemmatizer for the given language. This has two advantages: (1) isolating language-dependent primitives from the rest of the system, without requiring changes to the AQL language itself; and (2) leveraging newer primitive models as they become available, without requiring changes to existing AQL programs.

3.5 Transparency and Machine Learning

A common criticism of pure machine learning (ML) systems in the enterprise world is that statistical models are opaque to the application using them, making the results difficult to explain or be quickly fixed (Chiticariu et al., 2013). SystemT addresses this challenge by using a declarative language for specifying the TU program. Since the results are produced by constructs with well-understood semantics, it is possible to automatically generate explanations of why a certain output was or was not produced.

At the same time, SystemT has the flexibility to leverage ML techniques in the context of its overall declarative framework in two dimensions. First, primitive APIs and the user-defined interface (Sec. 3.4) allow for plugging in low-level NLP primitives, as well as trained models for higher-level tasks such as entity extraction. The former makes NLP primitives available to all AQL constructs. The latter allows AQL specifications to provide features to the model, post-process the result of the model, or use the model as building block in solving a higher-level task. Second, ML techniques are leveraged to learn AQL programs, thereby generating a deterministic, transparent model in lieu of a probabilistic one. Such algorithms can be incorporated in the SystemT IDEs (Sec. 3.6) to speed up AQL development.

3.6 Integrated Development Environments

SystemT provides integrated development environments (IDEs) designed for a wide spectrum of users. The professional IDE allows expert developers to create complex TU programs in AQL (Li et al., 2012). The visual IDE enables novice users and non-programmers to construct drag-and-drop TU programs without learning AQL (Li et al., 2015). Both IDEs leverage ML and human-computer interaction techniques as those summarized in (Chiticariu et al., 2015) to support typical development life cycles of TU tasks (Fig. 5).

3.7 Empirical Evaluation

In addition to theoretical studies of AQL expressivity and runtime performance, we have also evaluated SystemT empirically on multiple TU tasks. We show that extractors built in AQL yield results of comparable quality to the best published results

Domain	Application
Compliance	Multilingual named entity extraction for document retention
	Element extraction and classification in legal documents (e.g. contract, regulations)
	Named entity extraction for document retention and regulation compliance
Email/Online Chat	Entity and event extraction in emails and online chat for AI assistant
	Named entity extraction in emails for search
Finance	Extracting financial information from public records to estimate the true cost of water
	Extracting company fundamentals (e.g. financial metrics and key personnel) from regulatory filings to create a knowledge base
General domain	Building text understanding programs for entity extraction and sentiment analysis
	Building text understanding programs
Life science	Extracting features (e.g. entities and relations) from life science literature to speed up the discovery of new drugs
Material science	Extracting entities and relations from natural language and tables in material science literature to speed up the discovery for new materials
Security and privacy	Personal information extraction and redaction for security and privacy
Social media	Sentiment analysis over social media for indepth understanding of social behavior
Travel	Extracting information and sentiment from online reviews to build AI assist for travel

Table 1: Partial list of SystemT applications

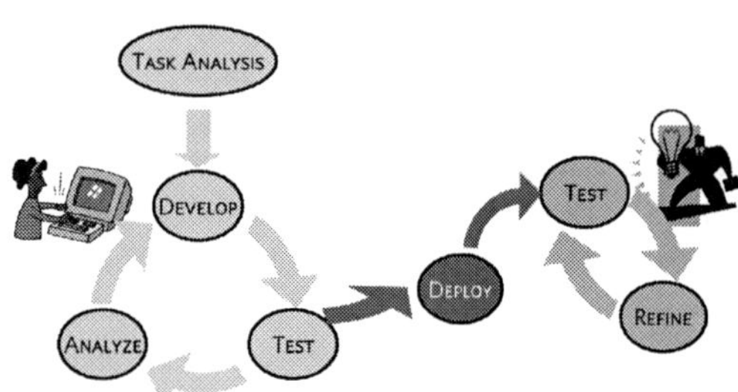

Figure 5: Development life cycles using SystemT

on several competition datasets, while achieving orders of magnitude speed-up in processing time, and requiring smaller memory utilization (Krishnamurthy et al., 2009; Chiticariu et al., 2010; Nagesh et al., 2012; Wang et al., 2017).

4 Impact of SystemT

Business Impact. Started as a research prototype, SystemT has been widely adopted within IBM and its clients. It is embedded in over 10 commercial product offerings and used in numerous internal and external projects[2] for a wide variety of enterprise applications, a small subset of which is highlighted in Table 1.

Research Impact. Various aspects of SystemT have been published in 40+ major research conferences and journals in diverse areas, including natural language processing, database systems, artificial intelligence and human-computer interaction. This is the first time that all aspects of the system, including design considerations and current functionality, are described in a single paper.

Education Impact. SystemT is available to teachers and students under a free academic license. We have developed a full graduate-level course on text understanding using SystemT, which has been taught in several universities. A version of this class has been made available[3] as a MOOC with 10,000+ students enrolled in less than 18 months.

5 Conclusion

In this paper, we discuss new challenges posed by enterprise applications to text understanding (TU) systems. We present SystemT, an industrial-strength system for developing end-to-end TU applications in a declarative fashion. We highlight the key design decisions and discuss how they help meet the needs of the enterprise setting. SystemT has been used to build enterprise applications in a wide range of domains, and is publicly available for commercial and academic usage.

References

Alan Akbik, Laura Chiticariu, Marina Danilevsky, Yonas Kbrom, Yunyao Li, and Huaiyu Zhu. 2016. Multilingual information extraction with PolyglotIE. In *COLING'16*.

Douglas E. Appelt and Boyan Onyshkevych. 1998. The common pattern specification language. In *Pro-*

---

[2] Example products exposing or embedding SystemT include: IBM BigInsights, IBM Streams, IBM Watson for Drug Discovery

[3] https://cognitiveclass.ai/learn/text_analytics/

ceedings of a Workshop held at Baltimore, Maryland, October 13-15, 1998, TIPSTER '98, pages 23–30.

Morton M. Astrahan, Mike W. Blasgen, Donald D. Chamberlin, Jim Gray, W. Frank King III, Bruce G. Lindsay, Raymond A. Lorie, James W. Mehl, Thomas G. Price, Gianfranco R. Putzolu, Mario Schkolnick, Patricia G. Selinger, Donald R. Slutz, H. Raymond Strong, Paolo Tiberio, Irving L. Traiger, Bradford W. Wade, and Robert A. Yost. 1979. System R: A relational data base management system. *IEEE Computer*, 12(5):42–48.

Kubilay Atasu, Raphael Polig, Christoph Hagleitner, and Frederick R. Reiss. 2013. Hardware-accelerated regular expression matching for high-throughput text analytics. In *FPL 2013*, pages 1–7.

Tyler Baldwin and Yunyao Li. 2015. An in-depth analysis of the effect of text normalization in social media. In *HLT-NAACL*, pages 420–429.

Branimir Boguraev. 2003. Annotation-based finite state processing in a large-scale nlp arhitecture. In *RANLP*, pages 61–80.

Xilun Chen, Laura Chiticariu, Marina Danilevsky, Alexandre Evfimievski, and Prithviraj Sen. 2017. A rectangle mining method for understanding the semantics of financial tables. In *International Conference on Document Analysis and Recognition (IC-DAR)*.

Laura Chiticariu, Rajasekar Krishnamurthy, Yunyao Li, Sriram Raghavan, Frederick R. Reiss, and Shivakumar Vaithyanathan. 2010. Systemt: An algebraic approach to declarative information extraction. ACL '10, pages 128–137.

Laura Chiticariu, Yunyao Li, and Frederick Reiss. 2015. Transparent machine learning for information extraction: State-of-the-art and the future. In *EMNLP*.

Laura Chiticariu, Yunyao Li, and Frederick R. Reiss. 2013. Rule-based information extraction is dead! long live rule-based information extraction systems! In *EMNLP 2013*, pages 827–832.

H. Cunningham, D. Maynard, and V. Tablan. 2000. JAPE: a Java Annotation Patterns Engine (Second Edition). Research Memorandum CS–00–10, Department of Computer Science, University of Sheffield.

Witold Drozdzynski, Hans-Ulrich Krieger, Jakub Piskorski, Ulrich Schäfer, and Feiyu Xu. 2004. Shallow processing with unification and typed feature structures — foundations and applications. *Künstliche Intelligenz*, 1:17–23.

Ronald Fagin, Benny Kimelfeld, Frederick Reiss, and Stijn Vansummeren. 2013. Spanners: a formal framework for information extraction. In *PODS 2013*, pages 37–48.

Ronald Fagin, Benny Kimelfeld, Frederick Reiss, and Stijn Vansummeren. 2016. A relational framework for information extraction. *SIGMOD Rec.*, 44(4):5–16.

Rajasekar Krishnamurthy, Yunyao Li, Sriram Raghavan, Frederick Reiss, Shivakumar Vaithyanathan, and Huaiyu Zhu. 2009. Systemt: A system for declarative information extraction. *SIGMOD Rec.*, 37(4):7–13.

Yunyao Li, Laura Chiticariu, Huahai Yang, Frederick Reiss, and Arnaldo Carreno-fuentes. 2012. WizIE: A best practices guided development environment for information extraction. In *ACL 2012 System Demonstrations*, pages 109–114.

Yunyao Li, Elmer Kim, Marc A. Touchette, Ramiya Venkatachalam, and Hao Wang. 2015. VINERy: A visual ide for information extraction. *Proc. VLDB Endow.*, 8(12):1948–1951.

Ajay Nagesh, Ganesh Ramakrishnan, Laura Chiticariu, Rajasekar Krishnamurthy, Ankush Dharkar, and Pushpak Bhattacharyya. 2012. Towards efficient named-entity rule induction for customizability. EMNLP-CoNLL '12, pages 128–138.

Raphael Polig, Kubilay Atasu, Heiner Giefers, Christoph Hagleitner, Laura Chiticariu, Frederick Reiss, Huaiyu Zhu, and Peter Hofstee. 2018. A hardware compilation framework for text analytics queries. *J. Parallel Distrib. Comput.*, 111:260–272.

Frederick Reiss, Sriram Raghavan, Rajasekar Krishnamurthy, Huaiyu Zhu, and Shivakumar Vaithyanathan. 2008. An algebraic approach to rule-based information extraction. In *ICDE 2008*, pages 933–942.

Marco Antonio Valenzuela-Escárcega, Gus Hahn-Powell, and Mihai Surdeanu. 2016. Odin's runes: A rule language for information extraction. In *LREC*. European Language Resources Association (ELRA).

Chenguang Wang, Doug Burdick, Laura Chiticariu, Rajasekar Krishnamurthy, Yunyao Li, and Huaiyu Zhu. 2017. Towards re-defining relation understanding in financial domain. In *DSMM'17*, pages 8:1–8:6.

Construction of the Literature Graph in Semantic Scholar

Waleed Ammar, Dirk Groeneveld, Chandra Bhagavatula, Iz Beltagy, Miles Crawford,
Doug Downey,[†] Jason Dunkelberger, Ahmed Elgohary, Sergey Feldman, Vu Ha,
Rodney Kinney, Sebastian Kohlmeier, Kyle Lo, Tyler Murray, Hsu-Han Ooi,
Matthew Peters, Joanna Power, Sam Skjonsberg, Lucy Lu Wang, Chris Wilhelm,
Zheng Yuan,[†] Madeleine van Zuylen, and Oren Etzioni
`waleeda@allenai.org`

Allen Institute for Artificial Intelligence, Seattle WA 98103, USA
[†]Northwestern University, Evanston IL 60208, USA

Abstract

We describe a deployed scalable system for organizing published scientific literature into a heterogeneous graph to facilitate algorithmic manipulation and discovery. The resulting literature graph consists of more than 280M nodes, representing papers, authors, entities and various interactions between them (e.g., authorships, citations, entity mentions). We reduce literature graph construction into familiar NLP tasks (e.g., entity extraction and linking), point out research challenges due to differences from standard formulations of these tasks, and report empirical results for each task. The methods described in this paper are used to enable semantic features in `www.semanticscholar.org`.

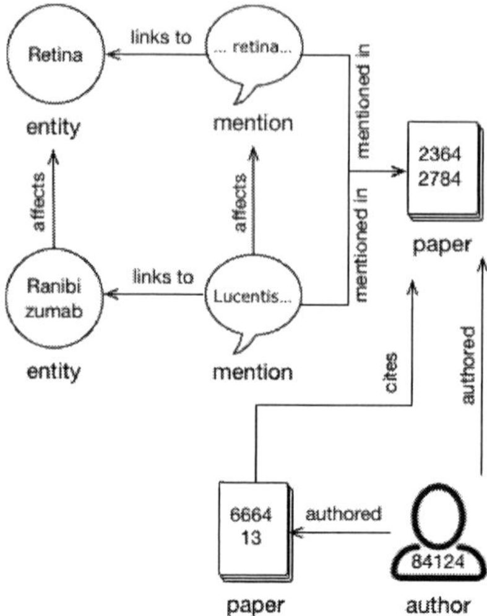

Figure 1: Part of the literature graph.

1 Introduction

The goal of this work is to facilitate algorithmic discovery in the scientific literature. Despite notable advances in scientific search engines, data mining and digital libraries (e.g., Wu et al., 2014), researchers remain unable to answer simple questions such as:

- What is the percentage of female subjects in depression clinical trials?

- Which of my co-authors published one or more papers on coreference resolution?

- Which papers discuss the effects of Ranibizumab on the Retina?

In this paper, we focus on the problem of extracting structured data from scientific documents, which can later be used in natural language interfaces (e.g., Iyer et al., 2017) or to improve ranking of results in academic search (e.g., Xiong et al.,

2017). We describe methods used in a scalable deployed production system for extracting structured information from scientific documents into *the literature graph* (see Fig. 1). The literature graph is a directed property graph which summarizes key information in the literature and can be used to answer the queries mentioned earlier as well as more complex queries. For example, in order to compute the Erdős number of an author X, the graph can be queried to find the number of nodes on the shortest undirected path between author X and Paul Erdős such that all edges on the path are labeled "authored".

We reduce literature graph construction into familiar NLP tasks such as sequence labeling, entity linking and relation extraction, and address some of the impractical assumptions commonly made in the standard formulations of these tasks. For example, most research on named entity recognition tasks report results on large labeled datasets such as CoNLL-2003 and ACE-2005 (e.g., Lample et al.,

84

Proceedings of NAACL-HLT 2018, pages 84–91
New Orleans, Louisiana, June 1 - 6, 2018. ©2017 Association for Computational Linguistics

2016), and assume that entity types in the test set match those labeled in the training set (including work on domain adaptation, e.g., Daumé, 2007). These assumptions, while useful for developing and benchmarking new methods, are unrealistic for many domains and applications. The paper also serves as an overview of the approach we adopt at www.semanticscholar.org in a step towards more intelligent academic search engines (Etzioni, 2011).

In the next section, we start by describing our symbolic representation of the literature. Then, we discuss how we extract metadata associated with a paper such as authors and references, then how we extract the entities mentioned in paper text. Before we conclude, we briefly describe other research challenges we are actively working on in order to improve the quality of the literature graph.

2 Structure of The Literature Graph

The literature graph is a *property graph* with directed edges. Unlike Resource Description Framework (RDF) graphs, nodes and edges in property graphs have an internal structure which is more suitable for representing complex data types such as papers and entities. In this section, we describe the attributes associated with nodes and edges of different types in the literature graph.

2.1 Node Types

Papers. We obtain metadata and PDF files of papers via partnerships with publishers (e.g., Springer, Nature), catalogs (e.g., DBLP, MED-LINE), pre-publishing services (e.g., arXiv, bioRxive), as well as web-crawling. Paper nodes are associated with a set of attributes such as 'title', 'abstract', 'full text', 'venues' and 'publication year'. While some of the paper sources provide these attributes as metadata, it is often necessary to extract them from the paper PDF (details in §3). We deterministically remove duplicate papers based on string similarity of their metadata, resulting in 37M unique paper nodes. Papers in the literature graph cover a variety of scientific disciplines, including computer science, molecular biology, microbiology and neuroscience.

Authors. Each node of this type represents a unique author, with attributes such as 'first name' and 'last name'. The literature graph has 12M nodes of this type.

Entities. Each node of this type represents a unique scientific concept discussed in the literature, with attributes such as 'canonical name', 'aliases' and 'description'. Our literature graph has 0.4M nodes of this type. We describe how we populate entity nodes in §4.3.

Entity mentions. Each node of this type represents a textual reference of an entity in one of the papers, with attributes such as 'mention text', 'context', and 'confidence'. We describe how we populate the 237M mentions in the literature graph in §4.1.

2.2 Edge Types

Citations. We instantiate a directed citation edge from paper nodes $p_1 \longrightarrow p_2$ for each p_2 referenced in p_1. Citation edges have attributes such as 'from paper id', 'to paper id' and 'contexts' (the textual contexts where p_2 is referenced in p_1). While some of the paper sources provide these attributes as metadata, it is often necessary to extract them from the paper PDF as detailed in §3.

Authorship. We instantiate a directed authorship edge between an author node and a paper node $a \longrightarrow p$ for each author of that paper.

Entity linking edges. We instantiate a directed edge from an extracted entity mention node to the entity it refers to.

Mention–mention relations. We instantiate a directed edge between a pair of mentions in the same sentential context if the textual relation extraction model predicts one of a predefined list of relation types between them in a sentential context.[1] We encode a symmetric relation between m_1 and m_2 as two directed edges $m_1 \longrightarrow m_2$ and $m_2 \longrightarrow m_1$.

Entity–entity relations. While mention–mention edges represent relations between mentions in a particular context, entity–entity edges represent relations between abstract entities. These relations may be imported from an existing knowledge base (KB) or inferred from other edges in the graph.

3 Extracting Metadata

In the previous section, we described the overall structure of the literature graph. Next, we discuss how we populate paper nodes, author nodes, authorship edges, and citation edges.

---

[1]Due to space constraints, we opted not to discuss our relation extraction models in this draft.

Although some publishers provide sufficient metadata about their papers, many papers are provided with incomplete metadata. Also, papers obtained via web-crawling are not associated with any metadata. To fill in this gap, we built the SCIENCEPARSE system to predict structured data from the raw PDFs using recurrent neural networks (RNNs).[2] For each paper, the system extracts the paper title, list of authors, and list of references; each reference consists of a title, a list of authors, a venue, and a year.

Preparing the input layer. We split each PDF into individual pages, and feed each page to Apache's PDFBox library[3] to convert it into a sequence of tokens, where each token has features, e.g., 'text', 'font size', 'space width', 'position on the page'.

We normalize the token-level features before feeding them as inputs to the model. For each of the 'font size' and 'space width' features, we compute three normalized values (with respect to current page, current document, and the whole training corpus), each value ranging between -0.5 to +0.5. The token's 'position on the page' is given in XY coordinate points. We scale the values linearly to range from $(-0.5, -0.5)$ at the top-left corner of the page to $(0.5, 0.5)$ at the bottom-right corner.

In order to capture case information, we add seven numeric features to the input representation of each token: whether the first/second letter is uppercase/lowercase, the fraction of uppercase/lowercase letters and the fraction of digits.

To help the model make correct predictions for metadata which tend to appear at the beginning (e.g., titles and authors) or at the end of papers (e.g., references), we provide the current page number as two discrete variables (relative to the beginning and end of the PDF file) with values 0, 1 and 2+. These features are repeated for each token on the same page.

For the k-th token in the sequence, we compute the input representation $\mathbf{i}_k$ by concatenating the numeric features, an embedding of the 'font size', and the word embedding of the lowercased token. Word embeddings are initialized with GloVe (Pennington et al., 2014).

Model. The input token representations are passed through one fully-connected layer and then

<hr>

[2]The SCIENCEPARSE libraries can be found at http://allenai.org/software/.

[3]https://pdfbox.apache.org

Field	Precision	Recall	F1
title	85.5	85.5	85.5
authors	92.1	92.1	92.1
bibliography titles	89.3	89.4	89.3
bibliography authors	97.1	97.0	97.0
bibliography venues	91.7	89.7	90.7
bibliography years	98.0	98.0	98.0

Table 1: Results of the SCIENCEPARSE system.

fed into a two-layer bidirectional LSTM (Long Short-Term Memory, Hochreiter and Schmidhuber, 1997), i.e.,

$$\overrightarrow{\mathbf{g}_k} = \text{LSTM}(\mathbf{W}\mathbf{i}_k, \overrightarrow{\mathbf{g}_{k-1}}), \mathbf{g}_k = [\overrightarrow{\mathbf{g}_k}; \overleftarrow{\mathbf{g}_k}],$$
$$\overrightarrow{\mathbf{h}_k} = \text{LSTM}(\mathbf{g}_k, \overrightarrow{\mathbf{h}_{k-1}}), \mathbf{h}_k = [\overrightarrow{\mathbf{h}_k}; \overleftarrow{\mathbf{g}_k}]$$

where W is a weight matrix, $\overleftarrow{\mathbf{g}_k}$ and $\overleftarrow{\mathbf{h}_k}$ are defined similarly to $\overrightarrow{\mathbf{g}_k}$ and $\overrightarrow{\mathbf{h}_k}$ but process token sequences in the opposite direction.

Following Collobert et al. (2011), we feed the output of the second layer $\mathbf{h}_k$ into a dense layer to predict unnormalized label weights for each token and learn label bigram feature weights (often described as a conditional random field layer when used in neural architectures) to account for dependencies between labels.

Training. The SCIENCEPARSE system is trained on a snapshot of the data at PubMed Central. It consists of 1.4M PDFs and their associated metadata, which specify the correct titles, authors, and bibliographies. We use a heuristic labeling process that finds the strings from the metadata in the tokenized PDFs to produce labeled tokens. This labeling process succeeds for 76% of the documents. The remaining documents are not used in the training process. During training, we only use pages which have at least one token with a label that is not "none".

Decoding. At test time, we use Viterbi decoding to find the most likely global sequence, with no further constraints. To get the title, we use the longest continuous sequence of tokens with the "title" label. Since there can be multiple authors, we use all continuous sequences of tokens with the "author" label as authors, but require that all authors of a paper are mentioned on the same page. If the author labels are predicted in multiple pages, we use the one with the largest number of authors.

Results. We run our final tests on a held-out set from PubMed Central, consisting of about 54K documents. The results are detailed in Table 1. We use a conservative evaluation where an instance is correct if it exactly matches the gold annotation, with no credit for partial matching.

To give an example for the type of errors our model makes, consider the paper (Wang et al., 2013) titled "Clinical review: Efficacy of antimicrobial-impregnated catheters in external ventricular drainage - a systematic review and meta-analysis." The title we extract for this paper omits the first part "Clinical review:". This is likely to be a result of the pattern "Foo: Bar Baz" appearing in many training examples with only "Bar Baz" labeled as the title.

4 Entity Extraction and Linking

In the previous section, we described how we populate the backbone of the literature graph, i.e., paper nodes, author nodes and citation edges. Next, we discuss how we populate mentions and entities in the literature graph using entity extraction and linking on the paper text. In order to focus on more salient entities in a given paper, we only use the title and abstract.

4.1 Approaches

We experiment with three approaches for entity extraction and linking:

I. Statistical: uses one or more statistical models for predicting mention spans, then uses another statistical model to link mentions to candidate entities in a KB.

II. Hybrid: defines a small number of hand-engineered, deterministic rules for string-based matching of the input text to candidate entities in the KB, then uses a statistical model to disambiguate the mentions.[4]

III. Off-the-shelf: uses existing libraries, namely (Ferragina and Scaiella, 2010, TagMe)[5] and (Demner-Fushman et al., 2017, MetaMap Lite)[6], with minimal post-processing to extract and link entities to the KB.

Approach	CS		Bio	
	prec.	yield	prec.	yield
Statistical	98.4	712	94.4	928
Hybrid	91.5	1990	92.1	3126
Off-the-shelf	97.4	873	77.5	1206

Table 2: Document-level evaluation of three approaches in two scientific areas: computer science (CS) and biomedical (Bio).

We evaluate the performance of each approach in two broad scientific areas: computer science (CS) and biomedical research (Bio). For each unique (paper ID, entity ID) pair predicted by one of the approaches, we ask human annotators to label each mention extracted for this entity in the paper. We use CrowdFlower to manage human annotations and only include instances where three or more annotators agree on the label. If one or more of the entity mentions in that paper is judged to be correct, the pair (paper ID, entity ID) counts as one correct instance. Otherwise, it counts as an incorrect instance. We report 'yield' in lieu of 'recall' due to the difficulty of doing a scalable comprehensive annotation.

Table 2 shows the results based on 500 papers using v1.1.2 of our entity extraction and linking components. In both domains, the statistical approach gives the highest precision and the lowest yield. The hybrid approach consistently gives the highest yield, but sacrifices precision. The TagMe off-the-shelf library used for the CS domain gives surprisingly good results, with precision within 1 point from the statistical models. However, the MetaMap Lite off-the-shelf library we used for the biomedical domain suffered a huge loss in precision. Our error analysis showed that each of the approaches is able to predict entities not predicted by the other approaches so we decided to pool their outputs in our deployed system, which gives significantly higher yield than any individual approach while maintaining reasonably high precision.

4.2 Entity Extraction Models

Given the token sequence $t_1, \ldots, t_N$ in a sentence, we need to identify spans which correspond to entity mentions. We use the BILOU scheme to encode labels at the token level. Unlike most formulations of named entity recognition problems (NER), we do not identify the entity type (e.g., protein,

---

[4]We also experimented with a "pure" rules-based approach which disambiguates deterministically but the hybrid approach consistently gave better results.

[5]The TagMe APIs are described at `https://sobigdata.d4science.org/web/tagme/tagme-help`

[6]We use v3.4 (L0) of MetaMap Lite, available at `https://metamap.nlm.nih.gov/MetaMapLite.shtml`

drug, chemical, disease) for each mention since the output mentions are further grounded in a KB with further information about the entity (including its type), using an entity linking module.

Model. First, we construct the token embedding $\mathbf{x}_k = [\mathbf{c}_k; \mathbf{w}_k]$ for each token t_k in the input sequence, where $\mathbf{c}_k$ is a character-based representation computed using a convolutional neural network (CNN) with filter of size 3 characters, and $\mathbf{w}_k$ are learned word embeddings initialized with the GloVe embeddings (Pennington et al., 2014).

We also compute context-sensitive word embeddings, denoted as $\mathbf{lm}_k = [\overrightarrow{\mathbf{lm}_k}; \overleftarrow{\mathbf{lm}_k}]$, by concatenating the projected outputs of forward and backward recurrent neural network language models (RNN-LM) at position k. The language model (LM) for each direction is trained independently and consists of a single layer long short-term memory (LSTM) network followed by a linear project layer. While training the LM parameters, $\overrightarrow{\mathbf{lm}_k}$ is used to predict t_{k+1} and $\overleftarrow{\mathbf{lm}_k}$ is used to predict t_{k-1}. We fix the LM parameters during training of the entity extraction model. See Peters et al. (2017) and Ammar et al. (2017) for more details.

Given the $\mathbf{x}_k$ and $\mathbf{lm}_k$ embeddings for each token $k \in \{1, \ldots, N\}$, we use a two-layer bidirectional LSTM to encode the sequence with $\mathbf{x}_k$ and $\mathbf{lm}_k$ feeding into the first and second layer, respectively. That is,

$$\overrightarrow{\mathbf{g}_k} = \text{LSTM}(\mathbf{x}_k, \overrightarrow{\mathbf{g}_{k-1}}), \mathbf{g}_k = [\overrightarrow{\mathbf{g}_k}; \overleftarrow{\mathbf{g}_k}],$$
$$\overrightarrow{\mathbf{h}_k} = \text{LSTM}([\mathbf{g}_k; \mathbf{lm}_k], \overrightarrow{\mathbf{h}_{k-1}}), \mathbf{h}_k = [\overrightarrow{\mathbf{h}_k}; \overleftarrow{\mathbf{h}_k}],$$

where $\overleftarrow{\mathbf{g}_k}$ and $\overleftarrow{\mathbf{h}_k}$ are defined similarly to $\overrightarrow{\mathbf{g}_k}$ and $\overrightarrow{\mathbf{h}_k}$ but process token sequences in the opposite direction.

Similar to the model described in §3, we feed the output of the second LSTM into a dense layer to predict unnormalized label weights for each token and learn label bigram feature weights to account for dependencies between labels.

Results. We use the standard data splits of the SemEval-2017 Task 10 on entity (and relation) extraction from scientific papers (Augenstein et al., 2017). Table 3 compares three variants of our entity extraction model. The first line omits the LM embeddings $\mathbf{lm}_k$, while the second line is the full model (including LM embeddings) showing a large improvement of 4.2 F1 points. The third line shows that creating an ensemble of 15 models further improves the results by 1.1 F1 points.

Model instances. In the deployed system, we use three instances of the entity extraction model

Description	F1
Without LM	49.9
With LM	54.1
Avg. of 15 models with LM	55.2

Table 3: Results of the entity extraction model on the development set of SemEval-2017 task 10.

with a similar architecture, but trained on different datasets. Two instances are trained on the BC5CDR (Li et al., 2016) and the CHEMDNER datasets (Krallinger et al., 2015) to extract key entity mentions in the biomedical domain such as diseases, drugs and chemical compounds. The third instance is trained on mention labels induced from Wikipedia articles in the computer science domain. The output of all model instances are pooled together and combined with the rule-based entity extraction module, then fed into the entity linking model (described below).

4.3 Knowledge Bases

In this section, we describe the construction of entity nodes and entity-entity edges. Unlike other knowledge extraction systems such as the Never-Ending Language Learner (NELL)[7] and OpenIE 4,[8] we use existing knowledge bases (KBs) of entities to reduce the burden of identifying coherent concepts. Grounding the entity mentions in a manually-curated KB also increases user confidence in automated predictions. We use two KBs:

UMLS: The UMLS metathesaurus integrates information about concepts in specialized ontologies in several biomedical domains, and is funded by the U.S. National Library of Medicine.

DBpedia: DBpedia provides access to structured information in Wikipedia. Rather than including all Wikipedia pages, we used a short list of Wikipedia categories about CS and included all pages up to depth four in their trees in order to exclude irrelevant entities, e.g., "Lord of the Rings" in DBpedia.

4.4 Entity Linking Models

Given a text span s identified by the entity extraction model in §4.2 (or with heuristics) and a reference KB, the goal of the entity linking model is to associate the span with the entity it refers to. A span and its surrounding words are collectively

---

[7] http://rtw.ml.cmu.edu/rtw/
[8] https://github.com/allenai/ openie-standalone

referred to as a mention. We first identify a set of candidate entities that a given mention may refer to. Then, we rank the candidate entities based on a score computed using a neural model trained on labeled data.

For example, given the string "... *database of facts, an ILP system will ...*", the entity extraction model identifies the span "ILP" as a possible entity and the entity linking model associates it with "Inductive_Logic_Programming" as the referent entity (from among other candidates like "Integer_Linear_Programming" or "Instruction-level_Parallelism").

Datasets. We used two datasets: i) a biomedical dataset formed by combining MSH (Jimeno-Yepes et al., 2011) and BC5CDR (Li et al., 2016) with UMLS as the reference KB, and ii) a CS dataset we curated using Wikipedia articles about CS concepts with DBpedia as the reference KB.

Candidate selection. In a preprocessing step, we build an index which maps any token used in a labeled mention or an entity name in the KB to associated entity IDs, along with the frequency this token is associated with that entity. This is similar to the index used in previous entity linking systems (e.g., Bhagavatula et al., 2015) to estimate the probability that a given mention refers to an entity. At train and test time, we use this index to find candidate entities for a given mention by looking up the tokens in the mention. This method also serves as our baseline in Table 4 by selecting the entity with the highest frequency for a given mention.

Scoring candidates. Given a mention (m) and a candidate entity (e), the neural model constructs a vector encoding of the mention and the entity. We encode the mention and entity using the functions **f** and **g**, respectively, as follows:

$$\mathbf{f}(m) = [\mathbf{v}_{m.name}; \mathrm{avg}(\mathbf{v}_{m.lc}, \mathbf{v}_{m.rc})],$$

$$\mathbf{g}(e) = [\mathbf{v}_{e.name}; \mathbf{v}_{e.def}],$$

where m.surface, m.lc and m.rc are the mention's surface form, left and right contexts, and e.name and e.def are the candidate entity's name and definition, respectively. $\mathbf{v}_{text}$ is a bag-of-words sum encoder for text. We use the same encoder for the mention surface form and the candidate name, and another encoder for the mention contexts and entity definition.

Additionally, we include numerical features to estimate the confidence of a candidate entity based on the statistics collected in the index described

	CS	Bio
Baseline	84.2	54.2
Neural	84.6	85.8

Table 4: The Bag of Concepts F1 score of the baseline and neural model on the two curated datasets.

earlier. We compute two scores based on the word overlap of (i) mention's context and candidate's definition and (ii) mention's surface span and the candidate entity's name. Finally, we feed the concatenation of the cosine similarity between **f**(m) and **g**(e) and the intersection-based scores into an affine transformation followed by a sigmoid nonlinearity to compute the final score for the pair (m, e).

Results. We use the Bag of Concepts F1 metric (Ling et al., 2015) for comparison. Table 4 compares the performance of the most-frequent-entity baseline and our neural model described above.

5   Other Research Problems

In the previous sections, we discussed how we construct the main components of the literature graph. In this section, we briefly describe several other related challenges we are actively working on.

Author disambiguation. Despite initiatives to have global author IDs ORCID and ResearcherID, most publishers provide author information as names (e.g., arXiv). However, author names cannot be used as a unique identifier since several people often share the same name. Moreover, different venues and sources use different conventions in reporting the author names, e.g., "first initial, last name" vs. "last name, first name". Inspired by Culotta et al. (2007), we train a supervised binary classifier for merging pairs of author instances and use it to incrementally create author clusters. We only consider merging two author instances if they have the same last name and share the first initial. If the first name is spelled out (rather than abbreviated) in both author instances, we also require that the first name matches.

Ontology matching. Popular concepts are often represented in multiple KBs. For example, the concept of "artificial neural networks" is represented as entity ID D016571 in the MESH ontology, and represented as page ID '21523' in DBpedia. Ontology matching is the problem of identifying semantically-equivalent entities across KBs or ontologies.[9]

Limited KB coverage. The convenience of grounding entities in a hand-curated KB comes at the cost of limited coverage. Introduction of new concepts and relations in the scientific literature occurs at a faster pace than KB curation, resulting in a large gap in KB coverage of scientific concepts. In order to close this gap, we need to develop models which can predict textual relations as well as detailed concept descriptions in scientific papers. For the same reasons, we also need to augment the relations imported from the KB with relations extracted from text. Our approach to address both entity and relation coverage is based on distant supervision (Mintz et al., 2009). In short, we train two models for identifying entity definitions and relations expressed in natural language in scientific documents, and automatically generate labeled data for training these models using known definitions and relations in the KB.

We note that the literature graph currently lacks coverage for important entity types (e.g., affiliations) and domains (e.g., physics). Covering affiliations requires small modifications to the metadata extraction model followed by an algorithm for matching author names with their affiliations. In order to cover additional scientific domains, more agreements need to be signed with publishers.

Figure and table extraction. Non-textual components such as charts, diagrams and tables provide key information in many scientific documents, but the lack of large labeled datasets has impeded the development of data-driven methods for scientific figure extraction. In Siegel et al. (2018), we induced high-quality training labels for the task of figure extraction in a large number of scientific documents, with no human intervention. To accomplish this we leveraged the auxiliary data provided in two large web collections of scientific documents (arXiv and PubMed) to locate figures and their associated captions in the rasterized PDF. We use the resulting dataset to train a deep neural network for end-to-end figure detection, yielding a model that can be more easily extended to new domains compared to previous work.

Understanding and predicting citations. The citation edges in the literature graph provide a wealth of information (e.g., at what rate a paper

is being cited and whether it is accelerating), and opens the door for further research to better understand and predict citations. For example, in order to allow users to better understand what impact a paper had and effectively navigate its citations, we experimented with methods for classifying a citation as important or incidental, as well as more fine-grained classes (Valenzuela et al., 2015). The citation information also enables us to develop models for estimating the potential of a paper or an author. In Weihs and Etzioni (2017), we predict citation-based metrics such as an author's h-index and the citation rate of a paper in the future. Also related is the problem of predicting which papers should be cited in a given draft (Bhagavatula et al., 2018), which can help improve the quality of a paper draft before it is submitted for peer review, or used to supplement the list of references after a paper is published.

6 Conclusion and Future Work

In this paper, we discuss the construction of a graph, providing a symbolic representation of the scientific literature. We describe deployed models for identifying authors, references and entities in the paper text, and provide experimental results to evaluate the performance of each model.

Three research directions follow from this work and other similar projects, e.g., Hahn-Powell et al. (2017); Wu et al. (2014): i) improving quality and enriching content of the literature graph (e.g., ontology matching and knowledge base population). ii) aggregating domain-specific extractions across many papers to enable a better understanding of the literature as a whole (e.g., identifying demographic biases in clinical trial participants and summarizing empirical results on important tasks). iii) exploring the literature via natural language interfaces.

In order to help future research efforts, we make the following resources publicly available: metadata for over 20 million papers,[10] meaningful citations dataset,[11] models for figure and table extraction,[12] models for predicting citations in a paper draft [13] and models for extracting paper metadata,[14] among other resources.[15]

---

[9]Variants of this problem are also known as deduplication or record linkage.

[10]http://labs.semanticscholar.org/corpus/
[11]http://allenai.org/data.html
[12]https://github.com/allenai/
deepfigures-open
[13]https://github.com/allenai/citeomatic
[14]https://github.com/allenai/science-parse
[15]http://allenai.org/software/

References

Waleed Ammar, Matthew E. Peters, Chandra Bhagavatula, and Russell Power. 2017. The ai2 system at semeval-2017 task 10 (scienceie): semi-supervised end-to-end entity and relation extraction. In *ACL workshop (SemEval)*.

Isabelle Augenstein, Mrinal Das, Sebastian Riedel, Lakshmi Vikraman, and Andrew D. McCallum. 2017. Semeval 2017 task 10 (scienceie): Extracting keyphrases and relations from scientific publications. In *ACL workshop (SemEval)*.

Chandra Bhagavatula, Sergey Feldman, Russell Power, and Waleed Ammar. 2018. Content-based citation recommendation. In *NAACL*.

Chandra Bhagavatula, Thanapon Noraset, and Doug Downey. 2015. TabEL: entity linking in web tables. In *ISWC*.

Ronan Collobert, Jason Weston, Léon Bottou, Michael Karlen, Koray Kavukcuoglu, and Pavel P. Kuksa. 2011. Natural language processing (almost) from scratch. In *JMLR*.

Aron Culotta, Pallika Kanani, Robert Hall, Michael Wick, and Andrew D. McCallum. 2007. Author disambiguation using error-driven machine learning with a ranking loss function. In *IIWeb Workshop*.

Hal Daumé. 2007. Frustratingly easy domain adaptation. In *ACL*.

Dina Demner-Fushman, Willie J. Rogers, and Alan R. Aronson. 2017. MetaMap Lite: an evaluation of a new Java implementation of MetaMap. In *JAMIA*.

Oren Etzioni. 2011. Search needs a shake-up. *Nature* 476 7358:25–6.

Paolo Ferragina and Ugo Scaiella. 2010. TAGME: on-the-fly annotation of short text fragments (by wikipedia entities). In *CIKM*.

Gus Hahn-Powell, Marco Antonio Valenzuela-Escarcega, and Mihai Surdeanu. 2017. Swanson linking revisited: Accelerating literature-based discovery across domains using a conceptual influence graph. In *ACL*.

Sepp Hochreiter and Jürgen Schmidhuber. 1997. Long short-term memory. *Neural computation* .

Srinivasan Iyer, Ioannis Konstas, Alvin Cheung, Jayant Krishnamurthy, and Luke S. Zettlemoyer. 2017. Learning a neural semantic parser from user feedback. In *ACL*.

Antonio J. Jimeno-Yepes, Bridget T. McInnes, and Alan R. Aronson. 2011. Exploiting mesh indexing in medline to generate a data set for word sense disambiguation. *BMC bioinformatics* 12(1):223.

Martin Krallinger, Florian Leitner, Obdulia Rabal, Miguel Vazquez, Julen Oyarzabal, and Alfonso Valencia. 2015. CHEMDNER: The drugs and chemical names extraction challenge. In *J. Cheminformatics*.

Guillaume Lample, Miguel Ballesteros, Sandeep K Subramanian, Kazuya Kawakami, and Chris Dyer. 2016. Neural architectures for named entity recognition. In *HLT-NAACL*.

Jiao Li, Yueping Sun, Robin J. Johnson, Daniela Sciaky, Chih-Hsuan Wei, Robert Leaman, Allan Peter Davis, Carolyn J. Mattingly, Thomas C. Wiegers, and Zhiyong Lu. 2016. Biocreative v cdr task corpus: a resource for chemical disease relation extraction. *Database : the journal of biological databases and curation* 2016.

Xiao Ling, Sameer Singh, and Daniel S. Weld. 2015. Design challenges for entity linking. *Transactions of the Association for Computational Linguistics* 3:315–328.

Mike Mintz, Steven Bills, Rion Snow, and Daniel Jurafsky. 2009. Distant supervision for relation extraction without labeled data. In *ACL*.

Jeffrey Pennington, Richard Socher, and Christopher D. Manning. 2014. GloVe: Global vectors for word representation. In *EMNLP*.

Matthew E. Peters, Waleed Ammar, Chandra Bhagavatula, and Russell Power. 2017. Semi-supervised sequence tagging with bidirectional language models. In *ACL*.

Noah Siegel, Nicholas Lourie, Russell Power, and Waleed Ammar. 2018. Extracting scientific figures with distantly supervised neural networks. In *JCDL*.

Marco Valenzuela, Vu Ha, and Oren Etzioni. 2015. Identifying meaningful citations. In *AAAI Workshop (Scholarly Big Data)*.

Xiang Wang, Yan Dong, Xiang qian Qi, Yi-Ming Li, Cheng-Guang Huang, and Lijun Hou. 2013. Clinical review: Efficacy of antimicrobial-impregnated catheters in external ventricular drainage - a systematic review and meta-analysis. In *Critical care*.

Luca Weihs and Oren Etzioni. 2017. Learning to predict citation-based impact measures. In *JCDL*.

Jian Wu, Kyle Williams, Hung-Hsuan Chen, Madian Khabsa, Cornelia Caragea, Alexander Ororbia, Douglas Jordan, and C. Lee Giles. 2014. CiteSeerX: AI in a digital library search engine. In *AAAI*.

Chenyan Xiong, Russell Power, and Jamie Callan. 2017. Explicit semantic ranking for academic search via knowledge graph embedding. In *WWW*.

Can Neural Machine Translation be Improved with User Feedback?

Julia Kreutzer[1][*] and **Shahram Khadivi**[3] and **Evgeny Matusov**[3] and **Stefan Riezler**[1,2]
[1]Computational Linguistics & [2]IWR, Heidelberg University, Germany
{kreutzer,riezler}@cl.uni-heidelberg.de
[3]eBay Inc., Aachen, Germany
{skhadivi,ematusov}@ebay.com

Abstract

We present the first real-world application of methods for improving neural machine translation (NMT) with human reinforcement, based on explicit and implicit user feedback collected on the eBay e-commerce platform. Previous work has been confined to simulation experiments, whereas in this paper we work with real logged feedback for offline bandit learning of NMT parameters. We conduct a thorough analysis of the available explicit user judgments—five-star ratings of translation quality—and show that they are not reliable enough to yield significant improvements in bandit learning. In contrast, we successfully utilize implicit task-based feedback collected in a cross-lingual search task to improve task-specific and machine translation quality metrics.

1 Introduction

In commercial scenarios of neural machine translation (NMT), the one-best translation of a text is shown to multiple users who can reinforce high-quality (or penalize low-quality) translations by explicit feedback (e.g., on a Likert scale) or implicit feedback (by clicking on a translated page). In such settings this type of feedback can be easily collected in large amounts. While bandit feedback[1] in form of user clicks on displayed ads is the standard learning signal for response prediction in online advertising (Bottou et al., 2013), bandit learning for machine translation has so far been restricted to simulation experiments (Sokolov et al., 2016b; Lawrence et al., 2017b;

Nguyen et al., 2017; Kreutzer et al., 2017; Bahdanau et al., 2017).

The goal of our work is to show that the gold mine of cheap and abundant real-world human bandit feedback can be exploited successfully for machine learning in NMT. We analyze and utilize human reinforcements that have been collected from users of the eBay e-commerce platform. We show that explicit user judgments in form of five-star ratings are not reliable and do not lead to downstream BLEU improvements in bandit learning. In contrast, we find that implicit task-based feedback that has been gathered in a cross-lingual search task can be used successfully to improve task-specific metrics and BLEU.

Another crucial difference of our work to previous research is the fact that we assume a counterfactual learning scenario where human feedback has been given to a historic system different from the target system. Learning is done offline from logged data, which is desirable in commercial settings where system updates need to be tested before deployment and the risk of showing inferior translations to users needs to be avoided. Our offline learning algorithms range from a simple bandit-to-supervised conversion (i.e., using translations with good feedback for supervised tuning) to transferring the counterfactual learning techniques presented by Lawrence et al. (2017b) from statistical machine translation (SMT) to NMT models. To our surprise, the bandit-to-supervised conversion proved to be very hard to beat, despite theoretical indications of poor generalization for exploration-free learning from logged data (Langford et al., 2008; Strehl et al., 2010). However, we show that we can further improve over this method by computing a task-specific reward scoring function, resulting in significant improvements in both BLEU and in task-specific metrics.

---

[*]The work for this paper was done while the first author was an intern at eBay.

[1]The fact that only feedback for a single translation is collected constitutes the "bandit feedback" scenario where the name is inspired by "one-armed bandit" slot machines.

Proceedings of NAACL-HLT 2018, pages 92–105
New Orleans, Louisiana, June 1 - 6, 2018. ©2017 Association for Computational Linguistics

2 Related Work

Sokolov et al. (2016a,b) introduced learning from bandit feedback for SMT models in an interactive online learning scenario: the MT model receives a source sentence from the user, provides a translation, receives feedback from the user for this translation, and performs a stochastic gradient update proportional to the feedback quality. Kreutzer et al. (2017) showed that the objectives proposed for log-linear models can be transferred to neural sequence learning and found that standard control variate techniques do not only reduce variance but also help to produce best BLEU results. Nguyen et al. (2017) proposed a very similar approach using a learned word-based critic in an advantage actor-critic reinforcement learning framework. A comparison of current approaches was recently performed in a shared task where participants had to build translation models that learn from the interaction with a service that provided e-commerce product descriptions and feedback for submitted translations (Sokolov et al., 2017). Lawrence et al. (2017b,a) were the first to address the more realistic problem of offline learning from logged bandit feedback, with special attention to the problem of exploration-free deterministic logging as is done in commercial MT systems. They show that variance reduction techniques used in counterfactual bandit learning (Dudík et al., 2011; Bottou et al., 2013) and off-policy reinforcement learning (Precup et al., 2000; Jiang and Li, 2016) can be used to avoid degenerate behavior of estimators under deterministic logging.

3 User Feedback

3.1 Explicit Feedback via Star Ratings

One way to collect reinforcement signals from human users of the eBay platform is by explicit ratings of product title translations on a five-point Likert scale. More specifically, when users visit product pages with translated titles, they can inspect the source when hovering with the mouse over the title. Then five stars are shown with the instruction to 'rate this translation'. A screenshot of an implementation of this rating interface is shown in Figure 1. The original title, the translation and the given star rating are stored. For the experiments in this paper, we focus on translations from English to Spanish. The user star rating data set contains 69,412 rated product titles with 148k

Figure 1: Screenshot of the 5-star rating interface for a product on `www.ebay.es` translated from English to Spanish.

individual ratings. Since 34% of the titles were rated more than once, the ratings for each title are averaged. We observe a tendency towards high ratings, in fact one half of the titles are rated with five stars (cf. Appendix C).

To investigate the reliability and validity of these ratings, we employed three bilingual annotators ('experts') to independently re-evaluate and give five-star ratings for a balanced subset of 1,000 product title translations. The annotators were presented the source title and the machine translation, together with instructions on the task provided in Appendix B. The inter-annotator agreement between experts is relatively low with Fleiss' $\kappa = 0.12$ (Fleiss, 1971). Furthermore, there is no correlation of the averaged 'expert' ratings and the averaged user star ratings (Spearman's $\rho = -0.05$). However, when we ask another three annotators to indicate whether they agree or disagree with a balanced subset of 2,000 user ratings, they agree with 42.3% of the ratings (by majority voting). In this binary meta-judgment task, the inter-annotator agreement between experts is moderate with $\kappa = 0.45$. We observe a strong tendency of the expert annotators to agree with high user ratings and to disagree with low user ratings. Two examples of user ratings, expert ratings and expert judgment are given in Table 1. In the first example, all raters agree that the translation is good, but in the second example, there is a strong disagreement between users and experts.

This analysis shows that it is generally not easy for non-professional users of the e-commerce platform, and even for expert annotators, to give star ratings of translations in the domain of user-generated product titles with high reliability. This problem is related to low validity, i.e., we do not know whether the users' response actually expresses translation quality, since we cannot control the influence of other factors on their judgment, e.g., the displayed image (see Figure 1), the prod-

Source Title	Title Translation	User Rating (avg)	Expert Rating (avg)	Expert Judgment (majority)
Universal 4in1 Dual USB Car Charger Adapter Voltage DC 5V 3.1A Tester For iPhone	Coche Cargador Adaptador De Voltaje Probador De Corriente Continua 5V 3.1A para iPhone	4.5625	4.33	Correct
BEAN BUSH THREE COLOURS: YELLOW BERGGOLD, PURPLE KING AND GREEN TOP CROP	Bean Bush tres colores: Amarillo Berggold, púrpura y verde Top Crop King	1.0	4.66	Incorrect

Table 1: Examples for averaged five-star user ratings, five-star expert ratings and expert judgments on the user ratings.

uct itself, or the users' general satisfaction with the e-commerce transaction, nor can we exclude the possibility that the user judgment is given with an adversarial purpose. Furthermore, we do not have control over the quality of sources[2], nor can we discern to which degree a user rating reflects fluency or adequacy of the translation.

3.2 Task-Based Implicit Feedback

Another form of collecting human reinforcement signals via the eBay e-commerce platform is to embed the feedback collection into a cross-lingual information retrieval task. The product title translation system is part of the search interaction of a user with the e-commerce platform in the following way: When a user enters a query in Spanish, it is first translated to English (query translation), then a search engine retrieves a list of matching products, and their titles are translated to Spanish and displayed to the user. As soon as the user clicks on one of the translated titles, we store the original query, the translated query, the source product title and its translation. From this collection we filter the cases where (a) the original query and the translated query are the same, or (b) more than 90% of the words from the query translation are not contained in the retrieved source title. In this way, we attempt to reduce the propagation of errors in query translation and search. This leaves us with a dataset of 164,065 tuples of Spanish queries, English product titles and their Spanish translations (15% of the original collection). Note that this dataset is more than twice the size of the explicit feedback dataset. An example is given in Table 2.

The advantage of embedding feedback collection into a search task is that we can assume that users who formulate a search query have a genuine intent of finding products that fit their need, and are also likely to be satisfied with product title translations that match their query, i.e., contain

terms from the query in their own language. We exploit this assumption in order to measure the quality of a product title translation by requiring a user to click on the translation when it is displayed as a result of the search, and then quantifying the quality of the clicked translation by the extent it matches the query that led the user to the product. For this purpose, we define a word-based matching function $\mathrm{match}(w, \mathbf{q})$ that evaluates whether a query $\mathbf{q}$ contains the word w:

$$\mathrm{match}(w, \mathbf{q}) = \begin{cases} 1, & \text{if } w \in \mathbf{q} \\ 0, & \text{otherwise.} \end{cases} \quad (1)$$

Based on this word-level matching, we compute a sequence-level reward for a sentence $\mathbf{y}$ of length T as follows:

$$\mathrm{recall}(\mathbf{y}, \mathbf{q}) = \frac{1}{T} \sum_{t=1}^{T} \mathrm{match}(y_t, \mathbf{q}). \quad (2)$$

4 Learning from User Feedback

Reward Functions. In reinforcement and bandit learning, rewards received from the environment are used as supervision signals for learning. In our experiments, we investigate several options to obtain a reward function $\Delta : \mathcal{Y} \to [0, 1]$ from logged human bandit feedback:

1. **Direct User Reward**: Explicit feedback, e.g., in the form of star ratings, can directly be used as reward by treating the reward function as a black box. Since human feedback is usually only available for one translation per input, learning from direct user rewards requires the use of bandit learning algorithms. In our setup, human bandit feedback has been collected for translations of a historic MT system different from the target system to be optimized. This restricts the learning setup to offline learning from logged bandit feedback.

2. **Reward Scoring Function**: A possibility to use human bandit feedback to obtain rewards for more than a single translation per input is

---

[2]Most titles consist of a sequence of keywords rather than a fluent sentence. See Calixto et al. (2017) for a fluency analysis of product titles.

Query	Translated Query	Title	Translated Title	Recall
candado bicicleta	bicycle lock	New Bicycle Vibration Code Moped Lock Bike Cycling Security Alarm Sound Lock	Nuevo código de vibración Bicicleta Ciclomotor alarma de seguridad de bloqueo Bicicleta Ciclismo Cerradura De Sonido	0.5

Table 2: Example for query and product title translation. 'candado' is translated to 'lock' in the query, but then translated back to 'cerradura' in the title. The recall metric would prefer a title translation with 'candado', as it was specified by the user.

to score translations either against a logged reference or a logged query. The first option requires a bandit-to-supervised conversion of data where high-quality logged translations are used as references against which BLEU or other MT quality metrics can be measured. The second option uses logged queries to obtain a matching score as in Equation 2.

3. **Estimated Reward**: Another option to extend bandit feedback to all translations is to learn a parametric model of rewards, e.g., by optimizing a regression objective. The reward function is known, but the model parameters need to be trained based on a history of direct user rewards or by evaluations of a reward scoring function.

In the following, we present how rewards can be integrated in various objectives for NMT training.

Maximum Likelihood Estimation by Bandit-to-Supervised Conversion. Most commonly, NMT models are trained with *Maximum Likelihood Estimation* (MLE, Equation 3) on a given parallel corpus of source and target sequences $D = \{(\mathbf{x}^{(s)}, \mathbf{y}^{(s)})\}_{s=1}^{S}$

$$L^{\text{MLE}}(\theta) = \sum_{s=1}^{S} \log p_\theta(\mathbf{y}^{(s)}|\mathbf{x}^{(s)}). \quad (3)$$

The MLE objective requires reference translations and is agnostic to rewards. However, in a *bandit-to-supervised conversion*, rewards can be used to filter translations to be used as pseudo-references for MLE training. We apply this scenario to explicit and implicit human feedback data in our experiments.

Reinforcement Learning by Minimum Risk Training. When rewards can be obtained for several translations per input instead of only for one as in the bandit setup, by using a reward estimate or scoring function, *Minimum Risk Training* (MRT, Equation 4) can be applied to optimize

NMT from rewards.

$$R^{\text{MRT}}(\theta) = \sum_{s=1}^{S} \sum_{\tilde{\mathbf{y}} \in \mathcal{S}(\mathbf{x}^{(s)})} q_\theta^\alpha(\tilde{\mathbf{y}}|\mathbf{x}^{(s)}) \, \Delta(\tilde{\mathbf{y}}), \quad (4)$$

where sample probabilities are renormalized over a subset of translation samples $\mathcal{S}(\mathbf{x}) \subset \mathcal{Y}(\mathbf{x})$: $q_\theta^\alpha(\tilde{\mathbf{y}}|\mathbf{x}) = \frac{p_\theta(\tilde{\mathbf{y}}|\mathbf{x})^\alpha}{\sum_{\mathbf{y}' \in \mathcal{S}(\mathbf{x})} p_\theta(\mathbf{y}'|\mathbf{x})^\alpha}$. The hyperparameter α controls the sharpness of q (see Shen et al. (2016)).

With sequence-level rewards, all words of a translation of length T are reinforced to the same extent and are treated as if they contributed equally to the translation quality. A word-based reward function, such as the match with a given query (Equation 1), allows the words to have individual weights. The following modification of the sequence-level MRT objective (Equation 4) accounts for word-based rewards $\Delta(y_t)$:

$$R^{\text{W-MRT}}(\theta) = \sum_{s=1}^{S} \sum_{\tilde{\mathbf{y}} \in \mathcal{S}(\mathbf{x}^{(s)})} \prod_{t=1}^{T}$$
$$\left[q_\theta^\alpha(\tilde{y}_t|\mathbf{x}^{(s)}, \tilde{\mathbf{y}}_{<t}) \, \Delta(y_t) \right], \quad (5)$$

where $\Delta(y_t)$ in our experiments is a matching score (1). In the following we use the bracketed prefix (W-) to subsume both sentence-level and word-level training objectives.

When output spaces are large and reward functions sparse, (W-)MRT objectives typically benefit from a warm start, i.e., pre-training with MLE. Following Wu et al. (2016), we furthermore adopt a linear combination of MLE and (W-)MRT to stabilize learning:

$$R^{\text{(W-)MIX}}(\theta) = \lambda \cdot R^{\text{MLE}}(\theta) + R^{\text{(W-)MRT}}(\theta).$$

Counterfactual Learning by Deterministic Propensity Matching. Counterfactual learning attempts to improve a target MT system from a log of source sentences, translations produced by a historic MT system, and obtained feedback $L = \{(\mathbf{x}^{(h)}, \mathbf{y}^{(h)}, \Delta(\mathbf{y}^{(h)}))\}_{h=1}^{H}$. For the special case of deterministically logged rewards

Lawrence et al. (2017b) introduced the *Deterministic Propensity Matching* (DPM) objective with self-normalization as a multiplicative control variate (Swaminathan and Joachims, 2015):[3]

$$R^{\text{DPM}}(\theta) = \frac{1}{H} \sum_{h=1}^{H} \Delta(\mathbf{y}^{(h)})\, \bar{p}_\theta(\mathbf{y}^{(h)}|\mathbf{x}^{(h)}), \quad (6)$$

where translation probabilities are reweighted over the current mini-batch $B \subset H, B \ll H$: $\bar{p}_\theta(\mathbf{y}^{(h)}|\mathbf{x}^{(h)}) = \frac{p_\theta(\mathbf{y}^{(h)}|\mathbf{x}^{(h)})}{\sum_{b=1}^{B} p_\theta(\mathbf{y}^{(b)}|\mathbf{x}^{(b)})}$. We additionally normalize the log probability of a translation $\mathbf{y}$ by its length $|\mathbf{y}|$: $p_\theta^{norm}(\mathbf{y}|\mathbf{x}) = \exp\left(\frac{\log p_\theta(\mathbf{y}|\mathbf{x})}{|\mathbf{y}|}\right)$.

Counterfactual Learning by Doubly Controlled Estimation. Lawrence et al. (2017b) furthermore propose the *Doubly Controlled* objective (DC, Equation 7) implementing the idea of doubly robust estimation (Dudík et al., 2011; Jiang and Li, 2016) for deterministic logs. In addition to learning from the historic reward for the logging system, the reward for other translations is estimated by a parametrized regression model that is trained on the log $\hat{\Delta}_\phi : \mathcal{Y} \to [0, 1]$. This objective contains both a multiplicative (probability reweighting) and an additive (reward estimate) control variate, hence the name.[4]

$$R^{\text{DC}}(\theta) = \frac{1}{H} \sum_{h=1}^{H} \left[\left(\Delta(\mathbf{y}^{(h)}) - \hat{\Delta}_\phi(\mathbf{y}^{(h)}) \right) \right.$$
$$\left. \times \bar{p}_\theta(\mathbf{y}^{(h)}|\mathbf{x}^{(h)}) + \sum_{\mathbf{y} \in \mathcal{S}(\mathbf{x}^{(h)})} \hat{\Delta}_\phi(\mathbf{y})\, p_\theta(\mathbf{y}|\mathbf{x}^{(h)}) \right]$$
$$(7)$$

As for MRT, the expectation over the full output space is approximated with a subset of k sample translations $\mathcal{S}(\mathbf{x}) \subset \mathcal{Y}(\mathbf{x})$.

Relative Rewards. With the objectives as defined above, gradient steps are dependent on the magnitude of the reward for the current training instance. In reinforcement learning, an average reward baseline is commonly subtracted from the current reward with the primary goal to reduce variance (Williams, 1992). As a side effect, the current reward is relativized, such that the gradient step is not only determined by the magnitude of the current rewards, but is put into relation with previous rewards. We found this effect to be particularly beneficial in experiments with suboptimal reward estimators or noisy rewards and therefore apply it to all instantiations of the DPM and DC objectives. For DPM, the running average of historic rewards $\bar{\Delta}_h = \frac{1}{h} \sum_{i=1}^{h} \Delta(\mathbf{y}^{(i)})$ is subtracted from the current reward. For DC we apply this to both types of rewards in Equation 7: 1) the logged reward $\Delta(\mathbf{y}^{(h)})$, from which we subtract its running average $\bar{\Delta}_h$ instead of the estimated reward $\hat{\Delta}_\phi(\mathbf{y}^{(h)})$, and 2) the estimated reward $\hat{\Delta}_\phi(\mathbf{y})$, from which we hence subtract the average estimated reward $\bar{\hat{\Delta}}_h = \frac{1}{h} \sum_{i=1}^{h} \frac{1}{k} \sum_{\mathbf{y}' \in \mathcal{S}(\mathbf{x}^{(i)})} \hat{\Delta}_\phi(\mathbf{y}')$.

5 Experiments

5.1 NMT Model

In our experiments, learning from feedback starts from a pre-trained English to Spanish NMT model that has not seen in-domain data (i.e., no product title translations). The NMT baseline model (BL) is a standard subword-based encoder-decoder architecture with attention (Bahdanau et al., 2015), implemented with TensorFlow (Abadi et al., 2015). The model is trained with MLE on 2.7M parallel sentences of out-of-domain data until the early stopping point which is determined on a small in-domain dev set of 1,619 product title translations. A beam of size 12 and length normalization (Wu et al., 2016) are used for beam search decoding. For significance tests we used approximate randomization (Clark et al., 2011), for BLEU score evaluation (lowercased) the multi-bleu script of the Moses decoder (Koehn et al., 2007), for TER computation the tercom tool (Snover et al., 2006). For MRT, DC and (W-)MIX models we set $k = 5$, for (W-)MIX models $\lambda = 0.5$ and $\alpha = 0.05$. For all NMT models involving random sampling, we report average results and standard deviation (in subscript) over two runs. Further details about training data and hyperparameters settings are described in Appendix D.

5.2 Reward Estimator

The model architecture for the reward estimator used in the DC objective is a bilingual extension of the convolutional neural network (CNN) for

---

[3]Lawrence et al. (2017b) propose reweighting over the whole log, but this is infeasible for NMT. For simplicty we refer to their DPM-R objective as DPM, and DC-R as DC.

[4]We find empirically that estimating $\hat{c}$ over the current batch as in objective $\hat{c}$DC in (Lawrence et al., 2017b) does not improve over the simple setting with $c = 1$.

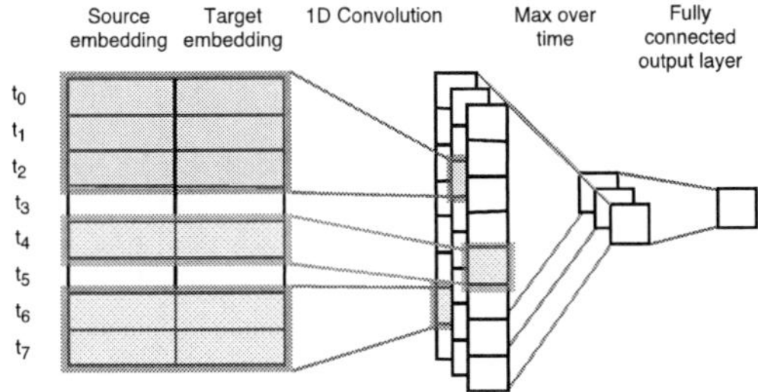

Figure 2: Model architecture for the reward estimator. This example has one filter for each filter size (3: purple, 1: green, 2: blue). Source and target sequences are padded up to a maximum length, here $T_{max} = 8$.

Data & Model	MSE	Macro-avg. Distance	Micro-Avg. Distance	Pearson's r	Spearman's ρ
Star ratings	0.1620	0.0065	0.3203	0.1240	0.1026
sBLEU	0.0096	0.0055	0.0710	0.8816	0.8675

Table 3: Results for the **reward estimators** trained and evaluated on human star ratings and simulated sBLEU.

sentence classification proposed by Kim (2014). Both source and target sequences are padded up to a pre-defined maximum sequence length T_{max}, their embeddings are concatenated and further processed by a 1D-Convolution over the time dimension with several filters of sizes from 2 to 15, which is then followed by a max-over-time pooling and fed to a fully-connected output layer (Figure 2). The model is trained to minimize the mean squared error (MSE) on the training portion of the logged feedback data (60k for simulated sentence-BLEU feedback, 62,470 for star rating feedback). The word embeddings of the reward estimator are initialized by the word embeddings of the trained baseline NMT system and fine-tuned further together with the other CNN weights. The best parameters are identified by early-stopping on the validation portion of the feedback data (2,162 for the simulation, 6,942 for the star ratings). Please find a detailed description of the model's hyperparameters in Appendix D.4.

Results for a stand-alone evaluation of the reward estimator on the validation portions of the feedback data are given in Table 3. The estimator models sBLEU much more accurately than the user star ratings. This is due to large variance and skew of the user ratings. An MSE-trained estimator typically predicts values around the mean, which is not a suitable strategy for such a skewed distribution of labels, but is successful for the prediction of normal-distributed sBLEU.

5.3 Explicit Star Rating Feedback

Counterfactual Bandit Learning. As shown in Table 4, counterfactual learning with DPM and DC on the logged star ratings as direct reward does not yield improvements over the baseline model in terms of corpus BLEU or TER. A randomization of feedback signals for translations gives the same results (DPM-random), showing that counterfactual learning from logged star ratings is equivalent to learning from noise. Evaluating the models in terms of estimated user reward, however, we find an improvement of +1.49 for DC, +0.04 for DPM over the baseline (53.93) (not shown in Table 4)—but these improvements do not transfer to BLEU because the reward model largely over-estimates the translation quality of translations with major faults. Hence it is not desirable to optimize towards this signal directly.

Bandit-to-Supervised Conversion. In the following setup, we utilize the user ratings to filter the log by using only five star rated translations, and perform supervised learning of MLE and MIX using sBLEU against pseudo-references as reward function. Table 4 shows that this filtering strategy leads to large improvements over the baseline, for MLE and even more for MIX, even though the data set size is reduced by 42%. However, around the same improvements can be achieved with a random selection of logged translations of the same size (MIX small, containing 55% five-star ratings). Using all logged translations for training MIX achieves the best results. This suggests that the model does not profit from the feedback, but mostly from being exposed to in-domain translations of the logging system. This effect is similar to training on pseudo-references created by back-translation (Sennrich et al., 2016b,a).

5.4 Task-Based Implicit Feedback

Bandit-to-Supervised Conversion. We apply the same filtering technique to the logged implicit feedback by treating translations with recall = 1 as references for training MIX with sBLEU (reduction of the data set by 62%). The results in Table 5 show that large improvements over the baseline can be obtained even without filtering, BLEU and TER scores being comparable to the ones observed for training on explicit user ratings.

Task-based Feedback. The key difference between the implicit feedback collected in the query-

Model	Test BLEU	Test TER
BL	28.38	57.58
DPM	28.19	57.80
DPM-random	28.19	57.64
DC	$28.41_{\pm 0.85}$	$64.25_{\pm 1.66}$
MLE (all)	31.98	51.08
MIX (all)	$\mathbf{34.47}_{\pm 0.06}$	$\mathbf{47.97}_{\pm 0.18}$
MIX (small)	$34.16_{\pm 0.09}$	$48.12_{\pm 0.33}$
MIX (stars $=$ 5)	$34.35_{\pm 0.11}$	$47.99_{\pm 0.13}$

Table 4: Results for models trained on **explicit user ratings** evaluated on the product titles test set. 'small' indicates a random subset of logged translations of the same size as the filtered log that only contains translations with an average rating of five stars ('stars $=$ 5'). The differences in BLEU are not significant at $p \leq 0.05$ between MIX models, but over other models.

Model	Test BLEU	Test TER
BL	28.38	57.58
MLE (all)	31.89	51.35
MIX (all)	$34.39_{\pm 0.08}$	$47.94_{\pm 0.24}$
MIX (small)	$34.13_{\pm 0.26}$	$48.27_{\pm 0.60}$
MIX (recall $=$ 1)	$34.17_{\pm 0.02}$	$47.72_{\pm 0.26}$
W-MIX	$\mathbf{34.52}_{\pm 0.02}$	$\mathbf{46.91}_{\pm 0.03}$

Table 5: Results for models trained on **implicit task-based** feedback data evaluated on the product titles test set. 'small' indicates a random subset of logged translations of the same size as the filtered log that only contains translations that contain all the query words ('recall $=$ 1'). The BLEU score of MIX (small) significantly differs from MIX (all) at $p \leq 0.05$, the score of MIX (recall $=$ 1) does not. Other differences are significant.

title data and the explicit user ratings, is that it can be used to define reward functions like recall or match (Equations 2, 1). For the experiments we train W-MIX, the word-based MRT objective (Equation 5) linearly combined with MLE, on the logged translations accompanying the queries (160k sentences). This combination is essential here, since the model would otherwise learn to produce translations that contain nothing but the query words. To account for user-generated language in the queries and subwords in the MT model, we soften the conditions for a match, counting tokens as a match that are part of a word w that is either contained in the query, or has edit distance to a word in the query with $dist(w, \mathbf{q}_i) < \max(3, 0.3 \times |w|)$.

Table 6 repeats the best MIX results from Table 4 and 5, and evaluates the models with respect to query recall. We also report the query recall for the logged translations and the out-of-domain baseline. These results are compared to W-MIX training on implicit feedback data described in Sec-

Logged	BL	MIX (Tab. 4)	MIX (Tab. 5)	W-MIX
65.33	45.96	$62.92_{\pm 0.56}$	$63.21_{\pm 0.24}$	$\mathbf{68.12}_{\pm 0.27}$

Table 6: **Query recall** results on the query test set, comparing the logged translations, the baseline and the best MIX models trained on logged translations (MIX (all) from Tables 4 and 5) with the W-MIX model trained via word-based query matching (W-MIX from Table 5).

tion 3.2. The development portion of the query-title dataset contains 4,065 sentences, the test set 2,000 sentences, which is used for query recall evaluation. The W-MIX model shows the largest improvement in query recall (12% points) and BLEU (6 points) over the baseline out of all tested learning approaches. It comes very close to the BLEU/TER results of the model trained on in-domain references, but surpasses its recall by far. This is remarkable since the model does not use any human generated references, only logged data of task-based human feedback. Appendix F contains a set of examples illustrating what the W-MIX learned.

6 Conclusion

We presented methods to improve NMT from human reinforcement signals. The signals were logged from user activities of an e-commerce platform and consist of explicit ratings on a five-point Likert scale and implicit task-based feedback collected in a cross-lingual search task. We found that there are no improvements when learning from user star ratings, unless the noisy ratings themselves are stripped off in a bandit-to-supervised conversion. Implicit task-based feedback can be used successfully as a reward signal for NMT optimization, leading to improvements both in terms of enforcing individual word translations and in terms of automatic evaluation measures. In the future, we plan transfer these findings to production settings by performing regular NMT model updates with batches of collected user behavior data, especially focusing on improving translation of ambiguous and rare terms based on rewards from implicit partial feedback.

Acknowledgements

The last author was supported in part by DFG Research Grant RI 2221/4-1. We would like to thank Pavel Petrushkov for helping with the NMT setup, and the anonymous reviewers for their insightful comments .

References

Martín Abadi, Ashish Agarwal, Paul Barham, Eugene Brevdo, Zhifeng Chen, Craig Citro, Greg S. Corrado, Andy Davis, Jeffrey Dean, Matthieu Devin, Sanjay Ghemawat, Ian Goodfellow, Andrew Harp, Geoffrey Irving, Michael Isard, Yangqing Jia, Rafal Jozefowicz, Lukasz Kaiser, Manjunath Kudlur, Josh Levenberg, Dan Mané, Rajat Monga, Sherry Moore, Derek Murray, Chris Olah, Mike Schuster, Jonathon Shlens, Benoit Steiner, Ilya Sutskever, Kunal Talwar, Paul Tucker, Vincent Vanhoucke, Vijay Vasudevan, Fernanda Viégas, Oriol Vinyals, Pete Warden, Martin Wattenberg, Martin Wicke, Yuan Yu, and Xiaoqiang Zheng. 2015. TensorFlow: Large-scale machine learning on heterogeneous systems. https://www.tensorflow.org/.

Dzmitry Bahdanau, Philemon Brakel, Kelvin Xu, Anirudh Goyal, Ryan Lowe, Joelle Pineau, Aaron Courville, and Yoshua Bengio. 2017. An actor-critic algorithm for sequence prediction. In *5th International Conference on Learning Representations*. Toulon, France.

Dzmitry Bahdanau, Kyunghyun Cho, and Yoshua Bengio. 2015. Neural machine translation by jointly learning to align and translate. In *Third International Conference on Learning Representations*. San Diego, California.

Léon Bottou, Jonas Peters, Joaquin Quiñonero-Candela, Denis X. Charles, D. Max Chickering, Elon Portugaly, Dipanakar Ray, Patrice Simard, and Ed Snelson. 2013. Counterfactual reasoning and learning systems: The example of computational advertising. *Journal of Machine Learning Research* 14:3207–3260.

Iacer Calixto, Daniel Stein, Evgeny Matusov, Pintu Lohar, Sheila Castilho, and Andy Way. 2017. Using images to improve machine-translating e-commerce product listings. In *Proceedings of the 15th Conference of the European Chapter of the Association for Computational Linguistics*. Valencia, Spain.

Jonathan H. Clark, Chris Dyer, Alon Lavie, and Noah A. Smith. 2011. Better hypothesis testing for statistical machine translation: Controlling for optimizer instability. In *Proceedings of the 49th Annual Meeting of the Association for Computational Linguistics: Human Language Technologies*. Portland, Oregon.

Miroslav Dudík, John Langford, and Lihong Li. 2011. Doubly robust policy evaluation and learning. In *Proceedings of the 28th International Conference on Machine Learning*. Bellevue, Washington.

Joseph L Fleiss. 1971. Measuring nominal scale agreement among many raters. *Psychological bulletin* 76(5):378.

Y Gal and Z Ghahramani. 2016. Dropout as a bayesian approximation: Representing model uncertainty in deep learning. In *33rd International Conference on Machine Learning*. New York City, NY.

Sébastien Jean, Kyunghyun Cho, Roland Memisevic, and Yoshua Bengio. 2015. On using very large target vocabulary for neural machine translation. In *Proceedings of the 53rd Annual Meeting of the Association for Computational Linguistics and the 7th International Joint Conference on Natural Language Processing*. Beijing, China.

Nan Jiang and Lihong Li. 2016. Doubly robust off-policy value evaluation for reinforcement learning. In *Proceedings of the 33rd International Conference on Machine Learning (ICML)*. New York, NY.

Yoon Kim. 2014. Convolutional neural networks for sentence classification. In *Proceedings of the 2014 Conference on Empirical Methods in Natural Language Processing*. Doha, Qatar.

Diederik Kingma and Jimmy Ba. 2014. Adam: A method for stochastic optimization. *arXiv preprint arXiv:1412.6980* .

Philipp Koehn, Hieu Hoang, Alexandra Birch, Chris Callison-Burch, Marcello Federico, Nicola Bertoldi, Brooke Cowan, Wade Shen, Christine Moran, Richard Zens, et al. 2007. Moses: Open source toolkit for statistical machine translation. In *Proceedings of the 45th Annual Meeting of the Association for Computational Linguistics: Interactive Poster and Demonstration Sessions*. Prague, Czech Republic.

Julia Kreutzer, Artem Sokolov, and Stefan Riezler. 2017. Bandit structured prediction for neural sequence-to-sequence learning. In *Proceedings of the 55th Annual Meeting of the Association for Computational Linguistics*. Vancouver, Canada.

John Langford, Alexander Strehl, and Jennifer Wortman. 2008. Exploration scavenging. In *Proceedings of the 25th International Conference on Machine Learning (ICML)*. Helsinki, Finland.

Carolin Lawrence, Pratik Gajane, and Stefan Riezler. 2017a. Counterfactual learning for machine translation: Degeneracies and solutions. In *Proceedings of the NIPS WhatIF Workshop*. Long Beach, CA.

Carolin Lawrence, Artem Sokolov, and Stefan Riezler. 2017b. Counterfactual learning from bandit feedback under deterministic logging : A case study in statistical machine translation. In *Proceedings of the 2017 Conference on Empirical Methods in Natural Language Processing*. Copenhagen, Denmark.

Hoa T. Le, Christophe Cerisara, and Alexandre Denis. 2017. Do convolutional networks need to be deep for text classification ? *arXiv preprint arXiv:1707.04108* .

Minh-Thang Luong and Christopher D Manning. 2015. Stanford neural machine translation systems for spoken language domains. In *Proceedings of the International Workshop on Spoken Language Translation*. Da Nang, Vietnam.

Khanh Nguyen, Hal Daumé III, and Jordan Boyd-Graber. 2017. Reinforcement learning for bandit neural machine translation with simulated human feedback. In *Proceedings of the 2017 Conference on Empirical Methods in Natural Language Processing*. Copenhagen, Denmark.

Doina Precup, Richard S. Sutton, and Satinder P. Singh. 2000. Eligibility traces for off-policy policy evaluation. In *Proceedings of the Seventeenth International Conference on Machine Learning (ICML)*. San Francisco, CA.

Rico Sennrich, Barry Haddow, and Alexandra Birch. 2016a. Edinburgh neural machine translation systems for wmt 16. In *Proceedings of the First Conference on Machine Translation*. Berlin, Germany.

Rico Sennrich, Barry Haddow, and Alexandra Birch. 2016b. Improving neural machine translation models with monolingual data. In *Proceedings of the 54th Annual Meeting of the Association for Computational Linguistics*. Berlin, Germany.

Rico Sennrich, Barry Haddow, and Alexandra Birch. 2016c. Neural machine translation of rare words with subword units. In *Proceedings of the 54th Annual Meeting of the Association for Computational Linguistics*. Berlin, Germany.

Shiqi Shen, Yong Cheng, Zhongjun He, Wei He, Hua Wu, Maosong Sun, and Yang Liu. 2016. Minimum risk training for neural machine translation. In *Proceedings of the 54th Annual Meeting of the Association for Computational Linguistics*. Berlin, Germany.

Matthew Snover, Bonnie Dorr, Richard Schwartz, Linnea Micciulla, and John Makhoul. 2006. A study of translation edit rate with targeted human annotation. In *Proceedings of the 7th Conference of the Association for Machine Translation in the Americas*. Cambridge, Massachusetts.

Artem Sokolov, Julia Kreutzer, Christopher Lo, and Stefan Riezler. 2016a. Learning structured predictors from bandit feedback for interactive nlp. In *Proceedings of the 54th Annual Meeting of the Association for Computational Linguistics*. Berlin, Germany.

Artem Sokolov, Julia Kreutzer, Stefan Riezler, and Christopher Lo. 2016b. Stochastic structured prediction under bandit feedback. In *Advances in Neural Information Processing Systems*. Barcelona, Spain.

Artem Sokolov, Julia Kreutzer, Kellen Sunderland, Pavel Danchenko, Witold Szymaniak, Hagen Fürstenau, and Stefan Riezler. 2017. A shared task on bandit learning for machine translation. In *Proceedings of the Second Conference on Machine Translation*. Copenhagen, Denmark.

Alexander L. Strehl, John Langford, Lihong Li, and Sham M. Kakade. 2010. Learning from logged implicit exploration data. In *Advances in Neural Information Processing Sytems (NIPS)*. Vancouver, Canada.

Adith Swaminathan and Thorsten Joachims. 2015. The self-normalized estimator for counterfactual learning. In *Advances in Neural Information Processing Systems (NIPS)*. Montreal, Canada.

Jörg Tiedemann. 2009. News from opus-a collection of multilingual parallel corpora with tools and interfaces. In *Recent advances in natural language processing*. volume 5, pages 237–248.

Ronald J Williams. 1992. Simple statistical gradient-following algorithms for connectionist reinforcement learning. *Machine learning* 8:229–256.

Yonghui Wu, Mike Schuster, Zhifeng Chen, Quoc V Le, Mohammad Norouzi, Wolfgang Macherey, Maxim Krikun, Yuan Cao, Qin Gao, Klaus Macherey, et al. 2016. Google's neural machine translation system: Bridging the gap between human and machine translation. *arXiv preprint arXiv:1609.08144* .

A Appendix Overview

Section B provides the instructions that were given to the annotators when judging MT quality. In Section C we provide histograms for simulated and explicit rewards. Section D contains details on the data and NMT model hyperparameters. In Section E we give results for simulation experiments on the e-commerce product title domain and a publicly available data set. Finally, we compare translation examples of different models in Section F.

B Annotation Instructions

B.1 Star Ratings

Please rate the translation quality of the segments on the scale from 1 to 5. Focus on whether or not the information contained in the source sentence is correctly and completely translated (ratings 1 - 4). Then, if you are ready to give a 4 based on the criteria below, check whether or not you can assign a 5 instead of the 4, focusing on remaining grammatical, morphological and stylistic errors. Remember that even a very fluent translation that looks like a human-produced sentence can receive a bad rating if it does not correctly convey all the information that was present in the source.

Assign the following ratings from 1 to 5:

1. Important information is missing and/or distorted in the translation, and the error is so severe that it may lead to erroneous perception of the described product. Or the translation contains profanities/insulting words.

2. Information from the source is partially present in the translation, but important information is not translated or translated incorrectly.

3. The most important information from the source is translated correctly, but some other less important information is missing or translated incorrectly.

4. All of the information from the source is contained in the translation. This should be the only criterion to decide between 1-3 and 4. It is okay for a 4-rated translation to contain grammatical errors, disfluencies, or word choice that is not very appropriate to the style of the input text. There might be errors in casing of named entities when it is clear from the context that these are named entities.

5. All of the information from the source is contained in the translation and is translated correctly. In contrast to a 4-rated translation, the translation is fluent, easy to read, and contains either no or very minor grammatical/morphological/stylistic errors. The brand names and other named entities have the correct upper/lower case.

B.2 Binary Judgment

The customers of the eBay e-commerce platform, when presented with a title translation on the product page, can hover with the mouse over the translation of the title and see the original (source) title in a pop-up window. There, they have the possibility to rate the translation with 1 to 5 stars.

The goal of this evaluation is to check the ratings - you have to mark "Agree" when you agree with the rating and "Disagree" otherwise. The rating (number from 1 to 5) is shown in the Reference line.

Note that eBay customers did not have any instructions on what the rating of 5 stars, 3 stars, or 4 stars means. Thus, the evaluation is subjective on their side. Please apply your common sense when agreeing or disagreeing with human judgment. The focus should be on adequacy (correct information transfer) as opposed to fluency.

C Rewards

C.1 Reward Distributions

Figure 3 shows the distribution of logged user star ratings, Figure 4 the distribution of sentence BLEU (sBLEU) scores for the simulation experiments with logged feedback. The logged translations for the user star ratings were generated by the production system, the logged translations for the simulation were generated by the BL NMT system.

D Training Details

D.1 Data

We conduct experiments on an English-to-Spanish e-commerce item titles translation task. The in-domain data for training with simulated feedback is composed of in-house eBay data (item titles, descriptions, etc.). The out-of-domain data for training the baselines contains only publicly available parallel corpora, that is Europarl, TAUS, and OpenSubtitles released by the OPUS project (Tiedemann, 2009). The out-of-domain

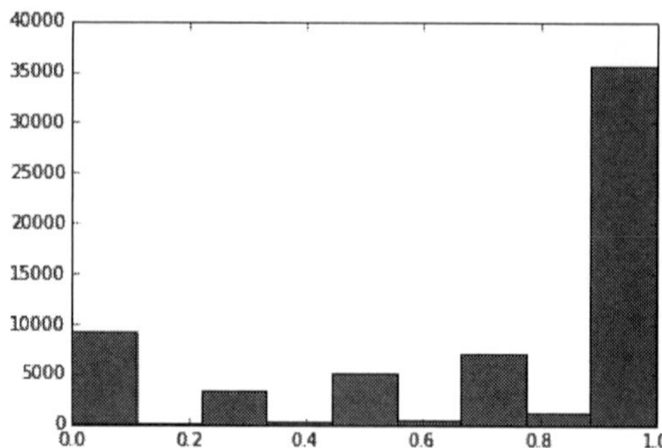

Figure 3: Distribution of user star ratings. The original ratings on a five-star scale are averaged per title and rescaled.

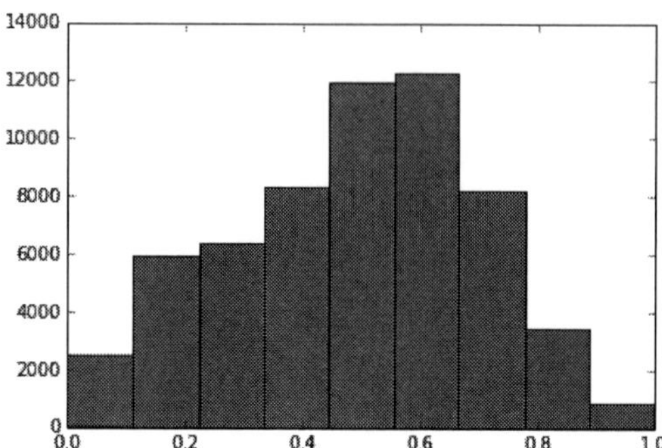

Figure 4: Distribution of sentence BLEUs of the product title training set when translated with the out-of-domain baseline for simulation experiments.

		En	Es
Train:	Sentences	2,741,087	
	Tokens	17,139,416	18,270,753
	Vocabulary	327,504	393,757
	Singletons	162,834	190,686
Dev.:	Sentences	1,619	
	Tokens	29,063	31,813
	Vocabulary	11,314	11,532
	OOVs	2,645	2,493
Test	Sentences	1000	
	Tokens	9,851	11,221
	Vocabulary	6,735	6,668
	OOVs	1,966	1,902

Table 7: Corpus statistics for the out-of domain training data and in-domain dev and test data.

Description	Size
User star ratings	69,412
... with 5 stars	40,064
Expert star ratings	1,000
Expert judgments	2,000
Query-title pairs	164,065
... with $recall = 1$	61,965
Title translations	62,162

Table 8: Data set sizes for collected feedback in number of sentences. The in-domain title translations are only used for simulation experiments.

data has been sub-sampled according to the similarity to the domain of the product title data, and 25% of the most similar sentence pairs have been selected. The corpus statistics for parallel data are shown in Table 7. Before calculating the corpus statistics, we apply pre-processing including tokenization and replacement of numbers and product specifications with a placeholder token (e.g., '6S', and '1080p'). Table 8 gives an overview of the type and the size of the translations with feedback.

D.2 NMT Model Architecture

The NMT has a bi-directional RNN encoder with one layer of 1000 GRUs, a decoder with 1000 GRUs, and source and target word embeddings of size 620. The vocabulary is generated from the out-of-domain training corpus with 40k byte-pair merges (Sennrich et al., 2016c) and contains 40813 source tokens and 41050 target tokens. The full softmax is approximated by 1024 samples as proposed in (Jean et al., 2015). Dropout (Gal and Ghahramani, 2016) is applied with probability $p = 0.1$ to the embedding matrices, with $p = 0.2$ to the input and recurrent connections of the RNNs.

D.3 NMT Training Hyperparameters

The out-of-domain model is trained with mini-batches of size 100 and L2 regularization with weight 1×10^{-7}, optimized with Adam (Kingma and Ba, 2014) with initial $\alpha = 0.0002$, then decaying α by 0.9 each epoch.

The remaining models are trained with constant learning rates and mini-batch size 30, regularization and dropout stay the same. The settings for the other hyperparameters are listed in Table 9. The estimator loss weight is only relevant for DC, where the pre-trained estimator gets further fine-tuned during DC training.

D.4 Reward Estimation

We find that for reward estimation a shallow CNN architecture with wide filters performs superior to a deeper CNN architecture (Le et al., 2017) and also to a recurrent architecture. Hence, we use one convolutional layer with ReLU activation of

Model	Adam's α	Length-Normalization	MRT α	Sample Size k	MIX λ	Estimator Loss Weight
Simulated Feedback						
MLE	0.002	-	-	-	-	-
MIX	0.002	-	0.005	5	0.05	-
EL	2×10^{-6}	-	-	-	-	-
DPM	2×10^{-6}	x	-	-	-	-
DPM-random	2×10^{-6}	x	-	-	-	-
DC	0.002	-	-	5	-	1000
Explicit Star Rating Feedback						
DPM	2×10^{-6}	x	-	-	-	-
DPM-random	2×10^{-6}	x	-	-	-	-
DC	2×10^{-6}	x	-	5	-	1000
MLE (all)	0.002	-	-	-	-	-
MIX (all)	0.002	-	0.005	5	0.05	-
MIX (small)	0.002	-	0.005	5	0.05	-
MIX (stars=5)	0.002	-	0.005	5	0.05	-
Implicit Task-Based Feedback						
MLE (all)	0.002	-	-	-	-	-
MIX (all)	0.002	-	0.005	5	0.05	-
MIX (small)	0.002	-	0.005	5	0.05	-
MIX (recall=1)	0.002	-	0.005	5	0.05	-
W-MIX	0.002	-	0.005	5	0.05	-

Table 9: Hyperparameter settings for training of the models.

n_f filters each for filter sizes from 2 to 15, capturing both local and more global features. For reward estimation on star ratings, $n_f = 100$ and on simulated sBLEU $n_f = 20$ worked best. Dropout with $p = 0.5$ is applied before the output layer for the simulation setting. We set $T_{max} = 60$. The loss of each item in the batch is weighted by inverse frequency of its feedback in the current batch (counted in 10 buckets) to counterbalance skewed feedback distributions. The model is optimized with Adam (Kingma and Ba, 2014) (constant $\alpha = 0.001$ for star ratings, $\alpha = 0.002$ for the simulation) on minibatches of size 30. Note that the differences in hyper-parameters between both settings are the result of tuning and do not cause the difference in quality of the resulting estimators. We do not evaluate on a separate test set, since their final quality can be measured in how much well they serve as policy evaluators in counterfactual learning.

E Simulated Bandit Feedback

Expected Loss. When rewards can be retrieved for sampled translations during learning, the Online Bandit Structured Prediction framework proposed by Sokolov et al. (2016a,b) can be applied for NMT, as demonstrated in Kreutzer et al. (2017); Sokolov et al. (2017). The *Expected Loss* objective (EL, Equation 8) maximizes[5] the expectation of a reward over all source and target sequences, and does in principle not require references:

$$R^{\text{EL}}(\theta) = \mathbb{E}_{p(\mathbf{x})p_\theta(\tilde{\mathbf{y}}|\mathbf{x})} \left[\Delta(\tilde{\mathbf{y}}) \right]. \qquad (8)$$

While we could not apply it to the logged user feedback since it was obtained offline, we can compare to its performance in a simulation setting with simulated rewards instead of human feedback. It is expected to outperform methods learning with logged feedback due to the exploration during learning. In the following simulation experiments, $\Delta(\tilde{\mathbf{y}})$ is computed by comparing a sampled translation $\tilde{\mathbf{y}} \sim p_\theta(\mathbf{y}|\mathbf{x})$ to a given reference translation $\mathbf{y}$ with smoothed sentence-level BLEU (sBLEU).

E.1 E-commerce Product Titles

We test several of the proposed learning techniques with an in-domain parallel corpus (62,162 sentences) of product titles where bandit feedback is simulated by evaluating a sampled translation against a reference using sBLEU. Similar to previous studies on SMT (Lawrence et al., 2017b),

---

[5]We use the terms reward or loss interchangeably depending on minimization or maximization contexts.

Learning	Model	Test BLEU	Test TER
Pre-trained	BL	28.38	57.58
Fully Supervised	MLE	31.72	53.02
	MIX	$34.79_{\pm 0.02}$	$48.56_{\pm 0.02}$
Online Bandit	EL	$31.78_{\pm 0.06}$	$51.11_{\pm 0.36}$
Counterfactual	DPM	30.19	56.28
	DPM-random	28.20	57.89
	DC	$31.11_{\pm 0.34}$	$55.05_{\pm 0.02}$

Table 10: Results for **simulation experiments** evaluated on the product titles test set.

Model	SMT	NMT (beam search)	NMT (greedy)
EP BL	25.27	27.55	26.32
NC BL	–	22.35	19.63
MLE	28.08	32.48	31.04
EL	–	28.02	27.93
DPM	26.24	27.54	26.36
DC	26.33	28.20	27.39

Table 11: BLEU results for simulation models evaluated on the News Commentary test set (`nc-test2007`) with beam search and greedy decoding. SMT results are from Lawrence et al. (2017b).

this reward is deterministic and does not contain user-dependent noise.

Supervised Fine-Tuning. When fine-tuning the baseline model on in-domain references (Luong and Manning, 2015), the model improves 3.34 BLEU (MLE in Table 10) on an in-domain test set (1,000 sentences). By tuning it on the same in-domain data for sBLEU with MIX, it gains another 3 BLEU points.

Bandit Learning. When feedback is given to only one translation per input (=online bandit feedback), the model (EL) achieves comparable performance to MLE training with references. When the feedback is logged offline for one round of deterministic outputs of the baseline model (=offline bandit feedback), we can still find improvements of 1.81 BLEU (DPM). With a reward estimator trained on this log, DC achieves even higher improvements of 3 BLEU. To test the contribution of the feedback in contrast to a simple in-domain training effect, we randomly perturbed the pairing of feedback signal and translation and retrain (DPM-random). This clearly degrades results, confirming feedback to be a useful signal rather than noise.

E.2 Results on Publicly Available Data

Simulation experiments were also run on publicly available data. We use the same data, preprocessing and splits as (Lawrence et al., 2017b) to compare with their French-to-English news experiments on counterfactual learning with deterministically logged feedback for statistical machine translation (SMT). The baseline model is trained with MLE on 1.6M Europarl (EP) translations, bandit feedback is then simulated from 40k News Commentary (NC) translations. For the comparison of full supervision vs. weak feedback, we train in-domain models with MLE on in-domain NC references: training only on in-domain data (NC BL), and fine-tuning the out-of-domain baseline (EP BL) on in-domain data (MLE). The results are given in Table 11. The NMT baselines outperform the SMT equivalents. With fully supervised fine-tuning the NMT models improve over the out-of-domain baseline (EP BL) by 5 BLEU points, outperforming also the in-domain baseline (NC BL). Moving to weak feedback, we still find improvements over the baseline by 0.5 BLEU with beam search and 1.6 BLEU with greedy decoding for online feedback (EL), and 0.6 BLEU with beam search and 1 BLEU with greedy decoding for counterfactual learning with DC. However, DPM performs worse than for SMT and those not manage to improve over the out-of-domain baseline. Nevertheless these results confirm that – at least in simulation settings – the DC objective is very suitable for counterfactual learning from bandit feedback for NMT, almost reaching the gains of learning from online bandit feedback.

F Examples

Table 12 gives an example where W-MIX training improved lexical translation choices. Table 13 lists two examples of W-MIX translations in comparison to the baseline and logged translations for given queries and product titles to illustrate the specific difficulties of the domain.

Title (en)	hall linvatec pro2070 powerpro ao <u>drill</u> synthes dhs & dcs <u>attachment</u> / warranty
Reference-0 (es)	hall linvatec pro2070 powerpro ao <u>taladro</u> synthes dhs & dcs <u>accesorio</u> / garantía
Reference-1 (es)	hall linvatec pro2070 powerpro synthes , <u>perforación</u> , <u>accesorio</u> de dhs y dcs , todo original , garantía
BL (es)	hall linvatec pro2070 powerpro ao <u>perforadora</u> synthes dhs & dcs <u>adjuntos</u> / garantía
MIX on star-rated titles (es)	hall linvatec pro2070 powerpro ao <u>perforadora</u> synthes dhs & dcs <u>adjuntos</u> / garantía
MIX on query-titles, small (es)	hall linvatec pro2070 powerpro ao <u>perforadora</u> synthes dhs & dcs <u>adjuntos</u> / garantía
MIX on query-titles, all (es)	hall linvatec pro2070 powerpro ao <u>taladro</u> synthes dhs & dcs adjuntos / garantía
W-MIX	hall linvatec pro2070 powerpro ao <u>taladro</u> synthes dhs & dcs <u>accesorio</u> / garantía

Table 12: Example for product title translation from the test set where W-MIX improved the lexical choice over BL and MIX on in-domain title set and MIX on full query-title set ('perforadora' vs 'taladro' as translation for 'drill', 'adjuntos' vs 'accesorio' as translation for 'attachment').

Title (en)	Unicorn Thread 12pcs Makeup <u>Brushes</u> Set Gorgeous Colorful <u>Foundation</u> Brush
Query (es)	unicorn <u>brushes</u> // makeup <u>brushes</u> // <u>brochas</u> de unicornio // <u>brochas</u> unicornio
Query (en)	unicorn <u>brushes</u> // makeup <u>brushes</u>
BL (es)	galletas de maquillaje de 12pcs
Log (es)	Unicorn Rosca 12 un. Conjunto de <u>Pinceles</u> para Maquillaje Hermosa Colorida <u>Base</u> Cepillo
W-MIX	unicornio rosca 12pcs <u>brochas</u> maquillaje conjunto precioso colorido <u>fundación</u> cepillo
Title (en)	12 × Men Women Plastic Shoe Boxes 33*20*12cm Storage Organisers Clear Large Boxes
Query (es)	cajas plasticas <u>para</u> zapatos
Query (en)	plastic shoe boxes
BL (es)	12 × hombres mujeres zapatos de plástico cajas de almacenamiento 33*20*12cm organizadores de gran tamaño
Log (es)	12 × Zapato De Hombre Mujer De Plástico Cajas Organizadores de almacenamiento 33*20*12cm cajas Grande Claro
W-MIX	12 × <u>para</u> hombres zapatos de plástico cajas de plástico 33*20*12cm almacenamiento organizador transparente grandes cajas

Table 13: Examples for product title translations of the logged query test set. In the first example, the W-MIX model improves the translation of "brushes", but also chooses a worse translation for "foundation" ("fundación" vs "base"). In the second example, one of the tricky parts is to translate the sequence of nouns "Men Women Plastic Shoe Boxes" and to disambiguate the relations between them. The BL model translates "shoes of plastic", the Log has "woman of plastic" and the W-MIX model makes it "shoes of plastic" and "boxes of plastic". The W-MIX model learns to use "para" from the query, but omits the translation of "women".

Accelerating NMT Batched Beam Decoding
with LMBR Posteriors for Deployment

Gonzalo Iglesias[†] **William Tambellini**[†] **Adrià De Gispert**[†‡]   **Eva Hasler**[†]   **Bill Byrne**[†‡]

[†]SDL Research

`{giglesias|wtambellini|agispert|ehasler|bbyrne}@sdl.com`

[‡]Department of Engineering, University of Cambridge, U.K.

Abstract

We describe a batched beam decoding algorithm for NMT with LMBR n-gram posteriors, showing that LMBR techniques still yield gains on top of the best recently reported results with Transformers. We also discuss acceleration strategies for deployment, and the effect of the beam size and batching on memory and speed.

1 Introduction

The advent of Neural Machine Translation (NMT) has revolutionized the market. Objective improvements (Sutskever et al., 2014; Bahdanau et al., 2015; Sennrich et al., 2016b; Gehring et al., 2017; Vaswani et al., 2017) and a fair amount of neural hype have increased the pressure on companies offering Machine Translation services to shift as quickly as possible to this new paradigm.

Such a radical change entails non-trivial challenges for deployment; consumers certainly look forward to better translation quality, but do not want to lose all the good features that have been developed over the years along with SMT technology. With NMT, real time decoding is challenging without GPUs, and still an avenue for research (Devlin, 2017). Great speeds have been reported by Junczys-Dowmunt et al. (2016) on GPUs, for which batching queries to the neural model is essential. Disk usage and memory footprint of pure neural systems are certainly lower than that of SMT systems, but at the same time GPU memory is limited and high-end GPUs are expensive.

Further to that, consumers still need the ability to constrain translations; in particular, brand-related information is often as important for companies as translation quality itself, and is currently under investigation (Chatterjee et al., 2017; Hokamp and Liu, 2017; Hasler et al., 2018). It is also well known that pure neural systems

reach very high fluency, often sacrificing adequacy (Tu et al., 2017; Zhang et al., 2017; Koehn and Knowles, 2017), and have been reported to behave badly under noisy conditions (Belinkov and Bisk, 2018). Stahlberg et al. (2017) show an effective way to counter these problems by taking advantage of the higher adequacy inherent to SMT systems via Lattice Minimum Bayes Risk (LMBR) decoding (Tromble et al., 2008). This makes the system more robust to pitfalls, such as over- and under-generation (Feng et al., 2016; Meng et al., 2016; Tu et al., 2016) which is important for commercial applications.

In this paper, we describe a batched beam decoding algorithm that uses NMT models with LMBR n-gram posterior probabilities (Stahlberg et al., 2017). Batching in NMT beam decoding has been mentioned or assumed in the literature, e.g. (Devlin, 2017; Junczys-Dowmunt et al., 2016), but to the best of our knowledge it has not been formally described, and there are interesting aspects for deployment worth taking into consideration.

We also report on the effect of LMBR posteriors on state-of-the-art neural systems, for five translation tasks. Finally, we discuss how to prepare (LMBR-based) NMT systems for deployment, and how our batching algorithm performs in terms of memory and speed.

2 Neural Machine Translation and LMBR

Given a source sentence $\mathbf{x}$, a sequence-to-sequence NMT model scores a candidate translation sentence $\mathbf{y} = y_1^T$ with T words as:

$$P_{NMT}(y_1^T|\mathbf{x}) = \prod_{t=1}^{T} P_{NMT}(y_t|y_1^{t-1}, \mathbf{x}) \quad (1)$$

where $P_{NMT}(y_t|y_1^{t-1}, \mathbf{x})$ uses a neural function $f_{NMT}(\cdot)$. To account for batching B neu-

Proceedings of NAACL-HLT 2018, pages 106–113
New Orleans, Louisiana, June 1 - 6, 2018. ©2017 Association for Computational Linguistics

ral queries together, our abstract function takes the form of $f_{NMT}(\mathbf{S}_{t-1}, \mathbf{y}_{t-1}, \mathbf{A})$ where $\mathbf{S}_{t-1}$ is the previous batch state with B state vectors in rows, $\mathbf{y}_{t-1}$ is a vector with the B preceding generated target words, and $\mathbf{A}$ is a matrix with the annotations (Bahdanau et al., 2015) of a source sentence. The model has a vocabulary size V.

The implementation of this function is determined by the architecture of specific models. The most successful ones in the literature typically share in common an attention mechanism that determines which source word to focus on, informed by $\mathbf{A}$ and $\mathbf{S}_{t-1}$. Bahdanau et al. (2015) use recurrent layers to both compute $\mathbf{A}$ and the next target word y_t. Gehring et al. (2017) use convolutional layers instead, and Vaswani et al. (2017) prescind from GRU or LSTM layers, relying heavily on multi-layered attention mechanisms, stateful only on the translation side. Finally, this function can also represent an ensemble of neural models.

Lattice Minimum Bayes Risk decoding computes n-gram posterior probabilities from an *evidence space* and uses them to score a *hypothesis space* (Kumar and Byrne, 2004; Tromble et al., 2008; Blackwood et al., 2010). It improves single SMT systems, and also lends itself quite nicely to system combination (Sim et al., 2007; de Gispert et al., 2009). Stahlberg et al. (2017) have recently shown a way to use it with NMT decoding: a traditional SMT system is first used to create an evidence space φ_e, and the NMT space is then scored left-to-right with both the NMT model(s) and the n-gram posteriors gathered from φ_e. More formally:

$$\hat{y} = \arg\max_y \sum_{t=1}^{T} (\Theta_0 + \overbrace{\sum_{n=1}^{4} \Theta_n P_{LMBR}(y_{t-n}^t | \varphi_e)}^{\mathbf{L}(y_{t-n}^{t-1}, y_t)} \\ + \lambda \log P_{NMT}(y_t | y_1^{t-1}, \mathbf{x})) \quad (2)$$

For our purposes $\mathbf{L}$ is arranged as a matrix with each row uniquely associated to an n-gram history identified in φ_e: each row contains scores for any word y in the NMT vocabulary.

$\mathbf{L}$ can be precomputed very efficiently, and stored in the GPU memory. The number of distinct n-gram histories is typically no more than 500 for our phrase-based decoder producing 200 hypotheses. Notice that such a matrix only containing P_{LMBR} contributions would be very sparse, but

it turns into a dense matrix with the summation of Θ_0. Both sparse and dense operations can be performed on the GPU. We have found it more efficient to compute first all the sparse operations on CPU, and then upload to the GPU memory and sum the constant Θ_0 in GPU[1].

3 NMT batched beam decoding

Algorithm 1 describes NMT decoding with LMBR posteriors using beam size B equal to the batch size. Lines 2-5 initialize the decoder; the number of time steps T is usually a heuristic function of the source length. $\mathbf{q}$ will keep track of the B best scores per time step, $\mathbf{b}$ and $\mathbf{y}$ are indices.

Lines 7-16 are the core of the batch decoding procedure. At each time step t, given $\mathbf{S}_{t-1}$, $\mathbf{y}_{t-1}$ and $\mathbf{A}$, f_{NMT} returns two matrices: $\mathbf{P}_t$, with size $B \times V$, contains log-probabilities for all possible candidates in the vocabulary given B live hypotheses. $\mathbf{S}_t$ is the next batch state. Each row in $\mathbf{S}_t$ is the vector state that corresponds to any candidate in the same row of $\mathbf{P}_t$ (line 8).

Lines 9, 10 add the n-gram posterior scores. Given the indices in $\mathbf{b}$ and $\mathbf{y}$ it is straightforward to read the unique histories for the B open hypotheses: the topology of the hypothesis space is that of a tree because an NMT state represents the entire live hypothesis from time step 0. Note that $b_{tj} < B$ is the index to access the previous word in $\mathbf{y}_{t-1}$. In effect, indices in $\mathbf{b}$ function as backpointers, allowing to reconstruct not only n-grams per time step, but also complete hypotheses. As discussed for Equation 2, these histories are associated to rows in our matrix $\mathbf{L}$. Function GETMATRIXBYROWS$(\cdot)$ simply creates a new matrix of size $B \times V$ by fetching those B rows from L. This new matrix is summed to $\mathbf{P}_t$ (line 10).

In line 11, we get the indices and scores in $\mathbf{P}_t + \mathbf{q}'_{t-1}$ of the top B hypotheses. These best hypotheses could come from any row in $\mathbf{P}_t$. For example, all B best hypotheses could have been found in row 0. In that case, the new batch state to be used in the next time step should contain copies of row 0 in the other $B - 1$ rows. This is achieved again with GETMATRIXBYROWS$(\cdot)$ in line 12.

Finally, lines 13-16 identify whether there are any end-of-sentence (EOS) candidates; the corre-

---

[1] Ideally we would want to keep $\mathbf{L}$ as a sparse matrix and sum Θ_0 on-the-fly. However this is not possible with Array-Fire 3.6.

Algorithm 1 Batch decoding with LMBR n-gram posteriors

1: **procedure** DECODENMT(x, **L**)
2:     $T \leftarrow$ Maximum target hypothesis length
3:     **b**, **y**, **q** indices and scores, with $\mathbf{b}_0 \leftarrow \mathbf{0}, \mathbf{y}_0 \leftarrow \mathbf{0}, \mathbf{q}_0 \leftarrow \mathbf{0}$
4:     **A** $\leftarrow$ Annotations for source sentence x
5:     $\mathbf{S}_0 \leftarrow$ Initial decoder state
6:     $F = \{\}$ ▷ Set of EOS survivors
7:     **for** t = 1 to T **do**
8:         $\mathbf{P}_t, \mathbf{S}_t \leftarrow f_{NMT}(\mathbf{S}_{t-1}, \mathbf{y}_{t-1}, \mathbf{A})$
9:         **h** $\leftarrow B$ histories identified through **b**, **y** and t
10:       $\mathbf{P}_t \leftarrow \mathbf{P}_t + $ GETMATRIXBYROWS(**L**, **h**)   ▷ Add LMBR contributions
11:       $\mathbf{b}_t, \mathbf{y}_t, \mathbf{q}_t \leftarrow$ TOPB$(\mathbf{P}_t + \mathbf{q}'_{t-1})$
12:       $\mathbf{S}_t \leftarrow$ GETMATRIXBYROWS$(\mathbf{S}_t, \mathbf{b}_t)$
13:       **for** j = 0 to $B - 1$ **do**
14:         **if** $y_{tj} = EOS$ **then**
15:           $F \leftarrow F \cup (\{t, j, q_{tj}\})$ ▷ Track indices and score
16:           $q_{tj} \leftarrow -\infty$ ▷ Mask out to prevent hypothesis extension
17:     **return** GETBESTHYPOTHESIS$(F, \mathbf{b}, \mathbf{y})$

---

sponding indices and score are pushed into stack F and these candidates are masked out (i.e. set to $-\infty$) to prevent further expansion. In line 17, GETBESTHYPOTHESIS(F) traces backwards the best hypothesis in F, again using indices in **b** and **y**. Optionally, normalization by hypothesis length happens in this step.

It is worth noting that:

1. If we drop lines 9, 10 we have a pure left-to-right NMT batched beam decoder.

2. Applying a constraint (e.g. for lattice rescoring or other user constraints) involves masking out scores in $\mathbf{P}_t$ before line 11.

3. Because the batch size is tied to the beam size, the memory footprint increases with the beam.

4. Due to the beam being used for both EOS and non EOS candidates, it can be argued that this empoverishes the beam and it could be kept in addition to non EOS candidates (either by using a bigger beam, or keeping separately). Empirically we have found that this does not affect quality with real models.

5. The opposite, i.e. that EOS candidates never survive in the beam for T time steps, can happen, although very infrequently. Several pragmatic backoff strategies can be applied in this situation: for example, running the decoder for additional time steps, or tracking all EOS candidates that did not survive in a separate stack and picking the best hypothesis from there. We chose the latter.

3.1 Extension to Sentence batching

In addition to batching all B queries to the neural model needed to compute the next time step for one sentence, we can do *sentence batching*: this is, we translate N sentences simultaneously, batching $B \times N$ queries per time step.

With small modifications, Algorithm 1 can be easily extended to handle sentence batching. If the number of sentences is N,

1. Instead of one set F to store EOS candidates, we need $F_1...F_N$ sets.

2. For every time step, $\mathbf{b}_t, \mathbf{y}_t$ and $\mathbf{q}_t$ need to be matrices instead of vectors, and minor changes are required in TOPB$(\cdot)$ to fetch the best candidates per sentence efficiently.

3. $\mathbf{P}_t$ and $\mathbf{S}_t$ can remain as matrices, in which case the new batch size is simply $B \cdot N$.

4. The heuristic function used to compute T is typically sentence specific.

4 Experiments

4.1 Experimental Setup

We report experiments on English-German, German-English and Chinese-English language

	WMT17			WAT	
	ger-eng	**eng-ger**	**chi-eng**	**eng-jpn**	**jpn-eng**
PBMT	28.9	19.6	15.8	33.4	18.0
FNMT	32.8	26.1	20.8	39.1	25.3
LNMT	33.7	26.6	22.0	40.4	26.1
TNMT	35.2	28.9	24.8	44.6	29.4
LTNMT	35.4	29.2	25.4	44.9	30.2
Best submissions	35.1	28.3	26.4	43.3	28.4

Table 1: Quality assessment of our NMT systems with and without LMBR posteriors for GRU-based (FNMT, LNMT) and Transformer models (TNMT, LTNMT). Cased BLEU scores reported on 5 translation tasks. The exact PBMT systems used to compute n-gram posteriors for LNMT and LTNMT systems are also reported. The last row shows scores for the best official submissions to each task.

pairs for the WMT17 task, and Japanese-English and English-Japanese for the WAT task. For the German tasks we use *news-test2013* as a development set, and *news-test2017* as a test set; for Chinese-English, we use *news-dev2017* as a development set, and *news-test2017* as a test set. For Japanese tasks we use the ASPEC corpus (Nakazawa et al., 2016).

We use all available data in each task for training. In addition, for German we use back-translation data (Sennrich et al., 2016a). All training data for neural models is preprocessed with the byte pair encoding technique described by Sennrich et al. (2016b). We use Blocks (van Merriënboer et al., 2015) with Theano (Bastien et al., 2012) to train attention-based single GRU layer models (Bahdanau et al., 2015), henceforth called **FNMT**. The vocabulary size is 50K. Transformer models (Vaswani et al., 2017), called here **TNMT**, are trained using the Tensor2Tensor package[2] with a vocabulary size of 30K.

Our proprietary translation system is a modular homegrown tool that supports pure neural decoding (FNMT and TNMT) and with LMBR posteriors (henceforce called **LNMT** and **LTNMT** respectively), and flexibly uses other components (phrase-based decoding, byte pair encoding, etcetera) to seamlessly deploy an end-to-end translation system.

FNMT/LNMT systems use ensembles of 3 neural models unless specified otherwise; TNMT/LTNMT systems decode with 1 to 2 models, each averaging over the last 20 checkpoints.

The Phrase-based decoder (**PBMT**) uses standard features with one single 5-gram language model (Heafield et al., 2013), and is tuned with standard MERT (Och, 2003); n-gram posterior probabilities are computed on-the-fly over rich translation lattices, with size bounded by the PBMT stack and distortion limits. The parameter λ in Equation 2 is set as 0.5 divided by the number of models in the ensemble. Empirically we have found this to be a good setting in many tasks.

Unless noted otherwise, the beam size is set to 12 and the NMT beam decoder always batches queries to the neural model. The beam decoder relies on an early preview of ArrayFire 3.6 (Yalamanchili et al., 2015)[3], compiled with CUDA 8.0 libraries. For speed measurements, the decoder uses one single CPU thread. For hardware, we use an Intel Xeon CPU E5-2640 at 2.60GHz. The GPU is a GeForce GTX 1080Ti. We report cased BLEU scores (Papineni et al., 2002), strictly comparable to the official scores in each task[4].

4.2 The effect of LMBR n-gram posteriors

Table 1 shows contrastive experiments for all five language pair/tasks. We make the following observations:

1. LMBR posteriors show consistent gains on top of the GRU model (LNMT vs FNMT rows), ranging from +0.5BLEU to +1.2BLEU. This is consistent with the findings reported by Stahlberg et al. (2017).

2. The TNMT system boasts improvements across the board, ranging from +1.5BLEU in German-English to an impressive +4.2BLEU in English-Japanese WAT

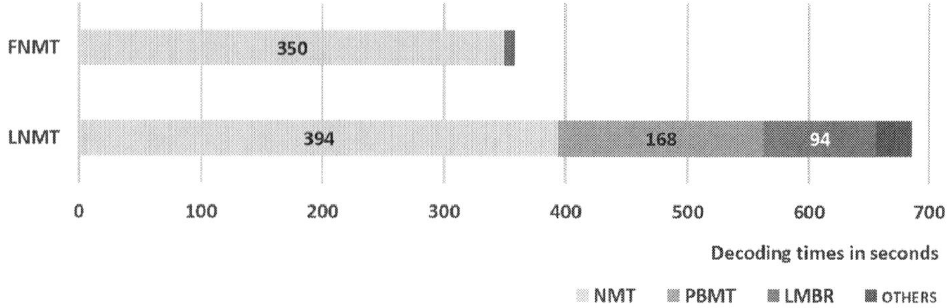

Figure 1: Accelerated FNMT and LNMT decoding times for newstest-2017 test set.

(TNMT vs LNMT). This is in line with findings by Vaswani et al. (2017) and sets new very strong baselines to improve on.

3. Further, applying LMBR posteriors along with the Transformer model yields gains in all tasks (LTNMT vs TNMT), up to +0.8BLEU in Japanese-English. Interestingly, while we find that rescoring PBMT lattices (Stahlberg et al., 2016) with GRU models yields similar improvements to those reported by Stahlberg et al. (2017), we did not find gains when rescoring with the stronger TNMT models instead.

4.3 Accelerating FNMT and LNMT systems for deployment

There is no particular constraint on speed for the research systems reported in Table 1. We now address the question of deploying NMT systems so that MT users get the best quality improvements at real-time speed and with acceptable memory footprint. As an example, we analyse in detail the English-German FNMT and LNMT case and discuss the main trade-offs if one wanted to accelerate them. Although the actual measurements vary across all our productised NMT engines, the trends are similar to the ones reported here.

In this particular case we specify a beam width of 0.01 for early pruning (Wu et al., 2016; Delaney et al., 2006) and reduce the beam size to 4. We also shrink the ensemble into one single big model[5] using the data-free shrinking method described by Stahlberg and Byrne (2017), an inexpensive way to improve both speed and GPU memory footprint.

In addition, for LNMT systems we tune phrase-based decoder parameters such as the distortion limit, the number of translations per source phrase and the stack limit. To compute n-gram posteriors we now only take a 200-best from the phrase-based translation lattice.

Table 2 shows a contrast of our English-German WMT17 research systems versus the respective accelerated ones.

	Research		Accelerated	
	BLEU	speed	BLEU	speed
FNMT	26.1	2207	25.2	9449
LNMT	26.6	263	25.7	4927

Table 2: Cased BLEU scores for *research* vs *accelerated* English-to-German WMT17 systems. Speed reported in words per minute.

In the process, both accelerated systems have lost 0.9 BLEU relative to the baseline. As an example, let us break down the effects of accelerating the LNMT system: using only 200-best hypotheses from the phrase-based translation lattice reduces 0.3 BLEU. Replacing the ensemble with a data-free shrunken model reduces another 0.2 BLEU and decreasing the beam size reduces 0.4 BLEU. The impact of reducing the beam size varies from system to system, although often does not result in substantial quality loss for NMT models (Britz et al., 2017).

It is worth noting that these two systems share exactly the same neural model and parameter values. However, LNMT runs 4500 words per minute (wpm) slower than FNMT. Figure 1 breaks down the decoding times for both the accelerated FNMT and LNMT systems. The LNMT pipeline also requires a phrase-based decoder and the extra component to compute the n-gram posterior probabil-

---

[5]The file size of each 3 individual models of the ensemble is 510MB; the size of the shrunken model is 1.2GB.

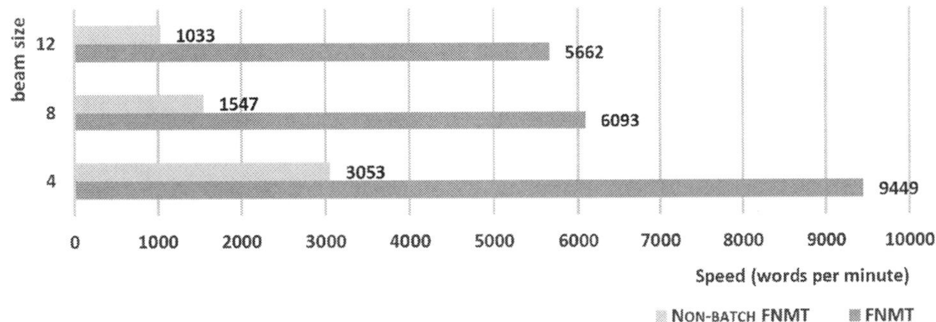

Figure 2: Batch beam decoder speed measured over newstest-2017 test set, using the accelerated FNMT system (25.2 BLEU for beam size = 4).

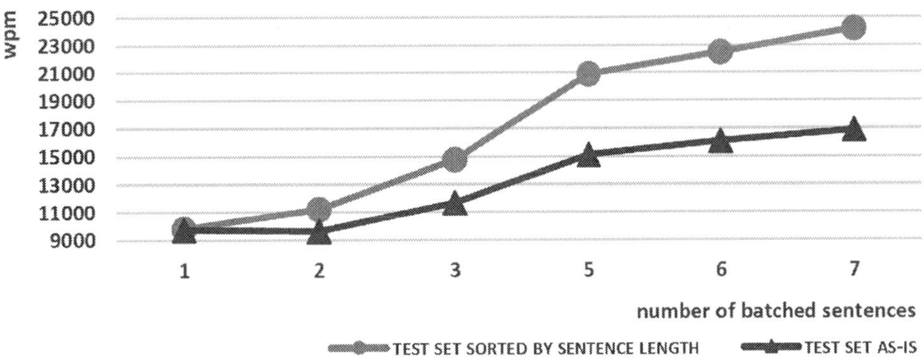

Figure 3: Batch beam decoder speed measured over newstest-2017 test set, using the accelerated eng-ger-wmt17 FNMT system (26.1 BLEU) with additional sentence batching, up to 7 sentences.

ities. In effect, while both are remarkably fast by themselves (e.g. the phrase-based decoder is running at 20000 wpm), these extra contributions explain most of the speed reduction for the accelerated LNMT system. In addition, the beam decoder itself is slightly slower for LNMT than for FNMT. This is mainly due to the computation of $\mathbf{L}$ as explained in Section 2. Finally, the respective GPU memory footprints for FNMT and LNMT are 4.1 and 4.8 GB.

4.4 Batched beam decoding and beam size

We next discuss the impact of using batch decoding and the beam size. To this end we use the accelerated FNMT system (25.2 BLEU, 9449 wpm) to decode with and without batching; we also widen the beam. Figure 2 shows the results.

The accelerated system itself with batched beam decoding and beam size of 4 is 3 times faster than without batching (3053 wpm). The GPU memory footprint is 1 GB bigger when batching

(4.1 vs 3.1 GB). As can be expected, widening the beam decreases the speed of both decoders. The relative speed-up ratio favours the batch decoder for wider beams, i.e. it is 5 times faster for beam size 12. However, because the batch size is tied to the beam size, this comes at a cost in GPU memory footprint (under 8 GB).

4.5 Sentence batching

As described in Section 3.1, it is straightforward to extend beam batching to sentence batching. Figure 3 shows the effect of sentence batching up to 7 sentences on our accelerated FNMT system.

Whilst the speed-up of our implementation is sub-linear, when batching 5 sentences the decoder runs at almost 21000 wpm, and goes beyond 24000 for 7 sentences. Thus, our implementation of sentence batching is 2.5 times faster on top of beam batching. Again, this comes at a cost: the GPU memory footprint increases as we batch more and more sentences together, up to 11 GB for

7 sentences, which approaches the limit of GPU memory.

Note that sentence batching does not change translation quality. For example, when translating 7 sentences, we are effectively batching 28 neural queries per time step. Indeed, each individual sentence is still being translated with a beam size of 4.

Figure 3 also shows the effect of sorting the test set by sentence length. Because sentences have similar lengths, less padding is required and hence we have less wasteful GPU computation. With 7 batched sentences the decoder would run at barely 17000 wpm, this is, 7000 wpm less due to not sorting by sentence length. A similar strategy is common for neural training (Sutskever et al., 2014; Morishita et al., 2017).

5 Conclusions

We have described a left-to-right batched beam NMT decoding algorithm that is transparent to the neural model and can be combined with LMBR n-gram posteriors. Our quality assessment with Transformer models (Vaswani et al., 2017) has shown that LMBR posteriors can still improve such a strong baseline in terms of BLEU. Finally, we have also discussed our acceleration strategy for deployment and the effect of batching and the beam size on memory and speed.

References

Dzmitry Bahdanau, Kyunghyun Cho, and Yoshua Bengio. 2015. Neural machine translation by jointly learning to align and translate. *ICLR*.

Frédéric Bastien, Pascal Lamblin, Razvan Pascanu, James Bergstra, Ian J. Goodfellow, Arnaud Bergeron, Nicolas Bouchard, and Yoshua Bengio. 2012. Theano: new features and speed improvements. Deep Learning and Unsupervised Feature Learning NIPS 2012 Workshop.

Yonatan Belinkov and Yonatan Bisk. 2018. Synthetic and natural noise both break neural machine translation. *ICLR*.

Graeme Blackwood, Adrià Gispert, and William Byrne. 2010. Efficient path counting transducers for minimum bayes-risk decoding of statistical machine translation lattices. In *Proceedings of ACL*, pages 27–32.

Denny Britz, Anna Goldie, Minh-Thang Luong, and Quoc Le. 2017. Massive exploration of neural machine translation architectures. In *Proceedings of EMNLP*, pages 1442–1451.

Rajen Chatterjee, Matteo Negri, Marco Turchi, Marcello Federico, Lucia Specia, and Frédéric Blain. 2017. Guiding neural machine translation decoding with external knowledge. In *Proceedings of WMT*, pages 157–168.

Brian Delaney, Wade Shen, and Timothy Anderson. 2006. An efficient graph search decoder for phrase-based statistical machine translation. In *Proceedings of IWSLT*.

Jacob Devlin. 2017. Sharp models on dull hardware: Fast and accurate neural machine translation decoding on the cpu. In *Proceedings of EMNLP*, pages 2820–2825.

Shi Feng, Shujie Liu, Nan Yang, Mu Li, Ming Zhou, and Kenny Q. Zhu. 2016. Improving attention modeling with implicit distortion and fertility for machine translation. In *Proceedings of COLING*, pages 3082–3092.

Jonas Gehring, Michael Auli, David Grangier, Denis Yarats, and Yann N. Dauphin. 2017. Convolutional sequence to sequence learning. *CoRR*, abs/1705.03122.

Adrià de Gispert, Sami Virpioja, Mikko Kurimo, and William Byrne. 2009. Minimum bayes risk combination of translation hypotheses from alternative morphological decompositions. In *Proceedings of NAACL-HLT*, pages 73–76.

Eva Hasler, Adrià de Gispert, Gonzalo Iglesias, and Bill Byrne. 2018. Neural machine translation decoding with terminology constraints. In *Proceedings of NAACL-HLT*.

Kenneth Heafield, Ivan Pouzyrevsky, Jonathan H. Clark, and Philipp Koehn. 2013. Scalable modified kneser-ney language model estimation. In *Proceedings of ACL*, pages 690–696.

Chris Hokamp and Qun Liu. 2017. Lexically constrained decoding for sequence generation using grid beam search. In *Proceedings of ACL*, pages 1535–1546.

Marcin Junczys-Dowmunt, Tomasz Dwojak, and Hieu Hoang. 2016. Is neural machine translation ready for deployment? A case study on 30 translation directions. *CoRR*, abs/1610.01108.

Philipp Koehn and Rebecca Knowles. 2017. Six challenges for neural machine translation. In *Proceedings of the First Workshop on Neural Machine Translation*, pages 28–39.

Shankar Kumar and William Byrne. 2004. Minimum bayes-risk decoding for statistical machine translation. In *Proceedings of NAACL-HLT*, pages 169–176.

Fandong Meng, Zhengdong Lu, Hang Li, and Qun Liu. 2016. Interactive attention for neural machine translation. In *Proceedings of COLING*, pages 2174–2185.

Bart van Merriënboer, Dzmitry Bahdanau, Vincent Dumoulin, Dmitriy Serdyuk, David Warde-Farley, Jan Chorowski, and Yoshua Bengio. 2015. Blocks and fuel: Frameworks for deep learning. *CoRR*, abs/1506.00619.

Makoto Morishita, Yusuke Oda, Graham Neubig, Koichiro Yoshino, Katsuhito Sudoh, and Satoshi Nakamura. 2017. An empirical study of mini-batch creation strategies for neural machine translation. In *Proceedings of the First Workshop on Neural Machine Translation*, pages 61–68.

Toshiaki Nakazawa, Manabu Yaguchi, Kiyotaka Uchimoto, Masao Utiyama, Eiichiro Sumita, Sadao Kurohashi, and Hitoshi Isahara. 2016. ASPEC: Asian scientific paper excerpt corpus. In *Proceedings of LREC*.

Franz Josef Och. 2003. Minimum error rate training in statistical machine translation. In *Proceedings of ACL*, pages 160–167.

Kishore Papineni, Salim Roukos, Todd Ward, and Wei-Jing Zhu. 2002. Bleu: a method for automatic evaluation of machine translation. In *Proceedings of ACL*, pages 311–318.

Rico Sennrich, Barry Haddow, and Alexandra Birch. 2016a. Improving neural machine translation models with monolingual data. In *Proceedings of ACL*, pages 86–96.

Rico Sennrich, Barry Haddow, and Alexandra Birch. 2016b. Neural machine translation of rare words with subword units. In *Proceedings of ACL*, pages 1715–1725.

K. C. Sim, W. J. Byrne, M. J. F. Gales, H. Sahbi, and P. C. Woodland. 2007. Consensus network decoding for statistical machine translation system combination. In *Proceedings of ICASSP*, volume 4, pages 105–108.

Felix Stahlberg and Bill Byrne. 2017. Unfolding and shrinking neural machine translation ensembles. In *Proceedings of EMNLP*, pages 1946–1956.

Felix Stahlberg, Adrià de Gispert, Eva Hasler, and Bill Byrne. 2017. Neural machine translation by minimising the bayes-risk with respect to syntactic translation lattices. In *Proceedings of EACL*, volume 2, pages 362–368.

Felix Stahlberg, Eva Hasler, Aurelien Waite, and Bill Byrne. 2016. Syntactically guided neural machine translation. In *Proceedings of ACL*, pages 299–305.

Ilya Sutskever, Oriol Vinyals, and Quoc V. Le. 2014. Sequence to sequence learning with neural networks. In *Proceedings of NIPS*, volume 2, pages 3104–3112, Cambridge, MA, USA. MIT Press.

Roy Tromble, Shankar Kumar, Franz Och, and Wolfgang Macherey. 2008. Lattice Minimum Bayes-Risk decoding for statistical machine translation. In *Proceedings of EMNLP*, pages 620–629.

Zhaopeng Tu, Yang Liu, Zhengdong Lu, Xiaohua Liu, and Hang Li. 2017. Context gates for neural machine translation. *Transactions of the Association for Computational Linguistics*, 5:87–99.

Zhaopeng Tu, Zhengdong Lu, Yang Liu, Xiaohua Liu, and Hang Li. 2016. Modeling coverage for neural machine translation. In *Proceedings of ACL*, pages 76–85.

Ashish Vaswani, Noam Shazeer, Niki Parmar, Jakob Uszkoreit, Llion Jones, Aidan N. Gomez, Lukasz Kaiser, and Illia Polosukhin. 2017. Attention is all you need. *CoRR*, abs/1706.03762.

Yonghui Wu, Mike Schuster, Zhifeng Chen, Quoc V. Le, Mohammad Norouzi, Wolfgang Macherey, Maxim Krikun, Yuan Cao, Qin Gao, Klaus Macherey, Jeff Klingner, Apurva Shah, Melvin Johnson, Xiaobing Liu, Lukasz Kaiser, Stephan Gouws, Yoshikiyo Kato, Taku Kudo, Hideto Kazawa, Keith Stevens, George Kurian, Nishant Patil, Wei Wang, Cliff Young, Jason Smith, Jason Riesa, Alex Rudnick, Oriol Vinyals, Greg Corrado, Macduff Hughes, and Jeffrey Dean. 2016. Google's neural machine translation system: Bridging the gap between human and machine translation. *CoRR*, abs/1609.08144.

Pavan Yalamanchili, Umar Arshad, Zakiuddin Mohammed, Pradeep Garigipati, Peter Entschev, Brian Kloppenborg, James Malcolm, and John Melonakos. 2015. ArrayFire - A high performance software library for parallel computing with an easy-to-use API.

Jingyi Zhang, Masao Utiyama, Eiichro Sumita, Graham Neubig, and Satoshi Nakamura. 2017. Improving neural machine translation through phrase-based forced decoding. In *Proceedings of IJCNLP*, pages 152–162.

Pieces of Eight: 8-bit Neural Machine Translation[*]

Jerry Quinn   **Miguel Ballesteros**
IBM Research,
1101 Kitchawan Road, Route 134 Yorktown Heights, NY 10598. U.S
jlquinn@us.ibm.com, miguel.ballesteros@ibm.com

Abstract

Neural machine translation has achieved levels of fluency and adequacy that would have been surprising a short time ago. Output quality is extremely relevant for industry purposes, however it is equally important to produce results in the shortest time possible, mainly for latency-sensitive applications and to control cloud hosting costs. In this paper we show the effectiveness of translating with 8-bit quantization for models that have been trained using 32-bit floating point values. Results show that 8-bit translation makes a non-negligible impact in terms of speed with no degradation in accuracy and adequacy.

1 Introduction

Neural machine translation (NMT) (Bahdanau et al., 2014; Sutskever et al., 2014) has recently achieved remarkable performance improving fluency and adequacy over phrase-based machine translation and is being deployed in commercial settings (Koehn and Knowles, 2017). However, this comes at a cost of slow decoding speeds compared to phrase-based and syntax-based SMT (see section 3).

NMT models are generally trained using 32-bit floating point values. At training time, multiple sentences can be processed in parallel leveraging graphical processing units (GPUs) to good advantage since the data is processed in batches. This is also true for decoding for non-interactive applications such as bulk document translation.

Why is fast execution on CPUs important? First, CPUs are cheaper than GPUs. Fast CPU computation will reduce commercial deployment costs. Second, for low-latency applications such as speech-to-speech translation (Neubig et al.,

2017a), it is important to translate individual sentences quickly enough so that users can have an application experience that responds seamlessly. Translating individual sentences with NMT requires many memory bandwidth intensive matrix-vector or matrix-narrow matrix multiplications (Abdelfattah et al., 2016). In addition, the batch size is 1 and GPUs do not have a speed advantage over CPUs due to the lack of adequate parallel work (as evidenced by increasingly difficult batching scenarios in dynamic frameworks (Neubig et al., 2017b)).

Others have successfully used low precision approximations to neural net models. Vanhoucke et al. (2011) explored 8-bit quantization for feedforward neural nets for speech recognition. Devlin (2017) explored 16-bit quantization for machine translation. In this paper we show the effectiveness of 8-bit decoding for models that have been trained using 32-bit floating point values. Results show that 8-bit decoding does not hurt the fluency or adequacy of the output, while producing results up to 4-6x times faster. In addition, implementation is straightforward and we can use the models as is without altering training.

The paper is organized as follows: Section 2 reviews the attentional model of translation to be sped up, Section 3 presents our 8-bit quantization in our implementation, Section 4 presents automatic measurements of speed and translation quality plus human evaluations, Section 5 discusses the results and some illustrative examples, Section 6 describes prior work, and Section 7 concludes the paper.

2 The Attentional Model of Translation

Our translation system implements the attentional model of translation (Bahdanau et al., 2014) consisting of an encoder-decoder network with an at-

---

[*] A piece of eight was a Spanish dollar that was divided into 8 reales, also known as Real de a Ocho.

Proceedings of NAACL-HLT 2018, pages 114–120
New Orleans, Louisiana, June 1 - 6, 2018. ©2017 Association for Computational Linguistics

tention mechanism.

The encoder uses a bidirectional GRU recurrent neural network (Cho et al., 2014) to encode a source sentence $\mathbf{x} = (x_1, ..., x_l)$, where x_i is the embedding vector for the ith word and l is the sentence length. The encoded form is a sequence of hidden states $\mathbf{h} = (h_1, ..., h_l)$ where each h_i is computed as follows

$$h_i = \begin{bmatrix} \overleftarrow{h_i} \\ \overrightarrow{h_i} \end{bmatrix} = \begin{bmatrix} \overleftarrow{f}(x_i, \overleftarrow{h}_{i+1}) \\ \overrightarrow{f}(x_i, \overrightarrow{h}_{i-1}) \end{bmatrix}, \qquad (1)$$

where $\overrightarrow{h_0} = \overleftarrow{h_0} = 0$. Here $\overleftarrow{f}$ and $\overrightarrow{f}$ are GRU cells.

Given $\mathbf{h}$, the decoder predicts the target translation $\mathbf{y}$ by computing the output token sequence $(y_1, ...y_m)$, where m is the length of the sequence. At each time t, the probability of each token y_t from a target vocabulary is

$$p(y_t|\mathbf{h}, y_{t-1}..y_1) = g(s_t, y_{t-1}, H_t), \qquad (2)$$

where g is a two layer feed-forward network over the embedding of the previous target word (y_{t-1}), the decoder hidden state (s_t), and the weighted sum of encoder states $\mathbf{h}$ (H_t), followed by a softmax to predict the probability distribution over the output vocabulary.

We compute s_t with a two layer GRU as

$$s'_t = r(s_{t-1}, y^*_{t-1}) \qquad (3)$$

and

$$s_t = q(s'_t, H_t), \qquad (4)$$

where s'_t is an intermediate state and $s_0 = \overleftarrow{h}_0$. The two GRU units r and q together with the attention constitute the conditional GRU layer of Sennrich et al. (2017). H_t is computed as

$$H_t = \begin{bmatrix} \sum_{i=1}^{l}(\alpha_{t,i} \cdot \overleftarrow{h}_i) \\ \sum_{i=1}^{l}(\alpha_{t,i} \cdot \overrightarrow{h}_i) \end{bmatrix}, \qquad (5)$$

where $\alpha_{t,i}$ are the elements of α_t which is the output vector of the attention model. This is computed with a two layer feed-forward network

$$\alpha'_t = v(\tanh(w(h_i) + u(s'_{t-1}))), \qquad (6)$$

where w and u are weight matrices, and v is another matrix resulting in one real value per encoder state h_i. α_t is then the softmax over α'_t.

We train our model using a program written using the Theano framework (Bastien et al., 2012). Generally models are trained with batch sizes ranging from 64 to 128 and unbiased Adam stochastic optimizer (Kingma and Ba, 2014). We use an embedding size of 620 and hidden layer sizes of 1000. We select model parameters according to the best BLEU score on a held-out development set over 10 epochs.

3   8-bit Translation

Our translation engine is a C++ implementation. The engine is implemented using the Eigen matrix library, which provides efficient matrix operations. Each CPU core translates a single sentence at a time. The same engine supports both batch and interactive applications, the latter making single-sentence translation latency important. We report speed numbers as both words per second (WPS) and words per core second (WPCS), which is WPS divided by the number of cores running. This gives us a measure of overall scaling across many cores and memory buses as well as the single-sentence speed.

Phrase-based SMT systems, such as (Tillmann, 2006), for English-German run at 170 words per core second (3400 words per second) on a 20 core Xeon 2690v2 system. Similarly, syntax-based SMT systems, such as (Zhao and Al-onaizan, 2008), for the same language pair run at 21.5 words per core second (430 words per second).

In contrast, our NMT system (described in Section 2) with 32-bit decoding runs at 6.5 words per core second (131 words per second). Our goal is to increase decoding speed for the NMT system to what can be achieved with phrase-based systems while maintaining the levels of fluency and adequacy that NMT offers.

Benchmarks of our NMT decoder unsurprisingly show matrix multiplication as the number one source of compute cycles. In Table 1 we see that more than 85% of computation is spent in Eigen's matrix and vector multiply routines (Eigen matrix vector product and Eigen matrix multiply). It dwarfs the costs of the transcendental function computations as well as the bias additions.

Given this distribution of computing time, it makes sense to try to accelerate the matrix operations as much as possible. One approach to increasing speed is to quantize matrix operations. Replacing 32-bit floating point math operations with 8-bit integer approximations in neural nets has been shown to give speedups and similar ac-

Time	Function
50.77%	Eigen matrix vector product
35.02%	Eigen matrix multiply
1.95%	NMT decoder layer
1.68%	Eigen fast tanh
1.35%	NMT tanh wrapper

Table 1: Profile before 8-bit conversion. More than 85% is spent in Eigen matrix/vector multiply routines.

curacy (Vanhoucke et al., 2011). We chose to apply similar optimization to our translation system, both to reduce memory traffic as well as increase parallelism in the CPU.

Our 8-bit matrix multiply routine uses a naive implementation with no blocking or copy. The code is implemented using Intel SSE4 vector instructions and computes 4 rows at a time, similar to (Devlin, 2017). Simplicity led to implementing 8-bit matrix multiplication with the results being placed into a 32-bit floating point result. This has the advantage of not needing to know the scale of the result. In addition, the output is a vector or narrow matrix, so little extra memory bandwidth is consumed.

Multilayer matrix multiply algorithms result in significantly faster performance than naive algorithms (Goto and Geijn, 2008). This is due to the fact that there are $O(N^3)$ math operations on $O(N^2)$ elements when multiplying NxN matrices, therefore it is worth significant effort to minimize memory operations while maximizing math operations. However, when multiplying an NxN matrix by an NxP matrix where P is very small (<10), memory operations dominate and performance does not benefit from the complex algorithm. When decoding single sentences, we typically set our beam size to a value less than 8 following standard practice in this kind of systems (Koehn and Knowles, 2017). We actually find that at such small values of P, the naive algorithm is a bit faster.

Time	Function
69.54%	8-bit matrix multiply
6.37%	Eigen fast tanh
2.06%	NMT decoder layer
0.95%	NMT tanh wrapper

Table 2: Profile after 8-bit conversion. Matrix multiply includes matrix-vector multiply. Matrix multiply is still 70% of computation. Tanh is larger but still relatively small.

Table 2 shows the profile after converting the matrix routines to 8-bit integer computation. There is only one entry for matrix-matrix and matrix-vector multiplies since they are handled by the same routine. After conversion, tanh and sigmoid still consume less than 7% of CPU time. We decided not to convert these operations to integer in light of that fact.

It is possible to replace all the operations with 8-bit approximations (Wu et al., 2016), but this makes implementation more complex, as the scale of the result of a matrix multiplication must be known to correctly output 8-bit numbers without dangerous loss of precision.

Assuming we have 2 matrices of size 1000x1000 with a range of values $[-10, 10]$, the individual dot products in the result could be as large as 10^8. In practice with neural nets, the scale of the result is similar to that of the input matrices. So if we scale the result to $[-127, 127]$ assuming the worst case, the loss of precision will give us a matrix full of zeros. The choices are to either scale the result of the matrix multiplication with a reasonable value, or to store the result as floating point. We opted for the latter.

8-bit computation achieves 32.3 words per core second (646 words per second), compared to the 6.5 words per core second (131 words per second) of the 32-bit system (both systems load parameters from the same model). This is even faster than the syntax-based system that runs at 21.5 words per core second (430 words per second). Table 3 summarizes running speeds for the phrase-based SMT system, syntax-based system and NMT with 32-bit decoding and 8-bit decoding.

System	WPCS
Phrase-based	170
Syntax-based	21.5
NMT 32-bit	6.5
NMT 8-bit	32.3

Table 3: Running speed (in words per core second) of the phrase-based SMT system, syntax-based system, NMT with 32-bit decoding and NMT with 8-bit decoding.

4 Measurements

To demonstrate the effectiveness of approximating the floating point math with 8-bit integer computation, we show automatic evaluation results on several models, as well as independent human evaluations. We report results on Dutch-English, English-Dutch, Russian-English, German-English and English-German models. Table 4 shows training data sizes and vocabulary sizes. All models have 620 dimension embeddings and 1000 dimension hidden states.

Lang	Training Sentences	Source Vocabulary	Target Vocabulary
En-Nl	17M	42112	33658
Nl-En	17M	33658	42212
Ru-En	31M	42388	42840
En-De	31M	57867	63644
De-En	31M	63644	57867

Table 4: Model training data and vocabulary sizes

4.1 Automatic results

Here we report automatic results comparing decoding results on 32-bit and 8-bit implementations. As others have found (Wu et al., 2016), 8-bit implementations impact quality very little.

In Table 6, we compared automatic scores and speeds for Dutch-English, English-Dutch, Russian-English, German-English and English-German models on news data. The English-German model was run with both a single model (1x) and an ensemble of two models (2x) (Freitag et al., 2017). Table 5 gives the number of sentences and average sentence length for the test sets used.

Lang	Test Sentences	Src Sent Length	Tgt Sent Length
En-Nl	990	22.5	25.9
Nl-En	990	25.9	22.5
Ru-En	555	27.2	35.2
En-De	168	51.8	46.0
De-En	168	46.0	51.8

Table 5: Test data sizes and sentence lengths

Speed is reported in words per core second (WPCS). This gives us a better sense of the speed of individual engines when deployed on multi-core systems with all cores performing translations. Total throughput is simply the product of WPCS and the number of cores in the machine. The reported speed is the median of 9 runs to ensure consistent numbers. The results show that we see a 4-6x speedup over 32-bit floating point de-

Lang	Mode	BLEU	Speed (WPSC)
En-Nl	32-bit	31.2	12.6
En-Nl	8-bit	31.2	58.9
Nl-En	32-bit	36.1	10.3
Nl-En	8-bit	36.3	45.8
Ru-En	32-bit	24.5	8.9
Ru-En	8-bit	24.3	51.4
De-En	32-bit	32.6	7.3
De-En	8-bit	32.2	37.5
En-De 2x	32-bit	30.5	7.1
En-De 2x	8-bit	30.6	33.7
En-De 1x	32-bit	29.7	15.9
En-De 1x	8-bit	29.7	71.3

Table 6: BLEU scores and speeds for 8-bit and 32-bit versions of several models. Speeds are reported in words per core second.

coding. German-English shows the largest deficit for the 8-bit mode versus the 32-bit mode. The German-English test set only includes 168 sentences so this may be a spurious difference.

4.2 Human evaluation

These automatic results suggest that 8-bit quantization can be done without perceptible degradation. To confirm this, we carried out a human evaluation experiment.

In Table 7, we show the results of performing human evaluations on some of the same language pairs in the previous section. An independent native speaker of the language being translated to/from different than English (who is also proficient in English) scored 100 randomly selected sentences. The sentences were shuffled during the evaluation to avoid evaluator bias towards different runs. We employ a scale from 0 to 5, with 0 being unintelligible and 5 being perfect translation.

Language	32-bit	8-bit
En-Nl	4.02	4.08
Nl-En	4.03	4.03
Ru-En	4.10	4.06
En-De 2x	4.05	4.16
En-De 1x	3.84	3.90

Table 7: Human evaluation scores for 8-bit and 32-bit systems. All tests are news domain.

The Table shows that the automatic scores shown in the previous section are also sustained

Source	Time	Sie standen seit 1946 an der Parteispitze
32-bit	720 ms	They **had been** at the **party leadership** since 1946
8-bit	180 ms	They **stood** at the **top of the party** since 1946.
Source	Time	So erwarten die Experten für dieses Jahr lediglich einen Anstieg der Weltproduktion von 3,7 statt der im Juni prognostizierten 3,9 Prozent. Für 2009 sagt das Kieler Institut sogar eine Abschwächung auf 3,3 statt 3,7 Prozent voraus.
32-bit	4440 ms	For this year, the experts expect only an increase in world production of 3.7 instead of the 3.9 percent forecast in June. In 2009, the Kiel Institute **predictated** a slowdown to **3.3 percent** instead of 3.7 **percent**.
8-bit	750 ms	For this year, the experts expect only an increase in world production of 3.7 instead of the 3.9 percent forecast in June. In 2009, the Kiel Institute **even forecast** a slowdown to **3.3%** instead of 3.7 **per cent**.
Source	Time	Heftige Regenfälle wegen "Ike" werden möglicherweise schwerere Schäden anrichten als seine Windböen. Besonders gefährdet sind dicht besiedelte Gebiete im Tal des Rio Grande, die noch immer unter den Folgen des Hurrikans "Dolly" im Juli leiden.
32-bit	6150 ms	Heavy rainfall due to "Ike" may cause **more severe** damage than its gusts of wind, particularly in densely populated areas in the Rio Grande valley, which **are still suffering** from the consequences of the "dolly" hurricane in July.
8-bit	1050 ms	Heavy rainfall due to "Ike" may cause **heavier** damage than its gusts of wind, particularly in densely populated areas in the Rio Grande valley, which **still suffer** from the consequences of the "dolly" hurricane in July.

Table 8: Examples of De-En news translation system comparing 32-bit and 8-bit decoding. Differences are in boldface. Sentence times are average of 10 runs.

Source	Time	Het is tijd om de kloof te overbruggen.
32-bit	730 ms	**It's** time to bridge the gap.
8-bit	180 ms	**It is** time to bridge the gap.
Source	Time	Niet dat Barientos met zijn vader van plaats zou willen wisselen.
32-bit	1120 ms	Not that Barientos would **want** to **change his father's place**.
8-bit	290 ms	Not that Barientos would **like** to **switch places with his father**.

Table 9: Examples of Nl-En news translation system comparing 32-bit and 8-bit decoding. Differences are in boldface. Sentence times are average of 10 runs.

by humans. 8-bit decoding is as good as 32-bit decoding according to the human evaluators.

5 Discussion

Having a faster NMT engine with no loss of accuracy is commercially useful. In our deployment scenarios, it is the difference between an interactive user experience that is sluggish and one that is not. Even in batch mode operation, the same throughput can be delivered with 1/4 the hardware.

In addition, this speedup makes it practical to deploy small ensembles of models. As shown above in the En-De model in Table 6, an ensemble can deliver higher accuracy at the cost of a 2x slowdown. This work makes it possible to translate with higher quality while still being at least twice as fast as the previous baseline.

As the numbers reported in Section 4 demonstrate, 8-bit and 32-bit decoding have similar average quality. As expected, the outputs produced by the two decoders are not identical. In fact, on a run of 166 sentences of De-En translation, only 51 were identical between the two. In addition, our human evaluation results and the automatic scoring suggest that there is no specific degradation by the 8-bit decoder compared to the 32-bit decoder. In order to emphasize these claims, Table 8 shows several examples of output from the two systems for a German-English system. Table 9 shows 2 more examples from a Dutch-English system.

In general, there are minor differences without any loss in adequacy or fluency due to 8-bit decoding. Sentence 2 in Table 8 shows a spelling error ("predictated") in the 32-bit output due to reassembly of incorrect subword units.[1]

6 Related Work

Reducing the resources required for decoding neural nets in general and neural machine translation in particular has been the focus of some attention in recent years.

Vanhoucke et al. (2011) explored accelerating convolutional neural nets with 8-bit integer decoding for speech recognition. They demonstrated that low precision computation could be used with no significant loss of accuracy. Han et al. (2015) investigated highly compressing image classification neural networks using network pruning, quantization, and Huffman coding so as to fit completely into on-chip cache, seeing significant improvements in speed and energy efficiency while keeping accuracy losses small.

Focusing on machine translation, Devlin (2017) implemented 16-bit fixed-point integer math to speed up matrix multiplication operations, seeing a 2.59x improvement. They show competitive BLEU scores on WMT English-French NewsTest2014 while offering significant speedup. Similarly, (Wu et al., 2016) applies 8-bit end-to-end quantization in translation models. They also show that automatic metrics do not suffer as a result. In this work, quantization requires modification to model training to limit the size of matrix outputs.

7 Conclusions and Future Work

In this paper, we show that 8-bit decoding for neural machine translation runs up to 4-6x times faster than a similar optimized floating point implementation. We show that the quality of this approximation is similar to that of the 32-bit version. We also show that it is unnecessary to modify the training procedure to produce models compatible with 8-bit decoding.

To conclude, this paper shows that 8-bit decoding is as good as 32-bit decoding both in automatic measures and from a human perception perspective, while it improves latency substantially.

In the future we plan to implement a multi-layered matrix multiplication that falls back to the naive algorithm for matrix-panel multiplications. This will provide speed for batch decoding for applications that can take advantage of it. We also plan to explore training with low precision for faster experiment turnaround time.

Our results offer hints of improved accuracy rather than just parity. Other work has used training as part of the compression process. We would like to see if training quantized models changes the results for better or worse.

References

Ahmad Abdelfattah, David Keyes, and Hatem Ltaief. 2016. Kblas: An optimized library for dense matrix-vector multiplication on gpu accelerators. *ACM Trans. Math. Softw.* 42(3):18:1–18:31. https://doi.org/10.1145/2818311.

Dzmitry Bahdanau, Kyunghyun Cho, and Yoshua Bengio. 2014. Neural machine translation by jointly learning to align and translate. *CoRR* abs/1409.0473.

Frédéric Bastien, Pascal Lamblin, Razvan Pascanu, James Bergstra, Ian J. Goodfellow, Arnaud Bergeron, Nicolas Bouchard, and Yoshua Bengio. 2012. Theano: new features and speed improvements. Deep Learning and Unsupervised Feature Learning NIPS 2012 Workshop.

KyungHyun Cho, Bart van Merrienboer, Dzmitry Bahdanau, and Yoshua Bengio. 2014. On the properties of neural machine translation: Encoder-decoder approaches. *CoRR* abs/1409.1259.

Jacob Devlin. 2017. Sharp models on dull hardware: Fast and accurate neural machine translation decoding on the cpu. In *Proceedings of the 2017 Conference on Empirical Methods in Natural Language Processing*. Association for Computational Linguistics, pages 2820–2825.

Markus Freitag, Yaser Al-Onaizan, and Baskaran Sankaran. 2017. Ensemble distillation for neural machine translation. *CoRR* abs/1702.01802.

Kazushige Goto and Robert A. van de Geijn. 2008. Anatomy of high-performance matrix multiplication. *ACM Trans. Math. Softw.* 34(3):12:1–12:25.

Song Han, Huizi Mao, and William J. Dally. 2015. Deep compression: Compressing deep neural network with pruning, trained quantization and huffman coding. *CoRR* abs/1510.00149.

Diederik P. Kingma and Jimmy Ba. 2014. Adam: A method for stochastic optimization. *CoRR* abs/1412.6980.

Philipp Koehn and Rebecca Knowles. 2017. Six challenges for neural machine translation. In *Proceedings of the First Workshop on Neural Machine Translation*. Association for Computational Linguistics, Vancouver, pages 28–39.

---

[1] In order to limit the vocabulary, we use BPE subword units (Sennrich et al., 2016) in all models.

Graham Neubig, Kyunghyun Cho, Jiatao Gu, and Victor O. K. Li. 2017a. Learning to translate in real-time with neural machine translation. In *Proceedings of the 15th Conference of the European Chapter of the Association for Computational Linguistics, EACL 2017, Valencia, Spain, April 3-7, 2017, Volume 1: Long Papers*. pages 1053–1062.

Graham Neubig, Chris Dyer, Yoav Goldberg, Austin Matthews, Waleed Ammar, Antonios Anastasopoulos, Miguel Ballesteros, David Chiang, Daniel Clothiaux, Trevor Cohn, Kevin Duh, Manaal Faruqui, Cynthia Gan, Dan Garrette, Yangfeng Ji, Lingpeng Kong, Adhiguna Kuncoro, Gaurav Kumar, Chaitanya Malaviya, Paul Michel, Yusuke Oda, Matthew Richardson, Naomi Saphra, Swabha Swayamdipta, and Pengcheng Yin. 2017b. Dynet: The dynamic neural network toolkit. *arXiv preprint arXiv:1701.03980* .

Rico Sennrich, Orhan Firat, Kyunghyun Cho, Alexandra Birch, Barry Haddow, Julian Hitschler, Marcin Junczys-Dowmunt, Samuel Läubli, Antonio Valerio Miceli Barone, Jozef Mokry, and Maria Nadejde. 2017. Nematus: a toolkit for neural machine translation. In *Proceedings of the Software Demonstrations of the 15th Conference of the European Chapter of the Association for Computational Linguistics*. Association for Computational Linguistics, Valencia, Spain, pages 65–68. http://aclweb.org/anthology/E17-3017.

Rico Sennrich, Barry Haddow, and Alexandra Birch. 2016. Neural machine translation of rare words with subword units. In *Proceedings of the 54th Annual Meeting of the Association for Computational Linguistics (Volume 1: Long Papers)*. Association for Computational Linguistics, Berlin, Germany, pages 1715–1725.

Ilya Sutskever, Oriol Vinyals, and Quoc V. Le. 2014. Sequence to sequence learning with neural networks. In *Advances in Neural Information Processing Systems 27: Annual Conference on Neural Information Processing Systems 2014, December 8-13 2014, Montreal, Quebec, Canada*. pages 3104–3112.

Christoph Tillmann. 2006. Efficient dynamic programming search algorithms for phrase-based smt. In *Proceedings of the Workshop on Computationally Hard Problems and Joint Inference in Speech and Language Processing*. Association for Computational Linguistics, Stroudsburg, PA, USA, CHSLP '06, pages 9–16.

Vincent Vanhoucke, Andrew Senior, and Mark Z. Mao. 2011. Improving the speed of neural networks on cpus. In *Deep Learning and Unsupervised Feature Learning Workshop, NIPS 2011*.

Yonghui Wu, Mike Schuster, Zhifeng Chen, Quoc V. Le, Mohammad Norouzi, Wolfgang Macherey, Maxim Krikun, Yuan Cao, Qin Gao, Klaus Macherey, Jeff Klingner, Apurva Shah, Melvin Johnson, Xiaobing Liu, Lukasz Kaiser, Stephan Gouws, Yoshikiyo Kato, Taku Kudo, Hideto Kazawa, Keith Stevens, George Kurian, Nishant Patil, Wei Wang, Cliff Young, Jason Smith, Jason Riesa, Alex Rudnick, Oriol Vinyals, Greg Corrado, Macduff Hughes, and Jeffrey Dean. 2016. Google's neural machine translation system: Bridging the gap between human and machine translation. *CoRR* abs/1609.08144.

Bing Zhao and Yaser Al-onaizan. 2008. Generalizing local and non-local word-reordering patterns for syntax-based machine translation. In *Proceedings of the Conference on Empirical Methods in Natural Language Processing*. Association for Computational Linguistics, Stroudsburg, PA, USA, EMNLP '08, pages 572–581. http://dl.acm.org/citation.cfm?id=1613715.1613785.

From dictations to clinical reports using machine translation

Greg P. Finley, Wael Salloum, Najmeh Sadoughi, Erik Edwards, Amanda Robinson, Mark Miller, David Suendermann-Oeft[*]
EMR.AI Inc.
San Francisco, CA, USA
`greg.finley@emr.ai`

Michael Brenndoerfer
University of California
Berkeley, CA, USA

Nico Axtmann
DHBW, Karlsruhe, Germany

Abstract

A typical workflow to document clinical encounters entails dictating a summary, running speech recognition, and post-processing the resulting text into a formatted letter. Post-processing entails a host of transformations including punctuation restoration, truecasing, marking sections and headers, converting dates and numerical expressions, parsing lists, etc. In conventional implementations, most of these tasks are accomplished by individual modules. We introduce a novel holistic approach to post-processing that relies on machine callytranslation. We show how this technique outperforms an alternative conventional system—even learning to correct speech recognition errors during post-processing—while being much simpler to maintain.

1 Introduction

Medical dictation is one of the most common ways of documenting clinical encounters (Rosenbloom et al., 2010). The dictated material needs to be transformed into a textual representation to be printed as a clinical letter or inserted into electronic medical record (EMR) systems. This can be done using one of the following techniques (Alapetite et al., 2009):

1) the speech recording is manually transcribed by a third party and returned to the physician for sign-off at a later point in time;

2) the recording is processed by a medical speech recognizer, controlled and corrected by a quality assurance team (mostly an external entity), and returned to the physician;

3) while the physician is dictating, a medical speech recognizer transforms the speech into text which is subject to immediate correction and sign-off by the physician.

---

[*]Patent pending.

```
this is doctor mike miller dictating
a maximum medical improvement slash
impairment rating evaluation for
john j o h n doe d o e social one
two three four five six seven eight
nine service i_d one two three four
five six seven eight nine service
date august eight two thousand
and seventeen subjective and
treatment to date the examinee is
a thirty nine year old golf course
maintenance worker with the apache
harding park who was injured on
eight seven two thousand seventeen
```

Figure 1: Raw output of a medical speech recognizer.

In this paper, we focus on the text processing that follows the application of automated speech recognition (ASR) in Techniques 2 and 3. The role of ASR is simply to transform spoken words into plain text, as exemplified in the excerpt of a medical dictation in Figure 1: ASR output is typi case insensitive and contains only alphabetic characters, transcribed verbatim including command words, repetitions, grammatical errors, etc.

In contrast, clinical letters follow rigorous formatting standards which require a sophisticated post-processor to transform the ASR output into a full-fledged letter. Major responsibilities of the post-processor include: truecasing, punctuation restoration, carrying out dictated commands (e.g., 'new paragraph', 'scratch that'), converting numerical and temporal expressions, formatting acronyms and abbreviations, numbering itemized lists, separating sections and section headers, and inserting physician "normals" (sections of boilerplate text or templates).

Figure 2 shows a post-processed version of the raw ASR output of Figure 1. This example makes

121

Proceedings of NAACL-HLT 2018, pages 121–128
New Orleans, Louisiana, June 1 - 6, 2018. ©2017 Association for Computational Linguistics

clear that many of the tokens of the ASR output need to be altered in order to create a properly formatted output document. In fact, informal experiments indicated that, on average, *more than half* of spoken tokens are subject to modification when preparing a clinical report from a dictation.

Conventional implementations of post-processors comprise a multitude of predominantly rule-based techniques (Sistrom et al., 2001; Liu et al., 2006; Frankel and Santisteban, 2011), mostly covering subsets of the operations listed above. There has been a fair amount of machine learning research on punctuation restoration (PR), which does constitute a significant component of post-processing, over the last two decades (Beeferman et al., 1998; Peitz et al., 2011). PR has even been addressed for medical ASR specifically, using methods such as finite state models for punctuation insertion (Deoras and Fritsch, 2008), or identifying punctuated tokens using recurrent neural networks (Salloum et al., 2017b).

Of course, PR is only one necessary module of a post-processing system. Typical modular approaches, especially those that are predominantly rule based, are subject to serious disadvantages in practical use. For one, the task may grow in complexity over time through the introduction of specific rules for certain hospitals or physicians. Another issue is that these systems must follow an ASR stage, where unforeseen errors (Johnson et al., 2014; Hodgson and Coiera, 2016; Edwards et al., 2017) may interfere destructively with post-processing, for which rules or models are typically designed or trained for idealized transcriptions.

In this paper, we present a holistic, data-driven approach to post-processing which makes use of recent advances in statistical machine translation, covering most of the aforementioned operations in a single shot and exhibiting accuracy superior to an existing modular system. After a brief introduction to machine translation in Section 2, we describe methods, data sets, and evaluation in Section 3 and experimental results in Section 4.

2   Machine translation

We approach the post-processing problem as a case of machine translation (MT), in which the source language is the raw ASR output as in Figure 1, and the target language is the final written letter from Figure 2—or, more accurately, a

This is Dr Mike Miller dictating a Maximum Medical Improvement/Impairment Rating Evaluation for John Doe.
SSN: 123-45-6789
Service ID: 123 456 789
Service Date: 08/08/17

Subjective and Treatment:
To date, the examinee is a 39 year-old golf course maintenance worker with the Apache Harding Park who was injured on 08/07/17.

Figure 2: Output of post-processor.

form that can be trivially converted into the final text, and in which formatting elements are represented themselves as words. To our knowledge, ours is the first system to frame ASR post-processing as MT, and one of very few described post-processing systems for the medical domain.

Most standard MT approaches require both parallel data (bitexts) and an additional quantity of data in the target language only, which is used to build a language model; likelihoods from both the translational and the language model are balanced during translation (Ney et al., 2000; Koehn et al., 2003, 2007; Lopez, 2008).

Koehn et al. (2003) introduce a phrase-based *statistical machine translation* (SMT) approach. Their model is defined based on Bayes' rule and includes the phrase translation probability, the language model for the target, and the distortion probability of the target language to account for occurrences of reordering. The phrase translation model and the distortion probabilities are trained on the aligned phrases of source and target language, and the language model is trained on the target language. During decoding, a sequence of translated phrases is chosen by performing a beam search to limit the set of phrase candidates.

3   Methods

In this section we describe our methods for preparing data for training, tuning, and evaluating our MT methods. To reframe the post-processing problem as MT is not a trivial matter—it requires careful attention to how training data is prepared, due to the requirements for MT and the peculiarities of medical text; we describe our methods for doing so in 3.2. Crucially, we also explore the integration of our models within a working production

Set	# Reports	# Words
Training	8,775	4,785,986 (Rep.) 5,363,580 (Tra.) 5,681,630 (Hyp.)
Tuning	500	276,551 (Rep.) 311,538 (Tra.) 305,672 (Hyp.)
Development	300	187,472 (Rep.) 211,740 (Tra.) 209,587 (Hyp.)
Test	300	177,756 (Rep.) 198,722 (Tra.) 196,198 (Hyp.)

Table 1: Statistics of the data sets used for training, tuning, development, and test.

system in 3.4, enabling us to evaluate the contribution of MT towards improving real-world results.

3.1 Data sources

All models and experiments in this paper use actual clinical notes. Reports and dictations from a variety of specialties at two different US hospitals were considered. As required under HIPAA, EMR.AI has a Business Associate Agreement with the Covered Entity that supplied the data.

We first identified a set of 9,875 reports for which we had manual transcriptions and ASR hypotheses available. This set was split into four smaller sets (see Table 3.1 for corpus statistics). The training set was used to generate source-to-target alignments and build the phrase and distortion models, as well as to train the monolingual language model. (The latter was trained on additional text as well, for a total of 23,754 reports and 14,208,546 words.) The tuning set was used for tuning the relative contribution of the various models for MT. The development set was used for evaluation along the way. Finally, we set aside a blind test set, used solely and exclusively for the results in this paper.

We also set out to test whether transcriptions or hypotheses make better training data. As the task is posed, hypotheses would seem more relevant; however, they are a noisier source of data than transcriptions, and it was not guaranteed that the needed correspondences could be learned through the noise. Therefore, for both training and tuning, we tried transcripts, hypotheses, or a combination of the two (nine separate conditions).

3.2 Finding parallel training samples

Although our data set contains dictations and their corresponding reports, these do not represent true bitexts of the type that are typically used for MT, for several reasons: boilerplate language or metadata may be added to the letter; whole sections may be reordered, or even inserted from prior notes in the patient's history; pleasantries, discontinuities, or corrections by the speaker will be omitted. Furthermore, notes can be thousands of words in length, and it is not practical to learn alignments from such long "sentences" given computational constraints.

To solve these problems, we developed a method to extract matching stretches of up to 100 words from the source and target, which can then be used as training samples. The procedure entails five major steps.

Text preprocessing. Punctuation, newlines, tabs, headings, and list items are separated from adjacent tokens and converted into dummy tokens. All digits become their own tokens.

Dynamic alignment. All matches and edits between source and target are determined using a dynamic program, similar to that used for Levenshtein distance but with key differences: matches are permitted between non-exact string matches if they are determined, in a previous run of the algorithm, to be possible substitutions; edits can be longer than one token; and extending an edit incurs a lesser penalty than beginning a new edit.

Merging edits. Short substitutions are merged together if there is an intervening single-word match between them, and the entire range is considered a substitution. The resulting edits allow for longer stretches of parallel sentence data.

Calculating confidence. For every edit, a score is calculated based on a mix of statistics (calculated from a prior run of the dynamic program), and a heuristic that assigns higher scores to longer substitutions, to shorter insertions or deletions, and to edits that are adjacent to other long edits.

Extracting sentences. An iterative algorithm traverses all edits and matches from left to right, building a parallel source–target "sentence" as it goes. A sentence ends when an edit of too low confidence is reached, or once it exceeds 100 words. In the latter case, the next sentence will start one-third of the way through the previous one, so sentences may overlap by up to 67 tokens.

Each extracted sentence becomes a training

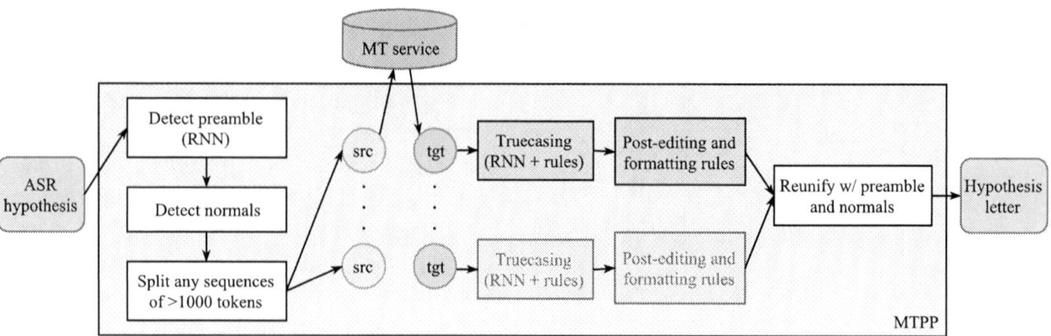

Figure 3: Basic design of the MTPP. Stages within the MTPP shaded in orange are responsible for transforming the MT target language ("tgt") into properly formatted written language.

sample. Any single-word string matches are also written as training samples—because this is not a typical MT problem in that the source and target "languages" are both English, we want to bias the system towards simply regurgitating input words it does not know how to translate. From 8,775 reports, this method generates many training samples: 4,402,612 for transcripts, 4,385,545 for hypotheses, and 8,788,157 for the combined set.

3.3 Model training

For the translation model, we employed typical statistical MT techniques. Optimal word-to-word alignments between source and target were learned using expectation maximization (Och and Ney, 2003). Subject to these alignments, parallel phrases of up to seven words in length were extracted. For the monolingual language model, we trained a 6-gram model with typical interpolation and backoff parameters.

The MT training stage yields a phrase substitution model and a distortion model. To determine the relative contribution of the phrase, distortion, and language models in computing translation option likelihoods, we tuned using minimum error rate training (Och, 2003): translate all text in a held-out tuning set, iteratively adjusting the weights of each contributing model until convergence on an error metric. We used an interpolation of word error rate (WER) and CDER (Leusch et al., 2006), which only assesses a single penalty for "block" movements. We include CDER to reduce the impact on tuning when entire sentences are reordered between the dictation and final letter; note that WER would assess numerous single-word insertion and deletion penalties in such a case.

3.4 Integration with medical post-processor

To use the MT system in production, it had to be integrated into a complete software product, which we refer to as the machine translation post-processor (MTPP), responsible for all stages of transformation between the raw ASR hypothesis and the generated report. Although the bulk of the decisions made during this process are handled by MT, the MTPP is responsible for selecting and preparing inputs for MT and transforming outputs into human-readable form. We present a simplified graphical overview of the MTPP in Figure 3.1.

At the first stage, the "preamble" (spoken metadata that is often not present in the final report) and any commands to insert a template are isolated and not sent to MT. Of the pieces that are subject to MT, any that exceed 1,000 tokens are split. The resulting chunks are sent to an MT daemon which has models pre-loaded into memory and can perform multiple translations in parallel. To each translated chunk, we apply truecasing and post-editing: several steps including joining digits, formatting headings, counting and labeling entries of numbered lists, etc. Finally, all chunks are unified and put into the correct order.

The preamble detector is based on a two-class recurrent neural network (RNN) classifier with pre-trained word embeddings and long short-term memory (LSTM) units, which tags tokens as either in- or out-of-preamble, then finds the split boundary according to a heuristic. The RNN truecaser has a similar architecture but predicts one of three classes for each token—all lowercase, first letter uppercase, or all uppercase—through one layer of softmax output shared across all time frames. This classifier was trained on automatically generated data from 15,635 reports. Truecasing is also supported through rule-based decisions as well as lists of truecased forms compiled from ontologies and prior reports, which include non-initial capitalizations ('pH', e.g.).

3.5 Evaluation

We assess performance of all models in two text domains: the *MT target domain*, which is the text format described in Section 3.2 in which numerals are split into individual digits, headers are surrounded by dummy tokens, and case is ignored; and the *post-processor error rate (PER) domain*. The latter is used to estimate the manual effort required to correct errors in the hypothesis report. PER can only be calculated from final outputs of a post-processor, and thus depends upon the integration described in Section 3.4.

PER is calculated similarly to WER except that it considers punctuation, newlines, and tabs as separate tokens, and it excludes any detected preamble from consideration (keeping the preamble leads to a slight increase in PER globally). PER is an especially harsh metric in real-world use, as it penalizes ASR errors, post-processing errors, and any other source of distance between the post-processor's output and the final letter following multiple rounds of manual review.

We measure PER of the MTPP against a baseline system, which was also developed internally within EMR.AI for specific use with clinical dictations. The baseline system employs a modular pipeline, where each module is responsible for a particular transformation—for instance, one detects a metadata-heavy "preamble" in the dictation (Salloum et al., 2017a); another converts spelled-out numbers to numerals, dates, etc. Some components of the system are rule based, while others rely on machine learning. This system had been the focus of significant development previously and was in regular production use prior to the advent of the MTPP.

4 Results

In the MT target domain, we present three standard measures of MT performance: WER, CDER, and BLEU. Results for all possible configurations of training and tuning data sources are given in Table 2. Note that these results are on a filtered test set: only source texts of 1,000 tokens or fewer were used (190 out of 300 in the test set), as this was found to be a point beyond which decoding

Tune \ Train	Hyp.	Tra.	Hyp. + Tra.	Metric
Hyp.	0.742	0.746	0.741	BLEU
	0.266	0.277	0.262	WER
	0.170	0.171	0.170	CDER
Tra.	**0.754**	0.745	0.747	BLEU
	0.259	0.276	**0.258**	WER
	0.164	0.171	0.167	CDER
Hyp. + Tra.	0.751	0.721	0.748	BLEU
	0.273	0.317	0.262	WER
	0.166	0.167	0.166	CDER

Table 2: Evaluation of test set on different training and tuning configurations with BLEU, WER, and CDER.

Tune \ Train	Hyp.	Tra.	Hyp. + Tra.
Hyp.	0.322	0.331	0.324
Tra.	0.324	0.338	**0.321**
Hyp. + Tra.	0.328	0.349	0.323

Table 3: Evaluation of the test set on different training and tuning configurations in terms of PER.

Method	PER	
	In: hyp.	In: tra.
No post-processing	0.619	0.574
Non-MT post-proc.	0.411	0.341
MTPP (best MT model)	**0.321**	**0.271**

Table 4: Comparison of PER in several conditions. Results are reported using ASR hypotheses as input ("In: hyp."), as in our other experiments, as well as using manual transcriptions as input ("In: tra.").

slowed considerably. Note that all BLEU are well above 0.7; these may appear to be exceptionally high scores, but note that our task here is *easier* than a "standard" translation task—to give some idea of a baseline, comparing the totally untranslated dictations in the test set to their matching reports yields a BLEU of 0.318 (as well as WER 0.514, CDER 0.483), which would be quite impossible in a case of translating between two different languages.

For the realistic evaluation of the complete system, we present PER measurements on final outputs of the MTPP in Table 3. Because the MTPP contains logic for breaking up the translation task across longer notes, no filtering is necessary and all 300 notes in the test set can be used. We must emphasize that these results cannot be compared with any quantities in Table 2, as they are measured in different domains entirely.

Tra.	…her mother was here and had them gave her **ibuprofen** as soon as she started …
Hyp.	…her mother was here and have him give her **an i_v profile** missing she started …
MTPP	…her mother was here and gave her **ibuprofen** missing, she started …
Tra.	in the meantime comma i will have **hospitalist come by and see** the patient …
Hyp.	in the meantime comma i will have **our hospital was combine to** the patient …
MTPP	In the meantime, I will have **hospitalist was come by and see** the patient …
Tra.	carafate one gram **a_c and h_s venlafaxine e_r** seventy five milligrams a day
Hyp.	carafate one gram **a_c_n_h_s meloxicam m e r** seventy five milligrams a day
MTPP	6. Carafate 1 g **before meals and at bedtime. / 7. Venlafaxine ER** 75 mg a day.

Table 5: Examples where the MTPP has "corrected" ASR errors. In each set of three lines, the first is the manual speech transcript, the second is the ASR hypothesis of the same audio, and the third is the output of the MTPP given the ASR hypothesis. Bolded text shows where the MTPP has generated output closer to the actual speech than to its input. Note, for the third example, that the abbreviation 'a.c.' (*ante cibum*) indicates to take the medication before meals, and 'h.s.' (*hora somni*) at bedtime.

The comparison of PER between all nine conditions suggests that the best results are achieved on training data that includes ASR hypotheses (test of proportions: $\chi^2 = 533$, $p < .001$, when comparing average PER with and without hypotheses in training). This is not a highly surprising result, as the evaluation task is to translate hypotheses, although we had wondered before if hypotheses were too noisy to constitute good training data. For tuning data, it appears that either hypotheses or transcripts yield good results, but a mixed set is always worse ($\chi^2 = 44.8$, $p < .001$, comparing average PER when tuned on the mix to PER when tuned on transcripts).

To quantify the impact of MT on post-processing accuracy, we also measured PER of the source hypotheses both before any post-processing and after passing through our baseline post-processor. Results are reported in Table 4. Overall, the MTPP results in a significant decrease in PER from the previous post-processor: a relative reduction of 21.9% error rate for hypotheses ($\chi^2 = 4102$, $p < .001$).

For further context, we also report PER using manual speech transcriptions as input (the rightmost column of Table 4). This is not a realistic use case, but we provide the measurements here to give a sense of the effect ASR errors have on typical PER measurements. The ASR WER of our MT test set was 0.142—much greater than the observed PER difference between hypotheses and transcripts, indicating that many formatting errors in PER occur on the same tokens as ASR errors.

4.1 Correcting ASR mistakes

For the MT models that learn from hypotheses, it was conceivable that they could actually learn to correct ASR mistakes by identifying common error patterns and how they are typically corrected in the final letter. To the MT system, there is no essential difference between, say, inserting formatting elements around a section header and replacing an erroneously recognized phrase with the intended phrase from the report; all words, numerals, and structural elements are tokens alike.

Indeed, we found several occurrences in our test set of phrases in MTPP output that were more similar to manual transcriptions of these dictations than to the ASR hypotheses that served as input to the MTPP. Refer to the examples in Table 5: each shows a transcript of a segment of speech (first line), the ASR hypothesis on that same segment (second line), and the output of the MTPP when given the ASR hypothesis as input (third line). In each, the MTPP output contains a bolded segment that is closer to the transcription than to the hypothesis. (Although note some incomplete cases, such as "hospitalist was come by and see" in the second example.) All of these examples were taken from the same test set as the other results in this paper. None of the transcriptions from the test set were ever seen by any system during training, tuning, or testing (all previous quantitative results used ASR hypotheses, not manual transcriptions, as the source language).

5 Discussion

Using MT for the post-processing task has numerous advantages over other approaches. Most obviously from our results, it achieves a high level of accuracy, even roundly outperforming a system containing numerous hand-designed rules and deep learning approaches that were trained on large amounts of annotated data.

Additionally, MT is a better solution for an adaptable and improvable system. The core of the system can be adapted to other dialects of English or even other languages by retraining the models. Even in the simplest use case, however, retraining can be periodically undertaken to improve performance on current data, accounting for possible changes over time in dictation or report writing style, as well as any ongoing development of the associated speech recognizer.

A final advantage is in the cost of maintaining the system. Although MT training has relatively high compute and memory requirements, there is very little cost in human time to retrain new models. Although our very best results did use transcriptions, our experiments demonstrate that the entire process can be reproduced fruitfully without them (and may even be subject to less unpredictability). To continuously improve a rule-based system, direct human intervention is required to write and validate new rules. For any supervised machine learning modules of a post-processor, human annotators may also be required.

6 Conclusion

In this paper we presented an overview of a complete and validated medical ASR post-processing system that relies on MT, as well as the novel processing methods required to ensure that MT is a viable approach for clinical dictations. Our strategy has multiple significant advantages compared to traditional rule-based approaches, and even other machine learning-based ones—not only does the MT design result in substantially reduced formatting errors, achieved in part by its ability to correct errors made by the speech recognizer in the first place, but it can also be retrained and improved fully automatically, without the need for costly manual adjustments.

References

Alexandre Alapetite, Henning B. Andersen, and Morten Hertzum. 2009. Acceptance of speech recognition by physicians: a survey of expectations, experiences, and social influence. *International journal of human-computer studies*, 67(1):36–49.

Doug Beeferman, Adam Berger, and John D. Lafferty. 1998. Cyberpunc: a lightweight punctuation annotation system for speech. In *Proc. of the International Conference on Acoustics, Speech, and Signal Processing (ICASSP)*, volume 2, pages 689–692. IEEE.

Anop Deoras and Juergen Fritsch. 2008. Decoding-time prediction of non-verbalized punctuation. In *Proc. of Interspeech*, pages 1449–1452, Brisbane, Australia. ISCA.

Erik Edwards, Wael Salloum, Greg P. Finley, James Fone, Greg Cardiff, Mark Miller, and David Suendermann-Oeft. 2017. Medical speech recognition: reaching parity with humans. In *Proc. of SPECOM*, volume LNCS 10458, pages 512–524. Springer.

Alan Frankel and Ana Santisteban. 2011. System and method for post processing speech recognition output. US Patent 7,996,223.

Tobias Hodgson and Enrico W. Coiera. 2016. Risks and benefits of speech recognition for clinical documentation: a systematic review. *Journal of the American Medical Informatics Association*, 23(e1):169–179.

Maree Johnson, Samuel Lapkin, Vanessa Long, Paula Sanchez, Hanna Suominen, Jim Basilakis, and Linda Dawson. 2014. A systematic review of speech recognition technology in health care. *BMC medical informatics and decision making*, 14(94):1–14.

Philipp Koehn, Hieu Hoang, Alexandra Birch, Chris Callison-Burch, Marcello Federico, Nicola Bertoldi, Brooke Cowan, Wade Shen, Christine Moran, Richard Zens, Chris Dyer, Ondrej Bojar, Alexandra Constantin, and Evan Herbst. 2007. Moses: Open source toolkit for statistical machine translation. In *Proc. of the 45th annual meeting of the ACL*, pages 177–180. ACL.

Philipp Koehn, Franz J. Och, and Daniel Marcu. 2003. Statistical phrase-based translation. In *Proc. of the Conference of the North American Chapter of the ACL on Human Language Technology*, volume 1, pages 48–54, Edmonton, Canada. ACL.

Gregor Leusch, Nicola Ueffing, and Hermann Ney. 2006. Cder: Efficient mt evaluation using block movements. In *Proc. of the 11th Conference of the European Chapter of the ACL*, pages 241–248, Trento, Italy. ACL.

David Liu, Mark Zucherman, and William B. Tulloss. 2006. Six characteristics of effective structured reporting and the inevitable integration with speech recognition. *Journal of digital imaging*, 19(1):98–104.

Adam Lopez. 2008. Statistical machine translation. *ACM computing surveys*, 40(3, article 8):1–49.

Hermann Ney, Sonja Niessen, Franz J. Och, Hassan Sawaf, Christoph Tillmann, and Stephan Vogel. 2000. Algorithms for statistical translation of spoken language. *IEEE transactions on speech and audio processing*, 8(1):24–36.

Franz J. Och. 2003. Minimum error rate training in statistical machine translation. In *Proc. of the 41st Annual Meeting of the ACL*, pages 160–167. ACL.

Franz J. Och and Hermann Ney. 2003. A systematic comparison of various statistical alignment models. *Computational Linguistics*, 29(1):19–51.

Stephan Peitz, Markus Freitag, Arne Mauser, and Hermann Ney. 2011. Modeling punctuation prediction as machine translation. In *Proc. of the International Workshop on Spoken Language Translation (IWSLT)*, pages 238–245. ISCA.

S. Trent Rosenbloom, William W. Stead, Joshua C. Denny, Dario Giuse, Nancy M. Lorenzi, Steven H. Brown, and Kevin B. Johnson. 2010. Generating clinical notes for electronic health record systems. *Applied clinical informatics*, 1(3):232–243.

Wael Salloum, Greg Finley, Erik Edwards, Mark Miller, and David Suendermann-Oeft. 2017a. Automated preamble detection in dictated medical reports. *BioNLP 2017*, pages 287–295.

Wael Salloum, Greg P. Finley, Erik Edwards, Mark Miller, and David Suendermann-Oeft. 2017b. Deep learning for punctuation restoration in medical reports. *Proc. of the 55th Annual Meeting of the ACL, Workshop on Biomedical Natural Language Processing (BioNLP)*, pages 159–164.

Chris L. Sistrom, Janice C. Honeyman, Anthony Mancuso, and Ronald G. Quisling. 2001. Managing predefined templates and macros for a departmental speech recognition system using common software. *Journal of digital imaging*, 14(3):131–141.

Benchmarks and models for entity-oriented polarity detection

Lidia Pivovarova,   Arto Klami,   Roman Yangarber
University of Helsinki, Finland
`first.last@cs.helsinki.fi`

Abstract

We address the problem of determining entity-oriented polarity in business news. This can be viewed as classifying the polarity of the sentiment expressed toward a given mention of a company in a news article. We present a complete, end-to-end approach to the problem. We introduce a new *dataset* of over 17,000 manually labeled documents, which is substantially larger than any currently available resources. We propose a *benchmark* solution based on convolutional neural networks for classifying entity-oriented polarity. Although our dataset is much larger than those currently available, it is small on the scale of datasets commonly used for training robust neural network models. To compensate for this, we use *transfer learning*—pre-train the model on a much larger dataset, annotated for a related but different classification task, in order to learn a good representation for business text, and then fine-tune it on the smaller polarity dataset.

1   Introduction

We report on research done in the context of PULS—a project for monitoring business news media (Du et al., 2016; Huttunen et al., 2013).[1] The system gathers 8,000–10,000 documents daily; each document is processed by a cascade of classifiers, including a named entity (NE) recognizer. A key NE in business news type is *company* or *organization*, which can be mentioned in a positive or negative context. For example, launching a new product or signing a new contract is viewed as a positive event; involvement in a product recall, bankruptcy or fraud is considered negative.

We focus on determining the *polarity* of a mention of a given company in news media. Polarity classification is important, since if a company appears in negative contexts frequently, it may affect

its reputation, impact its stock price, etc. Polarity prediction, as defined here, is similar to sentiment analysis (Liu and Zhang, 2012): both require the system to classify a span of text as positive or negative. However, there are crucial differences. Business news articles typically do not aim to express emotion or subjectivity—positive and negative events are usually described in a neutral tone. Thus, vocabularies of *affective terms*—e.g., *amazing* or *terrific*—commonly used in sentiment analysis, are not helpful for business polarity. Analysis should rather focus on *affective events* (Ding and Riloff, 2016), i.e., stereotypically positive or negative events. Further, business news employs genre-specific word usage; words seen as negative in "generic" contexts, may indicate a positive context here, and *vice versa*.Negative terms in (Hu and Liu, 2004), e.g., include *"cancer"*, which in business often appears in positive contexts, as when a pharmaceuticals unveil novel treatments.

While most work in sentiment analysis is done at the document level, we aim to classify *entity mentions* in text. This requires changes to document-based classification models. We explore two convolutional neural network (CNN) architectures, initially proposed for *document-level* classification, and adapt them for entity-oriented classification. The modified models have an additional input channel: the *focus*—the position(s) in text where a target company is mentioned. Focus helps the model distinguish among different companies mentioned in text and assign them polarity independently.

As far as we aware no suitable datasets exist for training models for entity-oriented polarity classification. We annotated a dataset of over 17,000 business news articles, which we release for public use, to provide a foundation for an eventual standard evaluation. Despite being much larger than any existing datasets for business polarity detection, it is still small compared to what is typically

---

[1] `http://newsweb.cs.helsinki.fi` or `http://puls.cs.helsinki.fi`

Proceedings of NAACL-HLT 2018, pages 129–136
New Orleans, Louisiana, June 1 - 6, 2018. ©2017 Association for Computational Linguistics

used when training CNNs for text classification.

We attempt to compensate for the small training data by transferring knowledge from a different corpus. The second corpus is large, but annotated for a different task: each document has a set of *event* labels; *some* of these may be mapped to polarity labels. We explore two strategies for knowledge transfer: i) manually mapping from event labels to polarity labels, and ii) pre-training CNNs for the event classification task, followed by unsupervised transfer of high-level features from event classification to polarity. We demonstrate that unsupervised transfer improves performance.

2   Related work

Sentiment analysis: Deep learning for sentiment analysis is an active area of research. Some methods learn vector representations for entire phrases (Dos Santos and Gatti, 2014; Socher et al., 2011); others learn syntactic tree structures (Tai et al., 2015; Socher et al., 2013). A simpler approach using CNNs (Kim, 2014) has demonstrated state-of-the-art performance (Tai et al., 2015).

Interest in applying sentiment mining to the business domain is spurred by important industry applications, such as analyzing the impact of news on financial markets (Ahmad et al., 2016; Van de Kauter et al., 2015; Loughran and McDonald, 2011). If a company frequently appears in news in negative contexts it may affect its reputation, impact its stock price, etc., (Saggion and Funk, 2009). Although news reports usually have a time lag, events reported in news have longer-term impact on investor sentiment and attitudes toward a given company (Boudoukh et al., 2013).

A major difficulty in training entity-oriented polarity models is the lack of publicly available datasets. In the corpus of 5,000 sentences published by Takala et al. (2014), most instances (sentences) contain no company name, and hence cannot be used for predicting polarity for specific entities. A dataset of 679 sentences in Dutch, annotated with entity-oriented business sentiment, was published by Van de Kauter et al. (2015). They demonstrate that a. in financial news, not all sentiment expressions within a sentence relate to the target company; b. sentiment is often expressed implicitly.

A shared task on fine-grained sentiment analysis of financial microblogs and news was held recently as part of SemEval (Cortis et al., 2017), and provided a small dataset containing company names.

This dataset contains only 1,000 news *headlines*, of which only 165 instances mention more than one company name, of which only 20 instances contain names with different polarities (positive for one company but negative for another). Thus, using entity-oriented methods on this dataset may not lead to an advantage in performance. Of the ten best-performing systems on the news sentiment task, many used sentence-level classification with no treatment of target company (Rotim et al., 2017; Cabanski et al., 2017; Ghosal et al., 2017; Kumar et al., 2017); others replace the target name with a special token (Mansar et al., 2017; Moore and Rayson, 2017; Jiang et al., 2017) or use company name as a feature (Kar et al., 2017), though none of the papers provide any evidence that special treatment of the target yields a gain in performance. In our experiments with the SemEval dataset (Pivovarova et al., 2017) a model with explicitly specified target worked slightly worse than a baseline.

The dataset that we release with this paper is 20 times larger and contains *entire* documents, where a given entity may be mentioned multiple times, with many different names mentioned in the same document. This corpus is suitable for experiments with entity-oriented polarity, and our experiments explicitly contrast models that take focus as an input against models that do not use the information about the target company's position.

Transfer learning: a.k.a. *inductive transfer*, is a technique for applying knowledge accumulated from solving one problem to improve the solution for a different problem. We use *feature transfer*, where the goal is to learn transferable representations for data, which are meaningful for multiple tasks (Pan and Yang, 2010; Bengio et al., 2013; Conneau et al., 2017), i.e., very general, low-level representations. On the other hand, one might consider two related tasks, and try to gain knowledge from one to help with the other. In such cases, one wishes to transfer representations at a much *higher level* (Glorot et al., 2011). An analysis of the trade-offs between generality and specificity of learned features can be found at (Yosinski et al., 2014). Deep learning with knowledge transfer has been previously applied to sentiment analysis in the context of domain adaptation (Glorot et al., 2011) and cross-lingual applications (Zhou et al., 2016). In our experiments, we apply knowledge transfer from event classification to sentiment analysis.

3   The Model

We train a classifier for entity-oriented polarity, which receives on input a text and a *"focus"* vector—the positions of mentions of the target company in text—and outputs the polarity for this company. For this purpose we extend state-of-the-art models in (Kim, 2014). The rationale for introducing focus is that polarity is not a feature of the text as a whole, but of each company mention; two company mentions in a text may have opposing polarities, and the model needs be able to distinguish them.

The architecture of the model is shown in Figure 1. The inputs are fed into the network as sentences of a fixed size, zero-padded; each word is a fixed-dimensional embedding vector complemented with a scalar indicating the *focus*. The focus vector is shown in darker grey in Figure 1, with the the company mention framed in red. This provides an additional dimension to the word embedding, and is crucial for distinguishing between instances that differ only in focus and polarity.

The inputs are fed into a layer of convolutional filters with multiple widths, optionally followed by deeper convolutional layers. The results of the last convolutional layer are max-pooled, producing a vector with one scalar per filter, which is then fed into a fully-connected layer with dropout regularization and a soft-max output layer. The output is a 2-dimensional vector that is a probability distribution over the two possible outcomes: positive and negative. In manual annotation we use five values: "very negative" [1 0], "somewhat negative" [.7 .3], "neutral" [.5 .5], "somewhat positive" [.3 .7] and "very positive" [0 1]. The model may output any possible distribution. The loss is cross-entropy between the network's output and the true distribution; the loss updates the weights via back-propagation.

We represent words by embeddings, trained using the GloVe algorithm (Pennington et al., 2014) on a corpus of 5 million news articles. Each article was pre-processed using lemmatization and the PULS NE recognition system. All NEs of the same type are mapped to the same special token; i.e., all company names have the same embedding, all person names another, etc. We continue to train the embeddings during polarity training by updating them at each iteration. This allows the model to learn properties of words significant for polarity, such as the difference between antonyms, which may not be captured well by the initial embeddings.

Class	# instances
very positive	2709
positive	4001
neutral	285

Class	# instances
very negative	2532
negative	4645
contradictory	146

Table 1: Class distribution in annotated data.

4   Data

The dataset contains 17,354 different documents with 19,689 company names. PULS clusters news into groups, each group containing documents describing the same story.[2] Then we manually annotate each group with business polarity of the most salient company names.

In our experiments, each training instance is the first five sentences in the document beginning from the first mention of the focus company. This choice was made because typically the beginning of an article carries information about the principal event, whereas later text contains background information which may mention the company, but where the polarity may be different. In case this processing results in identical instances, we remove duplicates, and keep only one copy.

The resulting dataset used in the experiments contains 14,172 distinct instances. The distribution of the data among the polarity classes is shown in Table 1. Instances labeled "contradictory" are not used for testing and training at present. The data were split into five folds for cross-validation.

We also have a separate, large collection of news articles (Pivovarova et al., 2013), which is annotated for *business events*—for example, *Merger, Contract, Investment, Product launch, Product recall, Fraud, Bankruptcy*—291 labels in all. An article may have multiple event labels. Some of these labels may imply (or strongly correlate with) positive or negative polarity. We attempt to exploit this large data to improve polarity prediction. To this end, we attempt two approaches, with several variations: **manual mapping** and **high-level feature transfer**.

For **manual mapping**, we manually selected those labels which we believe most clearly imply a polarity: e.g., *Investment, Product launch* and *Sponsorship* are considered positive, while *Fraud, Layoff* and *Bankruptcy* are negative; in all, we identified 26 "positive" and 12 "negative" labels. Using

---

[2]The grouping algorithm takes into account the semantic similarity of the keywords, and the distributions of NEs within the documents (Escoter et al., 2017)

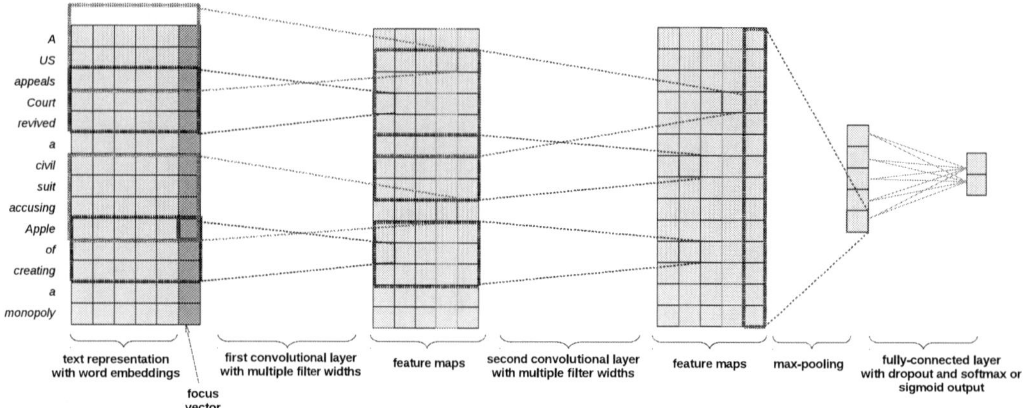

Figure 1: A model architecture with focus vector and two convolution layers

only these 38 event labels, we constructed a training set, removing documents with labels that result in no polarity, or conflicting polarities. Further, since it is impossible to know to which company the label refers, only documents whose headlines and the first sentence contain *exactly one* company mention were kept. (For example, if one company goes bankrupt and another acquires its assets—such documents are not used.)

The resulting dataset is highly skewed with 90% of the data positive. To assure that the positive and negative subsets have similar size, we apply *random undersampling* (Dendamrongvit and Kubat, 2010), i.e., we use a random subset of the positive documents. Of more than two million documents in the original event corpus, 100,000 have a non-ambiguous negative label and mention exactly one company. The resulting dataset consists of 200,000 documents; 10% is used as a development set to decide when to stop training. We use this newly generated 200K document *event corpus* in 2 ways:

Tuning: a two-stage learning procedure where the model is first trained using the event corpus, and then is tuned using the smaller polarity corpus.

Training on combined data: in this strategy, data from both corpora are mixed together, and used for training in random order.

In **high-level feature transfer**, we aim to reuse relatively high-level, task-specific features. We initially train a model to predict event types—using *all* event labels and *all* documents, irrespective of how many companies they mention. This requires a change in the models: because event labels are not mutually exclusive, we use a sigmoid function instead of soft-max in the topmost layer. After the event model is fully trained on the event labels, we strip off the last fully-connected layer of the network, replace it with a two-class output layer for polarity, and resume training using the smaller polarity dataset. We expect that the more task-specific features—ones obtained closer to the output layer— will be useful to determine polarity values, due to the latent relatedness between the two tasks. Thus, we keep almost the entire model, with the exception of the very final layer.

From the large dataset labeled with events, we use 10% as a development set, to determine when to stop training, and to find the best model; another 10% is used as a test set. Results from representative runs are shown in Table 2.

The bigger model gives better performance— with a much larger number of filters (1000 vs. 128). It is not possible to use such large models for learning polarity *without* transfer, because these models are trained on much smaller data and would quickly overfit. Therefore, in subsequent experiments we use two convolutional layers with filter sizes 3,4,5, with 128 filters of each size. [3]

5 Experiments

We present experiments with focus and knowledge transfer variants. Table 3 shows the results for each model variant, averaged across five-fold cross-validation. We report accuracy and cosine similar-

---

[3]The overall accuracy of the method can likely be improved further by careful tuning of hyper-parameters. Here we focus on the comparison of architectures, and defer hyper-parameters for future work.

Hyper-Parameters	rec	prec	F1
conv 2; filters 128; sizes {3,4,5}	35.85	75.42	48.53
conv 1; filters 1000; sizes {3,7,11}	50.80	58.13	**53.89**

Table 2: Event classification results

Transfer Strategy	Focus	Accuracy	Cosine
none	–	81.22	71.51
none	+	81.44	72.93
manual tuning	+	82.07	**73.98**
manual combined data	+	82.01	70.92
feature transfer	–	83.94	71.17
feature transfer	+	**84.44**	71.76
baseline (SVM)		52.02	

Table 3: Experimental results (multiplied by 100, for readability.)

ity between the model output and the annotation.

To compute accuracy as follows. In *annotation* we treat polarity detection as a *three-way* classification task; values inside $[-0.1, 0.1]$ are considered neutral; values further from 0.0 are positive or negative. However, for reasons presented below, the models do not do well on identifying neutral instances. Thus, in the experiments presented here, we evaluate prediction of *binary* polarity[4]: negative vs. positive or neutral. Accuracy measures how often a model *blunders*, and predicts negative polarity rather than positive or neutral, or vice versa.

Cosine similarity[5] is computed by collecting all of the model's polarity probabilities into one vector and one for the manually assigned polarities, and measuring the cosine between the vectors; also, polarities are mapped into the interval $[-1, 1]$. This gives a measure of closeness between model prediction and the ground truth, including differences between "positive" and "very positive" classes.

As the results show, accuracy and cosine similarity do not produce consistent rankings, because they measure different aspects of performance. From a practical, user-oriented point of view, it may be more important that a model avoid gross errors, rather than capturing subtle shades of polarity. In manual annotation we noticed that some distinctions ("positive" vs. "very positive") is far from

clear for human annotators. Thus, we are interested in the models that yield the best *accuracy*.

In addition, we used a SVM classifier as a baseline. The baseline does not use any information about the target company. We use a one-vs-all strategy to obtain three-way classification. For the baseline we report only the accuracy, since this method does not directly produce probabilities.

6 Discussion

Knowledge transfer: Table 3 shows that high-level feature transfer outperforms manual mapping. The main reason might be that feature transfer can benefit from a very large corpus of 2 million documents, while only 200,000 documents can be used with the manual mapping approach, which prevents us from training larger models due to over-fitting. The mapped dataset may suffer from other problems, resulting from how it is created. First, it contains no articles with *neutral* polarity—if an article has no positive or negative label, we cannot assume it to be neutral. For example, articles labeled *Corporate appointments* may have positive or negative polarity. Second, although we choose only the most "trusted" event labels for mapping to polarity, the dataset still contains noise: e.g., a document labeled as *Merger* and assumed to be positive may in fact discuss a canceled merger. Third, since we use only a small subset of the labels, the dataset is highly skewed and incomplete—most event types and data are not used. Most importantly, using manually mapped data, a model is trained to perform a task different from our target—it learns to dis-

---

[4]Due to the industry-level requirements: in business news negative polarity has important implications; "neutral" coverage may even be viewed mildly positive, as the entity mentioned is receiving (non-negative) publicity, etc.

[5]This is the official measure of the SemEval business polarity classification task (Cortis et al., 2017); we include it because it may be useful for indirect comparison of results.

	Example	Truth	+Focus	−Focus	Comment
1	**Valeant** to sell Dendreon unit to Sanpower for $820 million. Canada's **Valeant Pharmaceuticals International Inc.** said its affiliate will sell its Dendreon cancer business to Sanpower Group Co. Ltd. for $819.9 million, as the drugmaker continues to shed its non-core assets *to repay debt.*	-1.0	0.022	-0.322	The model without focus performs better since the company name is mentioned far away from the polarity expression and there is another name in between.
2	Samsung wins over **Apple** in $399 million patent appeal.	-1.0	-0.333	0.004	Model without focus fails: two companies with opposite polarities involved in same event.
3	**Facebook** CEO Mark Zuckerberg and his wife are dropping controversial suits they filed in December to buy small plots of land that are part of a [...] estate they own on the island of Kauai in Hawaii.	0.0	-0.743	-0.397	Text is about Facebook CEO, not the company itself. None of the models handle neutral company mentions well.

Table 4: Model comparison: CNN with/without focus using transfer. Company in focus is in bold

tinguish not positive vs. negative polarity, but one (sub-)set of event labels from another. We cannot assume that the model learns polarity patterns, only that polarity *correlates* with certain event types.

Focus: The results indicate that focus further improves performance.[6] On some test instances, models without focus outperforms models with focus—this happens when polarity expressions lie outside the filter window around the focus company, e.g., as in Example 1 in Table 4.

If two companies within the same text have opposite polarities, a model without focus can assign the correct polarity to at most one of them, as in example 2 in Table 4. Such cases are rare in our dataset; typically, when two companies are involved in the same event, they have the same polarity, e.g., when they strike a deal. Only 6% of instances in our dataset have a paired instance that has identical text but different focus and opposite polarity. Another case when focus is useful is when a document contains much background information, which may contain opposite polarity statements. Estimating the number of such cases is an arduous task. Since in some cases a model with focus performs worse than a model without focus, there is no clear gain in that regard. However, the best-performing transfer strategy works slightly better, as seen from Table 3.

Neutral polarity: Another observation is that all of our models have difficulty in detecting neutral polarities, as shown in Example 3 (which is about Facebook's CEO, rather than the company itself). Neutral examples are rare in our dataset, as shown in Table 1. This is probably the main reason why the models are unable to distinguish neutral polarity. This problem may be helped by annotating more neutral instances.

7 Conclusion

We address the problem of entity-oriented business polarity detection. The main contributions are: I. a dataset of 17,000 annotated documents, which is an order of magnitude larger than any previously available resources for this task;[7] II. we propose benchmark solutions to this problem, based on CNN architectures originally intended for document-level polarity classification, modified for *entity-oriented* polarity classification by explicitly incorporating *focus* into the model; III. we demonstrate that performance can be improved via *transfer learning*, by training a network on a much larger corpus, which is annotated for a different, distantly related task—namely, classification of event types.

We compare manual label mapping with transferring high-level features, and demonstrate that the latter approach performs better, and is less subjective; i.e., features relevant for finding event types work better than a simplistic mapping between the two tasks. The rationale behind this is that business polarity is latently inherent in the event types themselves: some event types carry a positive or negative polarity, while others do not indicate an unambiguous polarity. Therefore, attempting to map event labels directly to polarity is problematic.

For manual mapping of event labels, we can use only documents with exactly one company and "unambiguous" event labels, while for transfer learning we can use the entire event dataset, which lets us use much more data for training bigger models.

High-level feature transfer yields 15.8% error reduction—81% to 84% accuracy—as compared to using only the small polarity-annotated corpus.

---

[6]Results are statistically significant at $p < 0.05$ or lower.

[7]The corpus is available at `puls.cs.helsinki.fi/polarity`

Acknowledgements

This work was supported in part by Tekes (the Finnish Funding Agency for Technology and Innovation) Project *iMEDL: Digital Media Evolution through Deep Learning*, Grant number 5933/31/2017.

References

Khurshid Ahmad, JingGuang Han, Elaine Hutson, Colm Kearney, and Sha Liu. 2016. Media-expressed negative tone and firm-level stock returns. *Journal of Corporate Finance* 37:152–172.

Yoshua Bengio, Aaron Courville, and Pascal Vincent. 2013. Representation learning: A review and new perspectives. *IEEE transactions on pattern analysis and machine intelligence* 35(8):1798–1828.

Jacob Boudoukh, Ronen Feldman, Shimon Kogan, and Matthew Richardson. 2013. Which news moves stock prices? A textual analysis. Technical report, National Bureau of Economic Research.

Tobias Cabanski, Julia Romberg, and Stefan Conrad. 2017. HHU at SemEval-2017 task 5: Fine-grained sentiment analysis on financial data using machine learning methods. In *Proceedings of the 11th International Workshop on Semantic Evaluation (SemEval-2017)*. pages 832–836.

Alexis Conneau, Douwe Kiela, Holger Schwenk, Loic Barrault, and Antoine Bordes. 2017. Supervised learning of universal sentence representations from natural language inference data .

Keith Cortis, André Freitas, Tobias Dauert, Manuela Huerlimann, Manel Zarrouk, Siegfried Handschuh, and Brian Davis. 2017. Semeval-2017 task 5: Fine-grained sentiment analysis on financial microblogs and news. In *Proceedings of the 11th International Workshop on Semantic Evaluation (SemEval-2017)*. Association for Computational Linguistics, Vancouver, Canada, pages 510–526.

Sareewan Dendamrongvit and Miroslav Kubat. 2010. Undersampling approach for imbalanced training sets and induction from multi-label text-categorization domains. In *New Frontiers in Applied Data Mining*, Springer, pages 40–52.

Haibo Ding and Ellen Riloff. 2016. Acquiring knowledge of affective events from blogs using label propagation. In *Thirtieth AAAI Conference on Artificial Intelligence*.

Cícero Nogueira Dos Santos and Maira Gatti. 2014. Deep convolutional neural networks for sentiment analysis of short texts. In *COLING*. pages 69–78.

Mian Du, Lidia Pivovarova, and Roman Yangarber. 2016. PULS: natural language processing for business intelligence. In *Proceedings of the 2016 Workshop on Human Language Technology*. Go to Print Publisher, pages 1–8.

Llorenç Escoter, Lidia Pivovarova, Mian Du, Anisia Katinskaia, and Roman Yangarber. 2017. Grouping business news stories based on salience of named entities. In *15th Conference of the European Chapter of the Association for Computational Linguistics Proceedings of Conference, Volume 1: Long Papers*.

Deepanway Ghosal, Shobhit Bhatnagar, Md Shad Akhtar, Asif Ekbal, and Pushpak Bhattacharyya. 2017. IITP at SemEval-2017 task 5: an ensemble of deep learning and feature based models for financial sentiment analysis. In *Proceedings of the 11th International Workshop on Semantic Evaluation (SemEval-2017)*. pages 899–903.

Xavier Glorot, Antoine Bordes, and Yoshua Bengio. 2011. Domain adaptation for large-scale sentiment classification: A deep learning approach. In *Proceedings of the 28th international conference on machine learning (ICML-11)*. pages 513–520.

Minqing Hu and Bing Liu. 2004. Mining and summarizing customer reviews. In *Proceedings of the tenth ACM SIGKDD international conference on Knowledge discovery and data mining*.

Silja Huttunen, Arto Vihavainen, Mian Du, and Roman Yangarber. 2013. Predicting relevance of event extraction for the end user. In T. Poibeau, H. Saggion, J. Piskorski, and R. Yangarber, editors, *Multi-source, Multilingual Information Extraction and Summarization*, Springer Berlin, Theory and Applications of Natural Language Processing, pages 163–176.

Mengxiao Jiang, Man Lan, and Yuanbin Wu. 2017. ECNU at SemEval-2017 task 5: An ensemble of regression algorithms with effective features for fine-grained sentiment analysis in financial domain. In *Proceedings of the 11th International Workshop on Semantic Evaluation (SemEval-2017)*. pages 888–893.

Sudipta Kar, Suraj Maharjan, and Thamar Solorio. 2017. RiTUAL-UH at SemEval-2017 task 5: Sentiment analysis on financial data using neural networks. In *Proceedings of the 11th International Workshop on Semantic Evaluation (SemEval-2017)*. pages 877–882.

Yoon Kim. 2014. Convolutional neural networks for sentence classification. In *Proceedings of the Conference on Empirical Methods in Natural Language Processing (EMNLP)*.

Abhishek Kumar, Abhishek Sethi, Md Shad Akhtar, Asif Ekbal, Chris Biemann, and Pushpak Bhattacharyya. 2017. IITPB at SemEval-2017 task 5: Sentiment prediction in financial text. In *Proceedings of the 11th International Workshop on Semantic Evaluation (SemEval-2017)*. pages 894–898.

Bing Liu and Lei Zhang. 2012. A survey of opinion mining and sentiment analysis. In *Mining text data*, Springer, pages 415–463.

Tim Loughran and Bill McDonald. 2011. When is a liability not a liability? textual analysis, dictionaries, and 10-ks. *The Journal of Finance* 66(1):35–65.

Youness Mansar, Lorenzo Gatti, Sira Ferradans, Marco Guerini, and Jacopo Staiano. 2017. Fortia-FBK at SemEval-2017 task 5: Bullish or bearish? inferring sentiment towards brands from financial news headlines. *arXiv preprint arXiv:1704.00939* .

Andrew Moore and Paul Rayson. 2017. Lancaster A at SemEval-2017 task 5: Evaluation metrics matter: predicting sentiment from financial news headlines. *arXiv preprint arXiv:1705.00571* .

Sinno Jialin Pan and Qiang Yang. 2010. A survey on transfer learning. *IEEE Transactions on knowledge and data engineering* 22(10):1345–1359.

Jeffrey Pennington, Richard Socher, and Christopher D. Manning. 2014. GloVe: Global vectors for word representation. In *Empirical Methods in Natural Language Processing (EMNLP)*. pages 1532–1543.

Lidia Pivovarova, Llorenç Escoter, Arto Klami, and Roman Yangarber. 2017. HCS at SemEval-2017 task 5: Polarity detection in business news using convolutional neural networks. In *Proceedings of the 11th International Workshop on Semantic Evaluation (SemEval-2017)*. pages 842–846.

Lidia Pivovarova, Silja Huttunen, and Roman Yangarber. 2013. Event representation across genre. In *Proceedins of the 1st Workshop on Events: Definition, Detection, Coreference, and Representation*. NAACL HLT.

Leon Rotim, Martin Tutek, and Jan Šnajder. 2017. TakeLab at SemEval-2017 task 5: Linear aggregation of word embeddings for fine-grained sentiment analysis of financial news. In *Proceedings of the 11th International Workshop on Semantic Evaluation (SemEval-2017)*. pages 866–871.

Horacio Saggion and Adam Funk. 2009. Extracting opinions and facts for business intelligence. *RNTI Journal, E (17)* 119:146.

Richard Socher, Jeffrey Pennington, Eric H. Huang, Andrew Y. Ng, and Christopher D. Manning. 2011. Semi-supervised recursive autoencoders for predicting sentiment distributions. Association for Computational Linguistics, Stroudsburg, PA, USA, EMNLP '11.

Richard Socher, Alex Perelygin, Jean Y Wu, Jason Chuang, Christopher D Manning, Andrew Y Ng, and Christopher Potts. 2013. Recursive deep models for semantic compositionality over a sentiment treebank. In *Proceedings of the conference on empirical methods in natural language processing (EMNLP)*. Citeseer, volume 1631, page 1642.

Kai Sheng Tai, Richard Socher, and Christopher D Manning. 2015. Improved semantic representations from tree-structured long short-term memory networks. In *ACL*.

Pyry Takala, Pekka Malo, Ankur Sinha, and Oskar Ahlgren. 2014. Gold-standard for topic-specific sentiment analysis of economic texts. In *LREC*. pages 2152–2157.

Marjan Van de Kauter, Diane Breesch, and Véronique Hoste. 2015. Fine-grained analysis of explicit and implicit sentiment in financial news articles. *Expert Systems with Applications* .

Jason Yosinski, Jeff Clune, Yoshua Bengio, and Hod Lipson. 2014. How transferable are features in deep neural networks? In *Advances in neural information processing systems*. pages 3320–3328.

Guangyou Zhou, Zhao Zeng, Jimmy Xiangji Huang, and Tingting He. 2016. Transfer learning for cross-lingual sentiment classification with weakly shared deep neural networks. In *Proceedings of the 39th International ACM SIGIR conference on Research and Development in Information Retrieval*.

Selecting Machine-Translated Data for Quick Bootstrapping of a Natural Language Understanding System

Judith Gaspers
Amazon
Aachen, Germany
gaspers@amazon.de

Penny Karanasou
Amazon
Cambridge, UK
pkarana@amazon.co.uk

Rajen Chatterjee
University of Trento
Trento, Italy
chatterjee@unitn.it

Abstract

This paper investigates the use of Machine Translation (MT) to bootstrap a Natural Language Understanding (NLU) system for a new language for the use case of a large-scale voice-controlled device. The goal is to decrease the cost and time needed to get an annotated corpus for the new language, while still having a large enough coverage of user requests. Different methods of filtering MT data in order to keep utterances that improve NLU performance and language-specific postprocessing methods are investigated. These methods are tested in a large-scale NLU task with translating around 10 millions training utterances from English to German. The results show a large improvement for using MT data over a grammar-based and over an in-house data collection baseline, while reducing the manual effort greatly. Both filtering and postprocessing approaches improve results further.

1 Introduction

In recent years, there has been growing interest in voice-controlled devices, such as Amazon Alexa or Google home. This success makes the quick bootstrapping of corresponding systems, including NLU models, for new languages a prioritised goal. However, building a new NLU model for each language from scratch and gathering the necessary annotated corpora implies a significant amount of human time and effort both by annotators and scientists. In addition, this procedure is not scalable to supporting an increasing number of languages. On the other hand, a large amount of data is usually available for the language(s) that are already supported. Leveraging this source of data seems an obvious solution. In this paper,

we investigate the use of Machine Translation to translate existing data sources to a new target language and use them to bootstrap an NLU system for this target language.

A common procedure for data gathering for a new language starts by some grammar-generated data. Significant time and effort is consumed at this stage by language specialists to build grammars that offer a good coverage needed for a first working system. Once this first system reaches a certain performance threshold, it can be shared with beta users. This step allows more data that cover real user's queries to be generated. All existing data sources are then used to train the system that will be released to the final customers, once a new higher performance threshold is reached. Finally, when the system is released to the customers, customer data become available. Beta and customer data better cover the user utterances than grammar-generated data and are, thus, valuable for the development of a good and generalisable NLU system. However, it takes a significant amount of time and human annotation effort in order to have enough annotated beta, and later customer data, needed to build a good NLU system. Furthermore, having a system robust to new domains and features is very challenging and requires data with a wide coverage.

Machine Translation can be a useful tool for the quick expansion to new languages by automatically translating customer data from existing resources to new languages. This could decrease significantly the time needed to develop an NLU system that replies well to customer queries and is robust to new features. In this paper, we work with a large-scale system where around 10 millions annotated customer data are available for US English with a wide coverage of domains and features. We use this corpus to augment the training data of a new language. In particular, we will present our

---

The author Rajen Chatterjee conducted the work for this paper during an internship at Amazon, Cambridge, UK

Proceedings of NAACL-HLT 2018, pages 137–144
New Orleans, Louisiana, June 1 - 6, 2018. ©2017 Association for Computational Linguistics

experiments on applying our technique to bootstrap a German NLU system based on existing US English training data.

In addition, we explore ways to choose the "good" translations from the translated ones, i.e. the ones that improve the NLU performance. The investigated methods fall in the following categories. First, we investigate filtering based on MT quality. This method makes use of scores generated by the MT model to assign the quality of translations. The second method explores improving the NLU performance by making sure the filtered translations keep the semantic information required by the NLU system. In this case, the matching of the NLU labels after a backward translation task is used as the filtering criterion. Lastly, some language-specific post-processing is applied on the translation output. This includes resampling data with catalogues of the new language. Another post-processing step applied is to keep the original (EN) version of certain slots that the users tend to leave untranslated.

This paper is organised as follows. In Section 2, we give an overview of related literature. In Section 3, we present the methods for MT filtering for bootstrapping a new language while improving NLU performance. Next, we detail the experimental setup in section 4, including details on the used NLU and MT systems as well as the monolingual and bilingual corpora used. Afterwards, we present results in Section 5 before concluding the paper in Section 6 .

2   Background work

Many efforts to avoid or minimize this manual work have been made in the last few years using transfer learning, active learning and semi-supervised training. One of the successful approaches has been making use of an MT system to obtain annotated corpora. The results of such works depend on the availability of an MT system (general-purpose or in-domain), on the quality of the acquired translations and on the precision of NLU label-word alignment when passing from one language to another. García et al. (2012) combine multiple online general-purpose translation systems to achieve transferability between French and Spanish for a dialog system. Jabaian et al. (2011) study phrase-based translation as an alternative to Conditional Random Fields (CRF) to keep NLU label-word alignment info in the

decoding process. Lefèvre et al. (2010) propose the Semantic Tuple Classifiers (STC) model without any need for alignment information. Servan et al. (2010) translate the conceptual segments (i.e. NLU labeled) separately to maintain the chunking between source and target language but at the cost of degrading the translation quality.

There is a wide literature on assessing the MT quality. Evaluating the quality of MT output has been a topic in the Workshop of Machine Translation (WMT) since its beginnings (WMT06) and a separate task since 2008 ("Shared Evaluation Task" (WMT08)). Since 2012 a more specific "Quality Estimation Task" (WMT12) appears with a focus on deciding whether a translation is good and how to filter out translations that are not good enough. In addition, in 2017 (WMT17) other related topics appear including post-editing and bandit learning as specific tasks of correcting errors and improving MT quality by learning from feedback. A straight-forward method is using human translated data as the true reference and correct MT errors using this ground truth. Automatic Post-Editing (APE) can also improve MT quality by modifying MT output to the correct version (Chatterjee et al., 2017). Bandit learning (Sokolov et al., 2017) replaces human reference and post-edits by a weak user's feedback. This feedback is introduced in the training process in a reinforcement learning framework updating the gradient to maximize the rewards corresponding to user's feedback.

However, all previous method focus on improving MT quality (i.e. BLEU score) and not the NLU task of interest. Jabaian et al. (2011) add noise to translation data and use translation post-editing to increase the robustness of NLU to translation errors. Other methods include measuring the probability of a translated utterance by applying a target language LM, i.e. measuring if a translated utterance is typical, or computing the likelihood that an alignment between the source and the translated utterance is correct, as Klinger and Cimiano (2015) explore for the sentiment analysis task. We will do something similar in this paper by using directly the MT scores (alignment, translation and language model scores) as a measure of MT quality independent of the NLU tasks. In addition, we explore and extend a different approach for filtering which was presented by Misu et al. (2012). In order to select utterances among possibly erroneous translation results, the authors use back-translation results to check whether the translation result maintains the semantic meaning of the original sentence. The main difference though is that in the latter paper the method is applied using a very small dataset (less than 3k translated utterances) while we work with around 10 millions.

3 Method

In this paper, we explore bootstrapping of NLU models for a new language by translating training data from an NLU system for a different language. The training data is representative of user requests to voice-controlled assistants; annotations are projected from source to target utterances during MT decoding. Since the quality of NLU models trained on MT data depends heavily on the quality of the MT data, we explore different methods for filtering and post-processing. In the following, we describe all approaches in more detail.

3.1 Filtering

The goal of the filtering approaches is to choose "good" translations, i.e. we aim to keep primary translations in the training data which are likely to be useful for building NLU models. We explore two approaches for filtering, one based on MT system scores and one based on semantic information.

3.1.1 Filtering based on semantic information

Misu et al. (2012) remove erroneous machine translations in the NLU training data by using back-translations to measure whether the semantic information of a source utterance is retained in the translated utterance. In particular, they apply the following steps:

1. Label the source utterance with an NLU model
2. Translate the source utterance
3. Label the translated utterance by aligning with the result of step 1
4. Translate the translated utterance back into the source language
5. Label the back-translated utterance with an NLU model
6. Keep the target utterance, if the the recognised intents of steps 1 and 5 are the same

The authors present results with Japanese as the source and English as the target language, suggesting improved spoken language understanding results by filtering translations for the training data with their approach. Thus, this approach aims to keep translations for which some semantic information of utterances is retained, potentially avoiding errors in the NLU models trained on these data. We apply this approach in an adapted form, i.e. instead of the additional alignment step (3), we project labels using the MT system, i.e. we make use of the alignment model trained for the MT system. In addition, we extend the approach by 1) determining if the recognised slots are retained in addition to the intent, and 2) making use of the NLU model's confidence, i.e. we remove utterances retaining the intent, if the confidence of the NLU model is very low (< 0.1 on a scale from $0 - 1$).

3.1.2 Filtering based on MT scores

This approach explores the scores returned by the MT system for choosing translations from a training dataset. Since annotating the translations for quality judgement by humans is expensive, we considered to use the translation score as a quality metric that can give us relative quality judgement among a list of translations. In particular, we computed a threshold for each domain based on translation scores. The score we used is the weighted overall translation score as given by Moses MT toolkit and combining the scores of the translation model, the language model, the re-ordering score and some word penalty. To create a domain-wise threshold, given a translated utterance and its score, we first normalised the score by utterance length. Afterwards, we computed mean and standard deviation per domain. We then selected translations that have a score greater than or equal to the threshold. In this work, we evaluated different thresholds like mean of the translation scores, mean+stdev (standard deviation), mean+(0.5*stdev), and mean+(0.25*stdev).

3.2 Language-specific post-processing

Aiming to improve the quality of slot values in the translated data, we explore two strategies for language-specific post-processing.

3.2.1 Slot resampling

If data are translated from another language, slot values related to the countries in the source language might not model those of user requests in the target language. For example, when requesting a weather forecast, American customers would much more frequently ask for an American city than a German one. Thus, an utterance "how is the weather in New York" is likely to be much more frequent in the resulting training data than an utterance "how is the weather in Berlin", and consequently it would appear more frequently in the data after translation to German. This, however, doesn't seem to model language use by German customers well and can hence potentially degrade performance of statistical models trained on these data. Aiming to decrease the mismatch in slots values between source language and target language use, we used catalogs to resample slot values for slots where this seemed to be appropriate. In particular, we replaced slot values in the translated data using target language catalog entries corresponding to the slot. For instance, a catalog with German cities can be used to replace "New York" by "Berlin" in the previously mentioned example. For catalogs comprising information, which can be used for weighting catalog entities, we made use of it in that we sample entities according to weights, i.e. the higher the weight, the more often the corresponding entity is sampled. For example, the number of orders can be used to weight albums and population size can be used to weight cities.

3.2.2 Keeping some original slot values

Machine translation systems might incorrectly translate slot values which should not be translated. For example, in an utterance "play we are the champions by queen", the song title "we are the champions" and the band name "queen" should not be translated. While we can apply slot resampling to ingest existing slot values into such utterances, we also explore a different approach. In particular, in this approach we post-process the translated utterances to retain the slot values from the source language utterances for certain slots, such as artists or song titles.

4 Experimental setup

We ran experiments using US English as the source and German as the target language. Since we are interested in bootstrapping an NLU model for a new language which would first be deployed to beta customers, we evaluate our approach on German beta data. In the following, we first briefly describe the MT and NLU systems and subsequently the datasets.

4.1 MT and NLU systems

We used a phrase-based MT system which was built using Moses (Koehn et al., 2007) for a similar task, i.e. Question Answering (QA). The MT system is a multi-domain model trained on a mixture of internal and external parallel data sources, which are not from the QA domain; overall the out-of-domain data sources comprised 28,733,606 segments. The system was fine-tuned using a small manually created parallel corpus for QA, comprising 4,000 segments, and 424,921 in-domain target language segments were used for the target language model. Training data were preprocessed, in particular they were converted into spoken form before building the MT system to better match spoken user utterances of an NLU system. We used an MT system for a similar task rather than an MT system adapted for our data, because we would expect that suitable in-domain data for adaptation might not yet be available for early bootstrapping, i.e. when target language data have not yet been collected.

For building NLU models, we use Conditional Random Fields (Lafferty et al., 2001; Okazaki, 2007) for Named Entity Recognition and a Maximum Entropy classifier (Berger et al., 1996) for Intent Classification; we keep the sets of features, hyper-parameters and configuration constant for our experiments.

4.2 Datasets

We translated 10M of training data utterances from a US English NLU system. Overall, the data cover several domains with a large number of different intents and slots/named entities. We translated the data using the previously described MT system. NLU labels were kept and aligned during the MT decoding to project them from the English source utterances to the corresponding German translations. The final training dataset comprised 9,963,624 utterances.

For testing, we created a dataset collected from German Beta users; German test data were manually transcribed and annotated with intents and slots/named entities. The resulting test dataset comprised 119,772 utterances.

To create a baseline, we used an in-house data collection of 10k utterances, which were manually transcribed and annotated with intents and slots. While in-house data collections are costly and time-consuming, they constitute a reasonable approach for bootstrapping a model from scratch when customer data are not yet available.

The data amounts are summarised in Table 1.

Dataset	No. utt.
US EN→DE translated data (train)	9,963,624
DE Beta data (test)	119,772
In-house data collection (train)	10,000

Table 1: Number of utterances per dataset.

In addition, we created a grammar-based baseline. In particular, we randomly sampled utterances from grammars and created a training dataset from them. For this, we used around 200 grammars written by language experts covering (most) intents and slots supported by the NLU system. However, one of the domains was not covered by grammars, because it supports very diverse features and requests, which are difficult to capture by a grammar.

We report results by means of a semantic error rate (SemER) which is computed based on the number of insertions, deletions and substitutions for slots and the intent in a recognised utterance compared to a reference utterance, i.e.

$$\text{SemER} = \frac{\#\ (\text{slot + intent errors})}{\#\ (\text{slots + intents in reference})}$$

5   Results

First, we compare our approach to the baseline approaches based on grammars and an in-house data collection. For this, we trained NLU models on MT data, on the in-house data collection, on grammar-generated data as well as on MT data together with each baseline dataset. Subsequently, we evaluated the models on the German beta data test set. Results for model trained on the MT dataset and on the baseline datasets are presented in Table 2.

Training data	SemER (%)
Grammar-generated data (baseline)	55.44
In-house collection (baseline)	23.30
MT data	21.38
MT data + grammar-generated data	20.00
MT data + in-house collection	17.20

Table 2: Comparison for NLU models trained on MT data to our baseline models, i.e. models trained on grammar-generated data and models trained on an in-house data collection of 10k utterances.

As can be seen, the MT approach outperforms the grammar-based one by a large percentage (i.e. around 33% absolute in SemER), while requiring much less manual effort. In addition, training on both MT and grammar-generated data improves performance over training solely on either one of the datasets; the improvement of the joined approach is particularly large over training solely on grammar-generated data (i.e. around 35 % absolute in SemER). As noted before, the grammars did not cover one of the domains, yielding errors for its test utterances. To get an estimate of this impact, we removed all utterances from this domain from the test set and recomputed SemER for the grammar-based baseline. While SemER dropped to 34.23, there is still a large difference in performance compared to training on MT data and one domain is not supported at all, even though it is needed by the system. Compared to the grammar-based baseline, training on the in-house data collection yields a lower SemER of 23.3. Still, training on MT data outperforms this baseline as well, and combining MT data with the in-house data collection improves further over training solely on either one of the datasets (i.e. 17.2 for both vs 21.38 for MT and 23.3 for the in-house collection). Thus, MT data appear to be useful for both bootstrapping an NLU model from scratch and enhancing models trained on grammar-generated data or on an in-house data collection of 10k.

In the following, we evaluate whether our filtering and post-processing approaches can improve the quality of the MT training data further. Table 3 presents the results for our filtering approaches. While filtering based on semantic information yields an improvement in SemER over using MT data as they are, filtering based on MT scores only yields a slight improvement in one of the conditions. For filtering based on semantic information, our results confirm in a large-scale industry setting that training on utterances for which the intent is retained after back-translation is useful. In addition, our results show that performance can be improved further by either additionally removing utterances for which the slots are not retained or by removing utterances for which the confidence is very low. Here, removing low confidence utterances yields slightly better results. While we tested with 0.1 as a threshold, results might be improved further by optimising this threshold, potentially even per domain.

Approach(es)	Dataset size	SemER (%)
Translated data (baseline)	9,963,624	21.38
Sem. filtering, intents only	6,694,739	20.72 (-3.10)
Sem. filtering, intents + slots	6,194,498	20.60 (-3.64)
Sem. filtering, intents, exclude low confidence	6,500,127	20.32 (-4.97)
Filtering based on MT scores, mean	5,281,331	23.62 (+10.48)
Filtering based on MT scores, standard deviation	8,798,330	21.92 (+2.50)
Filtering based on MT scores, standard deviation, 0.25	6,286,603	21.05 (-1.54)
Filtering based on MT scores, standard deviation, 0.5	7,547,861	23.24 (+8.68)

Table 3: Results of the filtering approaches. Relative changes with respect to the baseline are given in parentheses.

Filtering based on MT scores decreases performance in all considered conditions, except mean+(0.25*stdev), which yields a very slight improvement. However, results were not consistent across domains, i.e., while overall SemER as well as SemER for several domains increased in most cases, it decreased for several domains with relative decreases of up to 48.35%. Here, manual inspection of the data indicates that this approach is not well-suited for domains comprising very diverse data, since one threshold based on a mean score cannot capture diverse data well. In addition, manual inspection revealed that a rather large percentage of the increase in SemER was due to removing ambiguous utterances, as these typically have a rather low MT score, but are sometimes very frequently used and hence need to be captured by the NLU system. For example, the German utterance "weiter" is frequently used, but can mean both "forward" and "resume" in English, implying also different user intents. Removing only this one utterance from the training data yielded around 2.5k errors, since this utterance is frequent in the test data. However, frequent errors could potentially be fixed manually with little effort by a rule-based approach. Since the approach based on MT scores yields improvements for certain domains, further investigations on the nature of datasets/domains it works well with could be interesting. Since it also yields improved results for some domains compared to the approach based on semantic information, further experiments investigating the combination of both approaches could potentially improve results further.

Table 4 shows the results of our language-specific post-processing approaches.

The results show that slot resampling has almost no impact on the error rates. The reason might be that the statistical model uses catalogs

Approach(es)	SemER (%)
Translated data (baseline)	21.38
Slot resampling	21.53 (+0.69)
Original slots	23.82 (+11.40)
Original slots + resampling	20.18 (-5.60)

Table 4: Results of the language-specific post-processing approaches. Relative changes in relation to the baseline are given in parentheses.

also as gazetteers, and hence already includes information on German entities during training. Future work might investigate the effect of slot resampling for models which do not use gazetteers. Keeping some original slot values degrades performance from 21.38% to 23.82%. One reason for the decrease in performance might be that keeping a few original slot values decreases the frequency of appearance of some German words that still appear in the test set and are requested by users in German. However, it is not consistent that some words or some slots are always in German or English, yielding some mismatches between translated training data and test data. Aiming to counterbalance the increase of English words' frequency, but also consider the original slot values, we combined both approaches. As can be seen in the table, the combined approach yields an improvement, i.e. SemER is 20.18% compared to 21.38% for training on MT data as they are. With 20.18%, this approach is also performing better than our best-performing filtering approach which yields 20.32% in SemER. One interesting question for future work will be to explore if combining filtering and language-specific post-processing approaches will improve results further.

Overall, compared to the grammar-based baseline, the best-performing post-processing approach yields a large improvement in SemER (20.18% vs 55.44%) and also yields results very similar to the NLU model trained on both the initial MT data and the grammar-generated data (20.18% vs 20.0%). However, our proposed post-processing approach can be applied automatically and quickly, while grammar writing is very costly and time-consuming.

6 Conclusion

Aiming to reduce time and costs needed to boot-strap an NLU model for a new language, in this paper we made use of MT data to build NLU models. In addition, we compared different techniques to filter and post-process the MT data, aiming to improve NLU performance further. These methods were evaluated in large-scale experiments for a voice-controlled assistant to bootstrap a German system using English data. The results when using MT data showed a large improvement in performance compared to a grammar-based baseline and outperformed a baseline using an in-house data collection. The applied filtering and post-processing techniques improved results further over using MT data as they are.

In future work, we plan to apply our approach to further languages and explore bootstrapping new domains for an existing NLU system.

Acknowledgments

We thank Steve Sloto, Greg Hanneman, Donna Gates and Patrick Porte for building the MT system and Fabian Triefenbach and Daniel Marcu for valuable comments on this paper.

References

Adam L Berger, Vincent J Della Pietra, and Stephen A Della Pietra. 1996. A maximum entropy approach to natural language processin. *Computational Linguistics* 22(1):39–71.

Rajen Chatterjee, Amin Farajian, Matteo Negri, Marco Turchi, Ankit Srivastava, Santanu Kumar Pal, and Bruno Kessler. 2017. Multi-source neural automatic post-editing: Fbkas participation in the wmt 2017 ape shared task. In *Proceedings of the Second Conference on Machine Translation,Copenhagen, Denmark*.

Fernando García, Lluís F. Hurtado, Encarna Segarra, Emilio Sanchis, and Giuseppe Riccardi. 2012. Combining multiple translation systems for spoken language understanding portability. In *2012 IEEE Spoken Language Technology Workshop (SLT), Miami, FL, USA, December 2-5, 2012*. pages 194–198.

B. Jabaian, L. Besacier, and F. Lefèvre. 2011. Combination of stochastic understanding and machine translation systems for language portability of dialogue systems. In *2011 IEEE International Conference on Acoustics, Speech and Signal Processing (ICASSP)*. pages 5612–5615.

Roman Klinger and Philipp Cimiano. 2015. Instance selection improves cross-lingual model training for fine-grained sentiment analysis. In *Proceedings of the Nineteenth Conference on Computational Natural Language Learning*. Association for Computational Linguistics, Beijing, China, pages 153–163.

Philipp Koehn, Hieu Hoang, Alexandra Birch, Chris Callison-Burch, Marcello Federico, Nicola Bertoldi, Brooke Cowan, Wade Shen, Christine Moran, Richard Zens, Chris Dyer, Ondřej Bojar, Alexandra Constantin, and Evan Herbst. 2007. Moses: Open source toolkit for statistical machine translation. In *Proceedings of the 45th Annual Meeting of the ACL on Interactive Poster and Demonstration Sessions*. ACL '07, pages 177–180.

John D. Lafferty, Andrew McCallum, and Fernando C. N. Pereira. 2001. Conditional random fields: Probabilistic models for segmenting and labeling sequence data. In *Proceedings of the Eighteenth International Conference on Machine Learning*. ICML '01, pages 282–289.

Fabrice Lefèvre, François Mairesse, and Steve J. Young. 2010. Cross-lingual spoken language understanding from unaligned data using discriminative classification models and machine translation. In *INTERSPEECH 2010, 11th Annual Conference of the International Speech Communication Association, Makuhari, Chiba, Japan, September 26-30, 2010*. pages 78–81.

T. Misu, E. Mizukami, H. Kashioka, S. Nakamura, and H. Li. 2012. A bootstrapping approach for slu portability to a new language by inducting unannotated user queries. In *2012 IEEE International Conference on Acoustics, Speech and Signal Processing (ICASSP)*. pages 4961–4964.

Naoaki Okazaki. 2007. Crfsuite: a fast implementation of conditional random fields (crfs). `http://www.chokkan.org/software/crfsuite/`.

Christophe Servan, Nathalie Camelin, Christian Raymond, Frédéric Béchet, and Renato de Mori. 2010. On the use of machine translation for spoken language understanding portability. In *Proceedings of the IEEE International Conference on Acoustics, Speech, and Signal Processing, ICASSP 2010, 14-19 March 2010, Sheraton Dallas Hotel, Dallas, Texas, USA*. pages 5330–5333.

Artem Sokolov, Julia Kreutzer, Kellen Sunderland, Pavel Danchenko, Witold Szymaniak, Hagen Fürstenau, and Stefan Riezler. 2017. A shared task on bandit learning for machine translation. *CoRR* abs/1707.09050.

WMT06. 2006. NAACL 2006 workshop on statistical machine translation. http://www.statmt.org/wmt06/.

WMT08. 2008. ACL 2008 third workshop on statistical machine translation - Shared task: Automatic evaluation of machine translation. http://www.statmt.org/wmt08/shared-evaluation-task.html.

WMT12. 2012. NAACL 2012 seventh workshop on statistical machine translation - Shared task: Quality estimation. http://www.statmt.org/wmt12/quality-estimation-task.html.

WMT17. 2017. EMNLP 2017 second conference on machine translation (WMT17). http://www.statmt.org/wmt17/index.html.

Fast and Scalable Expansion of Natural Language Understanding Functionality for Intelligent Agents

Anuj Goyal, Angeliki Metallinou, Spyros Matsoukas
Amazon Alexa Machine Learning
{anujgoya, ametalli, matsouka}@amazon.com

Abstract

Fast expansion of natural language functionality of intelligent virtual agents is critical for achieving engaging and informative interactions. However, developing accurate models for new natural language domains is a time and data intensive process. We propose efficient deep neural network architectures that maximally re-use available resources through transfer learning. Our methods are applied for expanding the understanding capabilities of a popular commercial agent and are evaluated on hundreds of new domains, designed by internal or external developers. We demonstrate that our proposed methods significantly increase accuracy in low resource settings and enable rapid development of accurate models with less data.

1 Introduction

Voice powered artificial agents have become widespread among consumer devices, with agents like Amazon Alexa, Google Now and Apple Siri being popular and widely used. Their success relies not only on accurately recognizing user requests, but also on continuously expanding the range of requests that they can understand. An ever growing set of functionalities is critical for creating an agent that is engaging, useful and human-like.

This presents significant scalability challenges regarding rapidly developing the models at the heart of the natural language understanding (NLU) engines of such agents. Building accurate models for new functionality typically requires collection and manual annotation of new data resources, an expensive and lengthy process, often requiring highly skilled teams. In addition, data collected from real user interactions is very valuable for developing accurate models but without an accurate model already in place, the agent will not enjoy widespread use thereby hindering collection of high quality data.

Presented with this challenge, our goal is to speed up the natural language expansion process for Amazon Alexa, a popular commercial artificial agent, through methods that maximize re-usability of resources across areas of functionality. Each area of Alexa's functionality, e.g., Music, Calendar, is called a *domain*. Our focus is to a) increase accuracy of low resource domains b) rapidly build new domains such that the functionality can be made available to Alexa's users as soon as possible, and thus start benefiting from user interaction data. To achieve this, we adapt recent ideas at the intersection of deep learning and transfer learning that enable us to leverage available user interaction data from other areas of functionality.

To summarize our contributions, we describe data efficient deep learning architectures for NLU that facilitate knowledge transfer from similar tasks. We evaluate our methods at a much larger scale than related transfer learning work in NLU, for fast and scalable expansion of hundreds of new natural language domains of Amazon Alexa, a commercial artificial agent. We show that our methods achieve significant performance gains in low resource settings and enable building accurate functionality faster during early stages of model development by reducing reliance on large annotated datasets.

2 Related Work

Deep learning models, including Long-Short term memory networks (LSTM) (Gers et al., 1999), are state of the art for many natural language processing tasks (NLP), such as sequence labeling (Chung et al., 2014), named entity recognition (NER) (Chiu and Nichols, 2015) and part of speech (POS) tagging (Huang et al., 2015).

Proceedings of NAACL-HLT 2018, pages 145–152
New Orleans, Louisiana, June 1 - 6, 2018. ©2017 Association for Computational Linguistics

Multitask learning is also widely applied in NLP, where a network is jointly trained for multiple related tasks. Multitask architectures have been succesfully applied for joint learning of NER, POS, chunking and supertagging tasks, as in (Collobert et al., 2011; Collobert and Weston, 2008; Søgaard and Goldberg, 2016).

Similarly, transfer learning addresses the transfer of knowledge from data-rich source tasks to under-resourced target tasks. Neural transfer learning has been successfully applied in computer vision tasks where lower layers of a network learn generic features that are transferred well to different tasks (Zeiler and Fergus, 2014; Krizhevsky et al., 2012). Such methods led to impressive results for image classification and object detection (Donahue et al., 2014; Sharif Razavian et al., 2014; Girshick et al., 2014) In NLP, transferring neural features across tasks with disparate label spaces is relatively less common. In (Mou et al., 2016), authors conclude that network transferability depends on the semantic relatedness of the source and target tasks. In cross-language transfer learning, (Buys and Botha, 2016) use weak supervision to project morphology tags to a common label set, while (Kim et al., 2017a) transfer lower layer representations across languages for POS tagging. Other related work addresses transfer learning where source and target share the same label space, while feature and label distributions differ, including deep learning methods (Glorot et al., 2011; Kim et al., 2017b), and earlier domain adaptation methods such as EasyAdapt (Daumé III, 2007), instance weighting (Jiang and Zhai, 2007) and structural correspondence learning (Blitzer et al., 2006).

Fast functionality expansion is critical in industry settings. Related work has focused on scalability and ability to learn from few resources when developing a new domain, and includes zero-shot learning (Chen et al., 2016; Ferreira et al., 2015), domain attention (Kim et al., 2017c), and scalable, modular classifiers (Li et al., 2014). There is a multitude of commercial tools for developers to build their own custom natural language applications, including Amazon Alexa ASK (Kumar et al., 2017), DialogFlow by Google (DialogFlow) and LUIS by Microsoft (LUIS). Along these lines, we propose scalable methods that can be applied for rapid development of hundreds of low resource domains across disparate label spaces.

3 NLU Functionality Expansion

We focus on Amazon Alexa, an intelligent conversational agent that interacts with the user through voice commands and is able to process requests on a range of natural language domains, e.g., playing music, asking for weather information and editing a calendar. In addition to this *built-in* functionality that is designed and built by internal developers, the Alexa Skills Kit (ASK) (Kumar et al., 2017) enables external developers to build their own *custom* functionality which they can share with other users, effectively allowing for unlimited new capabilities. Below, we describe the development process and challenges associated with natural language domain expansion.

For each new domain, the internal or external developers define a set of *intents* and *slots* for the target functionality. Intents correspond to user intention, e.g., 'FindRecipeIntent', and slots correspond to domain-specific entities of interest e.g.,'FoodItem'. Developers also define a set of commonly used utterances that cover the core use cases of the functionality, e.g., 'find a recipe for chicken'. We call those *core utterances*. In addition, developers need to create *gazetteers* for their domain, which are lists of slot values. For example, a gazetteer for 'FoodItem' will contain different food names like 'chicken'. We have developed infrastructure to allow internal and external teams to define their domain, and create or expand linguistic resources such as core utterances and gazetteers. We have also built tools that enable extracting *carrier phrases* from the example utterances by abstracting the utterance slot values, such as 'find a recipe for {FoodItem}'. The collection of carrier phrases and gazetteers for a domain is called a *grammar*. Grammars can be sampled to generate synthetic data for model training. For example, we can generate the utterance 'find a recipe for pasta' if the latter dish is contained in the 'FoodItem' gazetteer.

Next, developers enrich the linguistic resources available for a new domain, to cover more linguistic variations for intents and slots. This includes creating bootstrap data for model development, including collecting utterances that cover the new functionality, manually writing variations of example utterances, and expanding the gazetteer values. In general, this is a time and data intensive process. External developers can also continuously enrich the data they provide for their custom domain. However, external developers typically lack the time, resources or expertise to provide rich datasets, therefore in practice custom domains are significantly under-resourced compared to built-in domains.

Once the new domain model is bootstrapped using the collected datasets, it becomes part of Alexa's natural language functionality and is available for user interactions. The data from such user interactions can be sampled and annotated in order to provide additional targeted training data for improving the accuracy of the domain. A good bootstrap model accuracy will lead to higher user engagement with the new functionality and hence to a larger opportunity to learn from user interaction data.

Considering these challenges, our goal is to reduce our reliance on large annotated datasets for a new domain by re-using resources from existing domains. Specifically, we aim to achieve higher model accuracy in low resource settings and accelerate new domain development by building good quality bootstrap models faster.

4　Methodology

In this section, we describe transfer learning methods for efficient data re-use. Transfer learning refers to transferring the knowledge gained while performing a task in a *source* domain D_s to benefit a related task in a *target* domain D_t. Typically, we have a large dataset for D_s, while D_t is an under-resourced new task. Here, the target domain is the new built-in or custom domain, while the source domain contains functionality that we have released, for which we have large amounts of data. The tasks of interest in both D_s and D_t are the same, namely slot tagging and intent classification. However D_s and D_t have different label spaces Y_s and Y_t, because a new domain will contain new intent and slot labels compared to previously released domains.

4.1　DNN-based natural language engine

We first present our NLU system where we perform slot tagging (ST) and intent classification (IC) for a given input user utterance. We are inspired by the neural architecture of (Søgaard and Goldberg, 2016), where a multi-task learning architecture is used with deep bi-directional Recurrent Neural Networks (RNNs). Supervision for the different tasks happens at different layers. Our neural network contains three layers

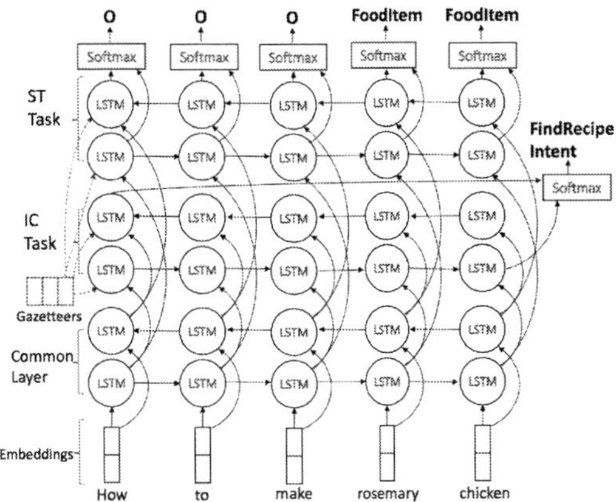

Figure 1: Multitask stacked bi-LSTM architecture for ST and IC, with a shared bottom layer, two separate top layers for ST and IC. Gazetteer features can be added as optional input to the ST and IC layers during the fine-tuning stage. (see also Sec. 4.2)

of bi-directional Long Short Term Memory networks (LSTMs) (Graves and Schmidhuber, 2005; Hochreiter and Schmidhuber, 1997). The two top layers are optimized separately for the ST and IC tasks, while the common bottom layer is optimized for both tasks, as shown in Figure 1.

Specifically let r_t^c denote the common representation computed by the bottommost bi-LSTM for each word input at time t. The ST forward LSTM layer learns a representation $r_t^{ST,f} = \phi(r_t^c, r_{t-1}^{ST})$, where ϕ denotes the LSTM operation. The IC forward LSTM layer learns $r_t^{IC,f} = \phi(r_t^c, r_{t-1}^{IC})$. Similarly, the backward LSTM layers learn $r_t^{ST,b}$ and $r_t^{IC,b}$. To obtain the slot tagging decision, we feed the ST bi-LSTM layer's output per step into a softmax, and produce a slot label at each time step (e.g., at each input word). For the intent decision, we concatenate the last time step from the forward LSTM with the first step of the backward LSTM, and feed it into a softmax for classification:

$$r_t^{slot} = r_t^{ST,f} \oplus r_t^{ST,b}, r^{intent} = r_T^{IC,f} \oplus r_1^{IC,b}$$
$$\hat{S}_t = softmax(W_s r_t^{slot} + b_s)$$
$$\hat{I} = softmax(W_I r^{intent} + b_I)$$

where $\oplus$ denotes concatenation. W_s, W_I, b_s, b_I are the weights and biases for the slot and intent softmax layers respectively. $\hat{S}_t$ is the predicted slot tag per time step (per input word), and $\hat{I}$ is the predicted intent label for the sentence.

The overall objective function for the multi-task network combines the IC and ST objectives.

Therefore we jointly learn a shared representation r_t^c that leverages the correlations between the related IC and ST tasks, and shares beneficial knowledge across tasks. Empirically, we have observed that this multitask architecture achieves better results than separately training intent and slot models, with the added advantage of having a single model, and a smaller total parameter size.

In our setup, each input word is embedded into a 300-dimensional embedding, where the embeddings are estimated from our data. We also use pre-trained word embeddings as a separate input, that allows incorporating unsupervised word information from much larger corpora (FastText (Bojanowski et al., 2016)). We encode slot spans using the IOB tagging scheme (Ramshaw and Marcus, 1995). When we have available *gazetteers* relevant to the ST task, we use gazetteer features as an additional input. Such features are binary indicators of the presence of an n-gram in a gazetteer, and are common for ST tasks (Radford et al., 2015; Nadeau and Sekine, 2007).

4.2 Transfer learning for the DNN engine

Typically, a new domain D_t contains little available data for training the multitask DNN architecture of Sec 4.1. We propose to leverage existing data from mature released domains (source D_s) to build generic models, which are then adapted to the new tasks (target D_t).

We train our DNN engine using labeled data from D_s in a supervised way. The source slot tags space Y_s^{slot} and intent label space Y_s^{intent} contain labels from previously released slots and intents respectively. We refer to this stage as *pre-training*, where the stacked layers in the network learn to generate features which are useful for the ST and IC tasks of D_s. Our hypothesis is that such features will also be useful for D_t. After pre-training is complete, we replace the top-most affine transform and softmax layers for IC and ST with layer dimensions that correspond to the target label space for intents and slots respectively, i.e., Y_t^{intent} and Y_t^{slot}. The network is then trained again using the available target labeled data for IC and ST. We refer to this stage as *fine-tuning* of the DNN parameters for adapting to D_t.

A network can be pre-trained on large datasets from D_s and later fine tuned separately for many low resource new domains D_t. In some cases, when developing a new domain D_t, new domain-specific information becomes available, such as domain gazetteers (which were not available at pre-training). To incorporate this information during fine-tuning, we add gazetteer features as an extra input to the two top-most ST and IC layers, as shown in Figure 1. We found that adding new features during fine-tuning significantly changes the upper layer distributions. Therefore, in such cases, it is better to train the ST and IC layers from scratch and only transfer and fine-tune weights from the common representation r_c of the bottom layer. However, when no gazetteers are available, it is beneficial to pre-train all stacked Bi-LSTM layers (common, IC and ST), except from the task-specific affine transform leading to the softmax.

4.3 Baseline natural language engine

While DNNs are strong models for both ST and IC, they typically need large amounts of training data. As we focus on under-resourced functionality, we examine an alternative baseline that relies on simpler models; namely a Maximum Entropy (MaxEnt) (Berger et al., 1996) model for intent classification and a Conditional Random Field (CRF) (Lafferty et al., 2001) model for slot tagging. MaxEnt models are regularized log-linear models that have been shown to be effective for text classification tasks (Berger et al., 1996). Similarly, CRFs have been popular tagging models in the NLP literature (Nadeau and Sekine, 2007) prior to the recent growth in deep learning. In our experience, these models require less data to train well and represent strong baselines for low resource classification and tagging tasks.

5 Experiments and Results

We evaluate the transfer learning methods of Section 4.2 for both custom and built-in domains, and compare with baselines that do not benefit from knowledge transfer (Sections 4.1, 4.3). We experiment with around 200 developer defined custom domains, whose statistics are presented in Table 1. Looking at the median numbers, which are less influenced by a few large custom domains compared to mean values, we note that typically developers provide just a few tens of example phrases and few tens of values per gazetteer (slot gazetteer size). Therefore, most custom domains are significantly under-resourced. We also select three new built-in domains, and evaluate them at various early stages of domain development. Here, we assume that variable amounts of training data gradually become available, including bootstrap and user interaction data.

We pre-train DNN models using millions of annotated utterances from existing mature built-in domains. Each annotated utterance has an associated domain label, which we use to make sure that the pre-training data does not contain utterances labeled as any of the custom or built-in target domains. After excluding the target domains, the pre-training data is randomly selected from a variety of mature Alexa domains covering hundreds of intents and slots across a wide range of natural language functionality. For all experiments, we use L1 and L2 to regularize our DNN, CRF and MaxEnt models, while DNNs are additionally regularized with dropout.

The test sets contain user data, annotated for each custom or built-in domain. For custom domains, test set size is a few hundred utterances per domain, while for built-in domains it is a few thousand utterances per domain. Our metrics include standard F1 scores for the SC and IC tasks, and a sentence error rate (SER) defined as the ratio of utterances with at least one IC or ST error over all utterances. The latter metric combines IC and ST errors per utterance and reflects how many utterances we could not understand correctly.

Data type	Mean	Median
number of intents	8.02	3
number of slots	2.07	1
slot gazetteer size	441.35	11
number of example phrases	268.11	42

Table 1: Statistics of data for around 200 developer defined custom domains

5.1 Results for custom developer domains

For the custom domain experiments, we focus on a low resource experimental setup, where we assume that our only target training data is the data provided by the external developer. We report results for around 200 custom domains, which is a subset of all domains we support. We compare the proposed transfer learning method, denoted as *DNN Pretrained*, with the two baseline methods described in sections 4.1 and 4.3, denoted as *DNN Baseline* and *CRF/MaxEnt Baseline*, respectively. For training the baselines, we use the available data provided by the developer for each domain, e.g., example phrases and gazetteers. From these resources, we create grammars and we sample them to generate 50K training utterances per

domain, using the process described in Section 3. This training data size was selected empirically based on baseline model accuracy. The generated utterances may contain repetitions for domains where the external developer provided a small amount of example phrases and few slot values per gazetteer. For the proposed method, we pre-train a DNN model on 4 million utterances and fine tune it per domain using the 50K grammar utterances of that domain and any available gazetteer information (for extracting gazetteer features). In Table 2, we show the mean and median across custom domains for $F1_{slot}$, $F1_{intent}$ and SER.

Table 2 shows that the CRF and MaxEnt models present a strong baseline and generally outperform the DNN model without pretraining, which has a larger number of parameters. This suggests that the baseline DNN models (without pretraining) cannot be trained robustly without large available training data. The proposed pre-trained DNN significantly outperforms both baselines across all metrics (paired t-test, $p < .01$). Median SER reduces by around 14% relative when we use transfer learning compared to both baselines. We are able to harness the knowledge obtained from data of multiple mature source domains D_s and transfer it to our under-resourced target domains D_t, across disparate label spaces.

To investigate the effect of semantic similarity across source and target domains we selected a subset of 30 custom domains with high semantic similarity with the source tasks. Semantic similarity was computed by comparing the sentence representations computed by the common bi-LSTM layer across source and target sentences, and selecting target custom domains with sentences close to at least one of the source tasks. For these 30 domains, we observed higher gains of around 19% relative median SER reduction. This corroborates observations of (Mou et al., 2016), that neural feature transferability for NLP depends on the semantic similarity between source and target. In our low resource tasks, we see a benefit from transfer learning and this benefit increases as we select more semantically similar data.

Our approach is scalable and is does not rely on manual domain-specific annotations, besides developer provided data. Also, pretrained DNN models are about five times faster to train during the fine-tuning stage, compared to training the model from scratch for each custom domain,

Approach	$F1_{Intent}$		$F1_{Slot}$		SER	
	Mean	Median	Mean	Median	Mean	Median
Baseline CRF/MaxEnt	94.6	96.6	80.0	91.5	14.5	9.2
Baseline DNN	91.9	95.9	85.1	92.9	14.7	9.2
Proposed Pretrained DNN *	**95.2**	**97.2**	**88.6**	**93.0**	**13.1**	**7.9**

Table 2: Results for around 200 custom developer domains. For F1, higher values are better, while for SER lower values are better. * denotes statistically significant SER difference compared to both baselines.

which speeds up model turn-around time.

5.2 Results for built-in domains

We evaluate our methods on three new built-in domains referred here as domain A (5 intents, 36 slot types), domain B (2 intents, 17 slot types) and domain C (22 intents, 43 slot types). Table 3 shows results for domains A, B and C across experimental early stages of domain development, where different data types and amounts of data per data type gradually become available. Core data refers to core example utterances, bootstrap data refers to domain data collection and generation of synthetic (grammar) utterances, and user data refers to user interactions with our agent. As described in Section 3, the collection and annotation of these data sources is a lengthy process. Here we evaluate whether we can accelerate the development process by achieving accuracy gains in early, low resource stages, and bootstrap a model faster.

For each data setting and size, we compare our proposed pretrained DNN models with the baseline CRF/MaxEnt baseline, which is the better performing baseline of Section 5.1. Results for the non pre-trained DNN baseline are similar, and omitted for lack of space. Our proposed DNN models are pre-trained on 4 million data from mature domains and then fine tuned on the available target data. The baseline CRF/MaxEnt models are trained on the available target data. Note that the datasets of Table 3 represent early stages of model development and do not reflect final training size or model performance. The types of target data slightly differ across domains according to domain development characteristics. For example, for domain B there was very small amount of core data available and it was combined with the bootstrap data for experiments.

Overall, we notice that our proposed DNN pre-training method improves performance over the CRF/MaxEnt baseline, for almost all data settings. As we would expect, we see the largest gains for the most low resource data settings. For example, for domain A, we observe a 7% and 5% relative

Train Set	Size	Method	$F1_{intent}$	$F1_{slot}$	SER
Domain A (5 intents, 36 slots)					
Core* data	500	Baseline	85.0	63.9	51.9
		Proposed	86.6	66.6	48.2
Bootstrap data*	18K	Baseline	86.1	72.8	49.6
		Proposed	86.9	73.8	47.0
Core + user data*	3.5K	Baseline	90.4	74.3	40.5
		Proposed	90.1	75.8	37.9
Core + bootstrap + user data	43K	Baseline	92.1	80.6	33.4
		Proposed	91.9	80.8	32.8
Domain B (2 intents, 17 slots)					
Bootstrap data*	2K	Baseline	97.0	94.7	10.1
		Proposed	97.8	95.3	6.3
User data	2.5K	Baseline	97.0	94.7	8.2
		Proposed	97.1	96.4	7.1
Bootstrap + user data*	52K	Baseline	96.7	95.2	8.2
		Proposed	97.0	96.6	6.4
Domain C (22 intents, 43 slots)					
Core* data	300	Baseline	77.9	47.8	64.2
		Proposed	85.6	46.6	51.8
Bootstrap data*	26K	Baseline	46.1	65.8	64.0
		Proposed	49.1	68.9	62.8
Core + bootstrap. + user data*	126K	Baseline	92.3	78.3	28.1
		Proposed	92.7	72.7	31.9

Table 3: Results on domains A, B and C for the proposed pretrained DNN method and the baseline CRF/MaxEnt method during experimental early stages of domain development. * denotes statistically significant SER difference between proposed and baseline

SER improvement on core and bootstrap data settings respectively. The performance gain we obtain on those early stages of development brings us closer to our goal of rapidly bootstrapping models with less data. From domains A and C, we also notice that we achieve the highest performance in settings that leverage user data, which highlights the importance of such data. Note that the drop in F_{intent} for domain C between core and bootstrap data is because the available bootstrap data did not contain data for all of the 22 intents of domain C. Finally, we notice that the gain from transfer learning diminishes in some larger data settings, and we may see degradation (domain C, 126K data setting). We hypothesize that as larger training data becomes available it may be better to not pre-train or pre-train with source data that are semantically similar to the target. We will investigate this as part of future work.

6 Conclusions and Future Work

We have described the process and challenges associated with large scale natural language functionality expansion for built-in and custom domains for Amazon Alexa, a popular commercial intelligent agent. To address scalability and data collection bottlenecks, we have proposed data efficient deep learning architectures that benefit from transfer learning from resource-rich functionality domains. Our models are pre-trained on existing resources and then adapted to hundreds of new, low resource tasks, allowing for rapid and accurate expansion of NLU functionality. In the future, we plan to explore unsupervised methods for transfer learning and the effect of semantic similarity between source and target tasks.

References

Adam L Berger, Vincent J Della Pietra, and Stephen A Della Pietra. 1996. A maximum entropy approach to natural language processing. *Computational linguistics*, 22(1):39–71.

John Blitzer, Ryan McDonald, and Fernando Pereira. 2006. Domain adaptation with structural correspondence learning. In *Proceedings of the 2006 conference on empirical methods in natural language processing*, pages 120–128. Association for Computational Linguistics.

Piotr Bojanowski, Edouard Grave, Armand Joulin, and Tomas Mikolov. 2016. Enriching word vectors with subword information. *arXiv preprint arXiv:1607.04606*.

Jan Buys and Jan A. Botha. 2016. Cross-lingual morphological tagging for low-resource languages. In *Proceedings of the Association for Computational Linguistics (ACL)*. Association for Computational Linguistics.

Yun-Nung Chen, Dilek Hakkani-Tür, and Xiaodong He. 2016. Zero-shot learning of intent embeddings for expansion by convolutional deep structured semantic models. In *Acoustics, Speech and Signal Processing (ICASSP), 2016 IEEE International Conference on*, pages 6045–6049. IEEE.

Jason PC Chiu and Eric Nichols. 2015. Named entity recognition with bidirectional lstm-cnns. *arXiv preprint arXiv:1511.08308*.

J. Chung, C. Gulcehre, K. Cho, and Y. Bengio. 2014. Empirical evaluation of gated recurrent neural networks on sequence modeling. In *NIPS 2014 Workshop on Deep Learning,*.

R. Collobert and J. Weston. 2008. A unified architecture for natural language processing: Deep neural networks with multitask learning. In *Proc. of International Conference of Machine Learning (ICML) 2008*.

Ronan Collobert, Jason Weston, Léon Bottou, Michael Karlen, Koray Kavukcuoglu, and Pavel Kuksa. 2011. Natural language processing (almost) from scratch. *Journal of Machine Learning Research*, 12(Aug):2493–2537.

Hal Daumé III. 2007. Frustratingly easy domain adaptation. In *Proceedings of the Association for Computational Linguistics (ACL)*. Association for Computational Linguistics.

DialogFlow. https://dialogflow.com.

Jeff Donahue, Yangqing Jia, Oriol Vinyals, Judy Hoffman, Ning Zhang, Eric Tzeng, and Trevor Darrell. 2014. Decaf: A deep convolutional activation feature for generic visual recognition. In *International conference on machine learning*, pages 647–655.

Emmanuel Ferreira, Bassam Jabaian, and Fabrice Lefèvre. 2015. Zero-shot semantic parser for spoken language understanding. In *Sixteenth Annual Conference of the International Speech Communication Association*.

Felix A Gers, Jürgen Schmidhuber, and Fred Cummins. 1999. Learning to forget: Continual prediction with lstm.

Ross Girshick, Jeff Donahue, Trevor Darrell, and Jitendra Malik. 2014. Rich feature hierarchies for accurate object detection and semantic segmentation. In *Proceedings of the IEEE conference on computer vision and pattern recognition*, pages 580–587.

Xavier Glorot, Antoine Bordes, and Yoshua Bengio. 2011. Domain adaptation for large-scale sentiment classification: A deep learning approach. In *Proceedings of the 28th international conference on machine learning (ICML-11)*, pages 513–520.

Alex Graves and Jürgen Schmidhuber. 2005. Framewise phoneme classification with bidirectional lstm and other neural network architectures. *Neural Networks*, 18(5):602–610.

Sepp Hochreiter and Jürgen Schmidhuber. 1997. Long short-term memory. *Neural computation*, 9(8):1735–1780.

Zhiheng Huang, Wei Xu, and Kai Yu. 2015. Bidirectional lstm-crf models for sequence tagging. *arXiv preprint arXiv:1508.01991*.

Jing Jiang and ChengXiang Zhai. 2007. Instance weighting for domain adaptation in nlp. In *ACL*, volume 7, pages 264–271.

J.-K. Kim, Y.-B. Kim, R. Sarikaya, and E. Fosler-Lussier. 2017a. Cross-lingual transfer learning for pos tagging without cross-lingual resources. In *Proc. of the 2017 Conference on Empirical Methods in Natural Language Processing (EMNLP)*, pages 2832–2838.

Young-Bum Kim, Karl Stratos, and Dongchan Kim. 2017b. Adversarial adaptation of synthetic or stale data. In *ACL*.

Young-Bum Kim, Karl Stratos, and Dongchan Kim. 2017c. Domain attention with an ensemble of experts. In *Annual Meeting of the Association for Computational Linguistics*.

Alex Krizhevsky, Ilya Sutskever, and Geoffrey E Hinton. 2012. Imagenet classification with deep convolutional neural networks. In *Advances in neural information processing systems*, pages 1097–1105.

Anjishnu Kumar, Arpit Gupta, Julian Chan, Sam Tucker, Björn Hoffmeister, Markus Dreyer, Stanislav Peshterliev, Ankur Gandhe, Denis Filiminov, Ariya Rastrow, Christian Monson, and Agnika Kumar. 2017. Just ASK: building an architecture for extensible self-service spoken language understanding. In *NIPS 2017 Workshop on Conversational AI*.

John Lafferty, Andrew McCallum, and Fernando CN Pereira. 2001. Conditional random fields: Probabilistic models for segmenting and labeling sequence data.

Q. Li, G. Tur, D. Hakkani-Tur, X. Li, T. Paek, A. Gunawardana, and C. Quirk. 2014. Distributed open-domain conversational understanding framework with domain independent extractors. In *Spoken Language Technology Workshop (SLT) 2014*.

LUIS. The Microsoft Language Understanding Intelligent Service (LUIS), https://www.luis.ai.

L. Mou, Z. Meng, R. Yan, G. Li, Y. Xu, L. Zhang, and Z. Jin. 2016. How transferable are neural networks in nlp applications. In *Proceedings of the 2016 conference on empirical methods in natural language processing*, pages 479–489.

D. Nadeau and S. Sekine. 2007. *A survey of named entity recognition and classification. Linguisticae Investigationes,*, volume 1. John Benjamins Publishing Company.

W. Radford, X. Carreras, and J. Henderson. 2015. Named entity recognition with document-specific kb tag gazetteers. In *Proc. of the 2015 Conference on Empirical Methods in Natural Language Processing (EMNLP)*, pages 512–517.

Lance Ramshaw and Mitch Marcus. 1995. Text chunking using transformation-based learning. In *Third Workshop on Very Large Corpora*.

Ali Sharif Razavian, Hossein Azizpour, Josephine Sullivan, and Stefan Carlsson. 2014. Cnn features off-the-shelf: an astounding baseline for recognition. In *Proceedings of the IEEE conference on computer vision and pattern recognition workshops*, pages 806–813.

Anders Søgaard and Yoav Goldberg. 2016. Deep multi-task learning with low level tasks supervised at lower layers. In *Proceedings of the 54th Annual Meeting of the Association for Computational Linguistics*, volume 2, pages 231–235.

Matthew D Zeiler and Rob Fergus. 2014. Visualizing and understanding convolutional networks. In *European conference on computer vision*, pages 818–833. Springer.

Bag of Experts Architectures for Model Reuse in Conversational Language Understanding

Rahul Jha, Alex Marin, Suvamsh Shivaprasad, and Imed Zitouni
Microsoft Corporation, Redmond, WA
{rajh,alemari,sushivap,izitouni}@microsoft.com

Abstract

Slot tagging, the task of detecting entities in input user utterances, is a key component of natural language understanding systems for personal digital assistants. Since each new domain requires a different set of slots, the annotation costs for labeling data for training slot tagging models increases rapidly as the number of domains grow. To tackle this, we describe Bag of Experts (BoE) architectures for model reuse for both LSTM and CRF based models. Extensive experimentation over a dataset of 10 domains drawn from data relevant to our commercial personal digital assistant shows that our BoE models outperform the baseline models with a statistically significant average margin of 5.06% in absolute F1-score when training with 2000 instances per domain, and achieve an even higher improvement of 12.16% when only 25% of the training data is used.

1 Introduction

Natural language understanding (NLU) is a key component of dialog systems for commercial personal digital assistants (PDAs) such as Amazon Alexa, Google Home, Microsoft Cortana and Apple Siri. The task of the NLU component is to map input user utterances into a semantic frame consisting of domain, intent and slots (Kurata et al., 2016). The semantic frame is used by the dialog manager for state tracking and action selection.

Slot tagging can be formulated as a sequence classification task where each input word in the user utterance must be classified as belonging to one of the slot types in a predefined schema (Sarikaya et al., 2016). In a standard NLU architecture, each new domain defines a new domain-specific schema for its slots. Figure 1 shows examples of annotated queries from three different domains relevant to a typical commercial digital

assistant. Since the schemas for different domains can vary, the usual strategy is to train a separate slot tagging model for each new domain. However, the number of domains increases rapidly as the PDAs are required to support new scenarios and training a separate slot tagging model for each new domain becomes prohibitively expensive in terms of annotation costs.

Travel
What are the $[best]_{rating}$ $[hotels]_{service}$ in $[Austin]_{location}$
I need a room from $[March\ 23rd]_{start\_date}$ to $[April\ 7th]_{end\_date}$

Flight Status
Check flight heading for $[New\ York]_{location}$ on $[October\ 16]_{start\_date}$ at $[3\ pm]_{start\_time}$
What time will $[Lufthansa]_{airline}$ flight $[182]_{flight}$ from $[Denver]_{location}$ land?

Real Estate
See $[houses]_{property\_type}$ $[for\ rent]_{listing\_type}$ in $[Houston]_{location}$
Find out if $[123\ main\ street]_{location}$ is on the market

Figure 1: Example utterances with the output slot tags for three different domains.

Even though different domains have different slot tagging schemas, some classes of slots appear across a number of domains, as suggested by the examples in Figure 1. Both **travel** and **flight status** have *date* and *time* related slots, and all three domains have the *location* slot. Reusing annotated data for these common slots would allow us to train models with better accuracy using less data. However, since both the input distribution and the label distribution are different across domains, we must use domain adaptation methods to train on the joint data (Daume, 2007; Kim et al.,

Proceedings of NAACL-HLT 2018, pages 153–161
New Orleans, Louisiana, June 1 - 6, 2018. ©2017 Association for Computational Linguistics

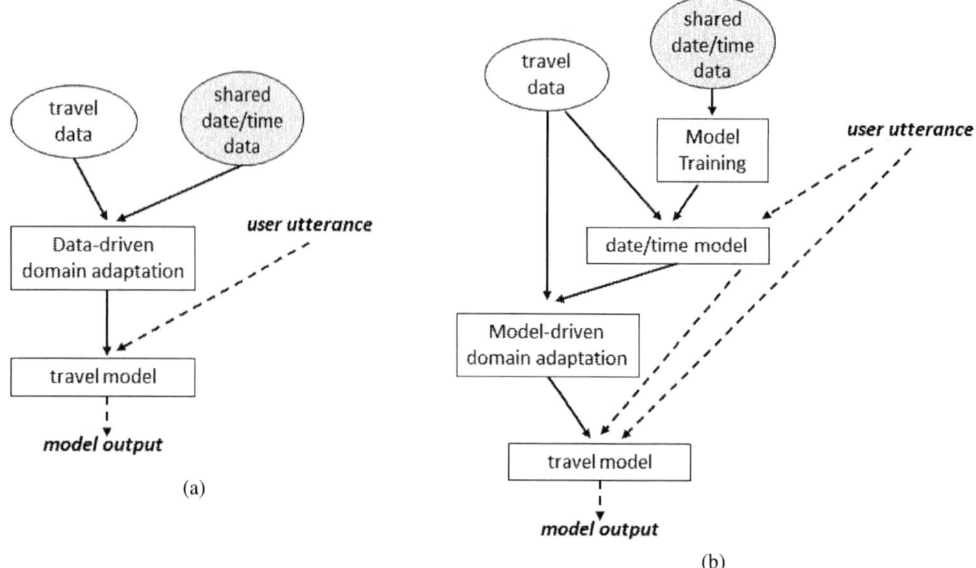

Figure 2: Examples for two different strategies for reusing annotated data from reusable slots. Figure (a) shows data-driven adaptation, while Figure (b) shows model-driven adaptation. Solid lines show the flow at training time, while the dashed lines show the flow at run-time for the deployed travel model. The model output at run-time is a slot-tagged user utterance.

2016c; Blitzer et al., 2006).

In this data-driven adaptation approach, we build a repository of annotated data containing date, time, location and other reusable slots. We then combine relevant data from the reusable repository with the domain specific data during model training. Figure 2(a) shows an example of this architecture where reusable date/time data is used for training travel domain.

A drawback of the data-driven adaptation approach is that as the repository of data for reusable slots grows, the training time for new domains increases. The training data for a new domain might be in the hundreds of samples, while the training data for the reusable slots might contain hundreds of thousands of samples. This increase in training time makes iterative refinement difficult in the initial design of new domains, which is when the ability to deploy new models quickly is crucial.

An alternative strategy is to use model-driven adaptation approaches (Kim et al., 2017b) as shown in Figure 2(b). Here, instead of retraining on the data for the reusable slots, we train "expert" models for these slots, and use the output of these models directly when training new domains. Using model-driven adaptation ensures that model training time is proportional to the data size of new

target domains, as opposed to the large data size for reusable slots, allowing for faster training.

In this paper, we present a model-driven adaptation approach for slot tagging called Bag of Experts (BoE). In Section 2, we first describe how this approach can be applied to two popular machine learning methods used for slot tagging: Long Short Term Memory (LSTM) and Conditional Random Fields (CRF) models. We then describe a dataset of 10 target domains and 2 reusable domains that we've collected for use in a commercial digital assistant, in Section 3. Using this data, we conduct experiments comparing the BoE models with their non-expert counterparts, and show that BoE models can lead to significant F1-score improvements. The experimental setup is described in Section 4.1 and the results are discussed in Section 4.3. This is followed by a survey of related work in Section 5 and the conclusion in Section 6.

2 Approaches

We first describe our LSTM and CRF models for slot tagging, followed by their BoE variants: LSTM-BoE and CRF-BoE. Tensorflow (Abadi et al., 2015) was used for implementing the LSTM models, while a custom C++ implementation was

Domain	#Train	#Test	#Dev	#Slots	Example Utterance
Fashion	5273	701	696	8	Show me the $[turtleneck]_{item}$ I wore $[last\ Tuesday]_{date}$
Flight Stat.	9481	553	492	9	Is flight $[283]_{flight\_number}$ at $[Kennedy\ airport]_{location}$ on time $[today]_{start\_date}$?
Deals	25598	1271	2036	5	Find $[mexican]_{category}$ deals in $[seattle]_{location}$
Purchase	5033	397	402	18	Buy the $[shirt]_{item}$ I was looking at $[yesterday]_{date}$
Real Estate	5633	525	498	7	Show me the $[rental]_{property\_type}$ at $[13\ Holt\ Street]_{location}$
Shopping	19725	1106	892	16	Find the $[Nov\ 2017]_{date}$ $[iphone]_{brand\_name}$ model
Soc. Net.	38450	432	441	21	Display $[Mike]_{username}$'s $[tweets]_{media\_type}$ from $[yesterday]_{date}$
Sports	20341	1048	1048	21	Display games $[this\ week]_{date}$ for $[texas\ tech]_{team\_name}$
Transport.	162951	19706	19724	17	$[Driving]_{transport\_type}$ directions to $[union\ station]_{location}$
Travel	49300	2027	1990	27	How much for $[2]_{number\_rooms}$ rooms at the $[Hilton]_{place\_name}$ in $[SF]_{location}$?

Table 1: List of target domains used for our experiments, along with some statistics and example utterances. The test and development data sets are sampled at 10% of the total annotated data. "Flight Stat." stands for "Flight Status", "Soc. Net." stands for "Social Network", and "Transport." stands for "Transportation".

used for the CRF models.

2.1 LSTM

For our LSTM model, we follow a standard bidirectional LSTM architecture (Huang et al., 2015; Ma and Hovy, 2016; Lample et al., 2016). Let $w_1...w_n$ denote the input word sequence. For every input word w_i, let f_i^C and b_i^C be the outputs of the forward and backward character level LSTMs respectively, and let m_i be the word embedding (initialized either randomly or with pre-trained embeddings). The input to the word level LSTMs, g_i, is the concatenation of these three vectors:

$$g_i = [f_i^C; b_i^C; m_i]$$

where both $f_i^C, b_i^C \in R^{25}$ and m_i has the same dimensions as the pre-trained embeddings. The forward and backward word level LSTMs take g_i as input and produce f_i^W and b_i^W, which are then concatenated to produce h_i:

$$h_i = [f_i^W, b_i^W]$$

where $f_i^W, b_i^W \in R^{100}$, making $h_i \in R^{200}$. h_i is then input to a dense feed forward layer with a softmax activation to predict the label probabilities for each word. We train using stochastic gradient descent with Adam (Kingma and Ba, 2015). To avoid overfitting, we also use dropout on top of m_i and h_i layers, with a default dropout keep probability of 0.8. We experiment with some variations of this default LSTM architecture, the results are described in Section 4.2.

2.2 LSTM-BoE

We now describe the LSTM Bag of Experts (LSTM-BoE) architecture. Let $e_1...e_k \in E$ be the set of reusable expert domains. For each expert e_j, we train a separate LSTM with the architecture described in Section 2.1. Let $h_i^{e_j}$ be the bi-directional word LSTM output for expert e_j on word w_i.

When training on a target domain, for each word w_i, we first compute the character level LSTMs f_i^C, b_i^C similarly to Section 2.1. We then compute a BoE representation for this word as:

$$h^E = \sum_{e_i \in E} h_i^{e_j}$$

The input to the word level LSTM for word w_i in the target domain is now a concatenation of the character level LSTM outputs (f_i^C, b_i^C), the word embedding m_i, and h^E:

$$g_i = [f_i^C; b_i^C; m_i; h^E]$$

g_i is then input to the word level LSTM for the target domain to produce h_i in the same way as Section 2.1. This architecture is similar to the one presented in (Kim et al., 2017b), with the exception that in their architecture, h^E is concatenated with the word level LSTM output h_i for the target domain. In our architecture, we add h^E before the word-level LSTM in order to capture long-range dependencies of label prediction for a word on expert predictions for context words.

2.3 CRF

Conditional Random Fields (CRF) are a popular family of models that have been proven to work well in a variety of sequence tagging NLP applications (Lafferty et al., 2001). For our experiments, we use a standard linear-chain CRF architecture with n-gram and context features.

In particular, for each token, we use unigram, bigram and trigram features, along with previous and next unigrams, bigrams, and trigrams for context length of up to 3 words. We also use a skip bigram feature created by concatenating the current unigram and skip-one unigram.

We train our CRF using stochastic gradient descent with L1 regularization to prevent overfitting. The L1 coefficient was set to 0.1 and we use a learning rate of 0.1 with exponential decay for learning rate scheduling (Tsuruoka et al., 2009).

2.4 CRF-BoE

Similar to the LSTM-BoE model, we first train a CRF model c_j for each of the reusable expert domains $e_j \in E$. When training on a target domain, for every query word w_i, a one-hot label vector l_i^j is emitted by each expert CRF model c_j.

The length of the label vector l_i^j is the number of labels in the expert domain, with the value corresponding to the label predicted by c_j for word w_i set to 1, and values for all other labels set to 0. For each word, the label vectors for all the expert CRF models are concatenated and provided as features for the target domain CRF training, along with the n-gram features.

3 Data

3.1 Target Domains

We built a dataset of 10 target domains for experimentation. Table 1 shows the list of domains as well as some statistics and example utterances. We treated these as new domains - that is, we do not have real interaction data with users for these domains. The annotated data is therefore prepared in two steps.

First, utterances are obtained using crowdsourcing, where workers are provided with prompts for different intents of a domain and asked to generate

Variation	Average Diff	P-val
Embeddings		
Glove (100)	$+1.61 \pm 0.71^*$	0.048
Glove (200)	$+2.01 \pm 0.64^*$	0.012
Glove (300)	$+1.92 \pm 0.94$	0.073
PDA Logs (500)	$+2.60 \pm 0.61^*$	0.002
Output Layer		
CRF	$+0.67 \pm 0.30$	0.054
Dropout (default keep probability 0.8)		
keep prob. = 0.5	$-2.53 \pm 0.62^*$	0.003
keep prob. = 0.6	$-1.60 \pm 0.31^*$	0.001
keep prob. = 0.7	-0.29 ± 0.28	0.330
keep prob. = 0.9	$+0.36 \pm 0.25$	0.176
keep prob. = 1.0	$+0.63 \pm 0.30$	0.065

Table 2: Average absolute F1-score improvement on the dev data for different LSTM variations. $*$ indicates the improvement is statistically significant with p-value < 0.05.

natural language utterances corresponding to those intents. Next, the generated utterances are annotated by a different set of crowd workers, using the slot schema for each domain. Inter-annotator agreement as well as manual inspection are used to ensure data quality in both stages.

The amount of data collected varies for each domain based on its complexity and business priority. Dataset size statistics for the data used in our experiments are presented in section 4.1. Test and dev data are sampled at 10% of the total annotated data, with stratified sampling used in order to preserve the distribution of the intents.

3.2 Reusable Domains

We experiment with two domains containing reusable slots: timex and location. The timex domain consists of utterances containing the slots *date*, *time* and *duration*. The location domain consists of utterances containing *location*, *location_type* and *place_name* slots. Both of these types of slots appear in more than 20 of a set of 40 domains developed for use in our commercial personal assistant, making them ideal candidates for reuse.[1]

---

[1] Several other candidate reusable domains exist, including: the **name** domain containing the slot *contact_name*; the **number** domain containing the slots *rating*, *quantity* and *price*; and the **reference** domain containing the slots *ordinal* (whose values include "first", "second" or "third") and *order_ref* (with values such as "before" or "after"). All of these slots appear in more than 25% of the available domains.

Data for these domains was sampled from the input utterances from our commercial digital assistant. Each reusable domain contains about a million utterances. There is no overlap between utterances in the target domains used for our experiments and utterances in the reusable domains. The data for the reusable domains is sampled from other domains available to the digital assistant, not including our target domains.

Grouping the reusable slots into domains in this way provides additional opportunities for a commercial system: the trained reusable domain models can be used in other related products which need to identify time and location related entities. Models trained on the timex and location data have F1-scores of 96% and 89% respectively on test data from their respective domains.

4 Experiments

4.1 Experimental Setup

We want to verify if BoE models can improve slot tagging performance by using the information from reusable domains. To simulate the low data scenario for the initial model training, we create three training datasets by sampling 2000, 1000 and 500 training examples from every domain. We use stratified sampling to maintain the input distribution of the intents across the three training datasets.

For each training dataset, we train the four models as described in Section 2 and compute the precision, recall and F1-score on the test data. Fixed seeds are used when training all models to make the results reproducible. Table 3 summarizes these results, with only F1-scores reported to save space. We describe these results in Section 4.3.

4.2 LSTM architecture variants

Using the dev data set for the 10 domains, we experimented with using different pretrained embeddings, dropout probabilities and a CRF output layer in our LSTM architecture. The results are summarized in Table 2. For each of the 10 domains, we trained using each variant with 10 different seeds, and computed the mean F1-score for each domain. For comparing two variants, we computed the mean difference in the F1-scores over the 10 domains and its p-value.

We tried word level Glove embeddings of 100, 200 and 300 dimensions as well as 500-dimensional word embeddings trained over the utterances from our commercial PDA logs. Both 100 and 200 dimensional Glove embeddings led to statistically significant improvements, but the word embeddings trained over our logs led to the biggest improvement. We also tried using a CRF output layer (Lample et al., 2016) and different values of dropout keep probability, but none of them gave statistically significant improvements over the default model. Based on this, we used PDA trained 500-dimensional word embeddings for our final experiments on test data.

4.3 Results and Discussion

Table 3(a) shows the F1-scores obtained by the different methods for the training data set of 2000 training instances for each of the 10 domains. LSTM based models in general perform better than the CRF based models. The LSTM models have a statistically significant average improvement of 3.14 absolute F1-score over the CRF models. The better performance of LSTM over CRF can be explained by the LSTM being able to use information over longer contexts to make predictions, while the CRF model is limited to at most the previous and next 3 words.

The results in Table 3(a) also show that both the CRF-BoE and LSTM-BoE outperform the basic CRF and LSTM models. LSTM-BoE has a statistically significant mean improvement of 1.92 points over LSTM. CRF-BoE also shows an average improvement of 2.19 points over the CRF model, but the results are not statistically significant. Looking at results for individual domains, the highest improvement for BoE models are seen for **transportation** and **travel**. This can be explained by these domains having a high frequency of *timex* and *location* slots, as shown in Table 4.

The **shopping** model shows a regression for BoE models, and a reason could be the low frequency of expert slots (Table 4). However, low frequency of expert slots does not always mean that BoE methods can't help, as shown by the improvement in the **purchase** domain. Finally, for **sports**, **social network** and **deals** domains, the LSTM-BoE improves over LSTM, while CRF-BoE does not improve over CRF. Our hypothesis is that given the query patterns for these domains, the dense vector output used by LSTM-BoE is able to transfer some information, while the categorical label output used by CRF-BoE is not.

Table 3(b) shows the results with 500 and 1000

Train size	2000			
Domain	**CRF**	**LSTM**	**CRF-BoE**	**LSTM-BoE**
Fashion	79.54	82.18	80.87	**83.21**
Purchase	66.24	77.56	70.09	**79.72**
Flight Status	87.60	89.86	89.30	**91.51**
Deals	83.74	85.69	83.59	**87.31**
Travel	66.39	71.02	72.81	**75.52**
Transportation	79.18	80.93	**89.65**	85.95
Sports	75.70	77.82	75.08	**79.43**
Social Network	81.71	81.02	81.65	**83.74**
Shopping	77.16	**81.67**	76.07	80.65
Real Estate	96.16	**97.07**	96.18	97.01
Average improvement		+3.14*	+2.19	+5.06*

(a)

Train size	500				1000			
Domain	**CRF**	**LSTM**	**CRF-BoE**	**LSTM-BoE**	**CRF**	**LSTM**	**CRF-BoE**	**LSTM-BoE**
Fashion	69.05	75.31	71.52	**76.85**	73.81	79.63	75.49	**80.07**
Purchase	53.12	63.58	54.52	**70.66**	61.04	**69.39**	62.23	64.46
Flight Status	78.03	84.33	82.59	**88.29**	84.14	88.12	86.17	**89.85**
Deals	69.82	78.31	72.66	**81.11**	78.60	81.58	78.01	**82.95**
Travel	47.66	58.71	64.28	**70.00**	57.37	65.77	67.53	**73.91**
Transportation	70.37	75.02	**87.12**	85.59	75.03	76.53	**88.21**	86.68
Sports	55.93	65.71	56.88	**68.94**	66.92	71.78	66.52	**71.96**
Social Network	69.73	78.08	66.59	**79.91**	78.45	**80.31**	75.78	79.27
Shopping	59.26	66.55	57.11	**71.10**	70.01	76.32	69.26	**77.04**
Real Estate	91.04	**93.66**	92.59	93.15	93.76	95.07	94.29	**95.34**
Average improvement		+7.52*	+4.19	+12.16*		+4.54*	+2.44	+6.24*

(b)

Table 3: F1-scores obtained by each of the four models for the 10 domains, with the highest score in each row marked as bold. Table (a) reports the results for 2000 training instances, and Table (b) reports the results for 500 and 1000 training instances. The average improvement is computed over the CRF model, with the ones marked * being statistically significant with p-value < 0.05. The average improvement of LSTM-BoE over LSTM is +1.92*, +1.70 and +4.63* for 2000, 1000, and 500 training instances respectively.

training data instances. Note that the improvements are even higher for the experiments with smaller training data. In particular, LSTM-BoE shows an improvement of 4.63 in absolute F1-score over LSTM when training with 500 instances. Thus, as we reduce the amount of training data in the target domain, the performance improvement from BoE models is even higher.

As an example, in the **purchase** domain, the LSTM-BoE model achieves an F1-score of 70.66% with only 500 training instances, while even with 2000 training instances the CRF model achieves an F1-score of only 66.24%. Thus the LSTM-BoE model achieves better F1-score with only one-fourth the training data. Similarly, for **flight status**, **travel**, and **transportation** domains, the LSTM-BoE model gets better performance with 500 training instances, compared to a CRF model with 2000 training instances. The LSTM-BoE architecture, therefore, allows us to reuse the domain experts to produce better performing models with much lower data annotation costs. As the target domain training data increases, the contribution due to domain experts goes down, but more experimentation is needed to establish the threshold at which it is no longer useful to add experts.

5   Related Work

Early methods for slot-tagging used rule-based approaches (Ward and Issar, 1994). Much of the later work on supervised learning focused on CRFs, for example (Sarikaya et al., 2016), or neural networks (Deoras and Sarikaya, 2013; Yao et al., 2013; Liu et al., 2015; Celikyilmaz and Hakkani-Tur, 2015). Unsupervised (or weakly-supervised) methods also were used for NLU tasks, primarily leveraging search query click logs (Hakkani-Tur et al., 2011a,b, 2013) and knowledge graphs (Tur et al., 2012; Heck and Hakkani-Tur, 2012; Heck et al., 2013); hybrid methods, for example as described in (Kim et al., 2015a; Celikyilmaz et al., 2015; Chen et al., 2016), also exist. Our approach

Domain	%Timex	%Location
Fashion	16.08	0.00
Purchase	3.83	0.00
Flight Status	23.42	33.01
Deals	0.00	21.07
Travel	4.79	32.91
Transportation	2.08	85.87
Sports	23.30	3.29
Social Network	5.63	16.83
Shopping	1.84	0.00
Real Estate	0.00	85.74

Table 4: Percentange of queries with timex and location slots in each of our target domains.

in this paper is a purely supervised one.

Transfer learning is a vast area of research, with too many publications for an exhaustive list. We discuss some of the recent work most relevant to our methods. In (Kim et al., 2015b), the slot labels from across different domains are mapped into a shared space using Canonical Correlation Analysis (CCA) and automatically-induced embeddings over the label space. These label representations allow mapping of label types between different domains, which makes it possible to apply standard data-driven domain adaptation approaches (Daume, 2007). They also introduce a model-driven adaptation technique based on training a hidden unit CRF (HUCRF) on the source domain, which is then used to initialize the training for the target domain. The limitation of this approach is that only one source domain can be used, while multiple experts can be used in the proposed BoE approach.

(Kim et al., 2016a) build a single, universal slot tagging model, and constrain the decoding process to subsets of slots for various domains; this process assumes that a mapping of slot tags in the new domain to the ones in the universal slot model has already been generated. A related work by (Kim et al., 2016b) directly predicts the required schema prior to performing the constrained decoding. These approaches are attractive because only one universal model needs to be trained, but do not work in cases when a new domain contains a mixture of new and existing slots. Our approach allows transfer of partial knowledge in such cases.

(Kim et al., 2016c) uses a neural version of the approach first described in (Daume, 2007), by using existing annotated data in a variety of domains

to adapt the slot tag models of new domains where the tag space is partly shared. The drawback of such data-driven domain adaptation is the increase in training time as more experts are added.

An expert-based adaptation, similar to the techniques applied in this paper, was first described in (Kim et al., 2017b). (Jaech et al., 2016) use multitask learning, training a bidirectional LSTM with character-level embeddings, trained jointly to produce slot tags for a number of travel-related domains. Finally, (Kim et al., 2017a) frame the problem of temporal shift in data of a single domain (and the related problem of bootstrapping a new domain with imperfectly-matched synthetic data) as one of domain adaptation, applying adversarial training approaches.

A number of researchers also investigated bootstrapping NLU systems using zero-shot learning. (Dauphin et al., 2014; Kumar et al., 2017) both investigated domain classification; most relevant to us is the work by (Bapna et al., 2017), who studied full semantic frame tagging using zero-shot learning, by projecting the tags into a shared embedding space, similar to work done by (Kim et al., 2015b).

6 Conclusion

We experimented with Bag of Experts (BoE) architectures for CRF and LSTM based slot tagging models. Our experimental results over a set of 10 domains show that BoE architectures are able to use the information from reusable expert models to perform significantly better than their non-expert counterparts. In particular, the LSTM-BoE model shows a statistically significant improvement of 1.92% over the LSTM model on average when training with 2000 instances. When training with 500 instances, the improvement of LSTM-BoE model over LSTM is even higher at 4.63%. For multiple domains, an LSTM-BoE model trained on only 500 instances is able to outperform a baseline CRF model trained over 4 times the data. Thus, the BoE approach produces high performing models for slot tagging at much lower annotation costs.

Acknowledgments

We would like to thank Ahmed El Kholy for his comments and feedback on an earlier version of this paper. Also, thanks to Kyle Williams and Zhaleh Feizollahi for their help with code and data collection.

References

Martín Abadi, Ashish Agarwal, Paul Barham, Eugene Brevdo, Zhifeng Chen, Craig Citro, Greg S. Corrado, Andy Davis, Jeffrey Dean, Matthieu Devin, Sanjay Ghemawat, Ian Goodfellow, Andrew Harp, Geoffrey Irving, Michael Isard, Yangqing Jia, Rafal Jozefowicz, Lukasz Kaiser, Manjunath Kudlur, Josh Levenberg, Dan Mané, Rajat Monga, Sherry Moore, Derek Murray, Chris Olah, Mike Schuster, Jonathon Shlens, Benoit Steiner, Ilya Sutskever, Kunal Talwar, Paul Tucker, Vincent Vanhoucke, Vijay Vasudevan, Fernanda Viégas, Oriol Vinyals, Pete Warden, Martin Wattenberg, Martin Wicke, Yuan Yu, and Xiaoqiang Zheng. 2015. TensorFlow: Large-scale machine learning on heterogeneous systems. Software available from tensorflow.org.

Ankur Bapna, Gokhan Tur, Dilek Hakkani-Tur, and Larry Heck. 2017. Toward zero-shot frame semantic parsing for domain scaling. In *Proc. Interspeech*.

John Blitzer, Ryan McDonald, and Fernando Pereira. 2006. Domain adaptation with structural correspondence learning. In *Proceedings of the 2006 Conference on Empirical Methods in Natural Language Processing*, EMNLP '06, pages 120–128, Stroudsburg, PA, USA. Association for Computational Linguistics.

Asli Celikyilmaz and Dilek Hakkani-Tur. 2015. Convolutional neural network based semantic tagging with entity embeddings. In *Proc. NIPS Workshop on Machine Learning for SLU and Interaction*.

Asli Celikyilmaz, Dilek Hakkani-Tur, Panupong Pasupat, and Ruhi Sarikaya. 2015. Enriching word embeddings using knowledge graph for semantic tagging in conversational dialog systems. In *In Proc. AAAI*.

Yun-Nung (Vivian) Chen, Dilek Hakkani-Tur, Gokhan Tur, Asli Celikyilmaz, Jianfeng Gao, and Li Deng. 2016. Syntax or semantics? knowledge-guided joint semantic frame parsing. In *IEEE Workshop on Spoken Language Technology*.

Hal Daume, III. 2007. Frustratingly Easy Domain Adaptation. In *Proc. ACL*, pages 256–263, Prague, Czech Republic. Association for Computational Linguistics.

Yann Dauphin, Gokhan Tur, Dilek Hakkani-Tur, and Larry Heck. 2014. Zero-shot learning and clustering for semantic utterance classification. In *International Conference on Learning Representations*.

Anoop Deoras and Ruhi Sarikaya. 2013. Deep belief network based semantic taggers for spoken language understanding. In *Proc. Interspeech*.

D. Hakkani-Tur, G. Tur, L. Heck, A. Celikyilmaz, A. Fidler, D. Hillard, R. Iyer, and S. Parthasarathy. 2011a. Employing web search query click logs for multi-domain spoken language understanding. In *Proc. ASRU*.

D. Hakkani-Tur, G. Tur, L. Heck, and E. Shriberg. 2011b. Bootstrapping domain detection using query click logs for new domains. In *Proc. Interspeech*.

Dilek Hakkani-Tur, Asli Celikyilmaz, Larry Heck, and Gokhan Tur. 2013. A weakly supervised approach for discovering new user intents from search query logs. In *Proc. Interspeech*.

Larry Heck and Dilek Hakkani-Tur. 2012. Exploiting the semantic web for unsupervised spoken language understanding. In *Proc. SLT*.

Larry Heck, Dilek Hakkani-Tur, and Gokhan Tur. 2013. Leveraging knowledge graphs for web-scale unsupervised semantic parsing. In *Proc. Interspeech*.

Zhiheng Huang, Wei Xu, and Kai Yu. 2015. Bidirectional LSTM-CRF models for sequence tagging. *CoRR*, abs/1508.01991.

Aaron Jaech, Larry Heck, and Mari Ostendorf. 2016. Domain adaptation of recurrent neural networks for natural language understanding. In *Proc. Interspeech*.

Young-Bum Kim, Minwoo Jeong, Karl Stratos, and Ruhi Sarikaya. 2015a. Weakly supervised slot tagging with partially labeled sequences from web search click logs. In *Proc. NAACL*.

Young-Bum Kim, Alexandre Rochette, and Ruhi Sarikaya. 2016a. Natural language model reusability for scaling to different domains. In *Proc. EMNLP*.

Young-Bum Kim, Karl Stratos, and Dongchan Kim. 2017a. Adversarial adaptation of synthetic or stale data. In *Proc. ACL*.

Young-Bum Kim, Karl Stratos, and Dongchan Kim. 2017b. Domain attention with an ensemble of experts. In *Proceedings of the 55th Annual Meeting of the Association for Computational Linguistics (Volume 1: Long Papers)*, volume 1, pages 643–653.

Young-Bum Kim, Karl Stratos, and Ruhi Sarikaya. 2016b. Domainless adaptation by constrained decoding on a schema lattice. In *Proc. COLING*.

Young-Bum Kim, Karl Stratos, and Ruhi Sarikaya. 2016c. Frustratingly easy neural domain adaptation. In *COLING*, pages 387–396.

Young-Bum Kim, Karl Stratos, Ruhi Sarikaya, and Minwoo Jeong. 2015b. New transfer learning techniques for disaparate label sets. In *Proc. ACL*.

Diederik P. Kingma and Jimmy Ba. 2015. Adam: A method for stochastic optimization. *ICLR*.

A. Kumar, P. R. Muddireddy, M. Dreyer, and B. Hoffmeister. 2017. Zero-shot learning across heterogeneous overlapping domains. In *Proc. Interspeech*.

Gakuto Kurata, Bing Xiang, Bowen Zhou, and Mo Yu. 2016. Leveraging sentence-level information with encoder lstm for semantic slot filling. In *Proceedings of the 2016 Conference on Empirical Methods in Natural Language Processing*, pages 2077–2083, Austin, Texas. Association for Computational Linguistics.

John D. Lafferty, Andrew McCallum, and Fernando C. N. Pereira. 2001. Conditional random fields: Probabilistic models for segmenting and labeling sequence data. In *Proceedings of the Eighteenth International Conference on Machine Learning*, ICML '01, pages 282–289, San Francisco, CA, USA. Morgan Kaufmann Publishers Inc.

Guillaume Lample, Miguel Ballesteros, Sandeep Subramanian, Kazuya Kawakami, and Chris Dyer. 2016. Neural architectures for named entity recognition. *NAACL-HLT*.

C. Liu, P. Xu, and R. Sarikaya. 2015. Deep contextual language understanding in spoken dialog systems. In *Proc. Interspeech*.

Xuezhe Ma and Eduard H. Hovy. 2016. End-to-end sequence labeling via bi-directional lstm-cnns-crf. *Proceedings of the 54th Annual Meeting of the Association for Computational Linguistics*, abs/1603.01354.

Ruhi Sarikaya, Paul A. Crook, Alex Marin, Minwoo Jeong, Jean-Philippe Robichaud, Asli Celikyilmaz, Young-Bum Kim, Alexandre Rochette, Omar Z. Khan, Derek (Xiaohu) Liu, Daniel Boies, Tasos Anastasakos, Zhaleh Feizollahi, Nikhil Ramesh, Hisami Suzuki, Roman Holenstein, Elizabeth Krawczyk, and Vasiliy Radostev. 2016. An overview of end-to-end language understanding and dialog management for personal digital assistants. IEEE.

Yoshimasa Tsuruoka, Jun'ichi Tsujii, and Sophia Ananiadou. 2009. Stochastic gradient descent training for l1-regularized log-linear models with cumulative penalty. In *Proceedings of the Joint Conference of the 47th Annual Meeting of the ACL and the 4th International Joint Conference on Natural Language Processing of the AFNLP: Volume 1 - Volume 1*, ACL '09, pages 477–485, Stroudsburg, PA, USA. Association for Computational Linguistics.

Gokhan Tur, Minwoo Jeong, Ye-Yi Wang, Dilek Hakkani-Tur, and Larry Heck. 2012. Exploiting the semantic web for unsupervised natural language semantic parsing. In *Proc. Interspeech*.

W. Ward and S. Issar. 1994. Recent improvements in the CMU spoken language understanding system. In *Proc. ACL*.

K. Yao, J. Zweig, M. Hwang, Y. Shi, and D. Yu. 2013. Recurrent neural networks for language understanding. In *Proc. Interspeech*.

Multi-lingual neural title generation for e-Commerce browse pages

Prashant Mathur and **Nicola Ueffing** and **Gregor Leusch**
MT Science Team
eBay
Kasernenstraße 25
Aachen, Germany

Abstract

To provide better access of the inventory to buyers and better search engine optimization, e-Commerce websites are automatically generating millions of easily searchable browse pages. A browse page groups multiple items with shared characteristics together. It consists of a set of slot name/value pairs within a given category that are linked among each other and can be organized in a hierarchy. This structure allows users to navigate laterally between different browse pages (i.e. browse between related items) or to dive deeper and refine their search. These browse pages require a title describing the content of the page. Since the number of browse pages is huge, manual creation of these titles is infeasible. Previous statistical and neural generation approaches depend heavily on the availability of large amounts of data in a language. In this research, we apply sequence-to-sequence models to generate titles for high- & low-resourced languages by leveraging transfer learning. We train these models on multi-lingual data, thereby creating one joint model which can generate titles in various different languages. Performance of the title generation system is evaluated on three different languages; English, German, and French, with a particular focus on low-resourced French language.

1 Introduction

Natural language generation (NLG) has a broad range of applications, from question answering systems to story generation, summarization etc. In this paper, we target a particular use case that is important for e-Commerce websites, which group multiple items on common pages called *browse pages* (BP). Each browse page contains an overview of various items which share some characteristics expressed as slot/value pairs.

For example, we can have a browse page for Halloween decoration, which will display different types like lights, figurines, and candy bowls. These different items of decoration have their own browse pages, which are linked from the BP for Halloween decoration. A ceramic candy bowl for Halloween can appear on various browse pages, e.g. on the BP for Halloween decoration, BP for Halloween candy bowls, as well as the (non Halloween-specific) BP for ceramic candy bowls.

To show customers which items are grouped on a browse page, we need a human-readable title of the content of that particular page. Different combinations of characteristics bijectively correspond to different browse pages, and consequently to different browse page titles.

Note that here, different from other natural language generation tasks described in the literature, slot names are already given; the task is to generate a title for a set of slots. Moreover, we do not perform any selection of the slots that the title should realize; but all slots need to be realized in order to have a unique title. E-Commerce sites may have tens of millions of such browse pages in many different languages. The number of unique slot-value pairs are in the order of hundreds of thousands. All these factors render the task of human creation of BP titles infeasible.

Mathur, Ueffing, and Leusch (2017) developed several different systems which generated titles for these pages automatically. These systems include rule-based approaches, statistical models, and combinations of the two. In this work, we investigate the use of neural sequence-to-sequence models for browse page title generation. These models have recently received much attention in the research community, and are becoming the new state of the art in machine translation (refer Section 4).

We will compare our neural generation models

Proceedings of NAACL-HLT 2018, pages 162–169
New Orleans, Louisiana, June 1 - 6, 2018. ©2017 Association for Computational Linguistics

against two state-of-the-art systems.

1. The baseline system for English and French implements a *hybrid* generation approach, which combines a rule-based approach (with a manually created grammar) and statistical machine translation (SMT) techniques. For French, we have monolingual data for training language model, which can be used in the SMT system. For English, we also have human-curated titles and can use those for training additional "translation" components for this hybrid system.

2. The system for German is an *Automatic Post-Editing (APE)* system – first introduced by Simard et al. (2007) – which generates titles with the rule-based approach, and then uses statistical machine translation techniques for automatically correcting the errors made by the rule-based approach.

In the following section, we describe a few of the previous works in the field of language generation from a knowledge base or linked data. Section 3 addresses the idea of *lexicalization* of a browse node in linear form along with the *normalization* step to replace the slot values with placeholders. Sequence-to-sequence models for generation of titles are described in Section 4, followed by a description of joint learning over multiple languages in Section 5. Experiments and results are described in Sections 6 and 7.

2   Related work

The first works on NLG were mostly focused on rule-based language generation (Dale et al., 1998; Reiter et al., 2005; Green, 2006). NLG systems typically perform three different steps: *content selection*, where a subset of relevant slot/value pairs are selected, followed by *sentence planning*, where these selected pairs are realized into their respective linguistic variations, and finally *surface realization*, where these linguistic structures are combined to generate text. Our use case differs from the above in that there is no selection done on the slot/value pairs, but all of them undergo the sentence planning step. In rule-based systems, all of the above steps rely on hand-crafted rules.

Data driven approaches, on the other hand, either try to learn each of the steps automatically from the data Barzilay and Lapata (2005)

Dale et al. (1998) described the problem of generating natural language titles and short descriptions of structured nodes which consist of slot/value pairs. There are many research which deal with learning a generation model from parallel data. These parallel data consist of the structured data and natural-language text, so that the model can learn to transform the structured data into text. Duma and Klein (2013) generate short natural-language descriptions, taking structured DBPedia data as input. Their approach learns text templates which are filled with the information from the structured data.

Mei et al. (September, 2015) use recurrent neural network (LSTM) models to generate text from facts given in a knowledge base. Chisholm et al. (2017) solve the same problem by applying a machine translation system to a linearized version of the pairs. Several recent papers tackle the problem of generating a one-sentence introduction for a biography given structured biographical slot/value pairs. One difference between our work and the papers above, (Mei et al., September, 2015), and (Chisholm et al., 2017), is that they perform selective generation, i.e. they run a selection step that determines the slot/value pairs which will be included in the realization. In our use case however, all slot/value pairs are relevant and need to be realized.

Serban et al. (2016) generate questions from facts (structured input) by leveraging fact embeddings and then employing placeholders for handling rare words. In their work, the placeholders are heuristically mapped to the facts, however, we map our placeholders depending on the neural attention (for details, see Section 4).

3   Lexicalization

Our first step towards title generation is verbalization of all slot/value pairs. This can be achieved by a rule-based approach as described in (Mathur et al., 2017). However, in the work presented here, we do not directly lexicalize the slot/value pairs, but realize them in a pseudo language first. For example, the pseudo-language sequence for the slot/value pairs in Table 1 is "*_brand* ACME *_cat* Cell Phones & Smart Phones *_color* white *_capacity* 32GB".[1]

---

[1] *_cat* refers to an e-Commerce category in the browse page.

Slot Name	Value
Category	*Cell Phones & Smart Phones*
Brand	*ACME*
Color	*white*
Storage Capacity	*32GB*

Table 1: Example of browse page slot/value pairs.

3.1 Normalization

Pseudo-language browse pages can still contain a large number of unique slot values. For example, there exist many different brands for smart phones (Samsung, Apple, Huawei, etc.). Large vocabulary is a known problem for neural systems, because rare or less frequent words tend to translate incorrectly due to data sparseness (Luong et al., 2015). At the same time, the softmax computation over the large vocabulary becomes intractable in current hardware. To avoid this issue, we normalize the pseudo-language sequences and thereby reduce the vocabulary size. For each language, we computed the 30 most frequent slot names and normalized their values via placeholders (Luong et al., August, 2015). For example, the lexicalization of *"Brand: ACME"* is *"_brand ACME"*, but after normalization, this becomes *_brand \$brand|ACME*. This representation means that the slot name *_brand* has the value of a placeholder *_brand* which contains the entity called "ACME". During training, we remove the entity from the normalized sequence, while keeping them during translation of development or evaluation set. The mapping of placeholders in the target text back to entity names is described in Section 4.

The largest reduction in vocabulary size would be achieved by normalizing all slots. However, this would create several issues in generation. Consider the pseudo-language sequence *"_bike Road bike _type Racing"*. If we replace all slot values with placeholders, i.e. *"_bike \$bike _type \$type"*, then the system will not have enough information for generating the title "Road racing bike". Moreover, the boolean slots, such as *"_comic Marvel comics _signed No"* would be normalized to placeholders as *"_comic \$comic _signed \$signed"*, and we would loose the information ("No") necessary to realize this title as "Unsigned Marvel comics".

3.2 Sub-word units

We applied another way of reducing the vocabulary, called byte pair encoding (BPE) (Sennrich et al., 2016), a technique often used in NMT systems (Bojar et al., 2017). BPE is essentially a data compression technique which splits each word into sub-word units and allows the NMT system to train on a smaller vocabulary. One of the advantages of BPE is that it propagates generation of unseen words (even with different morphological variations). However, in our use case, this can create issues, because if BPE splits a brand and generates an incorrect brand name in the target, an e-Commerce company could be legally liable for the mistake. In such case, one can first run the normalization with placeholders followed by BPE, but due to time constraints, we do not report experiments on the same.

4 Sequence-to-Sequence Models

Sequence-to-sequence models in this work are based on an encoder-decoder model and an attention mechanism as described by Bahdanau et al. (May, 2016). In this network, the encoder is a bi-directional RNN which encodes the information of a sentence $X = (x_1, x_2, \ldots x_m)$ of length m into a fixed length vector of size $|h_i|$, where h_i is the hidden state produced by the encoder for token x_i. Since our encoder is a bi-directional model, the encoded hidden state is $h_i = h_{i,fwd} + h_{i,bwd}$, where h_{fwd} and h_{bwd} are unidirectional encoders, running from left to right and right to left, respectively. That is, they are encoding the context to the left and to the right of the current token.

Our decoder is a simple recurrent neural network (RNN) consisting of gated recurrent units (GRU) (Cho et al., 2014) because of their computationally efficiency. The RNN predicts the target sequence $Y = (y_1, y_2, \ldots, y_j, \ldots, y_l)$ based on the final encoded state h. Basically, the RNN predicts the target token $y_j \in V$ (with target vocabulary V) and emits a hidden state s_j based on the previous recurrent state s_{j-1}, the previous sequence of words $Y_{j-1} = (y_1, y_2, \ldots, y_{j-1})$ and C_j, a weighted attention vector. The attention vector is a weighted average of all the hidden source states h_i, where $i = 1, \ldots, m$. Attention weight (a_{ij}) is computed between the hidden states h_i and s_j and is leveraged as a weight of that source state h_i. In generation, we make use of these alignment scores to align our placeholders.[2] The target placeholders are bijectively mapped to those

---

[2] These placeholders are not to be confused with the placeholder for a tensor.

source placeholders whose alignment score (a_{ij}) is the highest at the time of generation.

The decoder predicts a score for all the tokens in the target vocabulary, which is then normalized by a softmax function, and the token with the highest probability is predicted.

5 Multilingual Generation

In this section, we present the extension of our work from a single-language setting to multi-language settings. There have been various studies in the past that target neural machine translation from multiple source languages into a single target language (Zoph and Knight, Jan, 2016), from single source to multiple target languages (Dong et al., 2015) and multiple source to multiple target languages (Johnson et al., June, 2016). One of the main motivation of joint learning in above works is to improve the translation quality on a low-resource language pair via transfer learning between related languages. For example, Johnson et al. (June, 2016) had no parallel data available to train a Japanese-to-Korean MT system, but training Japanese-English and English-Korean language pairs allowed their model to learn translations from Japanese to Korean without seeing any parallel data. In our case, the amount of training data for French is small compared to English and German (cf. Section 6.1). We propose joint learning of English, French and German, because we expect that transfer learning will improve generation for French. We investigate the joint training of pairs of these languages as well the combination of all three.

On top of the multi-lingual approach, we follow the work of Currey et al. (2017) who proposed copying monolingual data on both sides (source and target) as a way to improve the performance of NMT systems on low-resource languages. In machine translation, there are often named entities and nouns which need to be translated verbatim, and this copying mechanism helps in identifying them. Since our use case is monolingual generation, we expect a large gain from this copying approach because we have many brands and other slot values which need to occur verbatim in the generated titles.

6 Experiments

6.1 Data

We have access to a large number of human-created titles (curated titles) for English and German, and a small number of curated titles for French. When generating these titles, human annotators were specifically asked to realize all slots in the title.

We make use of a large monolingual out-of-domain corpus for French, as it is a low-resource language. We collect item description data from an e-Commerce website and clean the data in the following way: 1) we train a language model (LM) on the small amount of French curated titles, 2) we tokenize the out-of-domain data, 3) we remove all sentences with length less than 5, 4) we compute the LM perplexity for each sentence in the out-of-domain data, 5) we sort the sentences in increasing order of their perplexities and 6) select the top 500K sentences. Statistics of the data sets are reported in Table 2.

Languages	Set	#Titles	#trg Tokens
English	Train	222k	1.5M
	Dev	1000	6682
	Test	1000	6633
German	Train	226k	1.9M
	Dev	1000	8876
	Test	500	4414
French	Train	10k	95k
	Monolingual	500k	5.54M
	Dev	486	6403
	Test	478	3886

Table 2: Training and test data statistics per language. 'k' and 'M' stands for thousand and million, respectively.

6.2 Systems

We compared the NLG systems in the single-, dual-, and multi-lingual settings.

Single-language setting: This is the baseline NLG system, a straightforward sequence-to-sequence model with attention as described in Luong et al. (August, 2015), trained separately for each language. The vocabulary is computed on the concatenation of both source and target data, and the same vocabulary is used for both source and target languages in the experiments.

We use Adam (Kingma and Ba, December, 2014) as a gradient descent approach for faster convergence. Initial learning rate is set to 0.0002 with a decay rate of 0.9. The dimension of word embeddings is set to 620 and hidden layer size to

1000. Dropout is set to 0.2 and is activated for all layers except the initial word embedding layer, because we want to realize all aspects, we cannot afford to zero out any token in the source. We continue training of the model and evaluate on the development set after each epoch, stopping the training if the BLEU score on the development set does not increase for 10 iterations.

Baselines: We compare our neural system with a **fair** baseline system (*Baseline 1*), which is a statistical MT system trained on the same parallel data as the neural system: the source side is the linearized pseudo-language sequence, and the target side is the curated title in natural language. *Baseline 2* is the either the hybrid system (for French and English) or the APE system (for German), both described in Section 1. These are **unfair** baselines, because (1) the hybrid system employs a large number of hand-made rules in combination with statistical models (Mathur, Ueffing, and Leusch, 2017), while the neural systems are unaware of the knowledge encoded in those rules, (2) the APE system and neural systems learn from same *amount* of parallel data, but the APE system aims at correcting rule-based generated titles, whereas the neural system aims at generating titles directly from a linearized form, which is a harder task. We compare our systems with the best performing systems of (Mathur et al., 2017), i.e. hybrid system for English and French, and APE system for German.

Multi-lingual setting: We train the neural model jointly on multiple languages to leverage transfer learning from a high-resource language to a low-resource one. In our multi-lingual setting, we experiment with three different combinations to improve models for French: 1) English+French (*en-fr*) 2) German+French (*de-fr*) 3) English+French+German (*en-fr-de*). English and French being close languages, we expect the *en-fr* system to benefit more from transfer learning across languages than any other combination. Although, as evident in Zoph and Knight (Jan, 2016), joint learning between the distant languages works better as they tend to disambiguate each other better than two languages which are close. For comparison, we also run a combination of two high-resource languages, i.e. English and German (*en-de*), to see if transfer learning works for them. It is important to note that in all multi-lingual sys-

tems the low-resourced language is over-sampled to balance the data.

We used the same design parameters on the neural network in both the single-language and the multi-lingual setting.

Normalized setting: On top of the systems above, we also experimented with the normalization scheme presented in Section 3.1. Normalization is useful in two ways: 1) It reduces the vocabulary size and 2) it avoids spurious generation of important aspect values (slot values). The second point is especially important in our case because this avoids highly sensitive issues such as brand violations. MT researches have observed that NMT systems often generate very fluent output, but have a tendency to generate inadequate output, i.e. sentences or words which are not related to the given input (Koehn and Knowles, June, 2017). We alleviate this problem through the normalization described above. After normalization, we see vocabulary reductions of 15% for French, 20% for German and as high as 35% for English.

As described in Section 5, we also use byte pair encoding, with a BPE code size of 30,000 for all systems (with BPE). We train the codes on the concatenation of source and target since (in this monolingual generation task) the vocabularies are very similar; the vocabulary size is around 30k for systems using BPE for both source and target.

7 Results

We evaluate our systems with three different automatic metrics: BLEU (Papineni et al., 2002), TER (Snover et al., 2006) and character F-Score (Popović, 2016). Note that BLEU and character F-score are quality metrics, i.e. higher scores mean higher quality, while TER is an error metric, where lower scores indicate higher quality. All metrics compare the automatically generated title against a human-curated title and determine sequence matches on the word or character level.

Table 3 summarizes results from all systems on the **English** test set. All neural systems are better than the fair *Baseline 1* system.

Normalization with tags (i.e. using placeholders) has a negative effect on English title quality both in the single-language setting *en* (67.1 vs. 68.4 BLEU) and in the dual-language setting *en-fr* (67.1 vs. 70.7 BLEU). However, title quality increases when using BPE instead (71.9 vs. 70.7 BLEU). On *en-de*, we observe gains

System	Norm.	BLEU↑	chrF1↑	TER↓
Baseline 1	n/a	64.2	82.9	26.5
Baseline 2	n/a	74.3	86.1	19.8
en	No	68.4	82.8	21.2
en	Yes(Tags)	67.1	82.5	21.7
en-fr	No	70.7	83.9	20.1
en-fr	Yes(Tags)	67.1	82.1	22.8
en-fr	Yes(BPE)	71.9	85.2	18.5
en-fr$_{big}$	Yes(BPE)	74.1	86.2	17.3
en-de	No	65.8	80.7	23.6
en-de	Yes(Tags)	67.1	82.8	22.3
en-de	Yes(BPE)	72.7	85.4	18.8
en-fr-de	Yes(BPE)	74.5	86.3	17.0

Table 3: Results on EN test, cased and detokenized.

both from normalization with tags and from BPE. Again, BPE normalization works best. Both dual-language systems with BPE achieve better performance that the best monolingual English system (71.9 and 72.7 vs. 68.4 BLEU).

The system *en-fr*$_{big}$ contains monolingual French data added via the copying mechanism, which improves title quality. It outperforms any other neural system and is on par with *Baseline 2* (unfair baseline), even outperforming it in terms of TER. The multi-lingual system *en-fr-de* is very close to *en-fr*$_{big}$ according to all three metrics.

System	Norm.	BLEU↑	chrF1↑	TER↓
Baseline 1	n/a	58.5	88.3	31.4
Baseline 2	n/a	79.4	90.7	17.1
de	No	78.2	87.0	20.7
de	Yes(Tags)	71.1	85.0	27.2
en-de	No	74.0	87.3	22.6
en-de	Yes(Tags)	65.6	84.0	30.2
en-de	Yes(BPE)	79.6	91.1	16.6
de-fr	No	77.2	88.9	18.9
de-fr	Yes(Tags)	63.3	83.0	30.7
de-fr	Yes(BPE)	77.6	89.0	19.2
de-fr$_{big}$	Yes(BPE)	80.0	91.6	16.2
en-fr-de	Yes(BPE)	80.6	92.0	15.3

Table 4: Results on DE test, cased and detokenized.

Table 4 collects the results for all systems on the **German** test set. For the single-language setting, we see a loss of 7 BLEU points when normalizing the input sequence, which is caused by incorrect morphology in the titles. When using placeholders, the system generates entities in the title in the exact form in which they occur in the input. In German, however, the words often need to be inflected. For example, the slot "_brand Markenlos" should be realized as "Markenlose" (Unbranded) in the title, but the placeholder generates the input form "Markenlos" (without suffix 'e'). This causes a huge deterioration in the word-level metrics BLEU and TER, but not as drastic in chrF1, which evaluates on the character level.

For German, there is a positive effect of transfer learning for both dual-language systems *en-de* and *de-fr*$_{big}$ with BPE (79.6 and 80.0 vs. 78.2 BLEU). However, the combination of languages hurts when we combine languages at token level, i.e. without normalization or with tags. The performance of systems with BPE is even on par with or better than the strong baseline of 79.4 BLEU, both for combinations of two and of three languages.

System	Norm.	BLEU↑	chrF1↑	TER↓
Baseline 1	n/a	44.6	77.7	44.3
Baseline 2	n/a	76.8	89.0	18.4
fr$_{small}$	No	23.0	52.0	71.1
fr$_{small}$	Yes(Tags)	27.4	56.2	60.1
fr$_{big}$	Yes(BPE)	29.5	57.3	58.5
fr$_{big}$	Yes(Both)	31.4	61.3	60.9
en-fr	No	22.5	51.3	69.6
en-fr	Yes(Tags)	20.1	47.1	70.3
en-fr	Yes(BPE)	21.6	50.7	73.9
en-fr$_{big}$	Yes(BPE)	32.6	61.8	51.2
de-fr	No	21.7	50.2	71.4
de-fr	Yes(Tags)	23.2	49.9	67.3
de-fr	Yes(BPE)	30.9	63.0	61.8
de-fr$_{big}$	Yes(BPE)	38.8	67.8	50.5
en-fr-de	Yes(BPE)	45.3	73.2	42.0

Table 5: Results on FR test, cased and detokenized.

System	Title
src	_cat Équipements de garage _brand Outifrance
ref	Équipements de garage Outifrance
fr$_{small}$	Équipements de suspension et de travail
fr$_{small,tags}$	Équipements de garage Outifrance
src	_cat Cylindres émetteurs d'embrayage pour automobiles _brand Vauxhall
ref	Cylindres émetteurs d'embrayage pour automobiles Vauxhall
fr$_{small}$	Perles d'embrayage pour automobile Vauxhall
fr$_{big}$	Cylindres émetteurs d'embrayage pour automobile Vauxhall
src	_cat Dessous de verre de table _brand Amadeus
ref	Dessous de verre de table Amadeus
fr$_{big}$	Guirlandes de verre Dunlop de table
en-fr-de	Dessous de verre de table Amadeus

Table 6: Examples from the french test set.

Table 5 summarizes the results from all systems on the **French** test set. The single-language *fr* NMT system achieves a low BLEU score compared to the SMT system Baseline 1 (23.0 vs. 44.6). This is due to the very small amount of parallel data, which is a setting where SMT typically outperforms NMT as evidenced in Zoph et al. (April, 2016). Normalization has a big positive impact on all French systems (e.g. 27.4

vs. 23.0 BLEU for *fr*).

The *de-fr* systems show a much larger gain from transfer learning than the *en-fr* systems, which validates Zoph and Knight (Jan, 2016)'s results, who show that transfer learning is better for distant languages than for similar languages.

For all three languages, copying monolingual data improves the NMT system by a large margin.

The multi-lingual *en-fr-de* (BPE) system (with copied monolingual data) is the best system for all three languages. It has the additional advantage of being one single model that can cater to all three languages at once.

Table 6 presents the example titles comparing different phenomena. The first block shows the usefulness of placeholders in system $fr_{small,tags}$ (i.e. fr_{small}, normalized with tags) where in comparison to fr_{small} the brand is generated verbatim. The second block shows the effectiveness of copying the data where "Cylindres" is generated correctly in the fr_{big} (with BPE) system in comparison to fr_{small}. The last block shows that reordering and adequacy in generation can be improved with the helpful signals from high-resourced English and German languages.

8 Conclusion

We developed neural language generation systems for an e-Commerce use case for three languages with very different amounts of training data and came to the following conclusions:

(1) The lack of resources in French leads to generation of low quality titles, but this can be drastically improved upon with transfer learning between French and English and/or German.

(2) In case of low-resource languages, copying monolingual data (even if out-of-domain) improves the performance of the system.

(3) Normalization with placeholders usually helps for languages with relatively easy morphology.

(4) It is important to over-sample the low-resourced languages in order to balance the high-& low-resourced data, thereby, creating a stable NLG system.

(5) For French, a low-resource language in our use case, the hybrid system which combines manual rules and SMT technology is still far better than the best neural system.

(6) The multi-lingual model has the best trade-off, as it achieves the best results among the neural systems in all three languages and it is one single model which can be deployed easily on a single GPU machine.

Acknowledgments

Thanks to our colleague Pavel Petrushkov for all the help with the neural MT toolkit.

References

Dzmitry Bahdanau, Kyunghyun Cho, and Yoshua Bengio. May, 2016. Neural machine translation by jointly learning to align and translate. *CoRR* abs/1409.0473 [cs.CL].

Regina Barzilay and Mirella Lapata. 2005. Collective content selection for concept-to-text generation. In *Proceedings of the Conference on Human Language Technology and Empirical Methods in Natural Language Processing*. Association for Computational Linguistics, Stroudsburg, PA, USA, HLT '05, pages 331–338.

Ondrej Bojar, Christian Buck, Rajen Chatterjee, Christian Federmann, Yvette Graham, Barry Haddow, Matthias Huck, Antonio Jimeno Yepes, Philipp Koehn, and Julia Kreutzer. 2017. Proceedings of the second conference on machine translation, volume 1: Research papers. In *Proceedings of the Conference on Human Language Technology and Empirical Methods in Natural Language Processing*. Association for Computational Linguistics, Copenhagen, Denmark.

Andrew Chisholm, Will Radford, and Ben Hachey. 2017. Learning to generate one-sentence biographies from Wikidata. In *Proceedings of the 15th Conference of the European Chapter of the Association for Computational Linguistics: Volume 1, Long Papers*. Association for Computational Linguistics, pages 633–642.

Kyunghyun Cho, Bart van Merrienboer, Dzmitry Bahdanau, and Yoshua Bengio. 2014. On the properties of neural machine translation: Encoder-decoder approaches. In *Proceedings of SSST@EMNLP 2014, Eighth Workshop on Syntax, Semantics and Structure in Statistical Translation, Doha, Qatar, 25 October 2014*.

Anna Currey, Antonio Valerio Miceli Barone, and Kenneth Heafield. 2017. Copied monolingual data improves low-resource neural machine translation. In *Proceedings of the Second Conference on Machine Translation*. Association for Computational Linguistics.

Robert Dale, Stephen J Green, Maria Milosavljevic, Cécile Paris, Cornelia Verspoor, and Sandra Williams. 1998. The realities of generating natural language from databases. In *Proceedings of the 11th Australian Joint Conference on Artificial Intelligence*. pages 13–17.

Daxiang Dong, Hua Wu, Wei He, Dianhai Yu, and Haifeng Wang. 2015. Multi-task learning for multiple language translation. In *ACL (1)*. The Association for Computer Linguistics.

Daniel Duma and Ewan Klein. 2013. Generating natural language from linked data: Unsupervised template extraction. In *Proceedings of the 10th International Conference on Computational Semantics (IWCS 2013) – Long Papers*. Association for Computational Linguistics, pages 83–94.

Nancy Green. 2006. Generation of biomedical arguments for lay readers. In *Proceedings of the Fourth International Natural Language Generation Conference*. Association for Computational Linguistics, Stroudsburg, PA, USA, INLG '06.

Melvin Johnson, Mike Schuster, Quoc V. Le, Maxim Krikun, Yonghui Wu, Zhifeng Chen, Nikhil Thorat, Fernanda B. Viégas, Martin Wattenberg, Greg Corrado, Macduff Hughes, and Jeffrey Dean. June, 2016. Google's multilingual neural machine translation system: Enabling zero-shot translation. *CoRR* abs/1611.04558 [cs.CL].

Diederik P. Kingma and Jimmy Ba. December, 2014. Adam: A method for stochastic optimization. *CoRR* abs/1412.6980 [cs.LG].

Philipp Koehn and Rebecca Knowles. June, 2017. Six challenges for neural machine translation. *CoRR* abs/1706.03872 [cs.CL].

Minh-Thang Luong, Hieu Pham, and Christopher D. Manning. August, 2015. Effective approaches to attention-based neural machine translation. *CoRR* abs/1508.04025 [cs.CL].

Thang Luong, Ilya Sutskever, Quoc V. Le, Oriol Vinyals, and Wojciech Zaremba. 2015. Addressing the rare word problem in neural machine translation. In *Proceedings of the 53rd Annual Meeting of the Association for Computational Linguistics and the 7th International Joint Conference on Natural Language Processing of the Asian Federation of Natural Language Processing, ACL 2015, July 26-31, 2015, Beijing, China, Volume 1: Long Papers*. pages 11–19.

Prashant Mathur, Nicola Ueffing, and Gregor Leusch. 2017. Generating titles for millions of browse pages on an e-commerce site. In *Proceedings of the International Conference on Natural Language Generation*.

Hongyuan Mei, Mohit Bansal, and Matthew R. Walter. September, 2015. What to talk about and how? Selective generation using LSTMs with coarse-to-fine alignment. *Computing Research Repository (CoRR)* abs/1509.00838 [cs.CL].

Kishore Papineni, Salim Roukos, Todd Ward, and Wei-Jing Zhu. 2002. BLEU: a method for automatic evaluation of machine translation. In *Proceedings of the 40th annual meeting on association for computational linguistics*. Association for Computational Linguistics, pages 311–318.

Maja Popović. 2016. chrF deconstructed: beta parameters and n-gram weights. In *Proceedings of the First Conference on Machine Translation*. Association for Computational Linguistics, Berlin, Germany.

Ehud Reiter, Somayajulu Sripada, Jim Hunter, and Ian Davy. 2005. Choosing words in computer-generated weather forecasts. *Artificial Intelligence* 167:137–169.

Rico Sennrich, Barry Haddow, and Alexandra Birch. 2016. Neural machine translation of rare words with subword units. In *Proceedings of the 54th Annual Meeting of the Association for Computational Linguistics (Volume 1: Long Papers)*. Association for Computational Linguistics, pages 1715–1725.

Iulian Vlad Serban, Alberto García-Durán, Çaglar Gülçehre, Sungjin Ahn, Sarath Chandar, Aaron C. Courville, and Yoshua Bengio. 2016. Generating factoid questions with recurrent neural networks: The 30m factoid question-answer corpus. In *Proceedings of the 54th Annual Meeting of the Association for Computational Linguistics, ACL 2016, August 7-12, 2016, Berlin, Germany, Volume 1: Long Papers*.

Michel Simard, Cyril Goutte, and Pierre Isabelle. 2007. Statistical phrase-based post-editing. In *In Proceedings of NAACL*.

Matthew Snover, Bonnie Dorr, Richard Schwartz, Linnea Micciulla, and John Makhoul. 2006. A study of translation edit rate with targeted human annotation. In *In Proceedings of Association for Machine Translation in the Americas*. pages 223–231.

Barret Zoph and Kevin Knight. Jan, 2016. Multisource neural translation. *CoRR* abs/1601.00710 [cs.CL].

Barret Zoph, Deniz Yuret, Jonathan May, and Kevin Knight. April, 2016. Transfer learning for low-resource neural machine translation. *arXiv:1604.02201 [cs.CL]*.

A Novel Approach to Part Name Discovery in Noisy Text

Nobal B Niraula, Daniel Whyatt, and Anne Kao
Boeing Research and Technology
Huntsville, Alabama and Seattle, Washington, USA
{nobal.b.niraula, daniel.whyatt, anne.kao}@boeing.com

Abstract

As a specialized example of information extraction, part name extraction is an area that presents unique challenges. Part names are typically multiword terms longer than two words. There is little consistency in how terms are described in noisy free text, with variations spawned by typos, ad hoc abbreviations, acronyms, and incomplete names. This makes search and analyses of parts in these data extremely challenging. In this paper, we present our algorithm, PANDA (Part Name Discovery Analytics), based on a unique method that exploits statistical, linguistic and machine learning techniques to discover part names in noisy text such as that in manufacturing quality documentation, supply chain management records, service communication logs, and maintenance reports. Experiments show that PANDA is scalable and outperforms existing techniques significantly.

1 Introduction

Part information plays a key role in manufacturing, maintenance, supplier management and customer support of any large complex system, such as an airplane, which may easily involve over 30,000 types of parts. Parts can be described by part numbers or nomenclature. Furthermore, a given part serving the same function can often be supplied by multiple suppliers, who may use different part numbers and do not always use the same nomenclature to describe functionally equivalent parts. In addition, part names are very frequent in the service descriptions and notes written by mechanics and engineers around the world. Due to time constraints, working conditions (maintenance mechanics do not work in an office environment), time crunch, and job focus (primarily getting the aircraft ready for on-time takeoff, not writing perfect English), compounded by the fact that many of those involved are not native speakers of English, the data often contains a high percentage of non-standard spellings and ad hoc shorthand notations and typos. Table 1 exemplifies these issues with real sample maintenance records.

lh side sidewall panel between sta 1600 and 1700 (pos 41l and 42l) worn
new electrical panel fitted iaw amm task xx-xx-lwr ctr display selected lt inop on display selector pnl.

Table 1: Sample maintenance records containing parts (*highlighted*), typos, and ad hoc abbreviations (*lh* for *left*, *pnl* for *panel*, *lwr* for *lower*, etc.)

In order to pinpoint types of issues involved in manufacturing, maintenance support, or supply chain management, it is crucial to identify the specific part involved. Importantly, a robust and scalable approach for extracting parts from text of the nature described above should never rely on simple matching from a list of predefined part names. It should also have a way of exploiting abundant free text data amassed over years.

While information extraction is a well-studied field, typically information extraction focuses on people, organization, time, location, event and their relationship. Part name extraction is much less studied. Part name extraction has the following unique properties. First, the language of part names as well as their context in these data sources is very domain-specific. This means that, not only is there nothing analogous to special word lists like people's first and last names or city, state and country names, but general language resources like WorldNet (Miller, 1995) and Freebase (Freebase, 2018) are also virtually useless. In addition, part names are often longer than the names of people, organizations, or locations and can be as long as 5-

Proceedings of NAACL-HLT 2018, pages 170–176
New Orleans, Louisiana, June 1 - 6, 2018. ©2017 Association for Computational Linguistics

7 words (e.g. *variable speed constant frequency cool fan*). Furthermore, it is often the case that a substring Y (e.g. *landing gear*) of a part name X (e.g. *main landing gear*) is also a valid part name. This creates a challenge for a system to identify X instead of Y as the part being mentioned. In addition, as noted above, the free text data containing the part names are often non-professionally authored and contain a high percentage of spelling variants (both ad hoc abbreviations and typos) and domain-specific acronyms. The spelling challenges do not just occur in part names, but occur throughout the free text, posing challenges for either traditional grammar-based parsing or n-gram approaches.

In this paper we present PANDA (Part Name Discovery Analytics), a fast and scalable method that exploits statistical, linguistic and supervised machine learning techniques in a unique way such that minimal human supervision is sufficient to discover thousands of part names from noisy text.

2   Related Work

Basic information extraction methods typically rely on language models and hand-crafted rules. The n-gram approach derives common strings from a large corpus and, together with hand-crafted rules, makes for an easy-to-implement way of inferring entities (Chandramouli, Subramanian, & Bal, 2013). A more sophisticated approach would define rules based on regular expressions over text content or their parts-of-speech tags to extract information. Noun-phrase identification is a typical approach under this category (Vilain and Day, 2000). Rule-based and language model-based systems are very effective in cases when the entities of interest follow specific patterns. However, when the text is very noisy, generating hand-crafted rules and patterns is cost-prohibitive and not feasible.

To our knowledge, there is only one previously published work specifically focusing on part name extraction (Chandramouli, Subramanian, & Bal, 2013). The authors propose an n-gram based approach which extracts part names from service logs. Given a list of basic part types (e.g. *valve*), they generate bigrams and trigrams ending with those part types and consider them as part candidates. The candidates are ranked using a mutual information metric. Furthermore, the authors found that Part-of-Speech (POS) based filtering improved the quality of prediction. While this work is unsupervised and easy to implement, it has important

limitations. First, it cannot predict any new part types, because it relies on predefined part types. Therefore, any part types which are not already known will be missed. Secondly, their system cannot extract part names which have more than three tokens. In our data, part names consisting of more than three tokens occur frequently (i.e. *left main landing gear, horizontal stabilizer trim actuator*). Importantly, all n-gram based approaches suffer from the pervasive misspellings and abbreviations in noisy data. They may not be able to extract *outflow vlv*, *trim act* or *door switche*, as the respective part types *valve*, *actuator* and *switch* are misspelled or written in a non-standard way.

To enable more flexibility and more power in extracting entities, machine learning methods, especially supervised learning methods, have become a natural choice in modern day information extraction. Typical machine learning methods considered include Hidden Markov Models (HMM) (Skounakis, Craven and Ray, 2003; Freitag and McCallum, 1999), and Conditional Random Fields (CRFs) (McCallum, 2002). The supervised systems learn a set of rules or models from the supplied hand-tagged samples for the training phase of machine learning. Once a new model is built based on training data, the model can be applied to new documents to extract entities. Rules and models learned by supervised techniques are effective for extracting information from the same genre of documents they are trained on, but they may perform poorly when applied to a different genre. In addition, acquiring the right training examples can be very expensive. Part information extraction is one such area which requires SME (Subject Matter Expert) knowledge and is thus not suited to crowd sourcing.

Recent approaches that address the scalability problem in training data associated with supervised machine learning include weakly-supervised methods (Pasca, 2007), bootstrapping techniques (Vilain and Day, 2000; Maedche, 2003), and active learning (Thompson, Callif and Mooney, 1999; Williams et al., 2015). Active learning starts with bootstrap samples creating an initial model and uses that model to select the most informative examples in order to minimize the annotation cost required to generate training examples. A new model is created with the new examples and the process continues until a stopping criteria is met. However, such iteration still requires SME involvement. When the free text data contain a high degree of noise, and the number of parts involved is in the tens of thousands, it is not clear how fast an active learning approach will converge. Besides, SMEs are very expensive and reducing their efforts in part name extraction process, as do ne by our method PANDA, offers a huge cost saving for a company.

Studies show that open-ended and domain independent information extraction systems do not work well for domain-specific information extraction (Etzioni et al., 2004). As such, existing approaches can be expected to perform poorly for part extraction, a domain specific information extraction problem. To this end, we propose a system that is tuned to extract parts from the target natural language text (e.g. maintenance logs). The proposed system is robust so that it can operate on noisy text and yet scalable as it demands very minimal supervision.

3   Part Name Discovery Analytics

The intent of Part Name Discovery Analytics (PANDA) is primarily to extract part information in the domain of aircraft to support vehicle health management by exploiting hundreds of thousands of free text records. However, its use can extend to any large data sets containing part name mentions. The primary design philosophy is to utilize machine learning capabilities and at the same time exploit linguistic knowledge of how part names are constructed in English. This allows discovery of new parts and at the same time minimizes the expensive training process required for supervised machine learning. Dealing with highly noisy data is a key requirement of this domain. Therefore, a non-learning based method would not meet our requirements. As we show later, PANDA learns to infer new part names from the noisy text.

We leverage the linguistic fact that the most important term in a multiword part name is the head noun (the "Head"), and in English, the Head is the last term in a multiword term. These Heads are terms such as *panel, valve, switch* etc. Although most people who are somewhat familiar with this domain can easily come up with 10-20 examples of these Heads, it is important to note that there is no knowledge base anywhere that contains all of them. By utilizing linguistic knowledge, we can automatically provide the most effective training examples to the machine learning algorithm, as well as greatly minimize SME review in providing crucial feedback for the machine learning process.

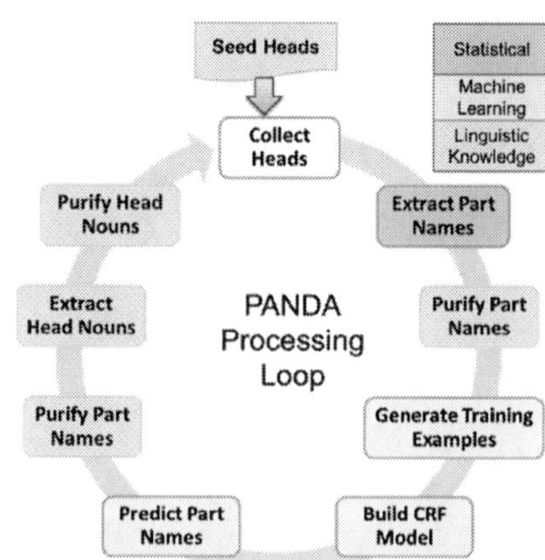

Figure 1: PANDA Processing Loop.

At a high level, PANDA cleverly shuttles between Heads and Heads plus modifiers, which are the full part names of interest. The requirement for SME's attention are focused on Heads. Since SME's need only review Heads, and not the full parts associated with each Head, the training is highly efficient.

Fig. 1 shows the architecture of PANDA. It consists of a loop which starts with seed Heads, a small set of basic part names such as *gear, panel, switch*, etc. The collected Heads are used to predict the part names in the Extract Part Names step (Section 3.1). The extracted part names are "purified" using several filtering mechanisms (Section 3.2). The purified parts are used to generate training examples (Section 3.3) for a CRF model (Section 3.4) which, in turn, is used to predict new part names in the data set (Section 3.5). The predicted part names are again purified (Section 3.2) and new Heads are extracted (Section 3.6). The extracted Heads themselves are also purified (Section 3.7). Finally, the purified Heads are added back to the earlier list forming a larger initial set of Heads. The loop is repeated until a stopping criteria is met (Section 3.8). Parts predicted by CRF and trie in the last run are collected as the final output.

3.1   Trie-based Part Name Prediction

The purpose of this step is to use part Heads and automatically generate complete part names that we need later to generate training examples for a machine learning model. To do this, we construct a data structure called a trie (Trie, 2018) from a large corpus such that the first level nodes are the given part Heads (e.g. *gear*) and their descendant nodes are the tokens appearing before them in the data set (see Fig. 2 below). This type of trie is computed by

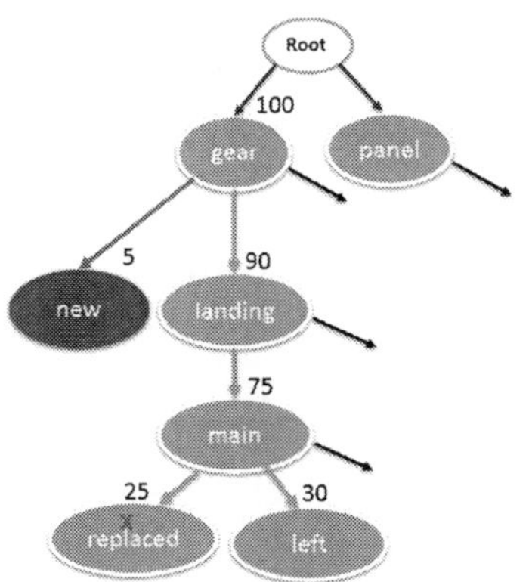

Figure 2: Sample trie generating parts *main landing gear* and *left main landing gear*.

scanning the tokens in reverse order, and is highly efficient. We then traverse the trie in depth-first fashion as long as it satisfies the minimum frequency criteria. We collect the potential part name sequence as we traverse. To further ensure better examples are used in the training example generation process, we could have a constraint to only use the Heads having certain minimum frequency.

3.2 Purify Part Names

As is the case of all machine learning methods, a significant amount of bad training samples may negatively impact the resulting model. Thus, to further improve the quality of part names predicted in the previous step, this step applies a number of heuristics based on POS features. For instance, a part name must not start with a verb or an article. If it does, we remove them and considered the remaining chunk as part name (e.g. *replaced main landing gear* becomes *main landing gear*). Similarly, PANDA requires that all part name tokens must either be nouns or adjectives.

3.3 Generate Training Examples

The goal of this phase is to generate training data for a machine learning model by annotating the data in the corpus with the part names resulting from the previous steps. Since the goal is to leverage patterns in the part names and their context to discover new part names, additional features need to be provided. PANDA currently employs k-previous and k-next word tokens and their POS tags as well as the POS tags of part names themselves as these features. The POS features can be generated using a POS Tagger such as Brill Tagger (Brill, 1992). Fig. 3 shows a sample annotated record with

the part name left main landing gear and corresponding POS-tags.

DT	JJ	NN	NN	NN	MD	RB	VB
The	left	main	landing	gear	will	not	retract

Figure 3: A sentence annotated with a part name.

3.4 Train a Sequence Model

The goal of this phase is to use the annotated corpus as training data to generate a model that identifies part names in the data. Any sequence model that extracts sequences of tokens, such as a CRF (Lafferty, McCallum and Pereira, 2001) or Long Short Term Memory network (Gers, Schmidhuber and Cummins, 1999), can be used at this phase. We use CRF in our experiments.

3.5 Predict Part Names

The goal of this phase is to use the sequence model trained in Section 3.4 on the corpus to extract new potential part names. The newly predicted parts are collected and purified using the approach presented in Section 3.2.

3.6 Extract Head Nouns

This step is to extract Heads from the newly identified potential part names in the machine learning output. It extracts the last token of the supplied part and returns that as the Head. For instance, it returns *cap* for *oil filter cap*.

3.7 Purify Head Nouns

The goal of this step is for PANDA to validate Heads generated in the previous phase. The feedback can be done with a human-in-the-loop (a SME). The SME will review all generated Heads and classify them into different categories, typically *Good* (e.g. *antenna*) or *Bad* (e.g. *inoperable*). Optionally, an additional category *Borderline* (e.g. *unit*) can be used. However, only *Good* Heads are used in the next iteration of the loop to generate additional new part names. *Borderline* heads will not be used to generate new part names for the training purpose, but will be accepted as potentially valid heads at the last run.

3.8 Stopping Criteria for the Loop

PANDA supports various types of stopping criteria. It can be stopped after a certain number of iterations or after a certain number of parts are generated, or after it reaches a certain ratio of bad vs. good new parts generated.

3.9 Part Prediction using PANDA

The parts collected after the final run can be used to extract the part names in new incoming records. Alternatively, the final CRF model can also be used to predict the parts. Or a combination of both of these can be used.

4 Experiments and Results

We conducted experiments using three major key data sources in the aerospace domain: (a) *Maintenance Logbook (MLB)* includes key maintenance condition, maintenance action and parts involved for issues identified on an aircraft. (b) *Schedule Interruption (SI)* includes records generated by dozens of major airlines at airports all over the world. It contains reasons for significant delays in departure or landing, often due to the condition of one or more parts/systems. (c) *Communication Systems (CS)* includes professional help desk type correspondence between an aircraft manufacturing company and airline operators. MLB and SI are very noisy (as shown in Table 1) compared to CS. All data sets contained multiple records, had comparable sizes of 1 million tokens each, and were subject to the same preprocessing steps and POS-tagging.

We ran PANDA on SI data set using 36 seed head nouns. We set PANDA to identify full part names of length up to 5 tokens with minimum frequency threshold of 1, to capture maximum recall, and allowed it to run till no new good Head was generated. The results are presented in Table 2. PANDA stopped after iteration 7 generating 9374 parts. SME's feedback to predicted Heads in each iteration as Good, Bad and Borderline heads, defined in Section 3.7, are also presented in the table. Starting from 36 initial Heads, PANDA was able to extract 382 (= 317 Good + 65 Borderline) new part Heads. This demonstrates PANDA's ability to infer new part Heads which are not known initially. This is crucial because all Heads are not known in advance and hundreds of new full parts may be associated with a single new Head.

Table 2 also shows the total number of parts collected up to a given iteration. It extracted 9374 full parts at the end of the final iteration but only required annotations of 780 part Heads. Since the annotation task only involves annotating the Heads and not the full parts, the annotation is very fast. As a reference, this whole experiment took less than 2 hours to complete. This demonstrates the scalability of PANDA in that it requires minimal human input in the training phase of machine learning. Since previously annotated Heads can be reused in subsequent experiments, PANDA will run even faster in the later experiments.

	Good	Bad	Borderline	Total Parts
Seed	36	-	-	-
Iter 1	98	97	19	3370
Iter 2	127	146	30	7853
Iter 3	48	95	9	8794
Iter 4	27	27	3	9020
Iter 5	12	18	2	9249
Iter 6	3	11	2	9283
Iter 7	2	4	0	9374
Total (1-7)	317	398	65	9374

Table 2: PANDA results showing annotation counts for Good, Bad and Borderline heads and total full parts on SI data set

	Heads	Parts
Baseline	36	979
PANDA	382	9374

Table 3: Baseline and PANDA extracted parts using same 36 seed heads

Next we sought to evaluate the quality of full parts generated by PANDA. However, no gold data set is currently available for that purpose. Also, evaluation in terms of recall by annotating all parts is not feasible, as annotating all 9374 full parts would be very costly. Therefore, we randomly selected 1000 parts for evaluation. PANDA scored 80.9% accuracy on this evaluation. This clearly shows that, though a SME only provides feedback on Heads during the training process, PANDA is still able to extract full part names from noisy data with a high degree of accuracy.

4.1 PANDA VS Baseline

As noted in Section 2, the only known algorithm in the literature to extract part names from free text is by Chandramouli, Subramanian, and Bal (2013). It considers parts as n-grams ending at provided heads and ranks them by a collocation measure. We implemented their best performing algorithm that purifies parts with POS tags as baseline. We ran both the baseline and PANDA to extract full part names of length up to 5 words from the SI data, with a minimum acceptable collocation value of 25 for the baseline. The results are shown in Table 3.

Since the baseline relies on provided Heads - 36 in this case - and has no way of inferring new part Heads and their corresponding parts, it suffers from low recall. PANDA, on the other hand can easily infer new Heads and associated parts. For instance, although *annunciator* was not in the initial Head list, PANDA was able to infer it and its variants such as *annunc*, *annuc*, and *ann*. In addition, PANDA extracted 32 types of annunciators such as *antiskid annunciator*, *door warn annunciator*, and *cabin zone temp annunc*.

In addition, PANDA captured the longest part name possible (a very specific part) while the baseline broke it down to its constituent chunks, creating parts that did not exist in the data set or were incorrect. Baseline results contained 186 such over-generated parts. In one example, when *access* always preceded *door panel*, PANDA only generated *access door panel*. In contrast, the baseline generated *door panel* (a non-existence part) as well as *access door panel*. Since *door panel* can easily be derived from *access door panel* (a specific part), PANDA still is able to identify generic parts, if they exist, in new incoming records without generating the parts that do not exist in the current data set, which may lead to error. For instance, the constituent part *one valve* that the baseline generates from *generator one valve* is not by itself a valid part.

Lastly, the baseline generated incorrect parts when there were more than one head in a part name. It extracted *temperature control valve*, *temperature control,* and *control valve* from the record containing "temperature control valve" as they were n-grams ending at known heads *control* and *valve*. In fact, out of 979 baseline parts, 466 were common with PANDA and the rest were either over-generated or invalid parts. These facts clearly demonstrate PANDA's superiority over the baseline model in terms of recall, learning ability for heads and parts, and accuracy of extracted parts.

4.2 PANDA on Diverse Data Sets

To test the generality of PANDA across different genres of part records, we ran PANDA on MLB, SI and BCS data sets for 5 iterations each. As noted above, MLB and SI are very noisy compared to BCS. Each of these experiments needed less than 2 hours. We report head annotation counts and total extracted parts in each of these data sets in Table 4. The results show that PANDA can process data sets of different genres with minimal annotations and can extract thousands of complex part names from them. As expected, fewer parts were discovered in BCS than in SI and MLB since it consisted of email conversations with boilerplate texts.

Data Set	Good	Bad	Borderline	Total Ann.	Total Parts
MLB	463	604	92	1159	8721
SI	312	379	63	754	9249
BCS	293	390	64	747	6554

Table 4: Head annotation counts and total parts across data sets of different part genre

4.3 Error Analysis

We identified some error types that affected PANDA results. First, there are certain parts that PANDA could not correctly extract due to its assumption that the last word of a part is the head of the part. From the text "Replaced handle of door", it could capture *handle* and *door* separately but not as *door handle* or *handle of door*. Such cases, however, were very rare. Second, POS-tagging errors affected some of PANDA's predictions. It captured *report generator drive* instead of *generator drive* due to *report* being incorrectly tagged as a noun. Third, a few parts were only partially captured due to the maximum part length setting. For instance *variable* was missed in the 6-word part *variable speed constant frequency cool fan*.

5 Conclusion and Future Work

We presented PANDA, a novel approach that discovers part names in noisy text. PANDA cleverly exploits the linguistic characteristics of part names in English to automatically generate full part names using basic part names. This automates the training example generation process, the most expensive step for building a supervised machine learning model. Experiments demonstrated that:

- PANDA required minimal human input for training the machine learning model
- PANDA was superior to the existing system in that it was able to infer new heads and parts and dramatically improved recall as compared to the existing system
- PANDA extracted high quality full parts
- PANDA can scale across diverse data sets

With these promising results, PANDA is currently being deployed to extract part names from several data sets for different aircraft models and subsystems. In the future, we plan to focus on the normalization of heads (e.g. *pnl* and *panal* to *panel*) and parts (e.g. *lft valve* and *left vlv* to *left valve*) from PANDA extracted results.

References

Brill, E. (1992, March). A simple rule-based part of speech tagger. In *Proceedings of the third conference on Applied natural language processing* (pp. 152-155). Association for Computational Linguistics.

Chandramouli, A., Subramanian, G., Bal, D., Ao, S. I., Douglas, C., Grundfest, W. S., & Burgstone, J. (2013). Unsupervised extraction of part names from service logs. In *Proceedings of the World Congress on Engineering and Computer Science* (Vol. 2).

Etzioni, O., Cafarella, M., Downey, D., Kok, S., Popescu, A. M., Shaked, T. & Yates, A. (2004, May). Web-scale information extraction in knowitall:(preliminary results). In *Proceedings of the 13th international conference on World Wide Web* (pp. 100-110). ACM.

Freebase. (2018). http://www.freebase.com. Retrieved January 2018.

Freitag, D., & McCallum, A. (1999, July). Information extraction with HMMs and shrinkage. In *Proceedings of the AAAI-99 workshop on machine learning for information extraction* (pp. 31-36).

Gers, F. A., Schmidhuber, J., & Cummins, F. (1999). *Learning to forget: Continual prediction with LSTM.*

Lafferty, J., McCallum, A., & Pereira, F. C. (2001). *Conditional random fields: Probabilistic models for segmenting and labeling sequence data.*

Miller, G. A. (1995). *WordNet: a lexical database for English.* Communications of the ACM, 38, 39-41.

McCallum, A. (2002, August). Efficiently inducing features of conditional random fields. In *Proceedings of the Nineteenth conference on Uncertainty in Artificial Intelligence* (pp. 403-410). Morgan Kaufmann Publishers Inc.

Maedche, A., Neumann, G., & Staab, S. (2003). Bootstrapping an ontology-based information extraction system. In *Intelligent exploration of the web* (pp. 345-359). Physica, Heidelberg.

Paşca, M. (2007, November). Weakly-supervised discovery of named entities using web search queries. In *Proceedings of the sixteenth ACM conference on Conference on information and knowledge management* (pp. 683-690). ACM.

Skounakis, M., Craven, M., & Ray, S. (2003, August). *Hierarchical hidden markov models for information extraction.* In IJCAI (pp. 427-433).

Thompson, C. A., Califf, M. E., & Mooney, R. J. (1999, June). Active learning for natural language parsing and information extraction. In *ICML* (pp. 406-414).

Trie. (2018). https://en.wikipedia.org/wiki/Trie. Retrieved January, 2018.

Vilain, M., & Day, D. (2000, September). Phrase parsing with rule sequence processors: an application to the shared CoNLL task. In *Proceedings of the 2nd workshop on Learning language in logic and the 4th conference on Computational natural language learning*-Volume 7 (pp. 160-162). Association for Computational Linguistics.

Williams, J. D., Niraula, N. B., Dasigi, P., Lakshmiratan, A., Suarez, C. G. J., Reddy, M., & Zweig, G. (2015). Rapidly scaling dialog systems with interactive learning. In *Natural Language Dialog Systems and Intelligent Assistants* (pp. 1-13). Springer, Cham.

Unsupervised Extraction of Part names from Service Logs. In Proceedings of the World Congress on Engineering and Computer Science, II, pp. 23-25.

The Alexa Meaning Representation Language

Thomas Kollar, Danielle Berry, Lauren Stuart, Karolina Owczarzak, Tagyoung Chung
{kollart, danijean, lsstuar, karowc, tagyoung}@amazon.com

Lambert Mathias, Michael Kayser, Bradford Snow, Spyros Matsoukas
{mathiasl, mikayser, brsnow, matsouka}@amazon.com

Abstract

This paper introduces a meaning representation for spoken language understanding. The Alexa meaning representation language (AMRL), unlike previous approaches, which factor spoken utterances into domains, provides a common representation for how people communicate in spoken language. AMRL is a rooted graph, links to a large-scale ontology, supports cross-domain queries, fine-grained types, complex utterances and composition. A spoken language dataset has been collected for Alexa, which contains $\sim$ 20k examples across eight domains. A version of this meaning representation was released to developers at a trade show in 2016.

1 Introduction

Amazon has developed Alexa, a voice assistant that has been deployed across millions of devices and processes voice requests in multiple languages. This paper addresses improvements to the Alexa voice service, whose core capabilities (as measured by the number of supported intents and slots) has expanded more than four-fold over the last two years. In addition more than ten thousand voice skills have been created by third-party developers using the Alexa Skills Kit (ASK). In order to continue this expansion, new voice experiences must be both accurate and capable of supporting complex interactions.

However, as the number of features has expanded, adding new features has become increasingly difficult for four primary reasons. First, requests with a similar surface form may belong to different domains, which makes it challenging to add features without degrading the accuracy of existing domains. For example, similar linguistic phrases such as *"order me an echo dot"* (e.g., for Shopping) have a similar form to phrases used for a ride-hailing feature such as, *"Alexa, order me*

a taxi". The second challenge is that a fixed flat structure is unable to easily support certain features (Gupta et al., 2006b), such as cross-domain queries or complex utterances, which cannot be clearly categorized into a given domain. For example, *"Find me a restaurant near the sharks game"* contains both local businesses and sporting events and *"Play hunger games and turn the lights down to 3"* requires a representation that supports assigning an utterance to two intents. The third challenge is that there is no mechanism to represent ambiguity, forcing the choice of a fixed interpretation for ambiguous utterances. For example, *"Play Hunger Games"* could refer to an audiobook, a movie, or a soundtrack. Finally, representations are not reused between skills, leading to the need for each developer to create a custom data and representations for their voice experiences.

In order to address these challenges and make Alexa more capable and accurate, we have developed two key components. The first is the Alexa ontology, a large hierarchical ontology that contains fine-grained types, properties, actions and roles. Actions represent a predicate that determines what the agent should do, roles express the arguments to an action, types categorize textual mentions and properties are relations between type mentions. The second component is the Alexa Meaning Representation Language (AMRL), a graph-based domain and language independent meaning representation that can capture the meaning of spoken language utterances to intelligent assistants. AMRL is a rooted graph where action, operators, relations and classes are labeled vertices and properties and roles are labeled edges. Unlike typical representations for spoken language understanding (SLU), which factors language understanding into the prediction of intents (non-overlapping actions) and slots (e.g., named entities) (Gupta et al., 2006a), our representation is

Proceedings of NAACL-HLT 2018, pages 177–184
New Orleans, Louisiana, June 1 - 6, 2018. ©2017 Association for Computational Linguistics

grounded in the Alexa ontology, which provides a common semantic representation for spoken language understanding and can directly represent ambiguity, complex nested utterances and cross-domain queries. Unlike similar meaning representations such as AMR (Banarescu et al., 2013), AMRL is designed to be cross-lingual, explicitly represent fine-grained entity types, logical statements, spatial prepositions and relationships and support type mentions. Examples of AMRL and the SLU representations can be seen in Figure 1.

The AMRL has been released via Alexa Skills Kit (ASK) built-in intents and slots in 2016 at a developers conference, offering coverage for eight of the ~20 SLU domains [1]. In addition to these domains, we have demonstrated that the AMRL can cover a wide range of additional utterances by annotating a sample from all first and third-party applications. We have manually annotated data for 20k examples using the Alexa ontology. This data includes the annotation of ~100 actions, ~500 types, ~20 roles and ~172 properties.

2 Approach

This paper describes a common representation for SLU, consisting of two primary components:

- The Alexa ontology - A large-scale hierarchical ontology developed to cover all spoken language usage.
- The Alexa meaning representation language (AMRL) - A rooted graph that provides a common semantic representation, is compositional and can support complex user requests.

These two components are described in the following sections.

2.1 The Alexa ontology

The Alexa ontology provides a common semantics for SLU. The Alexa ontology is developed in RDF and consists of five primary components:

- **Classes** A hierarchy of Classes, also referred to as types, is defined in the ontology. This hierarchy is a rooted tree, with finer-grained types at deeper levels. Coarse types that are children of THING include PERSON, PLACE, INTANGIBLE, ACTION, PRODUCT, CREATIVEWORK, EVENT and ORGANIZATION. Fine-grained types include MUSICRECORDING and RESTAURANT.

[1] https://amzn.to/2qDjNcJ

- **Properties** A given class contains a list of properties, which relate that class to other classes. Properties are defined in a hierarchy, with finer-grained classes inheriting the properties of its parent. There are range restrictions on the available types for both the domain and range of the property.
- **Actions** A hierarchy of actions are defined as classes within the ontology. ACTIONS cover the core functionality of Alexa.
- **Roles** ACTIONS operate on entities via roles. The most common role for an ACTION is the **.object** role, which is defined to be the entity on which the ACTION operates.
- **Operators and Relations** A hierarchy of operators and relations represent complex relationships that cannot be expressed easily as properties. Represented as classes, these include ComparativeOperator, Equals and Coordinator (Figure 2).

The Alexa ontology utilized schema.org as its base and has been updated to include support for spoken language. In addition, using schema.org as the base of the Alexa Ontology means that it shares a vocabulary used by more than 10 million websites, which can be linked to the Alexa ontology.

2.2 Alexa meaning representation language

AMRL leverages classes, properties, actions, roles and operators in the main ontology to create a compositional, graph-based representation of the meaning of an utterance. The graph-based representation conceptualizes each arc as a property and each node as an instance of a type; each type can have multiple parents. Conventions have been developed to annotate the AMRL for an utterance accurately and consistently. These conventions focus primarily on linguistic annotation, and only consider filled pauses, edits, and repairs in limited contexts. The conventions include:

- **Fine-grained type mentions** When an entity type appears in an utterance, the most fine-grained type will be annotated. For *"turn on the light"*, the mention *'light'* could be annotated as a DEVICE. However, there is a more appropriate finer-grained type, LIGHTING which will be selected instead.
- **Ambiguous type mentions** When more than one fine-grained type is possible, then the annotator will utilize a more coarse-grained

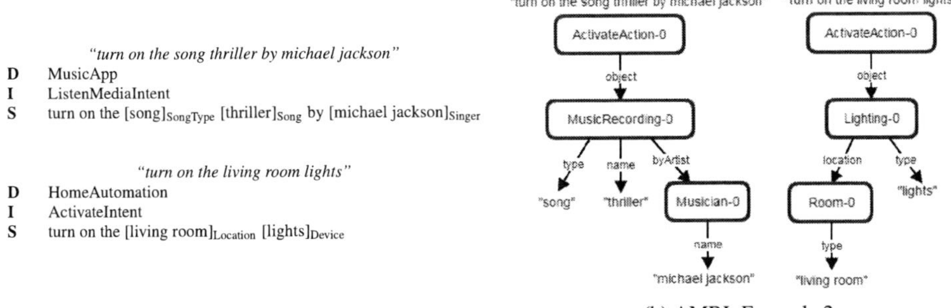

	"turn on the song thriller by michael jackson"
D	MusicApp
I	ListenMediaIntent
S	turn on the [song]$_{SongType}$ [thriller]$_{Song}$ by [michael jackson]$_{Singer}$

	"turn on the living room lights"
D	HomeAutomation
I	ActivateIntent
S	turn on the [living room]$_{Location}$ [lights]$_{Device}$

(a) SLU Example 1   (b) AMRL Example 2

Figure 1: This figure shows the SLU representation on the left and the AMRL representation on the right. The three components of the SLU representation, domain (D), intent (I) and slots (S) are shown. The intent is different (e.g., "ListenMediaIntent" vs. "ActivateIntent"), despite the presence of *"turn on"*. On the right are the same utterances represented in the AMRL. The nodes represent the instances of classes defined in an ontology, while the directed arcs connecting the class instances are properties. The root node of both graphs is the action, ACTIVATEACTION is shared across these two utterances, providing the domain-less annotation with a uniform representation for the same carrier phrase. "-0" indicates the first mention of a type in the utterance, and can be used used to denote co-reference across multiple dialog turns.

type in the hierarchy. This type should be the finest-grained type that still captures the ambiguity. For example, in the utterance *"play thriller'*, "thriller" can either be a MUSICAL-BUM or a MUSICRECORDING. Instead of selecting one of these a more coarse-grained type of MUSICCREATIVEWORK will be chosen. When the ambiguity would force fallback to the root class of the ontology THING, AMRL annotation chooses a sub-class and marks the usage of it as *uncertain*.

- **Properties** Properties are annotated when they are unambiguous. For example, *"find books by truman capote"*, the use of the **.author** property on the BOOK class is unambiguous. Similarly, for *"find books about truman capote"* the use of the **.about** property on the BOOK class is unambiguous.

- **Ambiguous property usage** When there is uncertainty in the property that should be selected for the representation, the annotator may fall back to a more generic property.

- **Property inverses** When a property can be annotated in two different directions, a canonical property is defined in the ontology and used for all annotations. For example, **.parentOrganization** has an inverse of **.subOrganization**. The former is selected as canonical for annotation flexibility and to eliminate cycles in the graph.

A few of these properties have special meaning at annotation time. Specifically, for the annotation of textual mentions there exist three primary properties: **.name**, **.value** and **.type**. The conventions for these properties are as follows:

- **.name** This is a nominal mention in the utterance, the **.name** property links the text to an instance of a class. **.name** is only used for mentions that are not a numeric quantity or enumeration. An example of **.name** for a MUSICIAN class would be *"madonna"*.

- **.value** This is defined in the same way as **.name** but is used for mentions that are numeric quantities or enumerations. For instance, *"two"* would be a **.value** of an INTEGER class.

- **.type** This is a generic mention of an entity type. For example, *"musician"* is a **.type** mention of the MUSICIAN class.

One action (NULLACTION) has a special meaning. This is annotated whenever a SLU query does not have an associated action or the action is unclear. This happens, for example, when someone says, *"temperature"*. In contrast, *"show me the temperature"* is annotated with the more specific DISPLAYACTION.

179

2.3 Expanded Language Support

AMRL has been used to represent utterances that are either not supported or challenging to support using standard SLU representations. The following section describes support for anaphora, complex and cross-domain utterances, referring expressions for locations and composition.

2.3.1 Anaphora

AMRL can natively support pronominal anaphora resolution both within the same utterance or across utterances. For example:

- Within utterance: *"Find the highest-rated toaster and show me its reviews"*
- Across utterances: *"What is Madonna's latest album" "Play it."*

Terminal nodes refer back to the same (unique) entity. An example annotation across multiple utterances can be seen in Figures 3a and 3b. Similar to the above, it can handle bridges within discourse, such as, "find me an italian restaurant" and "what's on its menu."

2.3.2 Inferred nodes

AMRL contains nodes that are not grounded in the text. For example, for the utterance, in Figure 2a there are two inferred nodes, one for the address of the restaurant and another for the address of the sports event. Not explicitly representing types has two primary benefits. First, certain linguistic phenomena such as anaphora are easier to support. Second, the representation is aligned to the ontology, which enables direct queries against the knowledge base. Inferred nodes are the AMRL way to perform reification.

2.3.3 Cross-domain utterances

Using the common semantics of AMRL means that parses do not need to obey domain boundaries. For example, these utterances would belong to two domains (e.g., sports and local search): *"Where is the nearest restaurant"* and *"What is happening at the Sharks game"*. AMRL, as in Figure 2a, can handle utterances that span multiple domains, such as the one shown in Figure 2a.

2.3.4 Conjunctions, disjunctions and negations

AMRL can cover logical expressions, where there can be an arbitrary combination of conjunctions, disjunctions, or conditional statements. Some examples of object-level or clause-level conjunctions include:

- Object-level conjunction: *"Add milk, bread, and eggs to my shopping list"*
- Clause-level conjunction: *"Restart this song and turn the volume up to seven"*

Conjunctions and disjunctions are represented using a Coordinator class. The ".value" property defined which logical operation is to be performed. Examples of the AMRL representation for these is shown in Figure 2b and 2c.

2.3.5 Conditional statements

Conditional statements are not usually represented in other formalisms. An example of a conditional statement is, *"when its raining, turn off the sprinklers"*. Time-based conditional statements are special cased due to their frequency in spoken language. For time-based expressions (e.g., *"when it is three p.m., turn on the lights"*), a startTime (or endTime) property is used on the action to denote the condition of when the action should start (or stop). For all other expressions, we use the ConditionalOperator, which has a "condition" property as well as a "result" property. When the condition is true, then the result would apply. The constrained properties are defining the arguments of the Equals operator. An example can be seen in Figure 4. A deterministic transformation from the simplified time-based scheme to ConditionalOperator form when greater consistency is desired.

2.3.6 Referring expressions for locations

AMRL can represent locations and their relationships. For simpler expressions that are common, such as "on" or "in," properties are used to represent the relationship between two entity mentions. For other spatial relations, such as "between" or "around," an operator is introduced. Two examples of spatial relationships can be seen in Figure 2d. In this example "beside" grounds to the relation being used (e.g., "beside") and uses two properties (e.g., constrained and target), which are the the first and second arguments to the spatial preposition.

2.3.7 Composition

AMRL supports composition, which enables reuse of types and subgraphs to represent utterances with similar meanings. For example, Figures 2e and 2f show the ability to create significantly different actions only by changing the type of the object of the utterance. Such substitution can occur

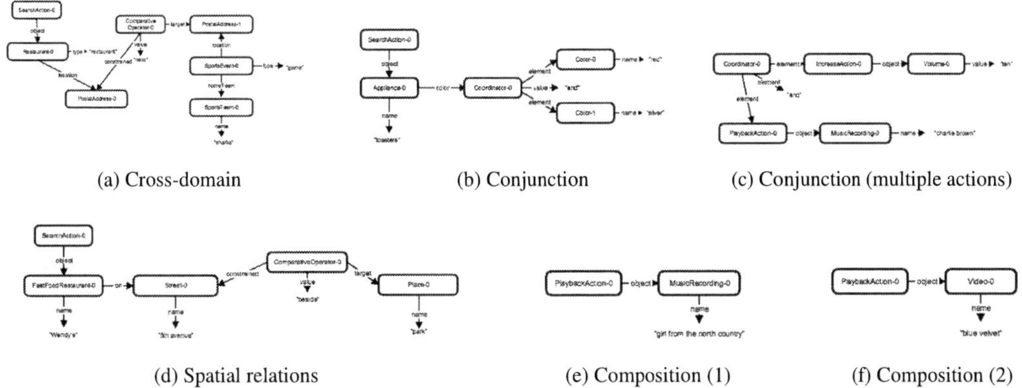

(a) Cross-domain   (b) Conjunction   (c) Conjunction (multiple actions)

(d) Spatial relations   (e) Composition (1)   (f) Composition (2)

Figure 2: Examples of complex queries. In (a) is the utterance *"find restaurants near the sharks game."*. In (b) is the utterance *"find red and silver toasters"*. In (c) is *"play charlie brown and turn the volume up to 10"*. In (d) is *"find the wendy's on 5th avenue beside the park."* In (e) and (f) are an illustration composition for, *"play girl from the north country"* and *"play blue velvet."*.

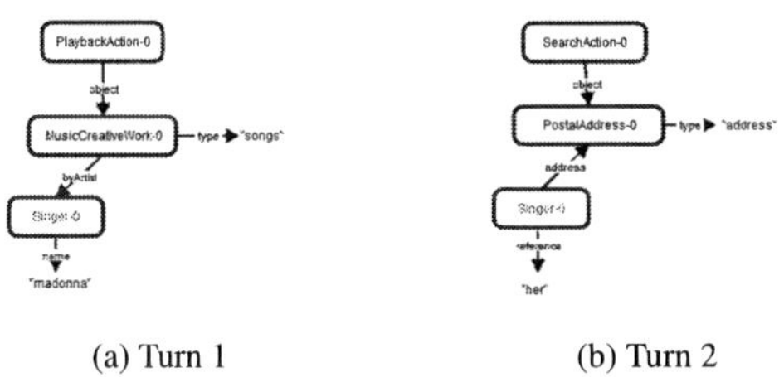

(a) Turn 1   (b) Turn 2

Figure 3: (a) shows the first turn of a conversation, *"play songs by madonna"* (b) shows the second turn of a conversation, *"what's her address"*. Because the node SINGER-0 has the same "-0" ID in both turns, the previous turn can be directly used to infer that the address should be for the person whose name is "Madonna."

anywhere in the annotation graph. PlaybackAction is used to denote playing of the entity referred to by the object role.

2.3.8 Unsupported features

Although many linguistic phenomena can be supported in AMRL, there are a few that have not been explicitly supported and are left for future work. These include existential and universal quantification and scoping and conventions for agency (most requests are imperative). In addition, there is currently no easy way to convert to first order logic (e.g., lambda calculus), due to conventions that simplify annotation, but lose information about operators such as spatial relationships.

3 Dataset

Data has been collected for the AMRL across many spoken language use-cases. The current domains that are supported include music, books, video, local search, weather and calendar. We have prototyped mechanisms to speed up annotation via paraphrasing (Berant and Liang, 2014) and conversion from our current SLU representation, in order to leverage the much larger data available. The primary mechanism we have for data-acquisition is via manual annotation. Tools have been developed in order to acquire the full graph annotated with all the properties, classes, actions and operators.

AMRL manual annotation is performed by data annotators in four stages. In the first stage an action is selected, for example ACTIVATEACTION in Figure 1b. The second stage defines the text spans in an utterance that link to a class in the ontology (e.g., "michael jackson" is a Musician type and "thriller" and "song" are MusicRecording types, the first is a **.name** mention, while the latter is a **.type** mention. The third stage creates connections between the classes and defines any missing nodes in the graph. In the final stage a skilled annotator reviews the graph for mistakes and and re-annotates it if necessary. There is a visualization of the semantic annotation available, enabling an annotator to verify that they have built the graph in a semantically accurate manner. Manual annotation happens at the rate of 40 per hour. The manually annotated dataset contains ∼20k annotated utterances and contains 93 unique actions,

181

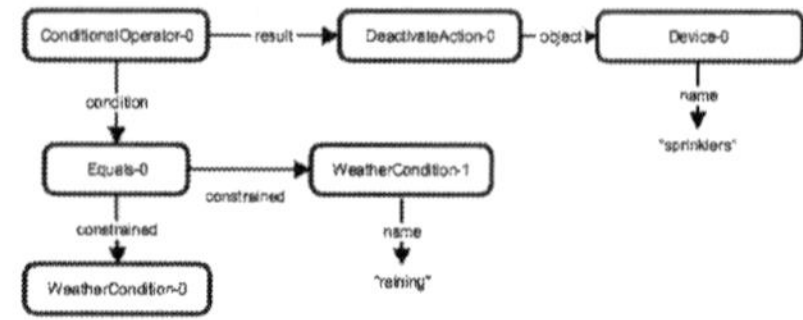

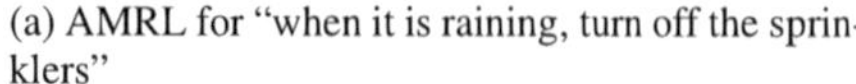

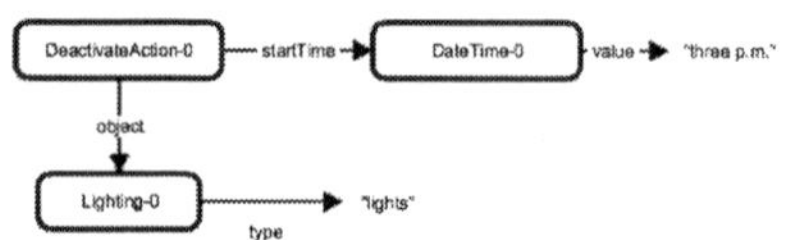

(a) AMRL for "when it is raining, turn off the sprinklers"

(b) AMRL for "when it is three p.m., turn on the lights."

Figure 4: Two examples of conditional statements. In (b) are the annotation for time-based conditions, while in (a) is a non-time based trigger.

448 types, 172 properties and 23 roles.

4   Parsing

Any graph parsing method can be used to predict AMRL given a natural language utterance. One approach is to use hyperedge replacement grammars (Chiang et al., 2013) (Peng et al., 2015), though these require large datasets in order to train accurate parsers. Alternatively, the graph can be linearized, as in (Gildea et al., 2017) and sequence to sequence or sequential models can be used to predict AMRL (Perera and Strubell, 2018). We have shown that AMRL full-parse accuracy is at 78%, though the serialization, use of embeddings from related tasks can improve parser accuracy. More details can be found in (Perera and Strubell, 2018).

5   Related Work

FreeBase (Bollacker et al., 2008) (now WikiData) and schema.org (Guha et al., 2016) are two common ontologies. Schema.org is widely used on the web and contains actions, types and properties. The Alexa ontology expands schema.org to cover types, properties and roles used in spoken language.

Semantic parsing has been investigated in the content of small domain-specific datasets such as GeoQuery (Wong and Mooney, 2006) and in the context of larger broad-coverage representations such as the Groningen Meaning Bank (GMB) (Bos et al., 2017), the Abstract Meaning Representation (AMR) (Banarescu et al., 2013), UCCA (Abend and Rappoport, 2013), PropBank (Kingsbury and Palmer, 2002), Raiment (Baker et al., 1998) and lambda-DCS (Kingsbury and Palmer, 2002). OntoNotes (Hovy et al., 2006), lambda-DCS s (Liang, 2013) (Baker et al., 1998), FrameNet (Baker et al., 1998), combinatory categorial grammars (CCG) (Steedman and Baldridge, 2011) (Hockenmaier and Steedman, 2007), universal dependencies (Nivre et al., 2016) are all related representations. A comparison of semantic representations for natural language semantics is described in Abend and Rappoport. Unlike these meaning representations for written language, AMRL covers question answering, imperative actions, and a wide range of new types and properties (e.g., smart home, timers, etc.).

AMR and AMRL are both rooted, directed, leaf-labeled and edge-labeled graphs. AMRL does not reuse PropBank frame arguments, covers predicate-argument relations, including a wide variety of semantic roles, modifiers, co-reference, named entities and time expressions (Banarescu et al., 2013). There are more than 1000 named-entity types in AMRL (AMR has around 80). Re-entrancy is not used in AMRL notation. In addition to the AMR "name" property, AMRL contains a "type" property for mentions of a type (or class) and a "value" property for the mention of numeric values. Anaphora is handled in AMRL for spoken dialog Poesio and Artstein (Gross et al., 1993). Unlike representations used for spoken language understanding (SLU) (Gupta et al., 2006b), AMRL represents both entity spans, complex natural language expressions, and fine-grained named-entity types.

6   Conclusions and Future Work

This paper develops AMRL, a meaning representation for spoken language. We have shown how it can be used to expand the set of supported use-cases to complex and cross-domain utterances, while leveraging a single compositional semantics. The representation has been released at AWS Re:Invent 2016 [2]. It is also being used as a representation for expanded support for complex utterances, such as those with sequential composi-

---

[2] https://amzn.to/2qDjNcJ

tion. Continued development of a common meaning representation for spoken language will enable Alexa to become capable and accurate, expanding the set of functionality for all Alexa users.

References

Omri Abend and Ari Rappoport. 2013. Universal conceptual cognitive annotation (ucca). In *ACL (1)*. pages 228–238.

Omri Abend and Ari Rappoport. 2017. The state of the art in semantic representation. In *Proceedings of the Association for Computational Linguistics*. Vancouver,CA.

Collin F. Baker, Charles J. Fillmore, and John B. Lowe. 1998. The berkeley framenet project. In *Proceedings of the 36th Annual Meeting of the Association for Computational Linguistics and 17th International Conference on Computational Linguistics - Volume 1*. Association for Computational Linguistics, Stroudsburg, PA, USA, ACL '98, pages 86–90. https://doi.org/10.3115/980845.980860.

Laura Banarescu, Claire Bonial, Shu Cai, Madalina Georgescu, Kira Griffitt, Ulf Hermjakob, Kevin Knight, Philipp Koehn, Martha Palmer, and Nathan Schneider. 2013. Abstract meaning representation for sembanking. In *Proceedings of the 7th Linguistic Annotation Workshop and Interoperability with Discourse*. Association for Computational Linguistics, Sofia, Bulgaria, pages 178–186. http://www.aclweb.org/anthology/W13-2322.

Jonathan Berant and Percy Liang. 2014. Semantic parsing via paraphrasing.

Kurt Bollacker, Colin Evans, Praveen Paritosh, Tim Sturge, and Jamie Taylor. 2008. Freebase: A collaboratively created graph database for structuring human knowledge. In *Proceedings of the 2008 ACM SIGMOD International Conference on Management of Data*. ACM, New York, NY, USA, SIGMOD '08, pages 1247–1250. https://doi.org/10.1145/1376616.1376746.

Johan Bos, Valerio Basile, Kilian Evang, Noortje Venhuizen, and Johannes Bjerva. 2017. The groningen meaning bank. In Nancy Ide and James Pustejovsky, editors, *Handbook of Linguistic Annotation*, Springer, volume 2, pages 463–496.

David Chiang, Jacob Andreas, Daniel Bauer, Karl Moritz Hermann, Bevan Jones, and Kevin Knight. 2013. Parsing graphs with hyperedge replacement grammars. In *ACL (1)*. pages 924–932.

Daniel Gildea, Nianwen Xue, Xiaochang Peng, and Chuan Wang. 2017. Addressing the data sparsity issue in neural amr parsing. In *EACL*.

Derek Gross, James Allen, and David Traum. 1993. The trains 91 dialogues .

R. V. Guha, Dan Brickley, and Steve Macbeth. 2016. Schema.org: Evolution of structured data on the web. *Commun. ACM* 59(2):44–51. https://doi.org/10.1145/2844544.

N. Gupta, G. Tur, D. Hakkani-Tur, S. Bangalore, G. Riccardi, and M. Gilbert. 2006a. The at&t spoken language understanding system. *IEEE Transactions on Audio, Speech, and Language Processing* 14(1):213–222. https://doi.org/10.1109/TSA.2005.854085.

Narendra Gupta, Gokhan Tur, Dilek Hakkani-Tur, Srinivas Bangalore, Giuseppe Riccardi, and Mazin Gilbert. 2006b. The AT&T spoken language understanding system. *Audio, Speech, and Language Processing, IEEE Transactions on* 14(1):213–222.

Julia Hockenmaier and Mark Steedman. 2007. Ccgbank: A corpus of ccg derivations and dependency structures extracted from the penn treebank. *Comput. Linguist.* 33(3):355–396. https://doi.org/10.1162/coli.2007.33.3.355.

Eduard Hovy, Mitchell Marcus, Martha Palmer, Lance Ramshaw, and Ralph Weischedel. 2006. Ontonotes: The 90% solution. In *Proceedings of the Human Language Technology Conference of the NAACL, Companion Volume: Short Papers*. Association for Computational Linguistics, Stroudsburg, PA, USA, NAACL-Short '06, pages 57–60. http://dl.acm.org/citation.cfm?id=1614049.1614064.

Paul Kingsbury and Martha Palmer. 2002. From treebank to propbank. In *LREC*. pages 1989–1993.

Percy Liang. 2013. Lambda dependency-based compositional semantics. *CoRR* abs/1309.4408. http://arxiv.org/abs/1309.4408.

Joakim Nivre, Marie-Catherine de Marneffe, Filip Ginter, Yoav Goldberg, Jan Hajic, Christopher D. Manning, Ryan McDonald, Slav Petrov, Sampo Pyysalo, Natalia Silveira, Reut Tsarfaty, and Daniel Zeman. 2016. Universal dependencies v1: A multilingual treebank collection. In Nicoletta Calzolari (Conference Chair), Khalid Choukri, Thierry Declerck, Sara Goggi, Marko Grobelnik, Bente Maegaard, Joseph Mariani, Helene Mazo, Asuncion Moreno, Jan Odijk, and Stelios Piperidis, editors, *Proceedings of the Tenth International Conference on Language Resources and Evaluation (LREC 2016)*. European Language Resources Association (ELRA), Paris, France.

Xiaochang Peng, Linfeng Song, and Daniel Gildea. 2015. A synchronous hyperedge replacement grammar based approach for amr parsing. In *CoNLL*. pages 32–41.

Vittorio Chung Tagyoung Kollar Thomas Perera and Emma Strubell. 2018. Multi-task learning for parsing the alexa meaning representation language. In *American Association for Artificial Intelligence (AAAI)*.

Massimo Poesio and Ron Artstein. 2008. Anaphoric annotation in the arrau corpus. In *LREC*.

Mark Steedman and Jason Baldridge. 2011. *Combinatory Categorial Grammar*, Wiley-Blackwell, pages 181–224. https://doi.org/10.1002/9781444395037.ch5.

Yuk Wah Wong and Raymond J Mooney. 2006. Learning for semantic parsing with statistical machine translation. In *Proceedings of the main conference on Human Language Technology Conference of the North American Chapter of the Association of Computational Linguistics*. Association for Computational Linguistics, pages 439–446.

Practical Application of Domain Dependent Confidence Measurement for Spoken Language Understanding Systems

Mahnoosh Mehrabani   **David Thomson** *   **Benjamin Stern**
Interactions LLC, Murray Hill, NJ, USA
`{mahnoosh, bstern}@interactions.com`

Abstract

Spoken Language Understanding (SLU), which extracts semantic information from speech, is not flawless, specially in practical applications. The reliability of the output of an SLU system can be evaluated using a semantic confidence measure. Confidence measures are a solution to improve the quality of spoken dialogue systems, by rejecting low-confidence SLU results. In this study we discuss real-world applications of confidence scoring in a customer service scenario. We build confidence models for three major types of dialogue states that are considered as different domains: how may I help you, number capture, and confirmation. Practical challenges to train domain-dependent confidence models, including data limitations, are discussed, and it is shown that feature engineering plays an important role to improve performance. We explore a wide variety of predictor features based on speech recognition, intent classification, and high-level domain knowledge, and find the combined feature set with the best rejection performance for each application.

1 Introduction

The purpose of an SLU system is to interpret the meaning of a speech signal (De Mori et al., 2008). SLU systems use Automatic Speech Recognition (ASR) to convert speech signal to the text of what was spoken (hypothesis), followed by semantic meaning extraction from the ASR hypothesis using Natural Language Processing (NLP). Semantic information that can be extracted from an utterance include the intent of speaker, as well as any entities such as names, products, numbers, places, etc., where depending on the application, one or more of these information are of importance.

While SLU systems have achieved considerable success during the past few decades, errors are in-

evitable in real applications due to a number of factors including noisy speech conditions, speaker variations such as accent, speaking style, inherent ambiguity of human language, lack of enough in-domain training data, etc. With the rise of virtual assistants and their increasing utilization from everyday voice inquiries on smart phones and voice commands in smart home scenarios to customer service applications, it is crucial to keep the accuracy of SLU systems above an acceptable threshold. Therefore, to keep the natural flow of conversation between human and automatic agent, using human agents when automatic system fails to provide an accurate response improves user satisfaction. However, the question is: "how do we know that SLU system failed?"

A confidence score is a scalar quantity that measures the reliability of an automatic system. In the literature, several studies have applied ASR-based feature vectors to train statistical models that predict word and/or utterance level confidence scores for ASR systems (Wessel et al., 2001; Jiang, 2005; Yu et al., 2011; White et al., 2007; Williams and Balakrishnan, 2009), and SLU systems (Hazen et al., 2002). Furthermore, semantic-based features have been applied in predicting confidence measures for spoken dialogue systems (San-Segundo et al., 2001; Sarikaya et al., 2005; Higashinaka et al., 2006; Jung et al., 2008), as well as other applications such as machine translation (Gandrabur et al., 2006).

The purpose of this study, is to show the importance of confidence modeling in real-world SLU applications, discuss practical challenges to train confidence models, and create a guideline to build efficient confidence models. We build domain-dependent semantic confidence models to improve the rejection of unreliable SLU results. Such rejection process is designed to maintain a high accuracy, while minimizing the number of rejected

Proceedings of NAACL-HLT 2018, pages 185–192
New Orleans, Louisiana, June 1 - 6, 2018. ©2017 Association for Computational Linguistics

utterances. Our experiments are based on improving rejection performance for three different types of dialogue states in a customer service scenario: opening (i.e., how may I help you), number capture (e.g., phone or account number), and confirmation (i.e., yes/no).

The contributions of this study are:

1. Building efficient confidence models based on domain-dependent feature engineering with limited labeled data for training, which makes confidence modeling process scalable for real applications.

2. Proposing an evaluation methodology for practical applications of rejection confidence scoring, based on which an operating point can be selected to balance cost vs. accuracy.

3. Comparing linear and nonlinear confidence models with limited training data, and proposing time-efficient nonlinear features that improve performance.

2 Problem Formulation

In this study we focus on improving confidence measure for SLU systems, where the input is a speech waveform and the output is the semantic information extracted from speech. We consider the semantic output of SLU system to be either true (i.e., all the relevant information required for the application is extracted correctly) or false. Confidence score $c \in \mathbb{R}$ in this context is a number associated with every pair of input utterance $x \in \mathbf{X}$ and estimated semantic output $\hat{y} \in \mathbf{Y}$, which computes how likely is the output of SLU system ($\hat{y}$) to be equal to the reference output (y).

When probabilistic models are used, posterior probability $P(y|x)$ can be applied as confidence score. However, proper normalization of posterior probabilities is important to obtain a reliable confidence score (Jiang, 2005). In this study, we define the SLU confidence measure as $P(\hat{y} = y|x, y)$. A statistical model is trained to predict the semantic correctness of SLU system. The posterior probability from this binary classifier is applied as confidence measure. While training a confidence model requires data, it outperforms unsupervised approaches. The features that are used to train the confidence model are functions of the input and output of SLU system: $f(x, y)$.

2.1 System Layout

Figure 1 illustrates the components of SLU system we used for our experiments including rejection based on confidence score. The main components of any SLU system are ASR and NL. However, we do not accept all the outputs of SLU system. A confidence model is used to decide wether or not the extracted semantic information by SLU system is accurate. The confidence model produces a score based on several predictor features including ASR scores, NL scores, and domain knowledge. If the confidence score is higher than a threshold, SLU result is accepted. The semantic information of rejected (i.e., more challenging) utterances is extracted by human labelers.

2.2 Evaluation Methodology

The performance of SLU system with an accept/reject backend, shown in Figure 1, can not simply be evaluated based on the accuracy of the output. An essential component of such system, is rejection confidence scoring, which depends on both confidence score and confidence threshold. Confidence modeling can be formulated as a binary classification problem, and be evaluated using standard measures such as Receiver Operating Characteristic (ROC) curve, or area under the curve (AUC). However, in a practical application, business objectives have to be considered in performance evaluations. In a virtual intelligent customer service scenario, it is important to maximize customer satisfaction while minimizing the cost. Customer satisfaction is directly related to the accuracy, and accuracy can be improved by using higher confidence threshold. Nevertheless, with a higher confidence threshold, more utterances that are labeled by the automated system are rejected and this will increase the cost of manual labeling. Therefore, there is a trade-off between cost (i.e., the number of rejected utterances) and precision (i.e., the accuracy of accepted utterances).

In this study, we focus on improving the confidence measurement to maintain the accuracy while reducing the rejection rate. To evaluate different confidence measures, we plot False Accept (FA) percentage on accepted utterances versus the rejection percentage. For the remaining of this study we call these plots FA-Rej. In production system, confidence threshold is set based on the required semantic accuracy for each application, and generally the higher the rejection, the lower is

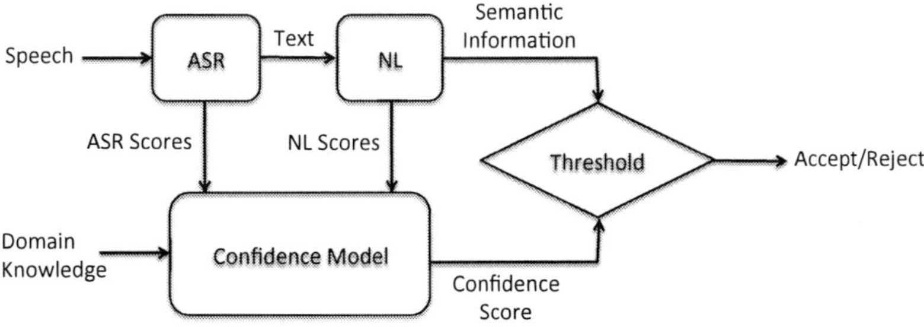

Figure 1: Flowchart of SLU system used for our experiments with an accept/reject backend based on confidence score to ensure the highest accuracy.

the error rate. If a FA-Rej plot has lower rejection rates at all FA rates compared to another plot, it shows a performance improvement.

2.3 Practical Challenges

The main challenge to build confidence models for a real-world application is data limitation. To train a confidence model, a dataset is required with true labels for each sample. In a customer service scenario, semantic information that should be captured, including intents, products, etc., vary from one client to the other. Furthermore, there are several dialog turns/states for each client with different intent sets. Our experiments show that training domain-dependent confidence models significantly improves performance. This makes the data preparation even more challenging, since creating labeled data for a large number of applications/clients is expensive. Therefore, in this study we focus on improving confidence measurement with minimum data.

We show the importance of feature engineering to select the best predictive feature set from a combination of ASR and NLP features, as well as using domain knowledge to improve performance of confidence models for each domain. In this context, domain is defined as a group of dialog states with similar intent types. We show that with low amounts of training data, Maximum Entropy (MaxEnt) model with a linear feature function is the most efficient classifier. We also apply several other classifiers including neural networks and random forest and compare performance for different feature sets. However due to train data limitations, nonlinear classifiers do not significantly outperform MaxEnt. Another advantage of MaxEnt is lower runtime, which is very important in practical applications.

2.4 Data Specification

We present results on three different types of dialogue states, which are widely used for customer service applications in automatic spoken dialogue systems. Our data is selected from real conversations between enterprise customers and the automatic agent. The first dialogue state is the response to an open-ended question, asking "how may I help you". For the remaining of this paper we call this dataset: "opening". In this dialogue state, the user is prompted to explain why they are calling customer service using natural language. The second dataset is based on a "number capture" dialogue state, where the system prompts users to provide an identification number, such as phone or account number. The third dataset is a "confirmation" dialogue state, where the user is prompted to confirm some information.

"Opening", "number capture", and "confirmation" datasets include approximately 15k, 11k, and 10k utterances, respectively. We use 10-fold cross validation for evaluation with a baseline MaxEnt model. These datasets were labeled manually to create the reference intents for each utterance. The "Opening" dataset consists of a large number of intents due to speakers being allowed to use an open language. Furthermore, an "opening" utterance might have more than one intent. For instance, if the speaker says: "I would like to talk to a live agent about my bill", the intent will be "live-agent/billing". In addition to intents, other semantic information such as products are also extracted from "opening" utterances.

For "number capture" dataset, if the speaker provides a number, SLU system is considered accurate if the hypothesized phone or account number exactly matches the reference number. We considered a few more intents for when speakers do not provide a number, such as "don't-have" (i.e., speaker does not have an account number) or "live-agent" (i.e., speaker would like to talk to a live agent). The main intents for "confirmation" dataset are: "true" and "false". A few other intents such as "live-agent" were also considered for this dialogue state. We used a statistical language model and intent classifier for "opening" and "confirmation" datasets, while a Speech Recognition Grammar Specification (SRGS), which is a rule-based language model that also provides the intent was used for "number capture". Note that our objective in this study is to improve rejection based on confidence modeling without any modifications in the SLU (i.e., ASR and NL) system.

3 Combining ASR and NL Features

During speech recognition, several scores are created that can be aggregated at word or utterance level and be applied to estimate ASR confidence. Since speech understanding process is a combination of speech recognition and natural language understanding of ASR hypothesis, additional semantic information and intent classification scores can also be used to predict the semantic confidence measure associated with a spoken utterance.

3.1 ASR Features

Previous studies have used a variety of speech recognition predictor features, such as posterior probabilities, acoustic and language model scores, n-best and lattice related scores, etc., to estimate the ASR confidence for different applications (Jiang, 2005; Yu et al., 2011; White et al., 2007; Williams and Balakrishnan, 2009; Hazen et al., 2002; San-Segundo et al., 2001). We examined several feature sets to achieve the best performance on rejecting the utterances with inaccurate semantic interpretation for "opening", "number capture", and "confirmation" domains. Particularly, two groups of ASR predictor features were applied: scores extracted from Word Confusion Network (WCN) (i.e., a compact representation of lattice (Mangu et al., 2000)), and delta scores that are based on comparing the best path score to an alternative path. Williams et al. (Williams and Balakrishnan, 2009) showed the effectiveness of these two feature types to estimate the probability of correctness for each item in an ASR n-best list.

The WCN feature set that we used includes utterance-level best path score, as well as statis-

Feature Number	Feature Description
F1	WCN utterance-level best path score
F2 – F4	Mean, min, max of WCN word-level scores
F5	Total number of paths in WCN
F6	Number of WCN segments
F7	Average utterance-level gdelta score
F8 – F10	Mean, min, max of gdelta word-level scores
F11	Average utterance-level udelta score
F12 – F14	Mean, min, max of udelta word-level scores
F15	Number of n-best
F16	Number of Speech frames
F17	Total number of frames

Table 1: List of ASR features

tics of word-level scores such as mean, min, max (adding standard deviation did not improve the results), total number of different paths in WCN, and number of segments in WCN. Delta feature set includes two categories: gdelta and udelta. Gdelta score is the log likelihood difference between the best path and the best path through garbage model (i.e., a filler model that is trained with non-speech and extraneous speech), while udelta is the log likelihood difference between the best path and best possible path without any language model constraint (if hopping from phone to phone was allowed). We used average utterance-level gdelta and udelta, as well as min, max, and mean of the word-level gdelta and udelta scores. Our best ASR feature set is a combination of WCN and delta feature sets with the addition of a few more features including number of speech frames, total number of frames, and number of n-best. Table 1 summarizes the ASR features that were used for confidence modeling in all three domains.

3.2 Semantic Features and NL Scores

As speech recognition errors contribute to semantic inaccuracy, ASR confidence predictor features, which mainly predict the probability of correctness of speech recognition hypothesis, can be applied in predicting the semantic confidence. Nevertheless, there are other factors that affect the semantic accuracy, even with an accurate ASR hypothesis. Such factors are related to the meaning interpreted from the text. Therefore, using semantic and high-level features that include domain knowledge can improve the rejection performance for an SLU system, especially with limited training data. A number of studies have applied semantic features for confidence prediction (San-Segundo et al., 2001; Sarikaya et al., 2005; Higashinaka et al., 2006; Jung et al., 2008). In this study, we identify domain-dependent features and show that semantic features based on domain knowledge for "opening" and "number capture" domains, as well as using statistical intent classifier scores for "opening" and "confirmation" dialogue states considerably improve performance.

Opening Dialogue State: Confidence predictor features based on word distribution and word identity have been previously studied (Yu et al., 2011; Huang et al., 2013). In this study, we created word distributions using a separate training dataset. Next, we tested various methods of creating predictor features based on the most common words in each application. For "opening" dataset this type of predictor features improved performance, and the best results were achieved by using the occurrence of top 450 words via a bag of words feature vector. Larger and smaller number of words were also tested, which deteriorated the performance. Furthermore, we tested using the word scores from WCN instead of binary occurrence vector, which did not improve the performance. Features based on significant or top words did not improve performance for "number capture" and "confirmation" datasets, which can be due to more limited vocabulary in those domains compared to "opening".

We also applied the top three intent scores from classifier as additional confidence predictor features, which significantly improved the results. For "opening" application, an SVM model was used to classify intents. Intent scores in this context are the raw scores computed based on classifier's decision function. Figure 2 shows the FA-Rej results of using NL features in addition to ASR features. As shown, compared to the best performance with ASR features, using significant words feature vector improves the performance. The best performance is achieved by combining ASR features with intent classifier scores. Our experiments show that when intent classification scores are used, adding the significant word feature vector deteriorates rejection performance. Figure 2 also shows the result of using the top intent score as final confidence measure for rejection, which has better performance than ASR features. How-

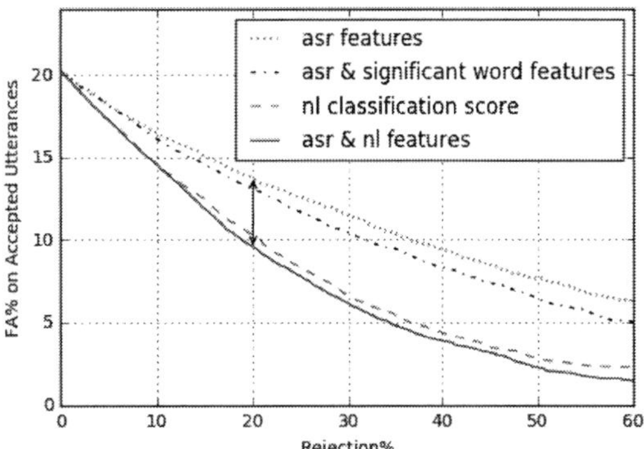

Figure 2: FA-Rej plots on "opening" dataset

ever, if intent classification scores are not available, the combination of ASR features and top word features obtains the best results.

Number Capture Dialogue State: The impact of using semantic and high-level features in addition to ASR features to predict semantic confidence for "number capture" application is shown in Figure 3. Since a rule-based grammar is used to perform speech recognition for this dataset, which also generates the intent (i.e., a sequence of digits or another intent), there are no intent classification scores to be applied to predicting the confidence. The additional feature set that we used as NL features include: encoded intent category, digit sequence length as a bag of words vector, binary feature showing the occurrence of the word 'oh', and binary feature comparing the first and second best intents. Our experiments show that using the length of digit sequence as a predictor feature vector improves confidence prediction. We used a 20-dimensional vector for length feature (the length of digit sequences in our dataset varied from zero to nineteen). Encoded intent identity (i.e., number, live agent, etc.) as another feature improved the performance for "number capture" domain. The occurence of the word 'oh' was used as another feature, since it is ambiguous and can mean 'zero' in a digit sequence or be used to show exclamation. Finally, the first and second intents based on the first best and second best ASR hypotheses were compared to generate another semantic feature that shows the certainty of SLU response. If both intents were numbers, but the digits did not exactly match, we set this feature to zero. As shown in Figure 3, using semantic features based on domain knowledge significantly improves the

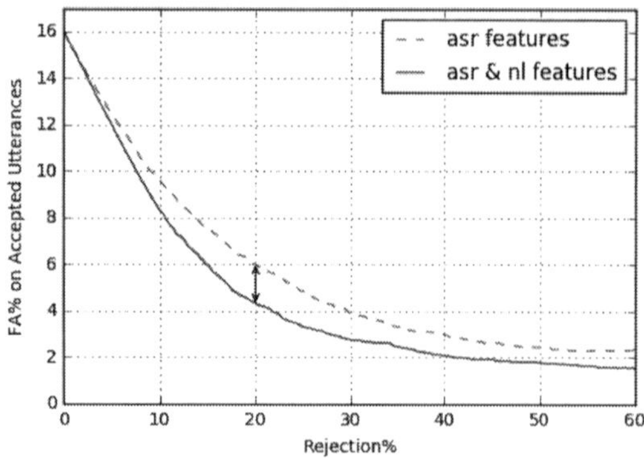

Figure 3: FA-Rej plots on "number capture" dataset

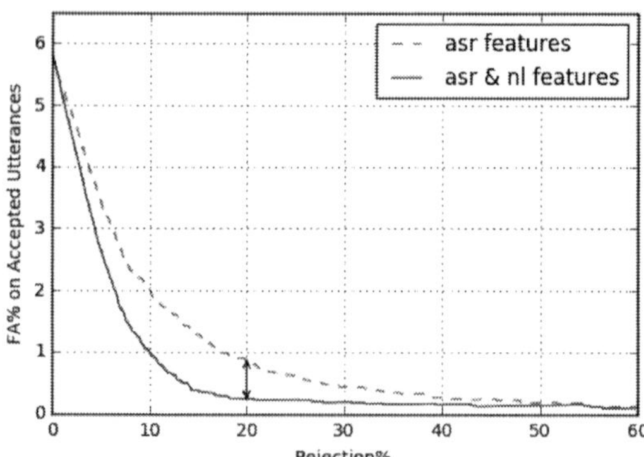

Figure 4: FA-Rej plots on "confirmation" dataset

rejection performance, and performance improvement (i.e., the difference between the number of utterances that have to be rejected to obtain a specific FA on accepted utterances) is higher at lower FA rates. This is especially of importance when the system is expected to have a high accuracy.

Confirmation Dialogue State: The result of integrating NL classification scores with ASR scores for "confirmation" dataset is compared to using ASR scores in Figure 4. As shown, considerable improvement is achieved by using intent classification scores. Due to the high accuracy of "confirmation" domain compared to the other domains, using other semantic features did not improve the performance.

Table 2 summarizes effective semantic and NL features for each domain. Relative performance improvement using the best semantic feature set in addition to ASR features at 20% rejection rate (i.e. when 80% of utterances are accepted based on confidence score) is shown in Table 3. As shown, while "confirmation" dialogue state achieves the highest accuracy compared to other applications, it has the highest relative improvement by using NL scores in addition to ASR scores. The difference in FA rates at 20% rejection when using ASR features versus using both ASR and NL features is illustrated by arrows in Figures 2-4.

4   Confidence Models

So far we have explored a variety of features using MaxEnt classifier with a linear feature function. In this section, we apply nonlinear feature functions with MaxEnt, as well as nonlinear models. Previous studies have shown the success of MaxEnt models for confidence prediction (Yu et al., 2011;

Feature(s)	Application(s)
NL classification scores	Opening, Confirmation
Occurrence of top words	Opening
Intent category	Number Capture
Length of digit sequence	Number Capture
Occurrence of "oh"	Number Capture
Comparing 1st and 2nd intents	Number Capture

Table 2: List of domain-dependent semantic features

	Opening	Number Capture	Confirmation
Performance Improvement	29.98 %	27.92 %	72.46 %

Table 3:   Relative performance improvement on accepted utterances at 20% rejection

White et al., 2007). The principle of maximum entropy states that given a set of training samples (x_i, y_i), the best estimation of the distribution $p(y|x)$ subject to a set of constraints is the one with the largest entropy (Jaynes, 1957). A typical constraint is that the empirical average from the training samples for each feature function $f_j(x, y)$ should match the expected value. The MaxEnt distribution with this constraint can be characterized with a log-linear form (White et al., 2007):

$$p(y|x) = \frac{exp(\sum_j \lambda_j f_j(x, y))}{\sum_y exp(\sum_j \lambda_j f_j(x, y))} \quad (1)$$

In this study, x is in fact a confidence predictor feature vector $\vec{x}$, and y is a binary random variable. The predictor feature vector includes binary, categorical, and continuous random variables.

As our baseline classifier, we used MaxEnt with a linear predictor feature function f. Philips et al. (Phillips et al., 2006) applied a number of methods to use nonlinear relations in data to improve performance of a MaxEnt classifier, from which we evaluated quadratic function and product of features. Furthermore, we tested binning, where bins were defined based on the Cumulative Distribution Function (CDF) of each continuous feature, which did not improve performance. In addition to the nonlinear feature functions proposed in previous studies, we used a logarithmic function of predictor features: $f(x) = \ln(|x| + \epsilon)$, where ϵ is a very small number used to prevent the log of zero. We also applied nonlinear models such as Neural Networks (NN) and Random Forest. The best NN performance was achieved using a feedforward fully-connected network with one hidden layer, and Adam (Kingma and Ba, 2014) optimizer. Due to limited training data, DNN with larger number of hidden layers did not show any improvements.

Our experiments showed that performance improvement using nonlinear methods is limited due to data limitation, and depends on the domain and the feature set. As shown in Figure 5 using logarithmic function of features that we proposed in this study, in addition to linear features improves the rejection performance for "number capture" when ASR features are used. The advantage of logarithmic features is time efficiency in both training and runtime compared to previously used nonlinear features. Figure 6 illustrates the performance improvement in low FA when applying nonlinear classifiers on "opening" dataset with the largest feature dimension (ASR features combined with top word features described in 3.2). However, with the best predictor feature set for each domain, nonlinear methods did not improve performance.

5 Discussion and Conclusions

The focus of this study was on the practical application of confidence measurement in rejecting unreliable SLU outputs with an important impact on the quality of spoken dialogue systems by re-prompting or using human annotations for challenging (e.g., noisy or vague) utterances. We performed a comprehensive feature engineering to identify the best set of features to train statistical semantic confidence models for three com-

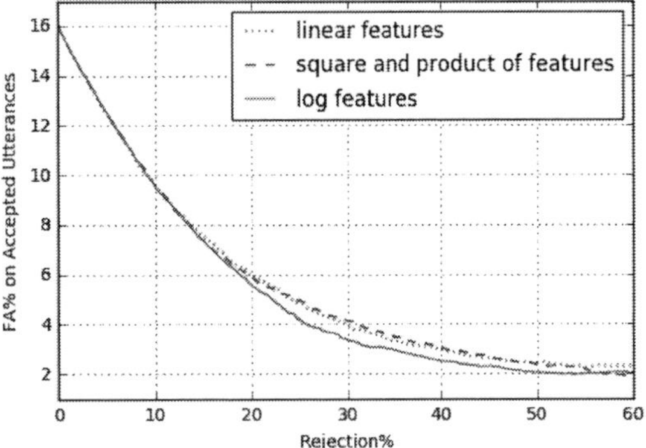

Figure 5: FA-Rej plots on "number capture" dataset with MaxEnt linear and nonlinear features

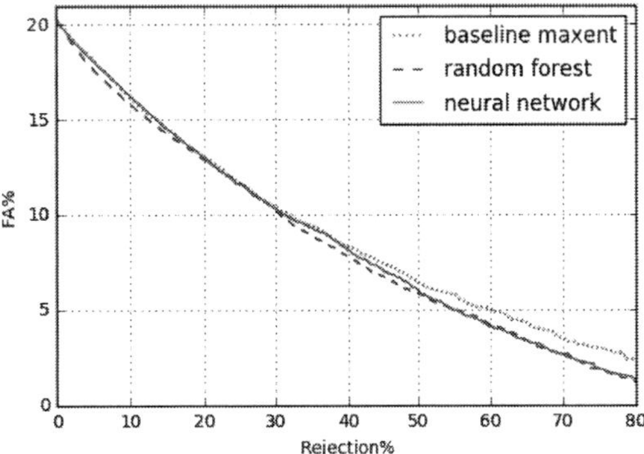

Figure 6: FA-Rej plots on "opening" dataset with baseline MaxEnt, random forest, and neural networks

mon types of dialogue states in a customer service scenario. It was shown that applying a combination of ASR confidence scores, NL-based features and domain-dependent predictors significantly improves the confidence measure performance. Our experiments showed that with a predictive set of features, MaxEnt is a proper classifier for confidence estimation in terms of performance and computational efficiency. Due to practical challenges, such as the limitation of application-specific supervised data to train confidence models and the importance of real-time rejection (and therefore confidence prediction), the application of more complex models requires a significant performance improvement.

References

Renato De Mori, Frédéric Bechet, Dilek Hakkani-Tur, Michael McTear, Giuseppe Riccardi, and Gokhan Tur. 2008. Spoken language understanding. *IEEE Signal Processing Magazine*, 25(3).

Simona Gandrabur, George Foster, and Guy Lapalme. 2006. Confidence estimation for nlp applications. *ACM Transactions on Speech and Language Processing (TSLP)*, 3(3):1–29.

Timothy J Hazen, Stephanie Seneff, and Joseph Polifroni. 2002. Recognition confidence scoring and its use in speech understanding systems. *Computer Speech & Language*, 16(1):49–67.

Ryuichiro Higashinaka, Katsuhito Sudoh, and Mikio Nakano. 2006. Incorporating discourse features into confidence scoring of intention recognition results in spoken dialogue systems. *Speech Communication*, 48(3):417–436.

Po-Sen Huang, Kshitiz Kumar, Chaojun Liu, Yifan Gong, and Li Deng. 2013. Predicting speech recognition confidence using deep learning with word identity and score features. In *Acoustics, Speech and Signal Processing (ICASSP), 2013 IEEE International Conference on*, pages 7413–7417. IEEE.

Edwin T Jaynes. 1957. Information theory and statistical mechanics. *Physical review*, 106(4):620.

Hui Jiang. 2005. Confidence measures for speech recognition: A survey. *Speech communication*, 45(4):455–470.

Sangkeun Jung, Cheongjae Lee, and Gary Geunbae Lee. 2008. Using utterance and semantic level confidence for interactive spoken dialog clarification. *JCSE*, 2(1):1–25.

Diederik Kingma and Jimmy Ba. 2014. Adam: A method for stochastic optimization. *arXiv preprint arXiv:1412.6980*.

Lidia Mangu, Eric Brill, and Andreas Stolcke. 2000. Finding consensus in speech recognition: word error minimization and other applications of confusion networks. *Computer Speech & Language*, 14(4):373–400.

Steven J Phillips, Robert P Anderson, and Robert E Schapire. 2006. Maximum entropy modeling of species geographic distributions. *Ecological modelling*, 190(3):231–259.

Rubén San-Segundo, Bryan Pellom, Kadri Hacioglu, Wayne Ward, and José M Pardo. 2001. Confidence measures for spoken dialogue systems. In *Acoustics, Speech, and Signal Processing, 2001. Proceedings.(ICASSP'01). 2001 IEEE International Conference on*, volume 1, pages 393–396. IEEE.

Ruhi Sarikaya, Yuqing Gao, Michael Picheny, and Hakan Erdogan. 2005. Semantic confidence measurement for spoken dialog systems. *IEEE Transactions on Speech and Audio Processing*, 13(4):534–545.

Frank Wessel, Ralf Schluter, Klaus Macherey, and Hermann Ney. 2001. Confidence measures for large vocabulary continuous speech recognition. *IEEE Transactions on speech and audio processing*, 9(3):288–298.

Christopher White, Jasha Droppo, Alex Acero, and Julian Odell. 2007. Maximum entropy confidence estimation for speech recognition. In *Acoustics, Speech and Signal Processing, 2007. ICASSP 2007. IEEE International Conference on*, volume 4, pages IV–809. IEEE.

Jason D Williams and Suhrid Balakrishnan. 2009. Estimating probability of correctness for asr n-best lists. In *Proceedings of the SIGDIAL 2009 Conference: The 10th Annual Meeting of the Special Interest Group on Discourse and Dialogue*, pages 132–135. Association for Computational Linguistics.

Dong Yu, Jinyu Li, and Li Deng. 2011. Calibration of confidence measures in speech recognition. *IEEE Transactions on Audio, Speech, and Language Processing*, 19(8):2461–2473.

Prediction for the Newsroom:
Which Articles Will Get the Most Comments?

Carl Ambroselli[1], Julian Risch[1], Ralf Krestel[1], and Andreas Loos[2]

[1]Hasso-Plattner-Institut, University of Potsdam, Prof.-Dr.-Helmert-Str. 2–3, 14482 Potsdam, Germany
[1]carl.ambroselli@student.hpi.de, julian.risch@hpi.de, ralf.krestel@hpi.de
[2]ZEIT online, Askanischer Platz 1, 10963 Berlin, Germany
[2]andreas.loos@zeit.de

Abstract

The overwhelming success of the Web and mobile technologies has enabled millions to share their opinions publicly at any time. But the same success also endangers this freedom of speech due to closing down of participatory sites misused by individuals or interest groups. We propose to support manual moderation by proactively drawing the attention of our moderators to article discussions that most likely need their intervention. To this end, we predict which articles will receive a high number of comments. In contrast to existing work, we enrich the article with metadata, extract semantic and linguistic features, and exploit annotated data from a foreign language corpus. Our logistic regression model improves F1-scores by over 80% in comparison to state-of-the-art approaches.

1 Exploding Comment Threads

In the last decades, media and news business underwent a fundamental shift, from one-directional to bi-directional communication between users on the one side and journalists on the other. The use of social media, blogs, and the possibility to immediately share, like, and comment digital content transformed readers into active and powerful agents in the media business. This shift from passive "consumers" to active "agents" deeply impacts both media and communication science and has many positive aspects.

However, the possibilities and powers can also be misused. Pressure groups, lobbyists, trolls, and others are effectively trying to influence discussions according to their (very different) interests. An easy approach consists in burying unwanted arguments or simply destroying a discussion by blowing it up. After such an attack, readers have to crawl through hundreds of nonsense and meaningless comments to extract meaningful and interesting arguments. Blowing up a thread can be

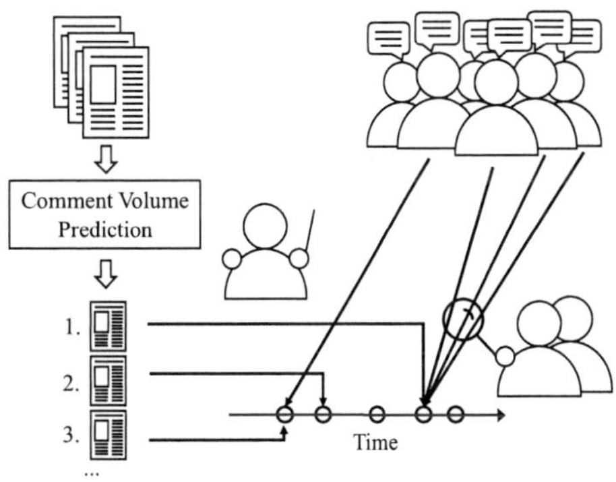

Figure 1: Integration of comment volume prediction into the newsroom workflow.

achieved by injecting provocative (but not necessarily off-topic) arguments into discussions. Bystanders are completing the goal of the destroyers, and they do so often unknowingly: with each — often well-intentioned — reaction to the provocation, they make it more difficult for others to follow the actual argumentation path and/or tree.

It is costly in terms of working power and time to keep the discussion area of a news site clean from attacks like that, and to watch the compliance of users ("netiquette"). As a reaction, many large online media sites worldwide closed their discussion areas or downsized them significantly (prominent examples of the last years are the Internet Movie Database, Bloomberg or the US-American National Public Radio). Other news provider and media sites, including us, take a different approach: A team of editors reads and filters comments on a 24/7-basis. This results in a huge workload with several thousand reader comments published each day. In its lifetime, an article receives between less than ten and more than 1500 comments; typical are about 100 to 150 comments. The number of published comments

Proceedings of NAACL-HLT 2018, pages 193–199
New Orleans, Louisiana, June 1 - 6, 2018. ©2017 Association for Computational Linguistics

presumably depends to a large extent on time, weather, and season as well as for each article on subject, length, style of writing, and author, among others.

Being able to predict which articles will receive high comment volume would be beneficial at two positions in the newsroom:

1. for the news director to schedule the publication of news stories, and

2. for scheduling team sizes and guiding the focus of the comment moderators and editors.

Figure 1 gives an overview of how comment volume prediction can be integrated into the workflow of a modern online news site. The incoming news articles are ranked based on the estimated number of comments they will attract. The news director takes these numbers into account in the decision process when to schedule which article for publication. This can balance the distribution of highly controversial topics across a day, giving not only readers and commenters the possibility to engage in each single one, but also distribute the moderation workload for comment editors evenly. Further, knowing which articles will receive many comments can help in the moderation process. Guiding the main focus of attention of moderators towards controversial topics not only facilitates efficient moderation, but also improves the quality of a comment thread. Our experience has shown that moderators entering the online discussion at an early stage can help keeping the discussion focused and fruitful.

In this paper, we study the task of identifying the weekly top 10% articles with the highest comment volume. We consider a new real-world dataset of 7 million news comments collected over more than nine years. In order to enrich our dataset and increase its meaningfulness, we propose to transfer a classifier trained on the English-language Yahoo News Annotated Comments Corpus (Napoles et al., 2017b) to our German-language dataset and leverage the additional class labels for comments in a post-publication prediction scenario. Experiments show that our logistic regression model based on article metadata, linguistic, and topical features outperforms state-of-the-art approaches significantly. Our contributions are summarized as (1) a transfer learning approach to learn early comments' characteristics, (2) an analysis of a new 7-million-comment dataset and

(3) an improvement of F1-score by 81% compared to state-of-the-art in predicting most commented articles.

2   Related Work

Related work on newsroom assistants focuses on comment volume prediction for pre-publication and post-publication scenarios. By the nature of news articles, the attention span after article publication is short and in practice post-publication prediction is valuable only within a short time frame. Tsagkias et al. (2009) classify online newspaper articles using random forests. First, they classify whether an article will receive any comments at all. Second, they classify articles as receiving a high or low amount of comments. The authors find that the second task is much harder and that predicting the actual number of comments is practically infeasible. Badari et al. (2012) conclude the same, analyzing Twitter activity as a popularity indicator for news: Predicting popularity as a regression task results in large errors. Therefore, the authors predict classes of popularity by binning the absolute numbers (1-20, 20-100, 100-2400 received tweets). However, predicting the number of received tweets includes modeling both, the user behavior and the platform, which is problematic. It is part of a platform's business secrets how content is internally ranked and distributed to users, making it hard to distinguish cause and effect from the outside. In our scenario, we even see no benefit in predicting the exact number of comments. Instead, we predict which articles belong to the weekly top 10% articles with the highest comment volume, which is one of the tasks defined by Tsagkias et al. (2009).

In a post-publication scenario, Tsagkias et al. (2010) consider the comments received within the first ten hours after article publication. Based on this feature, they propose a linear model to predict the final number of comments. Comparing comment behavior at eight online news platforms, they observe seasonal trends. Tatar et al. (2011) consider the shorter time frame of five hours after article publication to predict article popularity. They also use a linear model and find that neither adding publication time and article category to the feature set nor extending the dataset from three months to two years improves prediction results. Their survey on popularity prediction for web content summarizes features with good predictive capabilities and lists fields of application for popularity prediction (Tatar et al., 2012).

Rizos et al. (2016) focus on user comments to predict a discussion's controversiality. They extract a comment tree and a user graph from the discussion and investigate for example comment count, number of users, and vote score. The demonstrated improvement of popularity prediction with this limited, focused features motivates us to further explore content-based features of comments in our work.

Recently, research on deep learning (Nobata et al., 2016; Pavlopoulos et al., 2017) addresses (semi-) automation of the entire moderation task, but we see several issues that prevent us from putting these approaches into practice. First, the accuracy of these methods is not high enough. For example, reported recall (0.79) and precision (0.77) at the task of abusive language detection (Nobata et al., 2016) are not sufficient for use in production. With this recall, an algorithm would let pass every fifth inappropriate comment (containing hate speech, derogatory statements, or profanity), which is not acceptable. Pavlopoulos et al. (2017) address this problem by letting human moderators review comments that an algorithm could not classify with high confidence. Second, acceptance of these kind of black-box solutions is still limited in the community and the models lack comprehensibility. A compromise can be (ensemble) decision trees, because they achieve comparable results and can give reasons for their decisions (Kennedy et al., 2017). Still, moderators and users do not feel comfortable with machines deciding which comments are allowed to be published – not least because of fear of concealed censorship or bias.

3 Predicting High Comment Volume

For each news article, we want to predict whether it belongs to the weekly top 10% articles with the highest comment volume. We chose this relative amount to account for seasonal fluctuations and also to even out periods with low news worthiness. This traditional classification setting enables us to use established methods, such as logistic regression, to solve the task and provide explanations on why a particular article will receive many comments or not.

As a baseline to compare against, we implemented a random forest model with features from

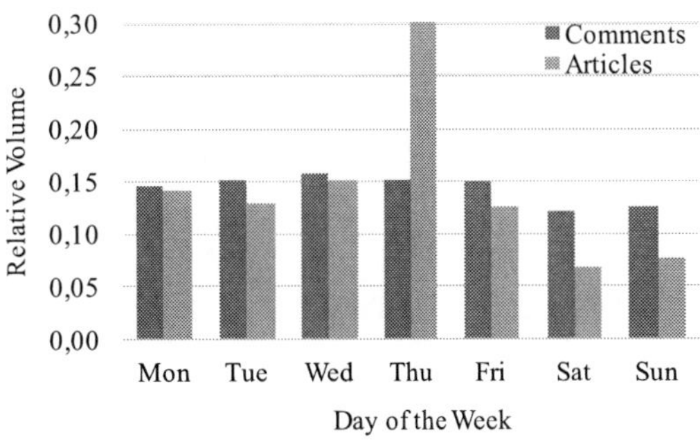

Figure 2: The number of received comments is not affected by a peek of article publications on Thursdays.

Tsagkias et al. (2009). For our approach we extend this feature set and categorize the features into five groups. Our **metadata** features consist of article publication time, day of the week, and whether the article is promoted on our Facebook page. We consider temperature and humidity during the hour of publication[1] and the number of "competing articles" as **context** features. Competing articles is the number of similar articles and the total number of articles published by our newspaper in the same hour. These articles compete for readers and user comments. Figure 2 visualizes how the number of received comments is not affected by the significantly higher number of published articles on Thursdays. The publication peek on Thursdays is caused by articles that are published in our weekly printed edition and at the same time published online one-to-one. Further, we incorporate **publisher** information, such as genre, department, and which news agency served as a source for the article. We include these features in order to study their impact and performance at comment volume prediction tasks and not in order to focus on engineering complex features.

In addition, we propose to leverage the article content itself. Starting with **headline** features, we use ngrams of length one to three as well as author provided keywords for the article. To capture topical information in the **body**, we rely on topic modeling and document embedding besides traditional bag-of-word (BOW) features. These guarantee that we also grasp some semantic representations of the articles. To this end, topic distributions, document embeddings, and word n-grams serve as semantic representa-

---

[1] as obtained for three large German cities, Berlin, Hamburg, and Frankfurt from http://www.dwd.de/

Table 1: Precision (P), recall (R), and F1-score for prediction of weekly top articles on the validation set.

Features	P	R	F1
Metadata	.12	.72	.21
Publication Time	.12	.74	.21
Promoted on Facebook	.29	.02	.01
Context	.13	.59	.22
Competing Articles	.11	.94	.20
Temperature and Humidity	.12	.27	.17
Publisher	.17	.85	.28
Author	.11	.96	.19
Genre	.16	.17	.17
Department	.15	.91	.26
Sources	.10	.38	.16
Medium	.11	.86	.20
Editor	.12	.82	.21
Headline	.15	.99	.26
Ngram 1-3 Words	.23	.48	.31
Keywords	.21	.57	.30
Body			
Doc2vec	.17	.63	.27
Stemmed BOW	.27	.61	.38
Topic model	.20	.66	.30

tions of articles. In order to model topics of news article bodies, we apply standard latent Dirichlet allocation (Blei et al., 2003). For the document embedding, we use a Doc2Vec implementation that downsamples higher-frequency words for the composition (Mikolov et al., 2013). We choose the vector length, number of topics, and window size based on F1-score evaluation on a validation set.

Despite recent advances of deep neural networks for natural language processing, there is a reason to focus on other models: For the application in newsrooms and the integration in semiautomatic processes, comprehensibility of the prediction results is very important. A black-box model — even if it achieved better performance — is not helpful in this scenario. Human moderators need to understand *why* the number of comments is predicted to be high or low. This comprehensibility issue justifies the application of decision trees and regression models, which allow to trace back predictions to their decisive factors. Table 1 lists precision, recall, and F1-score for the prediction of weekly top 10% articles with the highest comment volume. Especially the bag-of-words (BOW) and the topics of the article body, but also headline keywords and publisher metadata achieve

higher F1-score than the metadata features. The highest precision is achieved with the binary feature whether an article is promoted on Facebook, whereas author and competing articles achieve the highest recall.

3.1 Automatic Translation of Comments

Whether the first comment is a provocative question in disagreement with the article or an off-topic statement influences the route of further conversation. We assume that this assumption holds not only for social networks (Berry and Taylor, 2017), but also for comment sections at news websites. Therefore, we consider the tone and sentiment of the first comments received shortly after article publication as an additional feature. Typical layouts of news websites (including ours) list comments in chronological order and show only the first few comments to readers below an article. Pagination hides later received comments and most users do not click through dozens of pages to read through all comments. As a consequence, early comments attract a lot more attention and, with their tone and sentiment, influence comment volume to a larger extent. Presumably, articles that receive controversial comments in the first few minutes after publication are more likely to receive a high number of comments in total.

To classify comments as controversial or engaging, we need to train a supervised classification algorithm, which takes thousands of annotated comments. Such training corpora exist, if at all, mostly for English comments, while our comments are written in German. We propose to apply machine translation to overcome this language barrier: Given a German comment, we automatically translate it into English. From a classifier that has been trained on an annotated English dataset, we can derive automatic annotations for the translated comment. The derived annotations serve as another feature for our actual task of comment volume prediction.

We reimplemented the classifier by Napoles et al. (2017a) and train on their English dataset. The considered annotations consist of 12 binary labels: addressed audience (reply to a particular user or broadcast message to a general audience), agreement/disagreement with previous comment, informative, mean, controversial, persuasive, off-topic regarding the corresponding news article, neutral, positive, negative, and mixed sentiment. We au-

Table 2: ZOCC is of similar structure as YNACC but contains 700 times more labeled comments.

	YNACC	ZOCC
Comments	9160	6,831,741
Comment Threads	2400	192,647

tomatically translate all comments in our German dataset into English using the DeepL translation service[2]. For the translated comments, we automatically generate annotations based on Napoles et al.'s classifier. Thereby, we transfer the knowledge that the classifier learned on English training data to our German dataset despite its different language. This approach builds on the similar content style of both corpora, which is described in the next section.

4 Dataset

We consider two datasets that both contain user comments received by news articles with similar topics. First, our German 7-million-comment dataset, which we call Zeit Online Comment Corpus (ZOCC)[3] and second, the English 10k-comment Yahoo News Annotated Comments Corpus (YNACC) (Napoles et al., 2017b). ZOCC consists of roughly 200,000 online news articles published between 2008 and 2017 and 7 million associated user comments in German. Out of 174,699 users in total, 60% posted more than one comment, 23% more than 10 comments and 7% more than 100 comments. For both, articles and comments, extensive metadata is available, such as author list, department, publication date, and tags (for articles) and user name, parent comment (if posted in response), and number of recommendations by other users (for comments). Not surprisingly, ZOCC is following a popularity growth with an increasing number of articles and comments over time. While our newspaper published roughly 1,300 articles per month in 2010 and each article received roughly 20 comments on average, we nowadays publish roughly 1,500 articles per month, each receiving 110 comments on average. As both corpora's articles and comments cover a similar time span of several years and many different departments, they deal with a broad range of topics. While the majority of articles in YNACC is

about economy, ZOCC's major department is politics. More than 50% of the comments in ZOCC are posted in response to articles in the politics department, whereas in YNACC culture, society, and economy share an almost equal amount of around 20% each and politics on forth rank with 12%. On average, an article in ZOCC receives 90% of its comments within 48 hours, while it takes 61 hours for an article in YNACC. Despite their slight differences, both corpora cover most popular departments, which motivates the idea to transfer a classifier trained on YNACC to ZOCC. For YNACC, Napoles et al. propose a machine learning approach to automatically identify engaging, respectful, and informative conversations (2017a). By identifying weekly top 10% articles with the highest comment volume, we focus on a different task. Nonetheless, both corpora, ZOCC and YNACC, have similar properties: both corpora contain user comments posted in reaction to news articles across similar time span and similar topics. However, only the much smaller YNACC provides detailed annotations regarding, for example, comments' tone and sentiment.

5 Evaluation

We compare to the approach by Tsagkias et al. and evaluate on the same task (Tsagkias et al., 2009, 2010). Therefore, we consider a binary classification task, which is to identify the weekly top 10% articles with the largest comment volume. Table 3 lists our final evaluation results on the hold-out test set. We choose F1-score as our evaluation metric, since precision and recall are equally relevant in our scenario. On the one hand, we want to achieve high recall so that no important article and its discussion is overlooked. On the other hand, we have limited resources and cannot afford to moderate each and every discussion. A high precision is crucial so that our moderators focus only on articles that need their attention. All experiments are conducted using time-wise split with years 2014 to 2016 for training, January 2017 to March 2017 for validation, and April 2017 for testing. We find that our additional article and metadata features, but also the automatically annotated first comments outperform the baseline. Due to the diversity of the different features, their combination further improves the prediction results. In comparison to the approach by Tsagkias et al., we finally achieve an 81% larger F1-score.

[2]https://deepl.com
[3]http://www.zeit.de/

Table 3: Precision (P), recall (R), and F1-score of the baseline, all article and metadata features, annotations of comments shown on the first page, and all combined.

Features	P	R	F1
Tsagkias et al.	0.16	0.72	0.26
Article and metadata	0.26	0.75	0.39
1st page comments	0.29	0.50	0.36
Combined approach	0.42	0.52	0.47

Table 4: Precision (P) and recall (R) decline slightly after translation from English (E) into German (G).

Label	P(E)	R(E)	P(G)	R(G)
audience	.80	.80	.81	.82
agreement	.76	.18	.65	.09
informative	.55	.71	.51	.85
mean	.64	.52	.52	.37
controversial	.61	.90	.58	.94
disagreement	.60	.75	.58	.81
persuasive	.51	.89	.44	.97
off_topic	.67	.57	.66	.40
neutral	.68	.35	.62	.41
positive	.46	.13	.80	.10
negative	.70	.93	.71	.92
mixed	.45	.52	.40	.78

5.1 Automatically Translated Comments

With another experiment, we study the classification error introduced by translation. Therefore, we train two classifiers with the approach by Napoles et al.: First, we train and test a classifier on the original, English YNACC. Second, we automatically translate all comments in YNACC from English into German and use this translated data for training and testing of the second classifier. Comparing these two classifiers, we find that both precision and recall slightly decrease after translation, as shown in Table 4. Based on this result, we can assume that the translation of German comments into English introduces only a small error. Although YNACC and ZOCC differ in language, we can transfer a classifier that has been trained on YNACC to ZOCC. For each article, we use the labels assigned to the first four comments, which are visible on the first comment page below an article. The first four comments are typically received within very few minutes after article publication.

Table 5: Prediction of weekly top articles based on the number of comments received in the first x minutes after article publication.

Number of received comments	F1
after 2min	0.03
after 4min	0.03
after 8min	0.17
after 16min	0.33
after 32min	0.41
after 64min	0.45
sequence (after 2, 4, 8, 16, 32, 64min)	0.46

5.2 Number of Early Comments

As a baseline feature for comparison, we use the number of comments[4] received in a short time span after article publication. Annotated first page comments, but also article and metadata features significantly outperform the baseline until 32 minutes after article publication. After 32 minutes, the number of received comments outperforms every single feature (but not the combination of all our features). This is because the difference between final number of comments and so far received comments converges over time.

6 Conclusions

In this paper, we studied the task of predicting the weekly top 10% articles with the highest comment volume. This prediction helps to schedule the publication of news stories and supports moderation teams in focusing on article discussions that require most likely their attention. Our supervised classification approach is based on a combination of metadata and content-based features, such as article body and topics. Further, we automatically translate German comments into English to make use of a classifier pre-trained on English data: We classify the tone and sentiment of comments received in the first minutes after article publication, which improves prediction even further. On a 7-million-comment real-world dataset our approach outperforms the current state-of-the-art by over 81% larger F1-score. We hope that our prediction will help to reduce the number of cases where newspapers have no other choice but to close down a discussion section because of limited moderation resources.

---

[4]To allow for non-linear correlations, we pass the number of comments as an absolute count and a squared count.

References

Roja Bandari, Sitaram Asur, and Bernardo Huberman. 2012. The pulse of news in social media: Forecasting popularity. In *Proceedings of the International AAAI Conference on Web and Social Media (ICWSM)*. volume 12, pages 26–33.

George Berry and Sean J Taylor. 2017. Discussion quality diffuses in the digital public square. In *Proceedings of the International Conference on World Wide Web (WWW)*. ACM, pages 1371–1380. https://doi.org/10.1145/3038912.3052666.

David M. Blei, Andrew Y. Ng, and Michael I. Jordan. 2003. Latent dirichlet allocation. *J. Mach. Learn. Res.* 3:993–1022. http://dl.acm.org/citation.cfm?id=944919.944937.

George Kennedy, Andrew McCollough, Edward Dixon, Alexei Bastidas, John Ryan, Chris Loo, and Saurav Sahay. 2017. Technology solutions to combat online harassment. In *Proceedings of the Workshop on Abusive Language Online*. Association for Computational Linguistics, pages 73–77. http://www.aclweb.org/anthology/W17-3011.

Tomas Mikolov, Ilya Sutskever, Kai Chen, Greg Corrado, and Jeffrey Dean. 2013. Distributed representations of words and phrases and their compositionality. In *Proceedings of the International Conference on Neural Information Processing Systems (NIPS)*. Curran Associates Inc., USA, pages 3111–3119. http://dl.acm.org/citation.cfm?id=2999792.2999959.

Courtney Napoles, Aasish Pappu, and Joel R. Tetreault. 2017a. Automatically identifying good conversations online (yes, they do exist!). In *Proceedings of the International AAAI Conference on Web and Social Media (ICWSM)*. pages 628–631.

Courtney Napoles, Joel R. Tetreault, Aasish Pappu, Enrica Rosato, and Brian Provenzale. 2017b. Finding good conversations online: The yahoo news annotated comments corpus. In *Proceedings of the 11th Linguistic Annotation Workshop (LAW@EACL)*. pages 13–23. https://doi.org/10.18653/v1/W17-0802.

Chikashi Nobata, Joel R. Tetreault, Achint Thomas, Yashar Mehdad, and Yi Chang. 2016. Abusive language detection in online user content. In *Proceedings of the International Conference on World Wide Web (WWW)*. International World Wide Web Conferences Steering Committee, Republic and Canton of Geneva, Switzerland, pages 145–153. https://doi.org/10.1145/2872427.2883062.

John Pavlopoulos, Prodromos Malakasiotis, and Ion Androutsopoulos. 2017. Deep learning for user comment moderation. In *Proceedings of the Workshop on Abusive Language Online*. Association for Computational Linguistics, pages 25–35. http://www.aclweb.org/anthology/W17-3004.

Georgios Rizos, Symeon Papadopoulos, and Yiannis Kompatsiaris. 2016. Predicting news popularity by mining online discussions. In *Proceedings of the International Conference on World Wide Web (WWW)*. International World Wide Web Conferences Steering Committee, Republic and Canton of Geneva, Switzerland, pages 737–742. https://doi.org/10.1145/2872518.2890096.

Alexandru Tatar, Panayotis Antoniadis, Marcelo Dias de Amorim, and Serge Fdida. 2012. Ranking news articles based on popularity prediction. In *Proceedings of the International Conference on Advances in Social Networks Analysis and Mining (ASONAM)*. IEEE Computer Society, Washington, DC, USA, pages 106–110. https://doi.org/10.1109/ASONAM.2012.28.

Alexandru Tatar, Jérémie Leguay, Panayotis Antoniadis, Arnaud Limbourg, Marcelo Dias de Amorim, and Serge Fdida. 2011. Predicting the popularity of online articles based on user comments. In *Proceedings of the International Conference on Web Intelligence, Mining and Semantics (WIMS)*. ACM, New York, NY, USA, pages 67:1–67:8. https://doi.org/10.1145/1988688.1988766.

Manos Tsagkias, Wouter Weerkamp, and Maarten de Rijke. 2009. Predicting the volume of comments on online news stories. In *Proceedings of the International Conference on Information and Knowledge Management (CIKM)*. ACM, New York, NY, USA, pages 1765–1768. https://doi.org/10.1145/1645953.1646225.

Manos Tsagkias, Wouter Weerkamp, and Maarten de Rijke. 2010. News comments: Exploring, modeling, and online prediction. In *Proceedings of the European Conference on Information Retrieval Research (ECIR)*. Springer Berlin Heidelberg, Berlin, Heidelberg, pages 191–203. https://doi.org/10.1007/978-3-642-12275-0_19.

Demand-Weighted Completeness Prediction for a Knowledge Base

Andrew Hopkinson and **Amit Gurdasani** and **Dave Palfrey** and **Arpit Mittal**
Amazon Research Cambridge
Cambridge, UK
{hopkia, amitgurd, dpalfrey, mitarpit}@amazon.co.uk

Abstract

In this paper we introduce the notion of Demand-Weighted Completeness, allowing estimation of the completeness of a knowledge base with respect to how it is used. Defining an entity by its classes, we employ usage data to predict the distribution over relations for that entity. For example, instances of *person* in a knowledge base may require a birth date, name and nationality to be considered complete. These predicted relation distributions enable detection of important gaps in the knowledge base, and define the required facts for unseen entities. Such characterisation of the knowledge base can also quantify how usage and completeness change over time. We demonstrate a method to measure Demand-Weighted Completeness, and show that a simple neural network model performs well at this prediction task.

1 Introduction

Knowledge Bases (KBs) are widely used for representing information in a structured format. Such KBs, including Wikidata (Vrandečić and Krötzsch, 2014), Google Knowledge Vault (Dong et al., 2014), and YAGO (Suchanek et al., 2007), often store information as facts in the form of triples, consisting of two entities and a relation between them. KBs have many applications in fields such as machine translation, information retrieval and question answering (Ferrucci, 2012).

When considering a KB's suitability for a task, primary considerations are the number of facts it contains (Färber et al., 2015), and the precision of those facts. One metric which is often overlooked is *completeness*. This can be defined as the proportion of facts about an entity that are present in the KB as compared to an ideal KB which has every fact that can be known about that entity. For example, previous research (Suchanek et al., 2011; Min et al., 2013) has shown that between 69% and 99% of entities in popular KBs lack at least one relation that other entities in the same class have. As of 2016, Wikidata knows the father of only 2% of all people in the KB (Galárraga et al., 2017). Google found that 71% of people in Freebase have no known place of birth, and 75% have no known nationality (Dong et al., 2014).

Previous work has focused on a general concept of completeness, where all KB entities are expected to be fully complete, independent of how the KB is used (Motro, 1989; Razniewski et al., 2016; Zaveri et al., 2013). This is a problem because different use cases of a KB may have different completeness requirements. For this work, we were interested in determining a KB's completeness with respect to its query usage, which we term *Demand-Weighted Completeness*. For example, a relation used 100 times per day is more important than one only used twice per day.

1.1 Problem specification

We define our task as follows:

'Given an entity E in a KB, and query usage data of the KB, predict the distribution of relations that E must have in order for 95% of queries about E to be answered successfully.'

1.2 Motivation

Demand-Weighted Completeness allows us to predict both important missing relations for existing entities, and relations required for unseen entities. As a result we can target acquisition of sources to fill important KB gaps.

It is possible to be entirely reactive when ad-

Proceedings of NAACL-HLT 2018, pages 200–207
New Orleans, Louisiana, June 1 - 6, 2018. ©2017 Association for Computational Linguistics

dressing gaps in KB data. Failing queries can be examined and missing fields marked for investigation. However, this approach assumes that:

1. the same KB entity will be accessed again in future, making the data acquisition useful. This is far from guaranteed.

2. the KB already contains all entities needed. While this may hold for some use cases, the most useful KB's today grow and change to reflect a changing world.

Both assumptions become unnecessary with an abstract representation of entities, allowing generalization to predict usage. The appropriateness of the abstract representation can be measured by how well the model distinguishes different entity types, and how well the model predicts actual usage for a set of entities, either known or unknown.

Further, the Demand-Weighted Completeness of a KB with respect to a specific task can be used as a metric for system performance at that task. By identifying gaps in the KB, it allows targeting of specific improvements to achieve the greatest increase in completeness.

Our work is the first to consider KB completeness using the distribution of observed KB queries as a signal. This paper details a learning-based approach that predicts the required relation distributions for both seen and unseen class signatures (Section 3), and shows that a neural network model can generalize relation distributions efficiently and accurately compared to a baseline frequency-based approach (Section 6).

2 Related work

Previous work has studied the completeness of the individual properties or database tables over which queries are executed (Razniewski and Nutt, 2011; Razniewski et al., 2015). This approach is suitable for KBs or use cases where individual tables, and individual rows in those tables, are all of equal importance to the KB, or are queried separately.

Completeness of KBs has also been measured based on the cardinality of properties. Galárraga et al. (2017) and Mirza et al. (2016) estimated cardinality for several relations with respect to individual entities, yielding targeted completeness information for specific entities. This approach depends on the availability of relevant free text, and uses handcrafted regular expressions to extract the

```
barackObama:
    person:      1
    politician:  1
    democrat:    1
    republican:  0
    writer:      1
```

Figure 1: Class signature for *barackObama*. Other entities with the same class membership will have the same signature.

information, which can be noisy and doesn't scale to large numbers of relations.

The potential for metrics around completeness and dynamicity of a KB are explored in Zaveri et al. (2013), focusing on the task-independent idea of completeness, and the temporal currency, volatility and timeliness of the KB contents. While their concept of timeliness has some similarities to demand-weighted completeness in its task-specific 'data currency', we focus more on how the demand varies over time, and how the completeness of the KB varies with respect to that change in demand.

3 Representing Entities

3.1 Class Distributions

The data for a single entity does not generalize on its own. In order to generalize from observed usage information to unseen entities and unseen usage, and smooth out outliers, we need to combine data from similar entities. Such combination requires a shared entity representation, allowing combination of similar entities while preventing their confusion with dissimilar entities.

For this work, an entity may be a member of multiple classes (or types). We aggregate usage across multiple entities by abstracting to their classes. Membership of a class can be considered as a binary attribute for an entity, with the entity's membership of all the classes considered in the analysis forming a *class signature*.

For example, the entity *barackObama* is a *person*, *politician*, *democrat*, and *writer*, among other classes. He is not a *republican*. Considering these five classes as our class space, the class signature for *barackObama* would look like Figure 1.

Defining an entity by its classes has precedent in previous work (Galárraga et al., 2017; Razniewski et al., 2016). It allows consideration of entities and

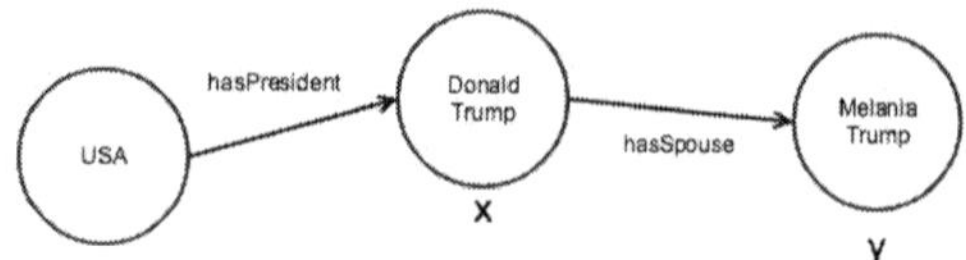

Figure 2: Graph representation of the facts needed to solve the query in Equation 1. The path walked by the query can branch arbitrarily, but maintains a directionality from initial entities to result entities.

```
USA:
    hasPresident:     13
    hasCapital:        8
    hasPopulation:     6
    ...
```

Figure 3: Absolute usage data for the entity *USA*.

class combinations not yet seen in the KB (though not entirely new classes).

3.2 Relation Distributions

KB queries can be considered as graph traversals, stepping through multiple edges of the knowledge graph to determine the result of multi-clause query. For example, the query:

$$y : \text{hasPresident}(\text{USA}, x) \wedge \text{hasSpouse}(y, x) \quad (1)$$

determines the spouse of the president of the United States by composing two clauses, as shown in Figure 2.

The demand-weighted importance of a relation R for an entity E is defined as the number of query clauses about E which contain R, as a fraction of the total number of clauses about E. For example, Equation 1 contains two clauses. As the first clause queries for the hasPresident relation of the USA entity, we attribute this occurrence of hasPresident to the USA entity. Aggregating the clauses for an entity gives a total entity usage of the form seen in Figure 3.

Since the distribution of relation usage is dominated by a few high-value relations (see Figure 6), we only consider relations required to satisfy 95% of queries.

3.3 Predicting Relations from Classes

Combining the two representation methods above, we aim to predict the relation distribution for a

```
barackObama:
    hasHeight:      0.16
    hasBirthdate:   0.12
    hasBirthplace:  0.08
    hasSpouse:      0.07
    hasChild:       0.05
```

Figure 4: An example of a predicted relation distribution for an individual entity. The values represent the proportion of usage of the entity that requires the given relation.

given entity (as in Figure 4) using the class membership for the entity (as in Figure 1). This provides the expected usage profile of an entity, potentially before it has seen any usage.

4 Data and Models

4.1 Our knowledge base

We make use of a proprietary KB (Tunstall-Pedoe, 2010) constructed over several years, combining a hand-curated ontology with publicly available data from Wikipedia, Freebase, DBPedia, and other sources. However, the task can be applied to any KB with usage data, relations and classes. We use a subset of our KB for this analysis due to the limitation of model size as a function of the number of classes (input features) and the number of relations (output features).

Our usage data is generated by our Natural Language Understanding system, which produces KB queries from text utterances. Though it is difficult to remove all biases and errors from the system when operated at industrial scale, we use a hybrid system of curated rules and statistical methods to reduce such problems to a minimum. Such errors should not impact the way we evaluate different models for their ability to model the data itself.

4.2 Datasets

To create a class signature, we first determine the binary class membership vector for every entity in the usage dataset. We then group entities by class signature, so entities with identical class membership are grouped together.

For each class signature, we generate the relation distribution from the usage data of the entities with that signature. In our case, this usage data is a random subset of query traffic against the KB taken from a specific period of time. The more usage a class signature has, the more fine-grained the

Dataset	Classes	Relations	Signatures
$D1_{small}$	4400	1300	12000
$D2_{medium}$	8000	2000	25000
$D3_{large}$	9400	2100	37000

Table 1: Dataset statistics.

```
person:
    hasName:      31
    hasAge:       18
    hasHeight:    11
    ...
```

Figure 5: Aggregated usage data for the class *person*.

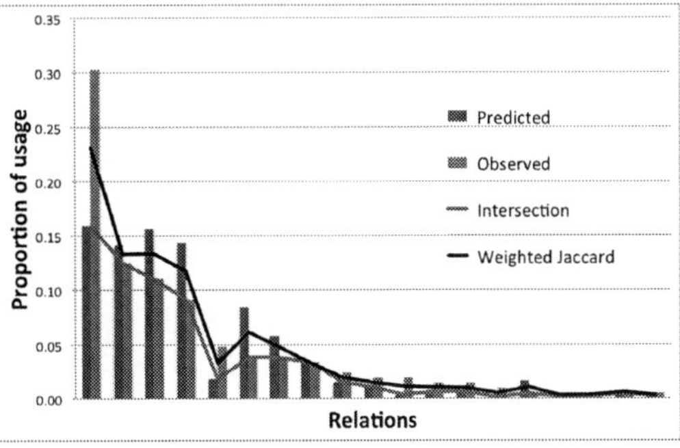

Figure 6: Example histogram of the predicted (using a neural model) and observed relation distributions for a single *class signature*, showing the region of intersection in green and the weighted Jaccard index in black.

distribution of relations becomes. The data is divided into 10 cross-validation folds to ensure that no class signature appears in both the validation and training sets.

We generate 3 different sizes of dataset for experimentation (see Table 1), to see how dataset size influences the models.

4.3 Relation prediction models

4.3.1 Baseline - Frequency-Based

In this approach, we compute the relation distribution for each individual class by summing the usage data for all entities of that class (see Section 3). This gives a combined raw relation usage as seen in Figure 5.

For every class in the training set we store this raw relation distribution. At test time, we compute the predicted relation distribution for a class signature as the normalized sum of the raw distributions of all its classes. However, these single-class distributions do not capture the influence of class co-occurrence, where the presence of two classes together may have a stronger influence on the importance of a relation than each class on their own. Additionally, storing distributions for each class signature does not scale, and does not generalize to unseen class combinations.

4.3.2 Learning-Based Approaches

To investigate the impact of class co-occurrence, we use two different learning models to predict the relation distribution for a given set of input classes. The vector of classes comprising the class signature is used as input to the learned models.

Linear regression. Using the normalized relation distribution for each class signature, we trained a least-squares linear regression model to predict the relation distribution from a binary vector of classes. This model has $(n \times m)$ parameters, where n is the number of input classes and m is the number of relations. We implemented our linear regression model using Scikit-learn toolkit (Pedregosa et al., 2011).

Neural network. We trained a feed-forward neural network using the binary class vector as the input layer, with a low-dimensional (h) hidden layer (with rectified linear unit as activation) followed by a softmax output layer of the size of the relation set. This model has $h(n + m)$ parameters, which depending on the value of h is significantly smaller than the linear regression model. The objective function used for training was Kullback-Liebler Divergence. We chose Keras (Chollet, 2015) to implement the neural network model. The model had a single 10-node Rectified Linear Unit hidden layer, with a softmax over the output.

5 Evaluation

We compare the predicted relation distributions to those observed for the test examples in two ways:

Weighted Jaccard Index. We modified the Jaccard index (Jaccard, 1912) to include a weighting term, which weights every relation with the mean weight in the predicted and observed distribution (see Figure 6). This rewards a correctly predicted relation without focusing on the proportion predicted for that relation, and is sufficient to define a set of important relations for a *class sig-*

nature. This is given by:

$$J = \frac{\sum\limits_{i} W(R_i) \times R_i \in (P \cap O)}{\sum\limits_{i} W(R_i) \times R_i \in (P \cup O)} \quad (2)$$

where P is the predicted distribution, O is the observed distribution, $W(R_i)$ is the mean weight of relation R_i in P and O. We also calculate false negatives (observed but not predicted) and false positives (predicted but not observed), by modifying the second term in the numerator of Equation 2 to give $P \backslash O$ and $O \backslash P$, rather than $P \cap O$.

Intersection. We compute the intersection of the two distributions (see Figure 6). This is a more strict comparison between the distributions which penalizes differences in weight for individual relations. This is given by:

$$I = \sum_{i} min(P(R_i), O(R_i)) \quad (3)$$

5.1   Usage Weighted Evaluation

We also evaluated the models using the Weighted Jaccard index and Intersection methods, but weighting by usage counts for each signature. This metric rewards the models more for correctly predicting relation distributions for common class signatures in the usage data. While unweighted analysis is useful to examine how the model covers the breadth of the problem space, weighted evaluation more closely reflects the model's utility for real usage data.

5.2   Temporal Prediction

Additionally, we evaluated the models on their ability to predict future usage. With an unchanging usage pattern, evaluation against future usage would be equivalent to cross-validation (assuming the same signature distribution in the folds). However, in many real world cases, usage of a KB varies over time, seasonally or as a result of changing user requirements.

Therefore we also evaluated a neural model against future usage data to measure how elapsed time affected model performance. The datasets T1, T2, and T3 each contain 3 datasets (of similar size to $D1_{small}$, $D2_{medium}$, and $D1_{large}$), and were created using usage data from time periods with a fixed offset, t. The base set was created at time t_0, T1 at time $t_0 + t$, T2 at time $t_0 + 2t$, and T3 at time $t_0 + 3t$. A time interval was chosen that reflected the known variability of the usage data,

Model	Jaccard	False Neg.	False Pos.
$D1_{small}$			
Freq.	0.604	0.084	0.311
Regr.	0.522	0.102	0.376
NN	**0.661**	0.036	0.303
$D2_{medium}$			
Freq.	0.611	0.101	0.287
Regr.	0.557	0.084	0.358
NN	**0.687**	0.035	0.278
$D3_{large}$			
Freq.	0.616	0.105	0.278
Regr.	0.573	0.080	0.347
NN	**0.700**	0.034	0.266

Table 2: Unweighted results for the three models on the three datasets.

such that we would expect the usage to not be the same.

6   Results

6.1   Cross-Validation

10-fold cross-validation results are shown in Table 2. The neural network model performs best, outperforming the baseline model by 6-8 percentage points. The regression model performs worst, trailing the baseline model by 4-8 percentage points.

6.1.1   Baseline

The baseline model shows little improvement with increasing amounts of data - the results from $D1_{small}$ to $D3_{large}$ (3x more data points) only improve by just over 1 percentage point. This suggests that this model is unable to generalise from the data, which is expected from the lack of class co-occurrence information in the model. Interestingly, the baseline model shows an increase in false negatives on the larger datasets, implying the lack of generalisation is more problematic for more fine-grained relation distributions.

6.1.2   Linear Regression

The linear regression model gives a much lower Jaccard measure than the baseline model. This is likely due to the number of parameters in the model relative to the number of examples. For $D1_{small}$, the model has approximately 6m parameters, with 12k training examples, making this an under-determined system. For $D3_{large}$ the number of parameters rises to 20m, with 37k training examples, maintaining the poor example:parameter ratio. From this we might expect the performance of the model to be invariant with the amount of data.

However, the larger datasets also have higher resolution relation distributions, as they are aggregated from more individual examples. This has the effect of reducing the impact of outliers in the data, giving improved predictions when the model generalises. We do indeed see that the linear regression model improves notably with larger datasets, closing the gap to the baseline model from 8 percentage points to 4.

6.1.3 Neural Network

The neural network model shows much better performance than either of the other two methods. The Jaccard score is consistently 6-8% above the regression model, with far fewer false negatives and smaller numbers of false positives. This is likely to be due to the smaller number of parameters of the neural model versus the linear regression model. For $D3_{large}$, the 10-node hidden layer model amounts to 115k parameters with 37k training examples, a far better ratio (though still not ideal) than for the linear regression model.

6.1.4 Weighted Evaluation

We include in Table 3 the results using the weighted evaluation scheme described in Section 5.1. This gives more usage-focused evaluation, emphasizing the non-uniform usage of different class signatures. The $D3_{large}$ neural model achieves 85% precision with a weighted evaluation. With the low rate of false negatives, this indicates that a similar model could be used to predict the necessary relations for KB usage.

6.2 Intersection

Table 4 gives measurements of the intersection metric. These show a similar trend to the Jaccard scores, with lower absolute values from the stricter evaluation metric. Although the Jaccard measure shows correct relation set prediction with a precision of 0.700, predicting the proportions for those relations accurately remains a difficult problem. The best value we achieved was 0.398.

Model	Jaccard	False Neg.	False Pos.
$D1_{small}$			
Freq.	0.779	0.066	0.123
Regr.	0.667	0.090	0.242
NN	**0.808**	0.032	0.159
$D2_{medium}$			
Freq.	0.816	0.059	0.094
Regr.	0.703	0.077	0.220
NN	**0.840**	0.037	0.123
$D3_{large}$			
Freq.	0.819	0.062	0.088
Regr.	0.720	0.069	0.210
NN	**0.850**	0.038	0.113

Table 3: Usage-weighted results for the three models on the three datasets.

Model	Freq.	Regr.	NN
Inter.	0.319	0.278	0.398

Table 4: Results for the three methods for the $D3_{large}$ dataset using the intersection metric. The difference between the methods is similar to the Jaccard measure above.

Interval	T1	T2	T3
$D1_{small}$	0.661	0.659	0.657
$D2_{medium}$	0.705	0.699	0.696
$D3_{large}$	0.712	0.708	0.704

Table 5: Results of training a neural model on all available data for $D1_{small}$ - $D3_{large}$, then evaluating on T1-T3. The values for $D2_{medium}$ and $D3_{large}$ are higher than cross-validation, as cross-validation never tests a model on examples used to train it. However, the T datasets contain all data from the specified period. The downward trend with increasing T is clear, but slight.

6.3 Unweighted Temporal Prediction

In addition to evaluating models on their ability to predict the behaviour of unseen class signatures, we also evaluated the neural model on its ability to predict future usage behaviour. The results of this experiment are given in Table 5.

We observe a very slight downward trend in the precision of the model using all three base datasets ($D1_{small}$ - $D3_{large}$), with a steeper (but still slight) downward trend for the larger datasets. This suggests that a model trained on usage data from one period of time will have significant predictive power on future datasets.

7 Measuring Completeness of a KB

Once we have a suitable model of the expected relation distributions for class combinations, we use the model to predict the expected relation distribution for specific entities in our KB. We then compare the predicted relation distribution to the observed relations for each specific entity. The completeness of an entity is given by the sum of the relation proportions for the predicted relations the entity has in the KB.

Any gaps for an entity represent relations that, if added to the KB, would have a quantifiable positive impact on the performance of the KB. By focussing on the most important entities according to our usage, we can target fact addition to have the greatest impact to the usage the KB receives.

By aggregating the completeness values for a set of entities, we may estimate the completeness of subsets of the KB. This aggregation is weighted by the frequency with which the entity appears in the usage data, giving a usage-weighted measure of the subset's completeness. These subsets can represent individual topics, individual classes of entity, or overall information about the KB as a whole.

For example, using the best neural model above on an unrepresentative subset of our KB, we evaluate the completeness of that subset at 58.3%. This not only implies that we are missing a substantial amount of necessary information for these entities with respect to the usage data chosen, but permits targeting of source acquisition to improve the entity completeness in aggregate. For example, if we are missing a large number of *hasBirthdate* facts for people, we might locate a source that has that information. We can quantify the benefit of that effort in terms of improved usage performance.

8 Conclusions and Future Work

We have introduced the notion of Demand-Weighted Completeness as a way of determining a KB's suitability by employing usage data. We have demonstrated a method to predict the distribution of relations needed in a KB for entities of a given class signature, and have compared three different models for predicting these distributions. Further, we have described a method to measure the completeness of a KB using these distributions.

For future work we would like to try complex neural network architectures, regularisation, and semantic embeddings or other abstracted relations to enhance the signatures. We would also like to investigate Good-Turing frequency estimation (Good, 1953).

References

François Chollet. 2015. Keras. `https://github.com/fchollet/keras`.

Xin Dong, Evgeniy Gabrilovich, Geremy Heitz, Wilko Horn, Ni Lao, Kevin Murphy, Thomas Strohmann, Shaohua Sun, and Wei Zhang. 2014. Knowledge Vault: A web-scale approach to probabilistic knowledge fusion. In *Proceedings of the 20th ACM SIGKDD International Conference on Knowledge Discovery and Data Mining*. ACM, New York, NY, USA, KDD '14, pages 601–610. `https://doi.org/10.1145/2623330.2623623`.

Michael Färber, Basil Ell, Carsten Menne, and Achim Rettinger. 2015. A comparative survey of DBpedia, Freebase, OpenCyc, Wikidata, and YAGO. *Semantic Web Journal, July* .

D. A. Ferrucci. 2012. Introduction to "this is watson". *IBM J. Res. Dev.* 56(3):235–249. `https://doi.org/10.1147/JRD.2012.2184356`.

Luis Galárraga, Simon Razniewski, Antoine Amarilli, and Fabian M. Suchanek. 2017. Predicting completeness in knowledge bases. In *Proceedings of the Tenth ACM International Conference on Web Search and Data Mining*. ACM, New York, NY, USA, WSDM '17, pages 375–383. `https://doi.org/10.1145/3018661.3018739`.

I. J. Good. 1953. The population frequencies of species and the estimation of population parameters. *Biometrika* 40(3-4):237. `https://doi.org/10.1093/biomet/40.3-4.237`.

Paul Jaccard. 1912. The distribution of the flora in the alpine zone.1. *New Phytologist* 11(2):37–50. `https://doi.org/10.1111/j.1469-8137.1912.tb05611.x`.

Bonan Min, Ralph Grishman, Li Wan, Chang Wang, and David Gondek. 2013. Distant supervision for relation extraction with an incomplete knowledge base. In *HLT-NAACL*. pages 777–782.

Paramita Mirza, Simon Razniewski, and Werner Nutt. 2016. Expanding Wikidata's parenthood information by 178%, or how to mine relation cardinalities. In *ISWC 2016 Posters & Demonstrations Trac.* CEUR-WS. org.

Amihai Motro. 1989. Integrity = validity + completeness. *ACM Trans. Database Syst.* 14(4):480–502. https://doi.org/10.1145/76902.76904.

F. Pedregosa, G. Varoquaux, A. Gramfort, V. Michel, B. Thirion, O. Grisel, M. Blondel, P. Prettenhofer, R. Weiss, V. Dubourg, J. Vanderplas, A. Passos, D. Cournapeau, M. Brucher, M. Perrot, and E. Duchesnay. 2011. Scikit-learn: Machine learning in Python. *Journal of Machine Learning Research* 12:2825–2830.

Simon Razniewski, Flip Korn, Werner Nutt, and Divesh Srivastava. 2015. Identifying the extent of completeness of query answers over partially complete databases. In *Proceedings of the 2015 ACM SIGMOD International Conference on Management of Data*. ACM, New York, NY, USA, SIGMOD '15, pages 561–576. https://doi.org/10.1145/2723372.2750544.

Simon Razniewski and Werner Nutt. 2011. Completeness of queries over incomplete databases. *VLDB* 4:749–760.

Simon Razniewski, Fabian M Suchanek, and Werner Nutt. 2016. But what do we actually know. *Proceedings of AKBC* pages 40–44.

Fabian Suchanek, David Gross-Amblard, and Serge Abiteboul. 2011. Watermarking for ontologies. *The semantic web–ISWC 2011* pages 697–713.

Fabian M. Suchanek, Gjergji Kasneci, and Gerhard Weikum. 2007. YAGO: A core of semantic knowledge. In *Proceedings of the 16th International Conference on World Wide Web*. ACM, New York, NY, USA, WWW '07, pages 697–706. https://doi.org/10.1145/1242572.1242667.

William Tunstall-Pedoe. 2010. True Knowledge: Open-domain question answering using structured knowledge and inference. *AI Magazine* 31(3):80–92. https://doi.org/10.1609/aimag.v31i3.2298.

Denny Vrandečić and Markus Krötzsch. 2014. Wikidata: A free collaborative knowledgebase. *Commun. ACM* 57(10):78–85. https://doi.org/10.1145/2629489.

Amrapali Zaveri, Anisa Rula, Andrea Maurino, Ricardo Pietrobon, Jens Lehmann, and Sören Auer. 2013. Quality assessment for linked open data: A survey.

Personalized neural language models for real-world query auto completion

Nicolas Fiorini
National Center for Biotechnology Information
National Library of Medicine, NIH
Bethesda, MD, USA
nicolas.fiorini@nih.gov

Zhiyong Lu
National Center for Biotechnology Information
National Library of Medicine, NIH
Bethesda, MD, USA
zhiyong.lu@nih.gov

Abstract

Query auto completion (QAC) systems are a standard part of search engines in industry, helping users formulate their query. Such systems update their suggestions after the user types each character, predicting the user's intent using various signals — one of the most common being popularity. Recently, deep learning approaches have been proposed for the QAC task, to specifically address the main limitation of previous popularity-based methods: the inability to predict unseen queries. In this work we improve previous methods based on neural language modeling, with the goal of building an end-to-end system. We particularly focus on using real-world data by integrating user information for personalized suggestions when possible. We also make use of time information and study how to increase diversity in the suggestions while studying the impact on scalability. Our empirical results demonstrate a marked improvement on two separate datasets over previous best methods in both accuracy and scalability, making a step towards neural query auto-completion in production search engines.

1 Introduction

Predicting the next characters or words following a prefix has had multiple uses from helping handicapped people (Swiffin et al., 1987) to, more recently, helping search engine users (Cai et al., 2016). In practice, most search engines today use query auto completion (QAC) systems, consisting of suggesting queries as users type in the search box (Fiorini et al., 2017). The task suffers from high dimensionality, because the number of possible solutions increases as the length of the target query increases. Historically, the query prediction task has been addressed by relying on query logs, particularly the popularity of past queries (Bar-Yossef and Kraus, 2011; Lu et al., 2009). The idea is to rely on the wisdom of the crowd, as popular

queries matching a typed prefix are more likely to be the user's intent.

This traditional approach is usually referred to as *MostPopularCompletion* (MPC)(Bar-Yossef and Kraus, 2011). However, the performance of MPC is skewed: it is very high for popular queries and very low for rare queries. At the extreme, MPC simply cannot predict a query it has never seen. This becomes a bigger problem in academic search (Lankinen et al., 2016), where systems are typically less used, with a wider range of possible queries. Recent advances in deep learning, particularly in semantic modeling (Mitra and Craswell, 2015) and neural language modeling (Park and Chiba, 2017) showed promising results for predicting rare queries. In this work, we propose to improve the state-of-the-art approaches in neural QAC by integrating personalization and time sensitivity information as well as addressing current MPC limitations by diversifying the suggestions, thus approaching a production-ready architecture.

2 Related work

2.1 Neural query auto completion

While QAC has been well studied, the field has recently started to shift towards deep learning-based models, which can be categorized into two main classes: semantic models (using Convolutional Neural Nets, or CNNs) (Mitra and Craswell, 2015) and language models (using Recurrent Neural Nets, or RNNs) (Park and Chiba, 2017). Both approaches are frequently used in natural language processing in general (Kim et al., 2016) and tend to capture different features. In this work, we focus on RNNs as they provide a flexible solution to generate text, even when it is not previously seen in the training data.

Yet, recent work in this field (Park and Chiba, 2017) suffers from some limitations. Most importantly, the probability estimates for full queries

Proceedings of NAACL-HLT 2018, pages 208–215
New Orleans, Louisiana, June 1 - 6, 2018. ©2017 Association for Computational Linguistics

are directly correlated to the length of the suggestions, consequently favoring shorter queries in some cases and hampering some predictions (Park and Chiba, 2017). By appending these results to MPC's and re-ranking the list with LambdaMART (Burges, 2010) in another step as suggested in previous work (Mitra and Craswell, 2015), they achieve state-of-the-art performance in neural query auto completion at the cost of a higher complexity and more computation time.

2.2 Context information

Still, these preliminary approaches have yet to integrate standards in QAC, e.g. query personalization (Koutrika and Ioannidis, 2005; Margaris et al., 2018) and time sensitivity (Cai et al., 2014). This integration has to differ from traditional approaches by taking full advantage of neural language modeling. For example, neural language models could be refined to capture interests of some users as well as their actual language or query formulation. The same can apply to time-sensitivity, where the probability of queries might change over time (e.g. for queries such as "tv guide", or "weather"). Furthermore, the feasibility of these approaches in real-world settings has not been demonstrated, even more so on specialized domains.

By addressing these issues, we make the following contributions in this work compared to the previous approaches:

- We propose a more straightforward architecture with **improved scalability**;

- Our method integrates **user information** when available as well as **time-sensitivity**;

- We propose to use a balanced beam search for ensuring **diversity**;

- We test on **a second dataset** and compare the generalizability of different methods in a specialized domain;

- Our method achieves **stronger performance** than the state of the art on both datasets.

Finally, our source code is made available in a public repository[1]. This allows complete **reproducibility of our results** and future comparisons.

3 Methods

3.1 Personalized neural Language Model

The justification of using a neural language model for the task of predicting queries is that it has been proven to perform well to generate text that has never been seen in the training data (Sutskever et al., 2011). Particularly, character-level models work with a finer granularity. That is, if a given prefix has not been seen in the training data (e.g. a novel or incomplete word), the model can use the information shared across similar prefixes to make a prediction nonetheless.

Recurrent Neural Network The difficulty of predicting queries given a prefix is that the number of candidates explodes as the query becomes longer. RNNs allow to represent each character (or word) of a sequence as a cell state, therefore reducing the dimensionality of the task. However, they also introduce the vanishing gradient problem during backpropagation, preventing them from learning long-term dependencies. Both gated recurrent units (GRU) (Cho et al., 2014) and long-short term memory cells (LSTMs) solve this limitation — albeit with a different approach — and are increasingly used. In preliminary experiments, we tried various forms of RNNs: vanilla RNNs, GRUs and LSTMs. GRUs performed similarly to LSTM with a smaller computational complexity due to fewer parameters to learn as was previously observed (Jozefowicz et al., 2015).

Word embedded character-level Neural Language Model The main novelty in (Park and Chiba, 2017) is to combine a character-level neural language model with a word-embedded space character. The incentive is that character-level neural language models benefit from a finer granularity for predictions but they lack the semantic understanding words-level models provide, and vice versa. Therefore, they encode text sequences using one-hot encoding of characters, character embedding and pre-trained word embedding (using word2vec (Mikolov et al., 2013)) of the previous word when a space character is encountered. Our preliminary results showed that the character embedding does not bring much to the learning, so we traded it with the context feature vectors below to save some computation time while enriching the model with additional, diverse information.

User representation We make the assumption that the way a user types a query is a function of their actual language/vocabulary, but also a function of their interests. Therefore, a language model could capture these user characteristics to better predict the query, if we feed the learner with the information. Each query q_i is a set of words such that $q_i = \{w_1, ..., w_n\}$. U is a column matrix and a user $u \in U$ is characterized by the union of words in their k past queries, i.e. $Q^u = \cup_{i=1}^{k} q_i$. The objective is to reduce, for each user, the vocabulary used in their queries to a vector of a dimensionality d of choice, or $Q^u \rightarrow \mathbb{R}^d$. We chose $d = 30$, in order to stay in the same computation order of previous work using character embedding (Park and Chiba, 2017). To this end, we adapted the approach *PV-DBOW* detailed in (Le and Mikolov, 2014). That is, at each training iteration, a random word w_i is sampled from Q^u. The model is trained by maximizing the probability of predicting the user u given the word w_i, i.e.:

$$\frac{1}{|U|} \sum_{u \in U} \sum_{w_i \in Q^u} log\, P(u|w_i). \qquad (1)$$

The resulting vectors are stored for each user ID and are used as input for the neural net (NN) (see Architecture section).

Time representation As an example, in the background data (see Section 4.1), the query "tv guide" appears 1,682 times and it is vastly represented in evening and nights. For this reason, we propose to integrate time features in the language model. While there has been more elaborated approaches to model it in the past (Shokouhi and Radinsky, 2012), we instead propose a straightforward encoding and leave the rest of the work to the neural net. For each query, we look at the time it was issued, consisting of hour x , minute y and second z, and we derive the following features:

$$\begin{aligned} & sin\left(\frac{2\pi(3600x + 60y + z)}{86400}\right), \\ & cos\left(\frac{2\pi(3600x + 60y + z)}{86400}\right). \end{aligned} \qquad (2)$$

This encoding has the benefit of belonging to $[-1, 1]$, which is a range comparable to the rest of the features. It is also capable to model cyclic data, which is important particularly around boundaries (e.g. considering a query at 11:55PM and another at 00:05AM). We proceed the same way to encode weekdays and we end up with four time features.

Overall architecture An overview of the architecture is proposed in Figure 1. The input of our neural language model is a concatenation of the vectors defined above, for each character and for each query in the training set. We use zero-padding after the "\n" character to keep the sequence length consistent, and the NN learns to recognize it. We feed this input vector into 2 layers of 1024 GRUs[2], each followed by a dropout layer (with a dropout rate of 50%) to prevent overfitting. Each GRU cell is activated with $ReLu(x) = x^+$ and gradients are clipped to a norm of 0.5 to avoid gradient exploding problems. The output of the second dropout layer is fed to a temporal softmax layer, which allows to make predictions at each state. The softmax function returns the probability $P(c_i|c_1, ..., c_{i-1})$ of the character c_i given the previous characters of the sequence, which is then used to calculate the loss function by comparing it to the next character in the target query. Instead of using the objective denoted in (Park and Chiba, 2017), we minimize the loss $\mathcal{L}$ defined as the average cross entropy of this probability with the reference probability $\hat{P}(c_i)$ across all queries, that is

$$\mathcal{L} =$$

$$-\frac{1}{|Q|} \sum_{q \in Q} \sum_{i=1}^{|q|-1} \hat{P}(c_{i+1}) \times log\, P(c_{i+1}|c_1, ..., c_i).$$

$$(3)$$

Q is the set of queries in the training dataset, $|Q|$ is the total number of queries in the set and $|q|$ is the number of characters in the query q. Convergence stabilizes around 5-10 epochs for the AOL dataset (depending on the model) and 15-20 epochs for the biomedical specialized dataset (see Section 4.1).

3.2 Balanced diverse beam search

The straightforward approach for decoding the most likely output sequence — in this case, a suffix given a prefix — is to use a greedy approach. That is, we feed the prefix into the trained NN and pick the most likely output at every step, until sequence is complete. This approach has a high

---

[2]It was reported that using more cells may not help the prediction while hurting computation (Park and Chiba, 2017).

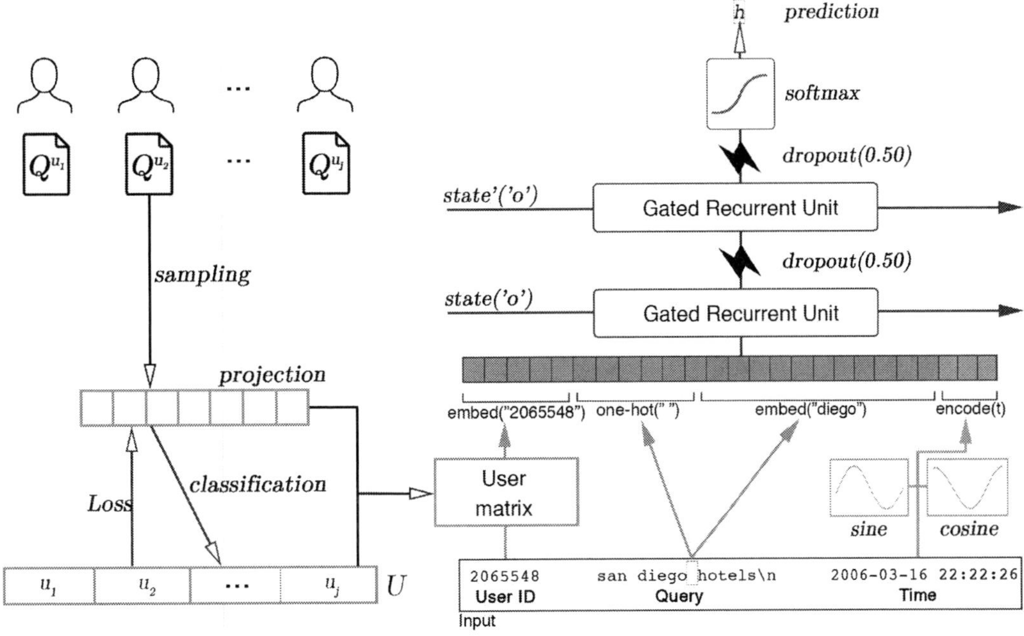

Figure 1: Architecture of our proposed model.

chance to output a locally optimal sequence and a common alternative is to use a beam search instead. We propose to improve the beam search by adding a greedy heuristic within it, in order to account for the diversity in the results. A similar suggestion has been made in (Vijayakumar et al., 2016), and our proposition differs by rebalancing the probabilities after diversity was introduced. In (Vijayakumar et al., 2016), at every step the most likely prediction is not weighted while all others are, by greedily comparing them. This approach effectively always prefers the most likely character over all other alternatives at each step. The first result will thus be the same as the local optimum using a greedy approach, which becomes problematic for QAC where order is critical. By rebalancing the probability of the most likely suggestion with the average diversity weight given to other suggestions, we make sure probabilities stay uniform yet suggestions are diverse. We use a normalized Levenshtein distance to assess the diversity.

4 Experiments

4.1 Dataset

The AOL query logs (Pass et al., 2006) are commonly used to evaluate the quality of QAC systems. We rely on a background dataset for the NN; training and validation datasets for lambdaMART integrations; and a test dataset for evaluations. Some adaptations are done to the AOL background dataset as in (Park and Chiba, 2017), such as removing the queries appearing less than 3 times or longer that 100 characters. For each query in the training, validation and test datasets, we use all possible prefixes starting after the first word as in (Shokouhi, 2013). We use the sets from (Park and Chiba, 2017) available online, enriched with user and time information provided in the original AOL dataset. In addition, we evaluate the systems on a second real-world dataset from a production search engine in the biomedical domain, PubMed (Fiorini et al., 2017; Lu, 2011; Mohan et al., 2018), that was created in the same manner. The biomedical dataset consists of 8,490,317 queries. The sizes of training, validation and test sets are comparable to those used for the AOL dataset.

4.2 Evaluation

Systems are evaluated using the traditional Mean Reciprocal Rank (MRR) metric. This metric assesses the quality of suggestions by identifying the rank of the real query in the suggestions given one of its prefixes. We also tested PMRR as introduced in (Park and Chiba, 2017) and observed the same trends in results as MRR, so we do not show them due to space limitation. Given the set of prefixes

P in the test dataset, MRR is defined as follows:

$$MRR = \frac{1}{|Q|} \sum_{r \in P} \frac{1}{r_p},\qquad(4)$$

where r_p represent the rank of the match. Paired t-tests measure the significance of score variations among systems and are reported in the Results section. We also evaluate prediction time as this is an important parameter for building production systems. The prediction time is averaged over 10 runs on the test set, on the same hardware for all models. We do not evaluate throughput but rather compare the time required by all approaches to process one prefix.

4.3 Systems and setups

We implemented the method in (Park and Chiba, 2017) and used their best-performing model as a baseline. We also compare our results to the standard **MPC** (Bar-Yossef and Kraus, 2011). For our method, we evaluate several incremental versions, starting with **NQAC** which follows the architecture detailed above but with the word embeddings and the one-hot encoding of characters only. We add the subscript **U** when the language model is enriched with user vectors and **T** when it integrates time features. We append **+D** to indicate the use of the diverse beam search to predict queries instead of a standard beam search. Finally, we also study the impact of adding MPC and LambdaMART (**+MPC, +λMART**).

5 Results

A summary of the results is presented in Table 1. Interestingly, our simple NQAC model performs similarly to the state-of-the-art on this dataset, called Neural Query Language Model (NQLM), on all queries. It is significantly less good for seen queries (-5.6%) and significantly better for unseen queries (+4.2%). Although GRUs have less expressive power than LSTMs, their smaller number of parameters to train allowed them to better converge than all LSTM models we tested, including that of (Park and Chiba, 2017). NQAC also benefits from a significantly better scalability (28% faster than NQLM) and thus seems more appropriate for production systems. When we enrich the language model with user information, it becomes better for seen queries (+1.9%) while being about as fast. Adding time sensitivity does not yield significant improvements on this dataset overall, but improves significantly the performance for seen queries (+1.7%). Relying on the diverse beam search significantly hurts the processing time (39% longer) while not providing significantly better performance. Our integration of MPC differs from previous studies. We noticed that for Web search, MPC performs extremely well and is computationally cheap (0.24 seconds). On the other hand, all neural QAC systems are better for unseen queries but struggle to stay under a second of processing time. Since identifying if a query has been seen or not is done in constant time, we route the query either to MPC or to NQAC_{UT} and we note the overall performance as NQAC_{UT}+MPC. This method provides a significant improvement over NQLM (+6.7%) overall while being faster on average. Finally, appending NQAC_{UT}'s results to MPC's and reranking the list with LambdaMART provides the best results on this dataset, but at the expense of greater computational cost (+60%).

While NQAC_{UT}+MPC appears clearly as the best compromise between performance and quality for the AOL dataset, the landscape changes drastically on the biomedical dataset and the quality drops significantly for all systems. This shows the potential difficulties associated with real-world systems, which particularly occur in specialized domains. In this case, the drop in performance is mostly due to the fact that biomedical queries are longer and it becomes more difficult for models to predict the entire query accurately only with the first keywords. While the generated queries make sense and are relevant candidates, the chance for generative models to predict the exact target query diminishes as the target query is longer because of combinatorial explosion. This is even more true when the target queries are diverse as in specialized domains (Islamaj Dogan et al., 2009; Névéol et al., 2011). For example, for the prefix "breast cancer", there are 1169 diverse suffixes in a single day of logs used for training. These include "local recurrence", "nodular prognosis", "hormone receptor", "circulating cells", "family history", "chromosome 4p16" or "herceptin review", to cite only a few. Hence, while the model predicts plausible queries, it is a lot more difficult to predict the one the user intended. The target query length also has an impact on prediction time, as roughly twice the time is needed for Web searches. MPC is the exception, however, it per-

Table 1: MRR results for all tested models on the AOL and biomedical datasets with their average prediction time in seconds.

Model	AOL dataset				Biomedical dataset			
	MRR			Time	MRR			Time
	Seen	Unseen	All		Seen	Unseen	All	
MPC (Bar-Yossef and Kraus, 2011)	**0.461**	0.000	0.184	**0.24**	0.165	0.000	0.046	**0.29**
NQLM(L)+WE+MPC+λMART (Park and Chiba, 2017)	0.430	0.306	0.356	1.33	0.159	0.152	0.154	2.35
Our models in this paper								
NQAC	0.406	0.319	0.354	0.94	0.155	0.139	0.143	1.73
$NQAC_U$	0.417	0.325	0.361	0.98	**0.191**	0.161	0.169	1.77
$NQAC_{UT}$	0.424	0.326	0.365	0.95	0.101	**0.195**	0.157	1.81
$NQAC_{UT}$+D	0.427	0.326	0.366	1.32	0.186	0.185	0.185	2.04
$NQAC_{UT}$+MPC	**0.461**	0.326	0.380	0.68	0.165	**0.195**	**0.187**	1.20
$NQAC_{UT}$+MPC+λMART	0.459	**0.330**	**0.382**	1.09	0.154	0.179	0.172	2.01

forms poorly even on seen queries (0.165). This observation suggests that more elaborate models are specifically needed for specialized domains. On this dataset, NQAC does not perform as well as NQLM and it seems this time that the higher number of parameters in NQLM is more appropriate for the task. Still, user information helps significantly for seen queries (+23%), probably because some users frequently check the same queries to keep up-to-date. Time sensitivity seems to help significantly unseen queries (+21%) while significantly hurting the quality for seen queries (-47%). Diversity is significantly helpful on this dataset (+19%) and provides a balance in performance for both seen and unseen queries. $NQAC_{UT}$+MPC yields the best overall MRR score for this dataset, and LambdaMART is unable to learn how to re-rank the suggestions, thus decreasing the score.

From these results, we draw several conclusions. First, MPC performs very well on seen queries for Web searches and it should be used on them. For unseen queries, the $NQAC_{UT}$ model we propose achieves a sub-second state-of-the-art performance. Second, it is clear that the field of application will affect many of the decisions when designing a QAC system. On a specialized domain, the task is more challenging: fast approaches like MPC perform too poorly while more elaborate approaches do not meet production requirements. $NQAC_U$ performs best on seen queries, $NQAC_{UT}$ on unseen queries. Finally, $NQAC_{UT}$+D provides an equilibrium between the two at a greater computational cost. Its overall MRR is similar to that of $NQAC_{UT}$+MPC but it is less redundant (see Table 2). Particularly, the system seems not to be limited anymore by the higher probability associated with shorter suggestions (e.g. "www google", a form of "www google com"), thus bringing more diversity. This aspect can be more useful for specialized domains where the range of possible queries is broader. Finally, we found that a lot more data was needed for the biomedical domain than for general Web search. After about a million queries, NQAC suggests meaningful and plausible queries for both datasets. However, for the biomedical dataset, the loss needs more epochs to stabilize than for the AOL dataset, mainly due to the combinatorial explosion mentioned above.

Table 2: Comparison of the 10 top query candidates from the baselines and our approach for the prefix "www".

MPC	(Park and Chiba, 2017)	NQAC+D
www google com	www google com	www google com
www yahoo com	www yahoo com	www myspace com
www myspace com	www myspace com	www mapquest com
www google	www google	www yahoo com
www ebay com	www hotmail com	www hotmail com
www hotmail com	www my	www bankofamerica com
www mapquest com	www myspace com	www chase com
www myspace	www mapquest com	www disneychannel com
www msn com	www yahoo	www myspace
www bankofamerica com	www disney channel com	www disney channel com

6 Conclusions and future work

To the best of our knowledge, we proposed the first neural language model that integrates user information and time sensitivity for query auto completion with a focus on scalability for real-world systems. Personalization is provided through pre-trained user vectors based on their past queries. By incorporating this information and by adapting the architecture, we were able to achieve state-of-the-art performance in neural query auto completion without relying on re-ranking, making this approach significantly more scalable in practice.

We studied multiple variants, their benefits and drawbacks for various use cases. We also demonstrate the utility of this method for specialized domains such as biomedicine, where the query diversity and vocabulary are broader and MPC fails to provide the same performance as in Web search. We also found that user information and diversity improve the performance significantly more than for Web search engines. To allow readers to easily reproduce, evaluate and improve our models, we provide all the code on a public repository.

The handling of time-sensitivity may benefit from a more elaborate integration, for example session-based rather than absolute time. Also, we evaluated our approaches on a general search setup for both datasets, while searches in the biomedical domain commonly contain fields (i.e. authors, title, abstract, etc.) which adds to the difficulty. The choice of a diversity metric is also important and could be faster or more efficient (e.g., using word embeddings to diversify the semantics of the suggestions). These limitations warrant further work and we leave them as perspectives.

Acknowledgement

This research was supported by the Intramural Research Program of the NIH, National Library of Medicine.

References

Ziv Bar-Yossef and Naama Kraus. 2011. Context-sensitive query auto-completion. In *Proceedings of the 20th international conference on World wide web*, pages 107–116. ACM.

Christopher JC Burges. 2010. From ranknet to lambdarank to lambdamart: An overview. *Learning*, 11(23-581):81.

Fei Cai, Maarten De Rijke, et al. 2016. A survey of query auto completion in information retrieval. *Foundations and Trends® in Information Retrieval*, 10(4):273–363.

Fei Cai, Shangsong Liang, and Maarten De Rijke. 2014. Time-sensitive personalized query auto-completion. In *Proceedings of the 23rd ACM international conference on conference on information and knowledge management*, pages 1599–1608. ACM.

Kyunghyun Cho, Bart Van Merriënboer, Dzmitry Bahdanau, and Yoshua Bengio. 2014. On the properties of neural machine translation: Encoder-decoder approaches. *arXiv preprint arXiv:1409.1259*.

Nicolas Fiorini, David J Lipman, and Zhiyong Lu. 2017. Cutting edge: Towards pubmed 2.0. *eLife*, 6:e28801.

Rezarta Islamaj Dogan, G Craig Murray, Aurélie Névéol, and Zhiyong Lu. 2009. Understanding pubmed® user search behavior through log analysis. *Database*, 2009.

Rafal Jozefowicz, Wojciech Zaremba, and Ilya Sutskever. 2015. An empirical exploration of recurrent network architectures. In *International Conference on Machine Learning*, pages 2342–2350.

Yoon Kim, Yacine Jernite, David Sontag, and Alexander M Rush. 2016. Character-aware neural language models. In *AAAI*, pages 2741–2749.

Georgia Koutrika and Yannis Ioannidis. 2005. A unified user profile framework for query disambiguation and personalization. In *Proceedings of workshop on new technologies for personalized information access*, pages 44–53.

Matti Lankinen, Hannes Heikinheimo, Pyry Takala, Tapani Raiko, and Juha Karhunen. 2016. A character-word compositional neural language model for finnish. *arXiv preprint arXiv:1612.03266*.

Quoc Le and Tomas Mikolov. 2014. Distributed representations of sentences and documents. In *International Conference on Machine Learning*, pages 1188–1196.

Zhiyong Lu. 2011. Pubmed and beyond: a survey of web tools for searching biomedical literature. *Database*, 2011.

Zhiyong Lu, W John Wilbur, Johanna R McEntyre, Alexey Iskhakov, and Lee Szilagyi. 2009. Finding query suggestions for pubmed. In *AMIA Annual Symposium Proceedings*, volume 2009, page 396. American Medical Informatics Association.

Dionisis Margaris, Costas Vassilakis, and Panagiotis Georgiadis. 2018. Query personalization using social network information and collaborative filtering techniques. *Future Generation Computer Systems*, 78:440–450.

Tomas Mikolov, Ilya Sutskever, Kai Chen, Greg S Corrado, and Jeff Dean. 2013. Distributed representations of words and phrases and their compositionality. In *Advances in neural information processing systems*, pages 3111–3119.

Bhaskar Mitra and Nick Craswell. 2015. Query auto-completion for rare prefixes. In *Proceedings of the 24th ACM international on conference on information and knowledge management*, pages 1755–1758. ACM.

Sunil Mohan, Nicolas Fiorini, Sun Kim, and Zhiyong Lu. 2018. A fast deep learning model for textual relevance in biomedical information retrieval. *CoRR*, abs/1802.10078.

Aurélie Névéol, Rezarta Islamaj Doğan, and Zhiyong Lu. 2011. Semi-automatic semantic annotation of pubmed queries: a study on quality, efficiency, satisfaction. *Journal of biomedical informatics*, 44(2):310–318.

Dae Hoon Park and Rikio Chiba. 2017. A neural language model for query auto-completion. In *Proceedings of the 40th International ACM SIGIR Conference on Research and Development in Information Retrieval*, pages 1189–1192. ACM.

Greg Pass, Abdur Chowdhury, and Cayley Torgeson. 2006. A picture of search. In *InfoScale*, volume 152, page 1.

Milad Shokouhi. 2013. Learning to personalize query auto-completion. In *Proceedings of the 36th international ACM SIGIR conference on Research and development in information retrieval*, pages 103–112. ACM.

Milad Shokouhi and Kira Radinsky. 2012. Time-sensitive query auto-completion. In *Proceedings of the 35th international ACM SIGIR conference on Research and development in information retrieval*, pages 601–610. ACM.

Ilya Sutskever, James Martens, and Geoffrey E Hinton. 2011. Generating text with recurrent neural networks. In *Proceedings of the 28th International Conference on Machine Learning (ICML-11)*, pages 1017–1024.

Andrew Swiffin, John Arnott, J Adrian Pickering, and Alan Newell. 1987. Adaptive and predictive techniques in a communication prosthesis. *Augmentative and Alternative Communication*, 3(4):181–191.

Ashwin K Vijayakumar, Michael Cogswell, Ramprasath R Selvaraju, Qing Sun, Stefan Lee, David Crandall, and Dhruv Batra. 2016. Diverse beam search: Decoding diverse solutions from neural sequence models. *arXiv preprint arXiv:1610.02424*.

Document-based Recommender System for
Job Postings using Dense Representations

Ahmed Elsafty[*] and **Martin Riedl**[†] and **Chris Biemann**[‡]

[*] XING SE, Hamburg, Germany

[†] IMS, Universität Stuttgart, Germany

[‡] Language Technology, Universität Hamburg, Germany

`ahmed.elsafty@xing.com,martin.riedl@ims.uni-stuttgart.de,`
`biemann@informatik.uni-hamburg.de`

Abstract

Job boards and professional social networks heavily use recommender systems in order to better support users in exploring job advertisements. Detecting the similarity between job advertisements is important for job recommendation systems as it allows, for example, the application of item-to-item based recommendations. In this work, we research the usage of dense vector representations to enhance a large-scale job recommendation system and to rank German job advertisements regarding their similarity. We follow a two-folded evaluation scheme: (1) we exploit historic user interactions to automatically create a dataset of similar jobs that enables an offline evaluation. (2) In addition, we conduct an online A/B test and evaluate the best performing method on our platform reaching more than 1 million users. We achieve the best results by combining job titles with full-text job descriptions. In particular, this method builds dense document representation using words of the titles to weigh the importance of words of the full-text description. In the online evaluation, this approach allows us to increase the click-through rate on job recommendations for active users by 8.0%.

1 Introduction

Recommender systems aim at providing recommendations for services that are targeted to specific users. The majority of such systems are applied in the field of e-commerce for e.g. product recommendations (Lu et al., 2015). In business-oriented networking platforms, recommender systems propose job recommendations to users.

In this deployment paper, we target the development of content-based methods for job recommendations focusing on German job advertisements. Based on our social online platform for professionals, 45% of the traffic is driven by recommendation services for job postings. Thus, improving

the job recommendations is expected to result in higher user interactions.

Our online platform's infrastructure consists of several recommendation stages in order to recommend job postings to users. In this paper, we focus on the so-called More-Like-This (MLT) component that recommends job postings based on previous users interactions with other job postings. Our current system consists of an ensemble of recommendation retrieval, filtering and re-ranking stages in order to recommend relevant job postings to users. For this, it exploits metadata of a job posting like keywords, disciplines and industries in which the job is categorized.

There are multiple issues when using exact keywords or category matching for ranking job postings. First, the document collection, with over 1 million job postings, is fairly huge and too diverse to fit into the small number of available categories, e.g. 22 disciplines such as *Law* or *Media*. Second, strict word matching leads to recall issues, for instance, *J2EE Developer* will not be similar to *Software Engineer*. Thus, employing a sparse vector representation is not appropriate for retrieving similarities between job postings. In addition, due to the cold start problem (Schein et al., 2002), using solely metadata of job postings or users is not suitable, especially for new users, for which only marginal or no information exists. Furthermore, metadata can be entirely missing or incorrect (e.g. outdated or on purpose).

Consequently, we will compute similarities between job postings based on dense vector representations. Recent document embedding techniques learn meaningful syntactic and semantic relationships based on word occurrences in the text. In this paper, we use dense vector representation of documents to score similarities between job postings based on their full-text descriptions and titles. First, we create a dataset for an offline eval-

Proceedings of NAACL-HLT 2018, pages 216–224

New Orleans, Louisiana, June 1 - 6, 2018. ©2017 Association for Computational Linguistics

uation consisting of similar job postings based on user co-interactions. Then, we construct an evaluation metric based on the classification of similar and non-similar items. Testing multiple embedding models and weighting functions, the best performance is achieved when building embeddings based on the job description with an increased weight for words that appear in the job title. Finally, the model is used in an online A/B test to assert its performance on live data.

2   Related Work

Recommendation systems can be divided into three categories (Resnick and Varian, 1997): content-based, collaborative filtering and hybrid models. Content-based recommender systems use items the user positively interacted with in the past, calculate similarity scores between item pairs and rank the new recommendations accordingly (Lops et al., 2011). Collaborative filtering approach suggest items to a given user, that other similar users positively interacted with (Koren and Bell, 2015). Hybrid methods combine both techniques (Burke, 2007). To avoid cold start problems, due to missing data, we focus on content-based approach here.

Dense numeric representations are commonly used to compute the similarity between content of documents (Hofmann, 2000) in order to reduce sparse count-based representations (Koren et al., 2009), which require huge amounts of memory. *Word2Vec* (Mikolov et al., 2013) has become a standard method that builds dense vector representations, which are the weights of a neural network layer predicting neighboring words. To retrieve a document representation, we compute the average of all vectors of the words in the documents. *Word2Vec* was also used for recommender systems to re-rank items based on vector correlations (Musto et al., 2015; Ozsoy, 2016). A modification that allows the usage of predicting arbitrary context in order to compute word representation is named *Word2VecF* and was introduced by Levy and Goldberg (2014). Document embedding techniques like *Doc2Vec* (Le and Mikolov, 2014) assigns each document a single vector, which gets adjusted with respect to all words in the document and all document vectors in the dataset. In an attempt to reduce *Doc2Vec* complexity and training corpus size dependencies, *Doc2VecC* (Chen, 2017) uses the same architecture as *Word2Vec*'s,

except that it samples words from the document in each training iteration by creating a document vector out of their average. The vector is then used to help predicting neighboring words during training.

To our best knowledge, no dataset is available to evaluate the performance of ranking similarities between jobs. Most similar is the dataset of the RecSys 2016 task (Abel et al., 2016). However, the task of this challenge was to learn the retrieval relevant documents based on user metadata and the approaches use supervised systems. In addition, datasets for document similarity exist, but do not focus on job postings. For the task of document similarity, the 20 Newsgroups (Lang, 1995) and TREC-AP (Lewis et al., 1996) datasets are commonly used. Here the task is to assign documents to a predefined category. Thus, the task is more related to document clustering than information retrieval of similar documents. Also related are semantic text similarity tasks, where two sentences have to be scored regarding their similarity with a score between 0 and 5 (Baudiš et al., 2016). Paraphrasing is another aspect that is important for document similarity. Bernhard and Gurevych (2008) introduced a dataset for paraphrasing both questions and answers in order to enhance the results for the information retrieval.

Related work was done by Fazel-Zarandi and Fox (2009), who introduced a method for matching jobs with job seekers. Whereas this fits to the RecSys 2016 task, this does not cover job posting retrieval of similar jobs. Furthermore, supervised approaches exist that predict jobs to candidate users e.g. Poch et al. (2014). In addition, Kessler et al. (2008) introduced a dataset based on French job offers and presented a system for ranking relevant jobs to candidates based on a jobs-to-candidates similarity metric.

3   Method

We hypothesize that job offers are semantically similar if the words used in its description are semantically similar. In addition, metadata of job offers like e.g. location of employee, title or qualifications are relevant for similarity computations.

3.1   Data Retrieval

Based on our job recommendation platform, we extract user interactions (bookmarks and reply intentions) from March 2014 to March 2017 as pairs of users and jobs. First, we remove users and jobs that have less than two interactions overall. Then, users are filtered out that have a number of overall lifetime interactions that exceeds the 99th percentile of all users. We consider such users as outliers. As click data of users is noisier than the bookmark data, we do not use clicks for the creation of this dataset.

Whereas our job recommendation platform features job postings in English and German, most users prefer German postings. This also affects our dataset, which comprises of 91% of German postings. While training semantic models for multiple languages is possible (e.g. Søgaard et al., 2017), we focus on German job postings, as found by a language detector[1].

3.2 Data Preprocessing

Before training, HTML tags, URLs and e-mails were removed using regular expressions, as early models showed a huge bias towards HR contact emails and job agencies that include boilerplate URLs in the job description footers. All special characters like non-alphabetical characters, interpunctuation and bullet points were removed. Initial semantic models required large vocabularies due to writing variations of the same word. For instance, the term *Java* occurs three times: *Java, java* and *JAVA*. Hence, we lowercase job posting texts and replace numbers with a placeholder (Abdelwahab and Elmaghraby, 2016). Finally, the document is stemmed using Snowball stemmer[2].

3.3 Ground Truth Construction

As manual annotation is expensive and time consuming – experts would have to go through N^2 jobs for completeness (where N is the sample size) – we automatically build a dataset using interactions of users from our job recommendation system. For building the dataset, we assume that two jobs are similar, if two or more users are interested in these two jobs. This assumption follows our intuition that users bookmark relevant jobs that are similar. However, this source of information can be noisy, due to random surfing, accidental clicks or when job postings are bookmarked for a friend and not for the profile owner. Hence, by selecting only jobs where several users co-interacted with, we can increase the probability that such jobs are similar.

In order to validate this assumption, a proper representative sample should be randomly selected and assessed by human experts. Since we did not have the resources for manual judgments, we compare the metadata from the job postings. For example, for 616,000 pairs of similar jobs, 70.02% of them share the same discipline. The other about 30% span across similar disciplines like e.g. *Marketing, Quality Assurance* and *Project Management* that have high topical overlap. However, discipline pairs exist that may not be considered as similar, like *Engineering & Technical* and *Management & Corporate Development*. Such "noise" in addition to slight diversity in bookmarked jobs is expected due to the automatic generation of the dataset. Nevertheless, such nontrivial discipline combinations have very low frequency. Better dataset construction approaches could involve increasing the number of users who co-interact with the job. Whereas this increases confidence, it decreases the dataset size drastically and could impose a bias for popular vs. rather sparingly sought disciplines.

Offline Evaluation Setup

The two jobs with the titles *Java Developer, Hamburg* and *Java Backend Developer, Stuttgart* are examples of two very similar job postings with different locations. Due to the location difference they fit to two different types of users: those who live close to Stuttgart and those close to Hamburg. For the creation of our dataset we consider the following: if there is no user co-interaction between two jobs, they will not be considered similar in the dataset. The same applies to similar jobs postings with large creation time stamp differences. For example, users that have been interested in jobs posted in 2014, might not be interested in similar jobs posted in 2017.

Inspired by the information retrieval-based evaluation approach by Le and Mikolov (2014), we created our dataset. In their approach, they created triples (s, p, n) that consists of a paragraph s, a similar paragraph p and a non-similar randomly sampled paragraph n. Inspired by this dataset, negative sampling in *Word2Vec* and cross validation, we extended the approach to construct a dataset of positive and negative samples as described in Algorithm 1. For each job, we create 10 folds of 10 similar and 40 non-similar jobs.

This algorithm returns a list of triplets consisting of the job j, a list of similar jobs Pos_f and a

---

Algorithm 1 Building the Evaluation Dataset

```
 1: procedure CREATE_DATASET(jobs)
 2:     output ← [ ]
 3:     for j in jobs do
 4:         for f = 1 … 10 do
 5:             Pos_f, Fold_f ← [ ], [ ]
 6:             for i = 1 … 10 do
 7:                 p_i ← random_similar_job
 8:                 Pos_f.append(p_i)
 9:                 Fold_f.append(p_i)
10:             for i = 1 … 40 do
11:                 n_i ← random_job
12:                 Fold_f.append(n_i)
13:             shuffle(Fold_f)
14:             output.append((j, Pos_f, Fold_f))
15:     return output              ▷ A list of triplets
```

shuffled list $Fold_f$ of similar and non similar job postings to the job j. During evaluation, every job posting in the shuffled $Fold_f$ is compared to the corresponding job j to compute a similarity score, which is used to rearrange $Fold_f$. The precision measure is used to compare the list cutout at 10 (retrieved), and the relevant job postings in Pos_f.

Sampling "negative job postings" from the entire dataset, we reduce the chance of fetching similar job postings that our dataset did not capture. To reduce the chance of false negatives, we increase the size of the dataset by randomly generating 10 lists for each job, resulting in a dataset of 112,000 distinct job postings and 12,000 shuffled lists.

In Figure 1, we show the similarity between job titles (we translated them from German to English) based on a *Doc2VecC* model (500 dim vectors, 10 window size, 15 negative sampling, 20 iterations) using *T-SNE*. The job colored in black (*Lean Java Expert Munich*) represents the job being evaluated, and the gray ones represent similar (positive) job postings sampled from our user interactions. The remaining jobs depict non-similar (negative) jobs sampled from the entire corpus. Based on the figure we have three observations: first, most positive jobs are closest to the queried job and focus on the same topic, namely Java development. Second, some of the "negative" jobs are relevant, e.g. *FrontEnd developer* and *Teamleader in IT Development*, and have a close distance to the queried job. Third, we observe multiple clusters: for example, in the upper right corner we observe a "media management" cluster, and in the center a

"project management" cluster.

4 Offline Evaluation

In this section, we first report results that are computed based on full-text job descriptions. Then, we exploit the performance using the job titles. To complete our experiments we show results for the combination of job titles and job descriptions.

In our experiments, we use commonly used hyperparameters (Siencnik, 2015; Levy et al., 2015; Yao et al., 2017). We tested different combinations of window size (2, 5, 10), model choice (skip-gram vs. continuous bag of words) and number of dimensions (100, 250, 500) and picked the following hyperparameters for the rest of the experiments: skip-gram model with vector size of 500, window size of 10, 15 words for negative sampling, 20 iterations and a threshold for the minimum count of 5.

Due to the ranking nature of the task, we report results based on the precision at 10 (P@10) score considering the ten highest ranked jobs. Since we have 10 positive similar job postings in each list, the P@10 can be interpreted as an average percentage of jobs in the top 10 which are actually similar and can have a maximum value of 100%.

Full-Text Job Description: As a baseline we represent each job as a word vector of TF-IDF scores based on the job description and use the cosine similarity for re-ranking the jobs (see Table 1). This baseline performs lowest with a P@10 score of 8.69% showing that such a sparse representation is insufficient to identify similarities between documents.

Model	Stem-med	Doc. Context	TF-IDF weights	P@10
TF-IDF				08.69 %
Word2Vec				54.84 %
Word2Vec	*			56.22 %
Word2VecF	*	*		61.12 %
Word2VecF	*	*	*	62.81 %
Doc2VecC	*			62.73 %
Doc2VecC	*		*	**64.23 %**

Table 1: Precision scores of word embedding models using full-text description only.

Using *Word2Vec*, we achieve a score of 54.85%, demonstrating that dense representations perform much better on our dataset than using sparse word representations. Stemming the documents yields to a further improvement (+1.38) and reduces the

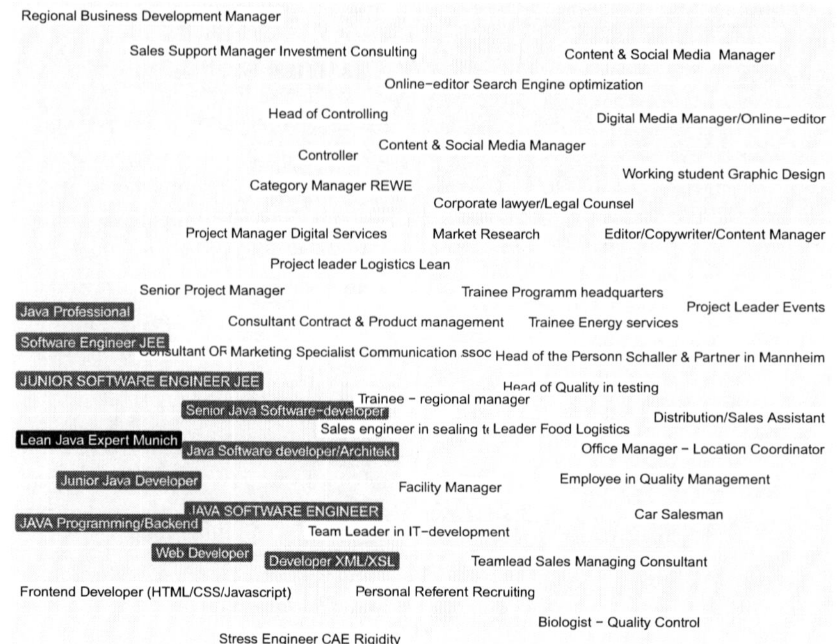

Figure 1: T-SNE representation of a sampled list after a model evaluation (job titles are translated from German to English).

training time, due to the smaller vocabulary size. Combining the stemmed representation with context information – we use the document IDs and compute the representation using *Word2VecF* – we achieve improvements of +4.9 points in comparison to the standard *Word2Vec* approach. In this setting, we predict the document ID for every word (unlike predicting its neighbors in *Word2Vec*). Such a "window" can be seen as a global context over the entire document, which performs better than using *Word2Vec* local context. By extending this model with *TF-IDF* scores, the performance is boosted by another +1.69 points to a score of 62.81%. In addition, we compute similarities with *Doc2VecC* using stemmed job descriptions as documents. This method performs best among the single tested models (62.73%), and scores highest when combined with *TF-IDF* weights achieving a score of 64.32%.

Job Title: Whereas the models mentioned above use the job description, most users click on jobs based on the title. Thus, we investigate building document vectors using solely title information using *Word2Vec* with stemmed words and *TF-IDF* weights. This experiment should reveal whether computational efforts can be reduced by using less information.

As shown in Table 2, *Word2Vec* using title vector yields a P@10 of 58.79%. Whereas these results are lower, they are still impressive, as we only have one "sentence" with an average of 4.8 words. In addition, we consider job titles as documents

Model	P@10
Word2Vec – 500 dim.	58.79%
Doc2Vec – 100 dim.	59.87 %
Doc2Vec – 250 dim.	60.03 %
Doc2Vec – 500 dim.	**61.23 %**
Doc2Vec – 500 dim. – Inferred	20.66 %

Table 2: Results using the title with various embeddings.

and use *Doc2Vec*. Given the small sentence size, it can be trained in reasonable time. In our experiments, we test this model with various dimensions (100, 250, 500) and keep the other parameters fixed.[3] Testing the effect of *Doc2Vec* on titles that have not been seen before, we achieve a low precision of 20.66%. This was tested by dropping the document vectors generated for our dataset after training, and using the model to infer the doc-

[3]We use a distributed bag of words model, window size of 10, minimum word count of 5 and a sampling rate of 1e-5.

ument vectors again. When predicting vectors for unseen documents, the model infers the title vector based on its words, however, information loss is to be expected. This implies that the model cannot be efficiently used in an online scenario or in a pipeline of streaming jobs since the entire model has to be retrained on the full data to obtain a better word coverage.

Title weighted description: Next, we combine *Doc2VecC* word vectors of the description weighted by the *TF-IDF* values with weights, indicating if a word is contained in the title. For the combination we use the following formula:

$$D(w_1, \ldots, w_k) = \frac{\sum_{i=1}^{k} TF\text{-}IDF(w_i) * V(w_i) * \lambda(w_i)}{\sum_{i=1}^{k} TF\text{-}IDF(w_i) * \lambda(w_i)}$$

$$\lambda(w_i) = \begin{cases} c, & \text{if } w_i \in \text{title}, c > 1.0 \\ 1, & \text{otherwise} \end{cases}$$

with $\lambda(w_i) = c$ with the constant $c > 1.0$ if w_i is contained in the title and $\lambda(w_i) = 1.0$ if the word w_i is not contained in the title.

When constructing the document vector D containing k words, all word vectors $V(w_i)$ are multiplied by their corresponding scalar *TF-IDF* values and the constant c if the word appears in the title. Then, the vectors are summed up and divided over the weights to calculate the weighted average. Based on findings in the previous section, we already know that the title provides enough information to distinguish jobs. Thus, weighting title words higher when averaging pulls the document vector a bit closer to the title in the vector space. Using $c = 5$, we achieve result with a precision score of 73.05%. It shows that by choosing a proper weighting function, we can achieve better results than changing the entire model. In industry, often not the best performing system is used, but the one which can also be applied efficiently to new and unseen data. Since word vectors are precomputed, document vectors can be computed online in the platform pipeline, such that vectors of new documents are available when needed by the recommender services.

5   Online Evaluation

The existing recommender system uses *Elasticsearch*[4] to retrieve job postings based on the user's

metadata, then exploits the user's previous interactions with job postings to rank the recommendations in a doc-to-doc similarity fashion via TF-IDF. This is used as a ranking baseline. For our online evaluations, we use the retrieval module from *Elasticsearch*, and plug our fastest and best performing job representation (title weighted *Doc2VecC*) model into a new system to re-rank the retrieved documents.

Before we performed the online evaluation, we analyzed whether the results with the *A/B* test will differ using different semantic representation, to prove whether the *A/B* test will lead to any meaningful result. For this, we re-rank the same retrieved recommendations for 2000 users sampled from the most active users on the platform.

As shown in Table 3, the intersected (common) recommendations (μ) between the two systems does not exceed 36% for all K ranks in the recommendation lists, with a decreasing standard deviation (σ). This reveals that the changes have huge impact on the rankings.

Top K	Intersection		Avg Distance (km)	
	μ	σ	$Existing$	New
4	30.1%	32.16%	287	179
10	35.5%	27.89%	293	188
20	35.4%	25.69%	325	195
50	34.1%	21.28%	336	192

Table 3: Pre-analysis for the A/B test. We show the mean and standard deviation of common recommendations returned by the systems on different ranks K, and the average distance of job postings to the user in kilometers (km).

In addition, we analyze the average distance in kilometers (km) of the recommended job postings to the user's location. The new model favors to rank jobs with closer distance at higher position: the top 4 recommendations are 30% closer and even 60% closer for the top 50 jobs. This is an important finding, as we hypothesize that users prefer jobs that are closer to their location. Job locations are usually included in the title, allowing vectors of cities to contribute higher in the title weighted averaging approach.

To perform the *A/B* test, we conduct a controlled experiment by selecting active users (with at least a single previous job interaction) and split them into two groups: one group gets job posting recommendations ranked by the *Elasticsearch*, and

---

[4] https://www.elastic.co

the second group gets job posting recommendations ranked by our best system (title weighted *Doc2VecC* model).

First, we apply an *A/A* test (Kohavi et al., 2009) to test for any split bias: both groups get recommendations from the existing system for 30 days. Then, the *A/B* test is conducted over the period of 20 days. The success metric is the Click-Through-Rate (CTR), which is the percentage of clicked items considering all items that have been shown to the users. Thus, the more items users interact with, the higher the CTR and the more successful is the algorithm.

	Group 1	**Group** 2
A/A test	20.000%	19.986%
A/B test	20.000%	21.600%

Table 4: Results of the A/A and A/B test with masked CTR to comply with the platform's policy.

Table 4 shows the results for the *A/A* and *A/B* test. To keep the true numbers proprietary to the company, we masked the absolute CTR values by normalizing group 1's real CTR to 20% and changing the clicks and group 2's CTR accordingly to preserve the ratios without showing confidential numbers. The *A/A* test shows negligible difference between the splits (-0.07%), showing no bias between the two groups. The experimental group 2 has a very noticeable relative difference of +8.00% more clicks per received recommendations using the title weighted description model.

To exemplify the difference between both systems, we show in Table 5 the top recommendations for a postdoctoral researcher who showed interest in three *Deep Learning Engineer* positions. Most of the recommendations of the existing system are software engineer associated job postings, while the new system suggests research oriented job postings with topics similar to the user's previous interactions like *data science*.

In contrast to offline evaluations, deploying models in productive pipelines must adhere to certain metrics, like request response time. As the recommender ranks over 300 jobs against multiple interactions per request, it shows a +9.90% increase in average response time compared to the existing indexed *Elasticsearch* model. While the new system's response time lies within our ac-

	Existing System	**New System**
1	IT project leader	Deep Learning in Autonomous cars
2	Software Engineer (Automotive)	Data Scientist
3	Senior Software Engineer (smart cars)	PhD researcher in Medical Imaging
4	Senior IT Consultant	Computer Linguist/ Analytics
5	Java Software Engineer	Researcher in single-cell Bioinformatics

Table 5: Ranked output from the existing and new system for a user with interest in *machine learning*.

ceptable ranges, it could be improved by reducing the model's vector dimensionality at the cost of its performance.

6   Conclusion and Future Work

In this paper, we have introduced a new method for automatically creating datasets for the offline evaluation of job posting similarities. Using such a silver standard dataset, we have evaluated the performance of different dense vector representations of documents in order to identify the most promising setup. Building dense representations based on full-text job descriptions yields the best results. However, computing representations for novel job postings becomes computational expensive, as the model has to be recomputed, as estimating representations for new documents results in much lower results. Building models from titles, the scores only slightly decrease, however, the computation of new models is much faster. In our experiments, we observe the best performance with a combined model, using the words within the title for weighting words in the description that allows to compute new representations in an online scenario. With this model, we yield a substantial 8% relative increase in CTR over the platform's previous system component.

In future work, we want to extend the weighting scheme by integrating ontology and keyword information in order to improve the similarity search.

References

Omar Abdelwahab and Adel Elmaghraby. 2016. UofL SemEval-2016 task 4: Multi domain word2vec for twitter sentiment classification. In *Proceedings of the 10th International Workshop on Semantic Evaluation, SemEval at NAACL-HLT*, pages 164–170, San Diego, CA, USA.

Fabian Abel, András A. Benczúr, Daniel Kohlsdorf, Martha Larson, and Róbert Pálovics. 2016. RecSys challenge 2016: Job recommendations. In *Proceedings of the 10th ACM Conference on Recommender Systems*, pages 425–426, Boston, MA, USA.

Petr Baudiš, Jan Pichl, Tomáš Vyskočil, and Jan Šedivý. 2016. Sentence pair scoring: Towards unified framework for text comprehension. volume Arxiv.

Delphine Bernhard and Iryna Gurevych. 2008. Answering Learners' Questions by Retrieving Question Paraphrases from Social Q&A Sites. In *Proceedings of the Third Workshop on Innovative Use of NLP for Building Educational Applications*, EANL '08, pages 44–52, Columbus, OH, USA.

Robin Burke. 2007. In *The Adaptive Web*, chapter Hybrid Web Recommender Systems, pages 377–408.

Minmin Chen. 2017. Efficient vector representation for documents through corruption. In *Proceedings of the International Conference on Learning Representations, ICLR*, Toulon, France.

Maryam Fazel-Zarandi and Mark S. Fox. 2009. Semantic Matchmaking for Job Recruitment: An Ontology-Based Hybrid Approach. In *Proceedings of the 3rd International SMR2 2009 Workshop on Service Matchmaking and Resource Retrieval in the Semantic Web, collocated with the 8th International Semantic Web Conference*, pages 3111–3119, Washington DC, USA.

Thomas Hofmann. 2000. Learning the similarity of documents: An information-geometric approach to document retrieval and categorization. In *Advances in Neural Information Processing Systems 12*, pages 914–920. Denver, CO, USA.

Rémy Kessler, Nicolas Béchet, Mathieu Roche, Marc El-Bèze, and Juan-Manuel Torres-Moreno. 2008. Automatic profiling system for ranking candidates answers in human resources. In *On the Move to Meaningful Internet Systems: OTM 2008 Workshops*, pages 625–634, Monterrey, Mexico.

Ron Kohavi, Roger Longbotham, Dan Sommerfield, and Randal M. Henne. 2009. Controlled experiments on the web: survey and practical guide. *Data Mining and Knowledge Discovery*, 18(1):140–181.

Yehuda Koren and Robert Bell. 2015. Advances in collaborative filtering. In *Recommender systems handbook*, pages 77–118.

Yehuda Koren, Robert Bell, and Chris Volinsky. 2009. Matrix factorization techniques for recommender systems. *Computer*, 42(8):42–49.

Ken Lang. 1995. Newsweeder: Learning to filter netnews. In *Machine Learning, Proceedings of the Twelfth International Conference on Machine Learning*, pages 331–339, Tahoe City, CA, USA.

Quoc V. Le and Tomas Mikolov. 2014. Distributed representations of sentences and documents. In *Proceedings of the 31th International Conference on Machine Learning, ICML*, pages 1188–1196, Beijing, China.

Omer Levy and Yoav Goldberg. 2014. Dependency-based word embeddings. In *Proceedings of the 52nd Annual Meeting of the Association for Computational Linguistics, ACL*, pages 302–308, Baltimore, MD, USA.

Omer Levy, Yoav Goldberg, and Ido Dagan. 2015. Improving distributional similarity with lessons learned from word embeddings. *Transactions of the Association for Computational Linguistics*, 3:211–225.

David D. Lewis, Robert E. Schapire, James P. Callan, and Ron Papka. 1996. Training algorithms for linear text classifiers. In *Proceedings of the 19th Annual International ACM SIGIR Conference on Research and Development in Information Retrieval, SIGIR'96*, pages 298–306, Zurich, Switzerland.

Pasquale Lops, Marco De Gemmis, and Giovanni Semeraro. 2011. Content-based recommender systems: State of the art and trends. In *Recommender systems handbook*, pages 73–105.

Jie Lu, Dianshuang Wu, Mingsong Mao, Wei Wang, and Guangquan Zhang. 2015. Recommender system application developments. *Decision Support Systems*, 74(C):12–32.

Tomas Mikolov, Ilya Sutskever, Kai Chen, Gregory S. Corrado, and Jeffrey Dean. 2013. Distributed representations of words and phrases and their compositionality. In *Proceedings of Advances in Neural Information Processing Systems, NIPS*, pages 3111–3119, Lake Tahoe, NV, USA.

Cataldo Musto, Giovanni Semeraro, Marco de Gemmis, and Pasquale Lops. 2015. Word embedding techniques for content-based recommender systems: An empirical evaluation. In *Poster Proceedings of the 9th ACM Conference on Recommender Systems, RecSys*, Vienna, Austria.

Makbule G. Ozsoy. 2016. From word embeddings to item recommendation. *CoRR*, abs/1601.01356.

Marc Poch, Núria Bel, Sergio Espeja, and Felipe Navio. 2014. Ranking Job Offers for Candidates: Learning Hidden Knowledge from Big Data. In *Proceedings of the Ninth International Conference on Language Resources and Evaluation LREC'14*, pages 2076 – 2082, Reykjavik, Iceland.

Paul Resnick and Hal R. Varian. 1997. Recommender systems. *Communications*, 40(3):56–58.

Andrew I. Schein, Alexandrin Popescul, Lyle H. Ungar, and David M. Pennock. 2002. Methods and metrics for cold-start recommendations. In *Proceedings of the 25th Annual International ACM SIGIR Conference on Research and Development in Information Retrieval*, SIGIR '02, pages 253–260, Tampere, Finland.

Scharolta Katharina Siencnik. 2015. Adapting word2vec to named entity recognition. In *Proceedings of the 20th Nordic Conference of Computational Linguistics, NODALIDA*, pages 239–243, Vilnius, Lithuania.

Anders Søgaard, Yoav Goldberg, and Omer Levy. 2017. A strong baseline for learning cross-lingual word embeddings from sentence alignments. In *Proceedings of the 15th Conference of the European Chapter of the Association for Computational Linguistics*, EACL, pages 765–774, Valencia, Spain.

Yao Yao, Xia Li, Xiaoping Liu, Penghua Liu, Zhaotang Liang, Jinbao Zhang, and Ke Mai. 2017. Sensing spatial distribution of urban land use by integrating points-of-interest and Google word2vec model. *International Journal of Geographical Information Science*, 31(4):825–848.

Author Index